SARCASM IN PAUL'S LETTERS

In this book, Matthew Pawlak offers the first treatment of sarcasm in New Testament studies. He provides an extensive analysis of sarcastic passages across the undisputed letters of Paul, showing where Paul is sarcastic, and how his sarcasm affects our understanding of his rhetoric and relationships with the early Christian congregations in Galatia, Rome, and Corinth. Pawlak's identification of sarcasm is supported by a dataset of 400 examples drawn from a broad range of ancient texts, including major case studies on Septuagint Job, the prophets, and Lucian of Samosata. These data enable the determination of the typical linguistic signals of sarcasm in ancient Greek, as well as its rhetorical functions. Pawlak also addresses several ongoing discussions in Pauline scholarship. His volume advances our understanding of the abrupt opening of Galatians, diatribe and Paul's hypothetical interlocutor in Romans, the 'Corinthian slogans' of First Corinthians, and the 'fool's speech' found within Second Corinthians 10–13.

MATTHEW PAWLAK is a postdoctoral researcher at the University of Tübingen. He completed his PhD in Theology and Religious Studies in 2020 at the University of Cambridge. His research has appeared in major academic journals across the disciplines of New Testament, Jewish Studies, Hebrew bible, and humour studies.

T0382126

SOCIETY FOR NEW TESTAMENT STUDIES

MONOGRAPH SERIES

General Editor: Edward Adams, *King's College, London*

182

SARCASM IN PAUL'S LETTERS

Sarcasm in Paul's Letters

MATTHEW PAWLAK

University of Tübingen, Germany

CAMBRIDGE
UNIVERSITY PRESS

Shaftesbury Road, Cambridge CB2 8EA, United Kingdom

One Liberty Plaza, 20th Floor, New York, NY 10006, USA

477 Williamstown Road, Port Melbourne, VIC 3207, Australia

314–321, 3rd Floor, Plot 3, Splendor Forum, Jasola District Centre, New Delhi – 110025, India

103 Penang Road, #05–06/07, Visioncrest Commercial, Singapore 238467

Cambridge University Press is part of Cambridge University Press & Assessment, a department of the University of Cambridge.

We share the University's mission to contribute to society through the pursuit of education, learning and research at the highest international levels of excellence.

www.cambridge.org
Information on this title: www.cambridge.org/9781009271905

DOI: 10.1017/9781009271929

© Cambridge University Press & Assessment 2023

First published 2023
First paperback edition 2024

A catalogue record for this publication is available from the British Library

ISBN   978-1-009-27191-2   Hardback
ISBN   978-1-009-27190-5   Paperback

Cambridge University Press & Assessment has no responsibility for the persistence or accuracy of URLs for external or third-party internet websites referred to in this publication and does not guarantee that any content on such websites is, or will remain, accurate or appropriate.

To Dad, Robin Pawlak,
for introducing me to sarcasm and to Paul.
To Mom, AnnaMaria Pawlak,
for pages 86, 170, 189
and so much besides.

CONTENTS

PREFACE

Where not otherwise indicated, all translations of non-English languages are my own. All biblical references marked NRSV are from the 2021 updated edition (NRSVue).

The article 'How to Be Sarcastic in Greek: Typical Means of Signaling Sarcasm in the New Testament and Lucian' (Matthew C. Pawlak, *HUMOR* 32.4 [2019]: 545–64) uses an earlier version of the dataset underlying the linguistic analysis of ancient Greek sarcasm found in Chapter 3 (§§3.1–3.2). The analysis presented in this book differs from the article in its scope, aims, language, and conclusions. While the article remains useful, the material in this book is more systematic and detailed, drawing on a significantly larger dataset.

Material in Chapter 4 (§4.1) of this book overlaps with the article 'Is Galatians an Ironic Letter? Θαυμάζω, Ancient Letter Writing Handbooks, and Galatians 1.6' (Matthew Pawlak, *Novum Testamentum* [2021]: 63: 249–70; doi:10.1163/15685365-12341694), although the chapter and article are ultimately different in purpose and scope. The article is an open access article, copyright Matthew Pawlak 2021, distributed under the terms of the CC BY 4.0 licence (https://creativecommons.org/licenses/by/4.0/legalcode). I direct readers interested in the relationship between the opening of Galatians and ancient epistolary conventions to the more detailed treatment of this subject in the article.

The chart on p.137 has been reproduced with the permission of the copyright holder from: King, Justin, 2018, *Speech-in-Character, Diatribe, and Romans 3:1–9: Who's Speaking When and Why It Matters*, BIS 163, Leiden: Brill, 269. Copyright 2018 by Koninklijke Brill NV, Leiden, The Netherlands.

Quotations marked NETS are taken from *A New English Translation of the Septuagint*, copyright 2007 by the International Organization for Septuagint and Cognate Studies, Inc., used by permission of Oxford University Press. All rights reserved.

ABBREVIATIONS

Abbreviations follow the Society of Biblical Literature (SBL) Handbook of Style, second edition. Abbreviations of classical texts follow the conventions of classics – Perseus abbreviations. Further abbreviations are as follows:

BDF	Blass Debrunner Funk
Chrysostom, *Comm. Gal.*	Alexander, Gross (trans.), n.d. 'The Commentary and Homilies of St. John Chrysostom, Archbishop of Constantinople, on the Epistles of St. Paul the Apostle to the Galatians and Ephesians,' pages 8–321 in *Saint Chrysostom: Homilies on Galatians, Ephesians, Philippians, Colossians, Thessalonians, Timothy, Titus, and Philemon*, edited by Philip Schaff, Nicene and Post-Nicene Fathers series (NPNF) 13, Edinburgh: T&T Clark (in-text reference is to NPNF page number).
Chrysostom, *Epist. Rom.*	Migne, J.-P. 1857, 'In Epistulam Ad Romanos (Homiliae 1–32)', pages 391–682 in *Patrologiae Cursus Completus (Series Graeca)*, MPG 60, Paris: Migne (Greek; accessed via TLG; in-text reference is to page number as indicated in TLG).
Jerome, *Comm. Gal.*	Cain, Andrew (trans.) 2010, *St. Jerome: Commentary on Galatians*, Fathers of the Church series (FC), Washington, DC: Catholic University of America Press (in-text reference is to section of Galatians addressed).

	Morris, J.B., and W.H. Simcox (trans.), n.d. 'The Homilies of St. John Chrysostom, Archbishop of Constantinople, on the Epistle of St. Paul the Apostle to the Romans', pages 604–997 in *Saint Chrysostom: Homilies on The Acts of the Apostles and the Epistle to the Romans*, edited by Philip Schaff, NPNF 11, Edinburgh: T&T Clark (in-text reference is to NPNF page number).
MT	Masoretic Text
NETS	A New English Translation of the Septuagint
NIV	New International Version
NPNF	Nicene and Post-Nicene Fathers
NRSV	New Revised Standard Version (updated edition)
Origen, *Comm.1 Cor*	Jenkins, C., 1908, 'Fragmenta ex commentariis in epistulam i ad Corinthios (in catenis)' in 'Documents: Origen on I Corinthians', *JTS* 9 & 10:9:232–47, 353–72, 500–14; 10:29–51 (Greek; accessed via TLG; in-text reference is to section as indicated in TLG).
Origen, *Comm. Rom.*	Scheck, Thomas (trans.), 2001, *Origen: Commentary on the Epistle to the Romans, Books 1–5*, FC, Washington, DC: Catholic University of America Press (in-text reference is to section in Scheck's edition).
TCNT	Twentieth Century New Testament
TLG	Thesaurus Linguae Graecae
VTG	Septuaginta: Vetus Testamentum Graecum

ACKNOWLEDGEMENTS

After the time spent bringing this work from an idea to a dissertation to a book, I find myself in the fortunate position of having many people to thank. I am grateful for the supervision I received from Simon Gathercole during the PhD at Cambridge. Simon's helpful and incisive comments on every draft of every chapter of the dissertation have been instrumental in developing this project. Thank you, Simon. I have also appreciated the supervision and support I have received from Michael Tilly and Jörg Frey over the course of my postdoctoral work. I would also like to thank Jim Aitken, Salvatore Attardo, Claude Cox, Katharine Dell, Marieke Dhont, Judith Lieu, Elizabeth Minchin, and Ryan Schellenberg for taking the time to read and provide feedback on chapters of the dissertation, as well as Sean Adams and James Carleton Paget for their helpful feedback at the examination.

I thank Kevin McGeough, whose Hebrew classes started me on the slippery slope towards academic research. I owe much of my foundation in biblical studies to Stephen Westerholm and Eileen Schuller. Informal conversations with fellow colleagues and grad students have provided much-needed support on everything from navigating PhD and post-PhD life to the minutiae of formatting and citation systems. For these conversations, I am grateful to Wally Cirafesi, Peter Day-Milne, Michael Dormandy, John Percival, Jordan Ryan, Daniel Stevens, and John VanMaaren.

This project has been made possible by the financial support of a full studentship from the Kirby Laing Foundation, a Doctoral Fellowship from the Social Sciences and Humanities Research Council of Canada, a postdoc funded by the DAAD PRIME programme, and short-term grants from the DAAD and the Canadian Commonwealth Scholarship Fund. I would also like to recognize Peterhouse for providing travel funding, a social community, and countless meals in Hall, and the theological faculties at Cambridge,

Tübingen, and Zürich. The support of all these organizations has been much appreciated. Thank you to the production team at Cambridge University Press for their work making this book a reality – und ich bedanke mich auch bei Lisa-Marie Gerle und Noah Stahl für ihre Hilfe mit dem Register.

Many thanks go to my family: to my parents, brothers, and sisters-in-law. Our weekly video calls across the Atlantic have been an irreplaceable source of happiness and good fun. Mom and Dad, your thanks are above. Thanks to Joshua and Tiffany for boosting my spirits across the years with a series of nephews and nieces, and I would recommend this book as a future bedtime story. I have appreciated consultations with Jesse and Alyssa on a variety of important subjects; thanks for making my life more entertaining. For all these and a thousand other things large and small that have shaped my values and etched their way into my personality and mannerisms, I will always be thankful.

I am convinced that at times there is nothing better for revitalizing one's academic work than thinking about anything but one's academic work. For this refreshment I am indebted to a community of outstanding friends, with a special shout-out to Antoine, Carolina, Jarred, Jordan, Peerapat, Peter, and William. Theresa was there for me literally from day one, and for everything she has been to me, I could never be grateful enough.

INTRODUCTION

A few years back, I was sitting in Evensong at the Peterhouse Chapel in Cambridge. During the service, the first scripture reading was taken from the Book of Job, the 26th chapter, beginning at the second verse: 'How you have helped one who has no power! How you have assisted the arm that has no strength! How you have counseled one who has no wisdom, and given much good advice!' (Job 26:2–3 NRSV). This was read in a tone that conveyed all the grace and solemnity appropriate to the liturgical setting. The passage sounded as if Job was addressing pious thanksgiving unto God. I must confess to having repressed a chuckle with some difficulty, knowing that what sounded so sincere in this context was Job's bitingly sarcastic indictment of his false comforters. While I do not fault a student reader for mistaking the tone of a passage for which they had no context, this situation well illustrates the exegetical importance of being able to accurately identify sarcasm. Simply put, taking a sarcastic utterance literally or reading a literal utterance sarcastically both have the potential to generate serious misreadings of a text.

With as much at stake for Pauline scholarship in determining whether a given statement is meant sincerely or sarcastically, it is surprising that there has been no dedicated study of sarcasm in Paul's letters. This work is meant to address this gap in scholarship, but not only for the sake of filling a void. Its first major contribution will be exegetical. I aim to determine systematically when Paul engages in sarcasm throughout his undisputed letters, and how the presence of sarcasm influences the interpretation of each passage. Because sarcasm is about implicit rather than explicit communication, sarcastic passages include some of the most difficult and disputed texts in the Pauline corpus. A methodologically grounded analysis of sarcasm can, therefore, bring a measure of clarity to several debated texts.

This analysis also contributes to the well-established study of Pauline rhetoric. Examining Paul's use of sarcasm throughout his undisputed letters enables investigation of how Paul uses sarcasm as a means of navigating his interactions with his congregations and opponents. The systematic scope of this research, surveying the full breadth of the undisputed letters rather than a single epistle, also creates an avenue for exploring how Paul's use of sarcasm differs depending on which congregation and situation he addresses and what this reveals about the tone of his relationships with different early Christian communities. With the Corinthian correspondence, we may also observe how these relationships develop over time.

However, with no previous studies of sarcasm in Paul, and very few even in classics, significant work remains to be done before we are ready to embark on our analysis of Paul. Much previous discussion of potentially sarcastic passages in Paul consists of commentators asserting whether a given verse is or is not ironic or sarcastic without sufficient supporting evidence. There have been a few dedicated studies of irony in Paul, but these tend to suffer from two methodological shortcomings. First, as we shall see in the next chapter, most Pauline scholarship is thoroughly out of date where irony research is concerned. Second, studies that treat 'irony' in general run the risk of ironing out the distinctions between different forms of irony, such as situational irony, verbal irony, and sarcasm. Because ironic situations and ironic comments are very different phenomena – both in terms of how they are communicated and recognized, and in terms of their functions – conflating different forms of irony leads to problematic conclusions. We cannot assume that what other scholars have argued about irony in Paul will necessarily hold true for sarcasm. Therefore, by focusing on sarcasm, a specific form of irony, this study can nuance previous discussions of irony in Paul.

With the field as it stands, three fundamental questions remain to be answered before we turn to Paul's letters: What is sarcasm? How is sarcasm expressed? And what does sarcasm do? These questions will form the basis of Part I of this study. The first chapter will address method and review the history of scholarship on sarcasm and irony in Paul. It will provide a detailed answer to the first question and a partial answer to the second. Here we provide an account of how the term *eirōneia* (εἰρωνεία) develops from its earliest references to the grammatical and rhetorical treatises of Paul's day, by which time it has come to mean something like what we call 'irony'. We focus especially on sarcasm (σαρκασμός) and how ancient authors define it in relationship to other forms of irony. We then lay out the major developments within the last several decades of irony studies, which have gone almost entirely unnoticed by previous Pauline scholarship. Surveying ancient and modern treatments of irony and sarcasm will enable us to disambiguate sarcasm from other forms of irony and facilitate the creation of a working definition of sarcasm that will serve throughout this project. Modern accounts of verbal irony will also furnish us with information about how sarcasm is normally expressed, allowing us to begin analyzing instances of sarcasm in ancient Greek texts.

The next two chapters will focus on the final two major questions – how sarcasm is communicated and its typical rhetorical functions. Our first comparative study on the Septuagint, which focuses on the texts where most of the evidence appears: the book of Job and the prophets, will address both issues to some extent with an especial focus on establishing the normal rhetorical functions of sarcasm in an ancient context. The next comparative study will look more broadly at ancient Greek texts, with special reference to the second-century satirist Lucian of Samosata – also including Aristophanes, the New Testament (outside Paul), and ancient satirical epigrams, among other texts. It will focus more on describing the typical signals for communicating sarcasm in ancient Greek.

These choices of comparative texts may strike some readers as unintuitive, especially when there is perhaps no ancient figure more associated with irony than Socrates, so here some preliminary justification is necessary. My choice to avoid Socrates, beyond discussion of his association with the term *eirōneia* in the next chapter, is intentional. As we shall see, the *eirōneia* attributed to Socrates is different from the use of irony as a figure of speech that we find in the later rhetoricians and grammarians. It is this latter form of irony that is associated with sarcasm, and is therefore the more relevant to this study. Furthermore, in her reassessment of the concept of Socratic irony, Lane questions whether much of Socrates' 'ironic praise' of his interlocutors – which, if ironic, would also be sarcastic (see Chapter 1, §1.1.2) – is really ironic at all.[1] Therefore, because the sort of *eirōneia* associated with Socrates in Plato is different from sarcasm, and because it is debatable whether Plato's Socrates makes use of

---

[1] Lane 2010, 249–57.

4   Introduction

sarcasm to a significant degree, Socrates would be a problematic point of comparison for a study of ancient sarcasm.

Why then the Septuagint? First, between the book of Job and the prophets, the Septuagint furnishes us with many, approximately thirty, examples of sarcasm with which to work. The Septuagint also has the advantage of being a Jewish text. Without intending to spark debate about Paul's self-identification *vis-à-vis* Judaism, Paul is at the very least 'circumcised on the eighth day, a member of the people of Israel, of the tribe of Benjamin, a Hebrew born of Hebrews' (Phil 3:5 NRSV), and intimately familiar with this body of texts. Furthermore, because of this familiarity, the Greek of the Septuagint impacts the way Paul writes in Greek. There is therefore linguistic overlap between the two corpora. While I will not argue that the use of sarcasm in the Septuagint directly influences Paul's use of sarcasm, greater linguistic and cultural overlap make for better analogical comparison.

With Paul writing in Greek, doubtless Hellenistic Jewish texts from the apocrypha, pseudepigrapha, and beyond would also make for interesting comparison. However, for our purposes, LXX *Job* and the prophets make for better case studies not only because of Paul's well-established familiarity with the Septuagint, but also for their relatively higher density of sarcasm. I have, to date, surveyed eleven Hellenistic Jewish texts for the presence of sarcasm, finding about ten examples. This is less sarcasm than we see in the book of Job, spread across a body of texts more than eight times as large. Considering these factors, LXX *Job* and the prophets simply allow for more detailed, focused analysis. I direct readers interested in Hellenistic Judaism to Appendix C, which lays out the examples of sarcasm I have found in these texts along with translations and notes.

Our next major case study leans more in the direction of classics. Being the first large-scale study of sarcasm in ancient Greek and having to establish the common signals that indicate sarcasm in this language create a need for assembling many examples of sarcasm. Lucian is the perfect author for this task. His works will furnish us with hundreds of examples of sarcasm.[2] This dataset will then be bolstered with an eclectic selection of ancient Greek texts – including the Hellenistic Jewish texts mentioned above – with the full chapter

---

[2] Although Lucian is not Paul's contemporary, he is closer to Paul's context than authors such as Plato and Aristophanes.

treating 400 examples of sarcasm in total. These data will provide considerable linguistic information about how ancient Greek speakers normally indicated sarcasm. While further research across time and dialects of Greek still has the potential to nuance these findings, the signals of sarcasm identified in our chapter on Lucian and other ancient Greek texts will play a significant role in facilitating the identification of sarcasm in Paul.

Following these chapters, Part II will take each of the undisputed Pauline letters in which sarcasm occurs in turn, beginning with Galatians, then Romans, and finally the Corinthian correspondence. For each letter I will exegete sarcastic passages, discuss how sarcasm fits into Paul's rhetoric in each letter, and provide pushback in places where previous scholarship has misidentified certain passages as ironic or sarcastic.

At the same time, much of this discussion will also be of interest to the New Testament generalist with no specific research interest in sarcasm or irony. Paul's opening in Galatians (1:6), which some consider an epistolary formula for expressing 'ironic rebuke', features in our chapter on the letter. Here I not only address whether this opening is sarcastic, but its relationship to similar letter openings across the documentary papyri. This enables the determination of whether Paul opens Galatians with a stock epistolary formula, and of the tone Gal 1:6 would probably convey.

Diatribe will play a major role in our discussion of Romans. To clarify the presence of sarcasm in certain rhetorical questions throughout the letter, I will offer a revised conception of authorial voice in dialogical passages. While this discussion is of direct relevance to scholars interested in the relationship between Romans and ancient diatribe, our conception of voice in Romans also contributes to the debate surrounding the identity of Paul's hypothetical interlocutor. Romans 13 has also generated considerable debate over the extent to which Paul's rhetoric submits to or subverts the imperial power of Rome. Our treatment of the passage contributes to this discussion by assessing the viability of ironic readings of Rom 13:1–7.

First Corinthians will provide the opportunity to address how closely or loosely the letter's often-discussed 'Corinthian slogans' represent the perspectives of the Corinthians. Establishing a broader range of possibilities beyond mere quotation will enable us to determine whether any slogans are likely to be sarcastic. I will also treat Paul's use of sarcasm in 1 Cor 8:1–11, a pericope which has (almost) never been considered ironic or sarcastic in past scholarship. This reading leads to a reassessment of Paul's rhetorical approach in dealing with the issue of idol-food. I then address the difficulties presented by 1 Cor 11:19, an exegetical crux that some interpreters have attempted to resolve with recourse to irony.

Paul's fool's speech in Second Corinthians has been the focal point for the lion's share of scholarship on Pauline irony. One of the major findings of our chapter on Second Corinthians will be the fact that Paul does not actually use sarcasm within the fool's speech itself. Paul does, however, use significant sarcasm throughout 2 Cor 10–13, although less frequently than he uses self-deprecating irony, *asteismos* in Greek. We shall define *asteismos* in §1.1.2 of the next chapter and discuss its rhetorical functions briefly in our work on Lucian. The relationship between sarcasm and *asteismos*, which we find only in 2 Cor 10–13, will be a major focus of our treatment of Second Corinthians. Our concluding chapter will review the major findings of the study and compare Paul's use of sarcasm across the letters surveyed.

PART I

What Is Sarcasm? How Is Sarcasm Expressed? What Does Sarcasm Do?

1

METHOD, DEFINING SARCASM, AND THE SCOPE OF THE PROJECT

This chapter will begin with a discussion of method before moving on to review Pauline scholarship on irony and sarcasm. We will be in a better position to assess Pauline scholarship having first treated irony and sarcasm in their own right. The first two sections, then, will survey ancient and modern treatments of these subjects.

These surveys will make an important methodological contribution to this study by defining my approach to irony and sarcasm and by focusing the scope of the project. Beginning with ancient discussions will ground the study in terminology relevant to Paul's linguistic context, providing a theoretical vocabulary for analyzing different forms of irony, including sarcasm, in language from Paul's day. Ancient treatments of irony and sarcasm, however, are not systematic accounts of language and there is much helpful nuance to be gained from modern scholarship. The first methodological contribution of modern irony research will be in narrowing the scope of this study by defining the relationships between different forms of irony. I will define sarcasm as a subcategory of verbal irony, which is itself distinct from other forms of irony. We will then go on to discuss the major paradigms for describing verbal irony that have been significant in recent scholarship before developing a working definition of sarcasm. I will not adopt a single approach to verbal irony but will instead consider each of the modern accounts as exegetical tools that can be used to explain why a given utterance is or is not sarcastic as we move forward with the study. Our working definition of sarcasm will aim to encapsulate as much of the insights of recent scholarship as possible while still maintaining continuity with the way sarcasm was defined in the ancient world.

Although surveying ancient and modern treatments of sarcasm and irony will provide a methodological framework for analyzing instances of sarcasm in ancient Greek texts, we will continue to develop our method for detecting sarcasm and evaluating its effects throughout this study. Determining how ancient Greek speakers normally communicated sarcasm and what its typical rhetorical functions were will be the major tasks of Chapters 2 and 3. These findings will create a baseline for comparison when we turn to the Pauline corpus itself.

Having surveyed ancient and modern discussions of sarcasm and irony, we will be well situated to evaluate the contributions of previous Pauline scholarship. Our review will focus on dedicated studies of irony or sarcasm in Paul, establishing which scholars will serve as conversation partners in discussing specific letters of Paul, and in what capacity past scholarship on Pauline irony will be relevant for our analysis of sarcasm. The background in modern irony research provided in §1.2 will enable us to fit Pauline scholarship into a chronology of developments in irony studies. This contextualization shows scholarship on Paul to have been significantly out of date in its understanding of irony, an issue that the present chapter aims to remedy.

1.1   Ancient Discussions of Irony and Sarcasm

We begin by overviewing ancient treatments of irony (*eirōneia*, εἰρωνεία). The concept of *eirōneia* develops over time, referring to patterns of behaviour in earlier works before becoming a dedicated figure of speech or trope as we move closer to Paul's historical context. We will focus on irony as a figure of speech in greater detail, as here we find specific reference to sarcasm (*sarkasmos*, σαρκασμός) as well as other forms of irony that will play a role in this study.

1.1.1   *eirōneia* from Aristophanes to Aristotle

The meaning of *eirōneia* changes over a few generations across the earliest extant texts to employ the term. Lane argues that in Aristophanes, *eirōneia* means something like 'concealing by feigning', an act associated with deception.[1] Aristophanes' *Wasps* provides an apt illustration: when Philocleon, who is obsessed with sitting on juries, is locked in his house to prevent him from sitting on a jury, he makes several desperate attempts at escaping (*Wasps*, 110–64). At one point, he claims he needs to take his donkey to the

---

[1] Lane 2006, 54–56; 2010, 248; cf. Vlastos 1987, 80–81.

market (*Wasps*, 165–173). Seeing through the scheme, one of his
captors remarks to another: 'What a pretext he dangled in front of
you [i.e. like bait on a hook], how cunningly deceptive' (οἵαν
πρόφασιν καθῆκεν, ὡς εἰρωνικῶς, *Wasps*, 174–75 [Lane]).
Here
Philocleon is behaving 'with *eirōneia*' (εἰρωνικῶς) because he is attempting to hide his true motives by deceptively pretending they are otherwise, making the scene fit well with Lane's definition of *eirōneia* in
Aristophanes.[2]

The description of the *eirōn* (εἴρων), the person characterized by
eirōneia, in Theophrastus lies closer to the Aristophanic meaning of
eirōneia as concealing by feigning than it does to Aristotle – whose
definition we will discuss presently.[3] Theophrastus portrays the *eirōn*
as someone who hides his real opinions and motives, 'he praises to
their faces those whom he has attacked in secret, and commiserates
with people he is suing if they lose their case' (*Char.* 1.2 [Rusten,
LCL]). Theophrastus assesses the *eirōn* negatively, characterizing
him as a non-committal coward who deceives to avoid responsibility
(*Char.* 1.2–6). We also find *eirōneia* depicted as the cowardly
avoidance of responsibility in Demosthenes (*Orat.* 4 [Phil 1], 7,
37; *Ex.* 14.3).

With Aristotle, *eirōneia* comes to mean self-deprecation: 'disavowing or downplaying qualities that one actually possesses'[4] (cf. *Eth.
Nic.* 1127a: ὁ δὲ εἴρων ἀνάπαλιν ἀρνεῖσθαι τὰ ὑπάρχοντα ἢ ἐλάττω
ποιεῖν). Aristotle's ethical works set virtues in contrast to their corresponding vices. Aristotle depicts *eirōneia* as a vice, a deficiency in
truthfulness (ἀλήθεια). Boastfulness (ἀλαζονεία) is *eirōneia*'s opposite
vice, an excess compared to truthfulness:

Ὁ δ᾽ ἀληθὴς καὶ ἁπλοῦς, ὃν καλοῦσιν αὐθέκαστον, μέσος τοῦ
εἴρωνος καὶ ἀλαζόνος· ὁ μὲν γὰρ ἐπὶ τὰ χείρω καθ᾽ αὑτοῦ
ψευδόμενος μὴ ἀγνοῶν εἴρων, ὁ δ᾽ ἐπὶ τὰ βελτίω ἀλαζών

The one who is truthful and straightforward, whom they
call forthright, lies between the self-deprecator [*eirōn*] and
the boaster. The self-deprecator is not at all ignorant of the

---

[2] For further discussion, and the above translation, see Lane 2006, 54–55. For other
uses of *eirōneia* in Aristophanes, see *Av.* 1211; *Nub.* 449.
[3] Theophrastus' *Characters* discusses traits of character rather than character types
in a literary sense (Rusten and Cunningham 1993, 12–13). The description of *eirōneia*
in Theophrastus does not therefore provide evidence for the *eirōn* as a stock character
in ancient Greek theatre or literature.
[4] Lane 2006, 79, cf. 77–80.

fact that they are deceptively portraying themself as lesser than they are, while the boaster claims to be better than they are (*Eth. Eud.* 1233b–1234a; cf. 1221a).

And in *Nicomachean Ethics* (1108a):

> In respect of truth then, the middle character may be called truthful, and the observance of the mean Truthfulness; pretence in the form of exaggeration is Boastfulness, and its possessor a boaster; in the form of understatement, Self-deprecation, and its possessor the self-deprecator ([προσποίησις] ἡ δ᾽ ἐπὶ τὸ ἔλαττον εἰρωνεία καὶ <ὁ ἔχων> εἴρων [Rackham, LCL]).

The *eirōn* therefore pretends (προσποίησις, *Eth. Nic.* 1108a) to lack qualities they possess; *eirōneia* is an intentional misrepresentation (ψευδόμενος μὴ ἀγνοῶν, *Eth. Eud.* 1233b) of the truth (ἀλήθεια).[5] Aristotle's definition of *eirōneia* goes on to replace the earlier meaning of the term attested in Aristophanes, and influence how later writers would read Plato.[6]

This Aristotelean definition of *eirōneia* does not apply to Philocleon in Aristophanes, whom we discussed above. Philocleon does not downplay the truth about himself or his personal qualities but engages in concealing by feigning to trick his captors into believing he has completely different motives than those he has.

While *eirōneia* is portrayed predominately as a negative quality in Aristotle (see also *Rh.* 1382b; *Physiognomica*, 808a) – as it was in Aristophanes, Theophrastus, and Demosthenes – it receives some concession due to association with Socrates. Aristotle admits that self-deprecation is better than boastfulness (ἀλαζονεία), especially when done tastefully – as he considers Socrates to have done (*Eth. Nic.* 1127a–b).

The use of *eirōneia* in Plato, and with respect to Plato's Socrates, is a matter of debate. As in Aristophanes, *eirōneia* remains a negative quality; when the term is applied to Socrates, it is used as an insult,[7]

---

[5] The initial definition of *eirōneia* in Theophrastus corresponds to Aristotle's definition: '*eirōneia*, in a nutshell, would seem to consist of pretending that one's deeds and words are worse than they are' (ἡ μὲν οὖν εἰρωνεία δόξειεν ἂν εἶναι, ὡς τύπῳ λαβεῖν, προσποίησις ἐπὶ χεῖρον πράξεων καὶ λόγων, *Char.* 1.1). This clashes with Theophrastus's own description of *eirōneia* (*Char.* 1.2–6, see p.11), and is probably a later addition dependent on Aristotle (Rusten and Cunningham 1993, 50n.1).

[6] See Lane 2010, 239–41.

[7] *Grg.* 489e; see Vlastos 1987, 82.

and as an accusation.[8] Lane argues that the Platonic references still carry the Aristophanic meaning,[9] whereas Vlastos sees something closer to Aristotle.[10]

At the very least, because the term *eirōneia* in Plato is used against Socrates rather than by or in support of Socrates, interpreters should not assume *a priori* that Plato means to associate Socrates with *eirōneia*.[11] Plato's Socrates is certainly accused of using *eirōneia*, but the exegetical question remains whether Plato portrays this accusation as valid. The use of the term 'Socratic irony' to describe Socrates' method of teaching or philosophical discussion also becomes problematic, insofar as it does not coincide with either the Aristophanic or Aristotelean definitions of *eirōneia* and should not be conflated therewith.[12]

We have now, agreeing with Lane, witnessed a development in *eirōneia*'s meaning from concealing by feigning in Aristophanes to self-deprecation in Aristotle. Much more could be said about early references to *eirōneia* and the behaviour of the *eirōn*, especially as they relate to Socrates in Plato. However, what is important to recognize for this study is that, despite common terminology, there is no necessary relationship between *eirōneia* as described from Aristophanes to Aristotle and the use of *eirōneia* as a figure of speech that we see in the later rhetoricians and grammarians. Because, as we shall see, sarcasm belongs to this second category of *eirōneia* as a figure of speech, it too should not be conflated with the use of the term *eirōneia* in early texts. Paul's use of sarcasm does not characterize him as an *eirōn* as described in Theophrastus or Aristotle. It does not set him in the tradition of Plato's Socrates, nor does it have anything to do with the modern literary construct 'Socratic irony'.

1.1.2   Sarcasm and Irony as Tropes: the Rhetoricians
        and Grammarians

We shall focus our treatment of *eirōneia* and sarcasm (*sarkasmos*, σαρκασμός) as tropes on the timeframe most relevant to Paul – the

---

[8] *Ap.* 37e–38a; *Resp.* 337a; *Symp.* 215a–222c.
[9] Lane 2006, 49–80; 2010, 247–49.
[10] Although he frames it in different terms (see Vlastos 1987, 87–95).
[11] Contra Nanos, who considers Plato to associate *eirōneia* with Socrates, and who considers this association positive (Nanos 2002, 35; cf. Forbes 1986, 10).
[12] For a strong critique of the concept of 'Socratic irony' as applied to Plato's Socrates, see Lane 2010, 237–57.

first century BCE to the second century CE.[13] By this time *eirōneia* has lost many of its negative connotations, largely thanks to association with Socrates.[14] Its meaning has also changed again. As we shall see, *eirōneia* discussed as a trope is distinct from the behaviour of the *eirōn* as defined from Aristophanes to Aristotle. Ancient treatments of irony as a figure of speech will be an important starting point for this project, because of how these texts associate irony with *sarkasmos*. Synthesizing these grammatical and rhetorical discussions of sarcasm reveals three significant patterns in how ancient authors go about defining it in relation to irony and other rhetorical techniques.[15]

The first pattern lies in how ancient authors connect sarcasm to other rhetorical techniques. Dating from as early as the first century BCE, the two grammars attributed to Tryphon contain the earliest extant treatments of *sarkasmos*.[16] Although neither of the Tryphonic grammars provide systematic taxonomies of tropes, there remains a clear connection between irony, sarcasm, and other comparable speech acts in these texts. Both group sarcasm and irony together along with a constellation of related terms such as self-deprecating irony (*asteismos*, ἀστεϊσμός), negation (*antiphrasis*, ἀντίφρασις), mockery (*myktērismos*, μυκτηρισμός), wit (*charientismos*, χαριεντισμός), and derision (*epikertomēsis*, ἐπικερτόμησις,[17] see Tryphon, *Trop.* 19–24; [Greg. Cor.][18] *Trop.* p). We may take this cluster of tropes as significant.

[13] Here I use 'trope' to refer to a constellation of terms employed by the rhetors and grammarians in describing sarcasm as a figure of speech (e.g. τρόπος, φράσις, λόγος). The differences in classification between these terms are slight and will not be a focus of this study. Quintilian also discusses *eirōneia* as a figure (*figura*), which differs from its use as a trope and which he connects to Socrates (*Inst.* 9.2.44–48). Quintilian's reception of Plato and Aristotle here certainly warrants further study. However, in this section we focus on irony as a trope, which provides the best inroad for investigating sarcasm.

[14] See Holland 2000, 87–90; Vlastos 1987, 84–85. Cf. Cicero, *De or.* 2.269–71.

[15] I begin to translate *eirōneia* and *sarkasmos* as 'irony' and 'sarcasm' here in recognition of the fact that in the rhetoricians and grammarians these terms start to coincide with what we in modern English refer to as irony and sarcasm; we will disambiguate modern constructions of irony in §1.2.1. To translate *eirōneia* as 'irony' in the early texts discussed throughout §1.1.1 would be misleading (cf. Lane 2006, 49).

[16] For discussion of the texts' dates and relationship to one another, see West 1965, 230–33, 235.

[17] See Chapter 3, n.90.

[18] The second Tryphonic grammar was originally (and erroneously) ascribed to Gregory of Corinth (see West 1965, 230–31).

These connections are even clearer in other treatments. Writing in the second century CE,[19] Alexander Numenius states, 'There are four sorts of irony: *asteismos, myktērismos, sarkasmos,* and *chleuasmos* (χλευασμός)'[20] (*Fig.* 18; cf. [Plutarch] *Vit. Hom.*II 706–8, 716–17, 721–22; Herodian, *Fig. Epitome* 16–17; Rhetorica Anonyma, *Trop.* 20).[21] Quintilian applies a multi-layered hierarchy, considering irony (*ironia/illusio*) a subcategory of allegory (*allegoria/inversio*)[22] and listing sarcasm[23] and related terms as species of irony (Quintilian, *Inst.* 8.6.44, 54, 57 [Butler, LCL]). The figure below summarizes how different authors draw connections between irony, sarcasm, and other tropes.

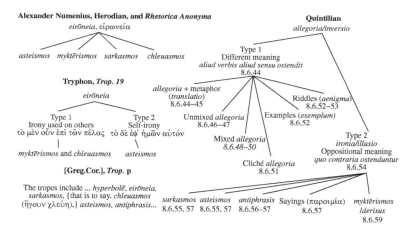

Figure 1 Categorization of tropes/figures of speech. Note that, in contrast to Alexander Numenius (*Fig.* 18), Herodian and Rhetorica Anonyma list irony's subtypes in the following order: *chleuasmos, myktērismos, sarkasmos, asteismos* (Herodian, *Fig. Epitome* 16–17; Rhetorica Anonyma, *Trop.* 20).

[19] Schmitz 1873, 1:123.
[20] Another form of mockery.
[21] Here Tryphon is less systematic, but still differentiates between self-irony (*asteismos*) and irony used on others (*myktērismos* and *chleuasmos,* Tryphon, *Trop.* 19, see Figure 1). The fact that Tryphon does not go on to define *chleuasmos,* but instead describes sarcasm (*Trop.* 20) may indicate that Tryphon sees *sarkasmos* and *chleuasmos* as basically synonymous (cf. n.26).
[22] Allegory here means a disjunction between the literal meaning of the words used and their intended meaning (*Inst.* 8.6.44; cf. Figure 1). It should not be confused with the modern English meaning of allegory.
[23] Which Quintilian leaves in Greek.

The close relationship between sarcasm and irony plays out in their definitions as well. In *De Tropis*, Tryphon, or someone writing in his name, defines irony as follows: 'Irony is a stylistic device that uses what is expressed literally to hint at an oppositional meaning, with pretence' (Εἰρωνεία ἐστι φράσις τοῖς ῥητῶς λεγο<μένοις αἰνιττο>μένη τοὐναντίον μεθ' ὑποκρίσεως, [Greg. Cor.] *Trop.* 15). Tryphon's definitions of sarcasm and irony here differ by only two Greek words. While irony is delivered 'with pretence' (μεθ' ὑποκρίσεως), sarcasm is spoken 'with mockery (*chleuasmos*)' (μετὰ χλευασμοῦ, [Greg. Cor.] *Trop.* 15–16). It is best to view this difference as additive. It is not that Tryphon considers sarcasm to lack pretence, but to communicate mockery in addition to pretence (ὑπόκρισις).[24] The expression of oppositional sentiment lies at the heart of other ancient definitions of irony and sarcasm as well (see [Plutarch] *Vit. Hom.*II 699–700, 716–7; Rhet. Anon. *Trop.* 20, 23).

It is important that we do not read Tryphon's 'oppositional meaning' (τοὐναντίον) too literally, as I have sought to do by avoiding the more restrictive translation 'the opposite'. The interpreter should not impose an unnecessary degree of rigidity on ancient definitions, which are brief and functional rather than systematic investigations into the nature of communication. Where we find more elaborated discussion in ancient authors, the focus is on the communication of affect rather than on strict semantic opposition. In Quintilian, sarcasm requires nothing more than 'censur[ing] with counterfeited praise' (*laudis adsimulatione detrahere*) or 'disguis[ing] bitter taunts in gentle words' (*tristia dicamus mollioribus verbis, Inst.* 8.6.55, 57, respectively [Butler, LCL]). This is a contrast in affect or evaluation – praise versus dispraise – not necessarily a difference in semantic meaning or contradiction in a matter of fact (cf. §1.2.2). Likewise, in Rhetorica Anonyma sarcasm 'expresses dishonour through kind words' (διὰ χρηστῶν ῥημάτων τὴν ἀτιμίαν ἐμφαίνων, *Trop.* 23).[25] Such sentiments are certainly oppositional to the literal message, but not necessarily its opposite.

---

[24] Consider the examples of irony and sarcasm in [Greg. Cor.] *Trop.* 15–16, which differ primarily in terms of the degree of mockery they express – the sarcastic being the greater – rather than in the presence of pretence (cf. Homer, *Od.* 17.397–408, 22.170–200).
[25] Cf. Phrynichus, *Praeparatio Sophistica*, A, concerning the expressions 'the noblest thief' (ἄριστος κλέπτειν), 'the noblest adulterer' (ἄριστος μοιχεύειν), and others like them: 'with the trope "sarcasm" such persons are praised in order to emphasize their wrongdoing' (σαρκασμοῦ τρόπῳ ἐπήνηται εἰς ὑπερβολὴν τοῦ κακοῦ).

The second significant pattern in ancient treatments of sarcasm is the way the grammarians connect it to different forms of mockery. We have already seen that in Tryphon sarcasm is expressed 'with mockery (*chleuasmos*)' (μετὰ χλευασμοῦ).[26] The overlap between sarcasm and different forms of mockery is most pronounced in the second-century grammar attributed to Herodian. While his definitions of the first three subcategories (εἴδη) of irony, *chleuasmos*, *myktērismos*, and *sarkasmos*, are quite distinct, the examples illustrating each term are similar. *chleuasmos* occurs, 'when laughing at the cowardly we might say, "what a manly soldier!"' *myktērismos*: 'What a deed you have done, friend, and a necessary one at that, that is, for so clever a man as yourself.' Both of these examples fit perfectly with the way Herodian defines sarcasm:

> Σαρκασμὸς δέ ἐστι λόγος τὴν ἀλήθειαν διὰ χρηστῶν ῥημάτων ἐμφαίνων, ὡς ὅταν τὸν ἐν προ<σ>λήψει τιμῆς κακοῖς περιπεσόντα καὶ διὰ τοῦτο ἀτιμαζόμενον ἐγγελῶντες εἴπωμεν 'εἰς μεγάλην δόξαν καὶ τιμὴν ἤγαγες σεαυτόν, ἑταῖρε'.

Sarcasm is an utterance that expresses the truth[27] through kind words, such as we might say while laughing at the person who in accepting an honour has fallen into wicked deeds and because of this is dishonoured: 'you, my friend, have won much glory and honour for yourself! (*Fig. Epit.* 16–17).

With the examples of three of Herodian's four species of irony fitting sarcasm's definition, a study of sarcasm has little to gain from trying to disentangle semantically these clearly overlapping speech acts. Instead, it will be sufficient to note that any given example of ancient Greek sarcasm could potentially be conceived of as an instance of *chleuasmos* or *myktērismos*. For our purposes, this is of no concern so long as it is also sarcastic. Ultimately, if we can take Herodian's word for it, the key difference between sarcasm and these other forms of mockery is a matter of delivery, that is, a distinction in the non-linguistic signals that accompany a given utterance.

---

[26] Cf. the gloss in Tryphon's list of tropes ([Greg. Cor.] *Trop.* p; Figure 1, p.15): 'sarcasm, {that is to say, *chleuasmos*}' (σαρκασμός, {ἤγουν χλεύη}).

[27] Rhetorica Anonyma's treatment of irony is so close to that of (Pseudo-) Herodian's that some sort of literary dependence must be the case. Here, Rhet. Anon. *Trop.* 23 has 'dishonour (ἀτιμίαν, cited p.16) instead of 'the truth' (ἀλήθειαν). This is probably a correction of Herodian, and not an unreasonable one.

We shall return to the issue of delivery presently; however, we must first concern ourselves with Herodian's fourth form of irony, which is simultaneously very like and unlike sarcasm. This last irony-type is *asteismos*, a speech act that we will encounter in Lucian, and that will play a significant role in our discussion of Second Corinthians.

In the Tryphonic tradition, *asteismos* is a self-deprecating form of irony (Ἀστεϊσμός ἐστι λόγος ἀφ᾽ ἑαυτοῦ διασυρτικὸς γενόμενος, Tryphon, *Trop.* 24),[28] 'a stylistic device that tactfully indicates something positive through words expressing oppositional meaning' (ἀστεϊσμός ἐστι φράσις διὰ τῶν ἐναντίων τὸ κρεῖττον ἠθικῶς ἐμφαίνουσα, [Greg. Cor.] *Trop.* 17). Classic examples include when 'someone who is rich says, "I myself am the poorest of all men," and the wrestler who defeats all his opponents claims to have lost to everybody.' (Tryphon, *Trop.* 24). Quintilian cites a more defensive example from Cicero, who employs *asteismos* to dismiss the accusations of others: 'We are seen as such typical "orators", since we've always imposed ourselves on the people' (*oratores visi sumus et populo imposuimus*, *Inst.* 8.6.55; cf. Cicero, *Letter Fragments*, 7.10).

asteismos is sarcasm's mirror image; instead of ironic praise used to mock another party, we have self-mocking irony for the sake of self-praise.[29] Resultantly, Quintilian requires only the words *et contra* to separate his examples of sarcasm and *asteismos* (*Inst.* 8.6.55).[30] While *asteismos* so conceived is similar to Aristotle's interpretation of *eirōneia* as discussed in §1.1.1, there remains an important

---

[28] Cf. Herodian, *Fig. Epit.* 16–17.

[29] The Greeks do not appear to have a specific term for the use of irony to compliment others, although this is possible. There is a whole class of insincere comments that Haiman describes as 'affectionate insults' that function similarly to *asteismos* but are targeted at others (see 1998, 22–23; see also Bruntsch and Ruch 2017, 1–13). Saying, 'You're just constantly underachieving', to ironically compliment a student who just got a distinction well illustrates the concept.

[30] There are textual difficulties in Quintilian's definition of *asteismos*. One variant reads, 'or with respect to a good thing' (*aut bonae rei*, *Inst.* 8.6.57). Following as it does a definition of sarcasm, this would have a similar function to *et contra* in 8.6.55, indicating that *asteismos* is similar to sarcasm, but is meant to compliment rather than criticize. Another variant may associate *asteismos* with *urbanitas* (for text critical notes, see Butler 1966, 3:332n.4, 3:333n.4). Such a connection fits with the definition of *asteismos* as witty quipping in the rhetoric ascribed to Demetrius (*Eloc.* 128–130). At the same time, *urbanitas* clashes with Quintilian's example of *asteismos*, which is clearly a case of self-deprecating irony. For this project we will focus on the more particular definition of *asteismos* as a self-deprecating form of irony rather than witty comments in general.

distinction.[31] Both the *eirōn* and the *asteist* downplay some positive trait that they consider themselves to possess. However, in *asteismos* the speaker's ultimate aim is to imply something positive about themself, while the *eirōn* communicates only their own modesty. Therefore, the *eirōn* and *asteist* alike might say, 'I am a mere fool', but only the *asteist* would thereby mean to imply 'I am actually wise'.

We now turn to the third significant feature of sarcasm particular to the ancient grammars. In discussing pseudo-Herodian we have already referred to certain performative features of ancient irony. These elements of tone and delivery are represented significantly enough across the grammars to suggest their being an integral part of how the Greeks conceived of sarcasm.[32]

We have already cited one of the definitions of sarcasm attributed to Tryphon. The other reads as follows: 'Sarcasm is showing the teeth while grinning' (Σαρκασμός ἐστι μέχρι τοῦ σεσηρέναι τοὺς ὀδόντας παραφαίνειν, Tryphon, *Trop.* 20). Here there is no description of what sorts of statements qualify as sarcastic, only a facial expression. This definition juxtaposes a degree of aggression ('showing the teeth', τοὺς ὀδόντας παραφαίνειν) with the ostensible positivity of a smile (σεσηρέναι).[33] The author of the *Vitae Homeri* also includes facial expression in their definition of sarcasm,[34] which reads like a synthesis of the two definitions attributed to Tryphon: 'There is a certain kind of irony, namely sarcasm, in which someone, through words of oppositional meaning, reproaches someone else while pretending to smile' (Ἔστι δέ τι εἶδος εἰρωείας καὶ ὁ σαρκασμός, ἐπειδάν τις διὰ τῶν ἐναντίων ὀνειδίζῃ τινι μετὰ προσποιήτου μειδιάματος, [Plutarch] *Vit. Hom.*II 716–717).[35]

---

[31] *asteismos* differs from Aristophanic *eirōneia* insofar as the former is not an attempt at concealment.

[32] That non-linguistic features are central to communicating irony in general is clear from Quintilian: '[Irony] is made evident to the understanding either by the delivery (*pronuntiatione*), the character of the speaker (*persona*) or the nature of the subject (*rei natura*)' (*Inst.* 8.6.54). Here *pronuntiatione* would be entirely a matter of how the ironic statement is performed. *Persona* could involve elements of both content and delivery; the speaker may characterize themself through words, gestures, tone, etc. *Rei natura* would function as a signal of irony in both written and spoken contexts.

[33] See Pawlak 2019, 551n.11. On sardonic smiling in ancient texts, see Lateiner 1995, 193–95; Halliwell 2008, 8–9, 93; Beard 2014, 73.

[34] For discussion and provenance, see Keaney and Lamberton 1996, 2, 7–10, 45–53.

[35] Interestingly, over a thousand years later, Rockwell found mouth movement to be significant for the expression of sarcasm (see 2001, 47–50).

In Herodian, the difference between sarcasm, *chleuasmos* (χλευασμός), and *myktērismos* (μυκτηρισμός) seems to be entirely a matter of delivery. Here we find *chleuasmos* delivered with insincere smiling (μειδιασμοῦ προ{σ}φερόμενος) and while laughing at the victim of a comment (ἐγγελῶντες). Sarcasm, too, is delivered with laughter directed at its target (ἐγγελῶντες, Herodian, *Fig. Epit.* 16–17). As for *myktērismos*, it involves the movement of the nostrils and something like a derisive snort (μετὰ τῆς τῶν ῥινῶν ἐπιμύξεως . . . πνεῦμα διὰ τῶν ῥινῶν συνεκφέροντες, Herodian, *Fig. Epit.* 16–17).[36]

Although nonverbal cues cannot help us exegete sarcasm millennia after the fact, these descriptions of a typical sarcastic facial expression reinforce the major features of how the ancient Greeks conceptualize sarcasm. The presence of an artificial smile concealing a look of hostility emphasizes the way sarcasm communicates a message oppositional to its literal appearance and the importance of pretence within that process. This pretence must be transparent enough to communicate the sarcast's negative message clearly, because the sarcast's ultimate aim is to express mockery, *chleuasmos* more specifically, as they laugh at (ἐγγελῶντες) the victim of their barb.

1.2   Modern Research on Verbal Irony

While ancient treatments of sarcasm and irony are an important starting point, the precision of modern research will be essential for developing the approach to irony that I will adopt throughout this study. We will create a focused scope for the project by elucidating the relationships between different forms of irony, namely situational and verbal irony, and by defining sarcasm as a subtype of verbal irony. We will then survey several paradigms for understanding verbal irony in modern scholarship. Because verbal irony is the broader category compared with sarcasm, most scholarship in recent years has focused thereon. However, most results are still generalizable to sarcasm.

In this survey, we will not have space to be fully systematic, but will instead focus on the concepts that have had the largest impact on the field. I will not adopt a single approach as the methodological lens for this study. While the accounts of verbal irony surveyed are

---

[36] Cf. Tryphon, *Trop.* 21.

nuanced and well-fleshed-out systems in their own right, they each have their own strengths and drawbacks. These paradigms will contribute methodologically to this study as exegetical tools: concepts that can be used to explain why a given text is an example of verbal irony. From there, it will remain to narrow our focus again from verbal irony to sarcasm by developing a working definition of sarcasm that will serve throughout the study.

1.2.1   Narrowing the Scope: from Irony to Verbal Irony
        to Sarcasm

This section will concern itself with demonstrating the utility of treating specific forms of irony instead of attempting a single analysis of irony in general. In making this case we shall focus on the two forms of irony most discussed in recent research, verbal irony and situational irony. From there, we will go on to clarify sarcasm's relationship to irony by defining it as a subspecies of verbal irony. We will go no further than this in defining sarcasm until we have explored scholarship on verbal irony.

There are a great many phenomena described under the umbrella 'irony'. Muecke lists no less than 19 – including ironies of fate, chance, and character alongside better-known forms such as dramatic, situational, verbal, and Socratic irony.[37] Early critical studies of irony, which we will go on to designate the 'First Quest' for the nature of irony (§1.3.1), were broad in their scope, leading to generalizations from one form of irony to the next.[38] But conceptual problems arise when treating multiple forms of irony together.

The verbal/situational irony divide will be a helpful way of illustrating this issue. At present, scholarship remains divided over whether there is any significant connection between these two forms of irony. Utsumi's implicit display theory is one of the most thoroughgoing attempts at making verbal irony dependent on situational irony.[39] Utsumi argues that verbal irony arises when a speaker implicitly makes reference to an 'ironic environment' and expresses

---

[37] Muecke 1969, 4. Cf. Colston 2017, 19.

[38] Although Muecke is capable of making fine distinctions between different ironies, he goes on to generalize about 'the ironist' and irony's morality in ways that efface these distinctions (see ibid., 216–47; see also Kierkegaard 1966, 336–42).

[39] For other attempts at connecting verbal and situational irony, see Shelley 2001, 811–14; Colston 2017, 19–42. For scholarship on situational irony, see Shelley 2001, 775–814; Lucariello 1994, 129–44.

a negative evaluation thereof. This ironic environment consists of a situation in which the speaker's expectations at a given time have failed.[40] Utsumi illustrates his paradigm using the following example: 'a mother asked her son to clean up his messy room, but he was lost in a comic book. After a while, she discovered that his room was still messy.' She remarks, 'This room is totally clean!'[41] The mother alludes to her failed expectation (that the room should be clean), thereby communicating implicit negative evaluation.

But one can just as easily conceive of verbal irony without an ironic environment, that is, without any situational irony, as the following anecdote illustrates:

> It often rains in England. It rained yesterday. The forecast says it will rain today. Knowing these things, when I step outside into the rain, I still say, 'My, what lovely weather!'

While I suspect most interpreters would view this comment as an instance of verbal irony, even sarcasm, there is no irony in the underlying situation. My expectations have been fulfilled exactly. As such, it appears that verbal irony overlaps with situational irony in some cases, but not others.

Because there is no fundamental overlap between situational and verbal irony, it is methodologically problematic to draw conclusions about an author's use of irony in general without respecting the differences between different forms of irony.[42] Concerning the many forms of irony, Wilson writes, 'There is no reason to assume that all these phenomena work in the same way, or that we should be trying to develop a single general theory of irony *tout court* ... in other words, irony is not a natural kind.'[43] We cannot assume that two things are meaningfully related just because they share the label 'irony'. There is no *prima facie* reason why an ironic situation, such as a police station being robbed, and an ironic comment, such as saying 'How lovely!' after stubbing one's toe, should be formed by the same mechanisms or have comparable rhetorical effects when communicated. Indeed, situational irony is a matter of interpretation: situations can be construed as ironic independent of whether,

---

[40] Utsumi 2000, 1783–85, 1803–4.

[41] Ibid. 1779, 1783–84.

[42] This methodological issue remains even if some generic relationship or common underlying mechanism between situational and verbal irony could be demonstrated.

[43] Wilson 2006, 1725. Sperber and Wilson do, however, consider *verbal* irony a 'natural kind' (1998, 289–92).

in the case of written texts, the author considered the situation ironic. Verbal irony, however, is an act of communication from one speaker to another party.[44]

As we shall see in §1.3, failure to draw distinctions between different forms of irony has been a persistent problem in scholarship on Paul. As a corrective, this study will now narrow in scope from irony in general to verbal irony, leaving situational and other forms of irony largely behind. It remains now to briefly discuss the relationship between sarcasm and verbal irony before moving on to contemporary treatments of verbal irony.

In current scholarship, there is disagreement over sarcasm's relationship to verbal irony. Certain scholars see some but not complete overlap, arguing that sarcasm consists of intentionally hurtful utterances that can be ironic but need not be. Another perspective considers sarcasm a subtype of verbal irony. From this viewpoint, all sarcastic statements are instances of verbal irony, but not all instances of verbal irony are sarcastic.[45] In order to maintain continuity with the thrust of ancient thought, I will adopt this latter position. We have therefore left irony-in-general behind to avoid invalid generalizations between ironic comments and situations. Before moving on from verbal irony to a working definition of sarcasm, we will first explore contemporary scholarship concerning what verbal irony is and how it works.

1.2.2   Counterfactuality and Verbal Irony

English dictionaries often describe irony as 'the expression of meaning through the use of words which normally mean the opposite'.[46] This definition, which Colston terms a 'lay account' of irony,[47] has its basis in the sorts of descriptions we find among the ancient Greek rhetoricians and grammarians. But, as discussed in §1.1.2, it is important to remember that when pushed to a systematic account of verbal irony, this strict notion of opposition does not do justice to the ancient discussions, with their emphasis on pretence and on dispraise-through-praise.

---

[44] Cf. Haiman 1998, 20.
[45] For a review of perspectives, see Attardo 2000b, 795.
[46] E.g., Waite 2013, 484–85.
[47] Colston 2019, 112–13.

Although earlier modern treatises on irony are more nuanced than such dictionary definitions, they still conceive of irony semantically, that is, in terms of meaning. For Booth, the detection of verbal irony[48] begins with 'reject[ing] the literal meaning' of a statement.[49] However, this semantic account of irony, the idea that verbal irony consists of saying the opposite of or something conflicting with what one means, has been largely abandoned since the late 1970s (see §1.3.2).[50]

The first significant flaw with the semantic approach is worth illustrating with a short parable, as it will become essential to our exegesis of sarcasm in Paul later on:

> An undergraduate sits in lectures. As the talk carries on, she finds herself next to a student who treats the professor's questions like a game of University Challenge, chirping quick answers and dominating the conversation. In a moment of irritation at the end of class, she mutters, perhaps a little too loudly, 'My, aren't you clever!'[51]

This example, henceforth The Parable of the Disgruntled Undergraduate, represents a clear instance of verbal irony – sarcasm more specifically.[52] Sarcastic statements of this kind constitute a major problem for traditional semantic accounts of irony, which require the expression of meaning in conflict with the literal utterance. Inexplicable by these paradigms, the above example contains a sarcastic statement that also happens to be factually true; the irritating student clearly is clever. Verbally ironic statements therefore need not be false. They may simultaneously express their literal meaning and imply more.

The second flaw with semantic approaches to verbal irony is the fact that not all ironic statements are propositional; sometimes there is no opposite meaning. Wilson illustrates this problem as follows: 'Bill is a neurotically cautious driver who keeps his petrol tank full,

---

[48] Booth uses the term 'stable irony', a concept that is close to, but somewhat different from, verbal irony (see Booth 1974, 1–14).

[49] Ibid, 10; see also 39–41. Cf. Muecke 1969, 23, 52–54; 1982, 40–41, 100; Kierkegaard 1966, 264–65, 272–73.

[50] For an early refutation, see Sperber and Wilson 1981, 295–96.

[51] Example adapted from Kumon-Nakamura, Glucksberg, and Brown 1995, 4–6; cf. Wilson 2006, 1726; Camp 2012, 596.

[52] It also fits nicely with Quintilian's 'censur[ing] with counterfeited praise' (*Inst.* 8.6.55 [Butler, LCL]).

never fails to indicate when turning and repeatedly scans the horizon for possible dangers.' The following ironic imperative (uttered by Bill's passenger), 'Don't forget to use your indicator', and the ironic question 'Do you think we should stop for petrol?' are not declarative.[53] It is therefore difficult to conceive of imperatives and questions as having opposite meanings implied through irony, even though the above examples demonstrate that they can be used ironically.[54]

Because of the problems illustrated by these examples, scholars have had to move beyond semantics in describing verbal irony. But this is not to say that opposition cannot still feature in much verbal irony. Research has demonstrated that clearly counterfactual statements are significantly more likely to be interpreted ironically than their factual counterparts.[55] Therefore, while verbal irony may not require the inversion of meaning, obvious incongruity between what is said and what is meant remains an important signal of its presence.

1.2.3 The Echoic Account

The echoic account of verbal irony was developed in the late 1970s by Sperber and Wilson.[56] This account comes out of a broader approach to linguistics known as Relevance Theory (RT).[57] RT purports that effective communication seeks to obtain maximum relevance, to generate the greatest possible 'contextual effect', while requiring a minimum of 'mental effort' to understand.[58] One may illustrate this concept using two hypothetical SBL presentations: Presenter A reads his highly esoteric paper in monotone. It quickly becomes evident that the only people in the room listening are those with strongly overlapping research areas (high contextual effect); the rest consider checking their emails to require lower mental effort. Presenter B explains her research clearly and dynamically. Even those from unrelated fields tune in thanks to the accessibility of the

---

[53] Wilson 2006, 1726.

[54] See Popa-Wyatt 2014, 131; cf. Sperber and Wilson 1981, 295.

[55] Kreuz and Glucksberg 1989, 382; cf. Kreuz and Roberts 1995, 27; Katz and Pexman 1997, 30–32, 36–38; Pexman, Ferretti, and Katz 2000, 202–3, 220.

[56] See 'Les ironies comme mentions' (1978). Published in English as 'Irony and the Use-Mention Distinction' (1981).

[57] RT also owes its genesis to Sperber and Wilson (see Sperber and Wilson 1986; Wilson and Sperber 2012).

[58] Wilson and Sperber 1992, 67–68.

presentation (low mental effort), and for those whose work is directly related, we have reached optimal relevance (high contextual effect, low mental effort).

Sperber and Wilson argue that all verbal irony can be described as instances of echoic mention. In contrast to *use*, where the words employed are the speaker's own, *mention* makes reference to the statements, thoughts, or expectations of others.[59] This is the difference between a child who stubs his toe and yells, 'Ow, crap!' (use) and his older brother who runs off shouting, 'Mom, mom! Matt said a bad word!' (mention). But Sperber and Wilson do not consider every instance of mention to be ironic. The echoic account defines verbal irony as instances of echoic mention implicitly referring to the speech or perspective of another party, not for the sake of conveying information (as in the above example of mention), but to express evaluation – that is, an affective response to the statement/thought mentioned.[60]

These echoes should not be thought of as citations, or even as reasonable approximations of another person's position, but can be quite loose. Sperber and Wilson use the example of a rained-out country walk where someone comments, 'What lovely weather!' If someone in the party had predicted nice weather, the ironic echo would be explicit. However, even if no such comment had been made, the quip could still refer to the general expectation that people go on walks to enjoy nice weather.[61] Irony therefore obtains relevance not by conveying reliable information about the proposition mentioned, but by expressing a speaker's feelings or perspective thereon.[62]

The echoic account is not without its critics. Haiman considers the paradigm 'restrictive',[63] and attempts have been made to demonstrate that there are cases of verbal irony that are entirely non-echoic.[64] At the same time, recourse to more indirect echoes, such

---

[59] See Sperber and Wilson 1981, 303–6.

[60] Sperber and Wilson 1981, 306–11; see also Wilson and Sperber 1992, 53–76; Wilson and Sperber 2012, 123–45. This perspective develops over time. Wilson and Sperber go on to replace the notion of irony as echoic mention with the broader concept of irony as a subtype of 'echoic use', itself a subtype of 'attributive use' (see 2012, 128–34).

[61] Sperber and Wilson 1981, 310.

[62] Wilson and Sperber 2012, 128–29.

[63] Haiman 1998, 25–26.

[64] Clark and Gerrig 1984, 123; Seto 1998, 239–56. For Sperber and Wilson's response, see 1998, 283–89.

as the echoing of social norms or expectations, can make the paradigm feel rather vague. As Simpson puts it,

> [T]he problem is simply that we can never know what exactly it is that [the ironist] is echoing, which means that if the echoic argument is to be sustained, then some anterior discourse event has to be invented, come hell or high water, to justify the echoic function.[65]

At some point one wonders whether the ironic echo becomes too faint to be useful.

Despite these drawbacks, the echoic account continues to exert influence within irony studies and remains useful for our purposes. Throughout this study we will encounter several instances of sarcasm that are best explained as echoic, and we will find that the explicit use of echoic mention functions as a significant indicator of sarcasm in ancient Greek texts.[66]

1.2.4   The Pretence Account

Clark's and Gerrig's pretence account of verbal irony emerges in response to the echoic paradigm and aims to resolve some of its problems. Clark and Gerrig consider verbal irony to occur when a speaker pretends to make a statement sincerely and also pretends that their audience will receive it as such. But this pretence is meant to be transparent to the speaker's actual audience, who recognize the remark as ironic.[67] They illustrate this phenomenon using a speaker who exclaims, 'See what lovely weather it is', under drizzly conditions:

> [T]he speaker is pretending to be an unseeing person … explaining to an unknowing audience how beautiful the weather is. She intends the addressee to see through the pretense … and to see that she is thereby ridiculing the sort

---

[65] Simpson 2003, 116.
[66] See Chapter 3, §3.1.1.3. Cf. Pawlak 2019, 549–50. The echoic account has also become the starting point for a number of spin-off paradigms – such as the echoic reminder and allusional pretence perspectives – which take it in different directions or combine its ideas with other hypotheses (see Kreuz and Glucksberg 1989, 374–86; Kumon-Nakamura, Glucksberg, and Brown 1995, 3–21; Attardo 2000b, 793–824; Popa-Wyatt 2014, 127–65).
[67] Clark and Gerrig 1984, 122.

of person who would make such an exclamation ... the sort of person who would accept it, and the exclamation itself.[68]

This articulation of the pretence account has since been revised. The multi-layered pretence that Clark and Gerrig describe above is too complex to account for what is going on when many speakers engage in verbal irony. Every ironic comment need not involve the appropriation of another persona and an address to a pretended, naïve audience.[69]

Responding to various issues and critiques, Currie streamlines the pretence perspective.[70] Currie considers verbal irony to occur when 'pretending to assert or whatever, one pretends to be a certain kind of person—a person with a restricted or otherwise defective view of the world or some part of it'.[71] This pretence can be broken down into two distinct elements, the pretending itself, and the evaluation of the ironic utterance's target represented in the 'defective outlook'.[72] Currie's revised pretence account has the advantage of not requiring a pretended address to a credulous audience, nor does it require an audience at all.[73]

At its best, the pretence account can integrate examples of verbal irony where proposed echoes are vague or that are difficult to describe as echoic at all. It also has some affinities to Sperber and Wilson's account. The use of verbal irony to express evaluation remains constant across both paradigms, while here pretence replaces the echoic mechanism.[74]

Additionally, pretending features in ancient accounts of irony and sarcasm – creating continuity between modern and ancient discussions – recall Tryphon's 'with pretence' (μεθ' ὑποκρίσεως, *Trop.* 15) and *Vitae Homeri*'s insincere smiling (μετὰ προσποιήτου μειδιάματος, [Plutarch] *Vit. Hom.*II 717; see §1.1.2).

Just as echoic irony invites us to think less in terms of semantics and more in terms of mention and evaluation, the pretence paradigm enables us to consider verbal irony in terms of sincerity versus

---

[68] Clark and Gerrig 1984, 122.

[69] For further criticism of the pretence account, see Sperber 1984, 130–36; Kreuz and Glucksberg 1989, 384.

[70] For Currie's interaction with the echoic paradigm, see 2006, 111–13, 122–28.

[71] Ibid. 116.

[72] Ibid. 115–19.

[73] I.e., one can be sarcastic with no one else around (Currie 2006, 114–15).

[74] For Sperber and Wilson's critique of pretence theory, including Currie's revision, see Wilson 2006, 1734–41; 2013, 48–54; Wilson and Sperber 2012, 134–45.

insincerity –a distinction that will play a significant role in interpreting ancient sarcasm, both Pauline and otherwise.

1.2.5 Constraint Satisfaction: How We Process Verbal Irony

In addition to addressing verbal irony's nature, scholarship has also devoted considerable resources to exploring the ways in which humans process verbal irony. In an early study, Booth describes the interpretation of irony as a step-by-step process – even if these steps 'are often virtually simultaneous' – beginning when one finds reason to reject the literal interpretation of an utterance.[75] Recent research has so vindicated not Booth's steps but his intuition about the rapidity and seamlessness of verbal irony recognition that we may no longer speak of irony processing as linear at all. This revised understanding of verbal irony processing is known as the parallel constraint satisfaction approach (CS). It hypothesizes that irony processing occurs early and is non-linear.

Studies have shown that the interpretation of ironic cues begins 'in the earliest moments of processing the remarks, suggesting that participants were integrating all available information as soon as it was relevant'.[76] In an eye-tracking study, subjects presented with an ironic statement and visual prompts representing ironic and literal interpretations did not show a tendency towards looking at the object representing a literal reading first.[77] Katz's research adds a temporal dimension, finding that sarcastic statements are processed rapidly, often in less than a second. This does not require consideration and rejection of the literal meaning of an utterance, but instead, 'the same processes are involved in processing for literal and sarcastic intent on-line'.[78]

Early, simultaneous processing does not mean that the interpreter never processes the literal meaning of an utterance during irony

---

[75] See Booth 1974, 10–13. For a more recent, linear approach to verbal irony processing, see Giora 1997, 183–202; Giora and Fein 1999, 425–33; Giora 2007, 269–79; Fein, Yeari, and Giora 2015, 1–26. We will not treat this perspective in detail. The most recent, methodologically nuanced studies support constraint satisfaction (see n.77).

[76] Pexman 2008, 287; cf. Pexman, Ferretti, and Katz 2000, 201–20.

[77] Kowatch, Whalen, and Pexman 2013, 304–13. Studies on brain activity during irony processing have also supported CS (Akimoto et al. 2017, 42–46; Spotorno et al. 2013, 1–9).

[78] Katz 2009, 88.

recognition, only that they need not go through the literal to comprehend the ironic. This point is methodologically important. CS demonstrates that we cannot limit our search for verbal irony only to instances where one is forced to reject an utterance's literal meaning. To do so ignores both what verbal irony is (§1.2.2) and how we process it. Parallel processing means using all available data to reach the most plausible of several possible interpretations.[79] Neither the literal nor the ironic reading should be given an *a priori* advantage.[80]

Therefore, if we want our method for identifying verbal irony to respect the way humans actually process it, ironic cues – the linguistic and contextual means by which speakers and authors signal irony to their audiences – become essential. Here too we have much to learn from CS.

In 2012 Campbell and Katz used sarcasm production and rating tasks to test whether certain cues theorized as essential to the nature of verbal irony were necessary to the interpretation of sarcasm.[81] These cues included some of those already discussed, such as echoic mention and pretence, in addition to others.[82] Campbell and Katz found that while each irony-signal was important and in some cases sufficient to characterize a statement as sarcastic, no single cue was necessary.[83] This means that we can create neither a linear method for interpreting ironic statements, nor a checklist of essential cues. Instead, the 'comprehension of language, in general, including non-literal and sarcastic language, involves utilizing all of the information that a person has at his or her command at any one point in time'.[84]

With the cues of verbal irony being essential to its recognition, but not fixed, it becomes important to determine what signals can tip the balance in favour of an ironic reading. While studies such as Campbell's and Katz's (above) have made significant progress with modern English, ancient Greek is largely unexplored territory.[85]

---

[79] See Campbell and Katz 2012, 477.
[80] Cf. Sim 2016, 118.
[81] Campbell and Katz 2012, 462–76.
[82] Ibid. 2012, 459–62.
[83] Ibid. 468–73, 476–78. This finding does not necessarily invalidate previous models of verbal irony. Just because a participant does not recognize the presence of a specific feature, pretence for example, in a sarcastic statement does not mean that this feature was not present in the first place (cf. ibid. 477).
[84] Ibid. 477.
[85] Although Minchin's work on Homer is a helpful starting point (2010a; 2010b). For further work on modern English, see Attardo 2000a, 3–20; Haiman 1990,

Therefore, one of the major tasks of Chapter 3 will be elucidating the linguistic and contextual signals of sarcasm in ancient Greek texts.

1.2.6   Sarcasm: Towards a Working Definition

Although we have presented no definitive solution to the nature of verbal irony, each of the paradigms reviewed contributes conceptual information that will be useful in identifying and exegeting specific instances of sarcasm throughout Paul's letters. Recognizing the fundamental differences between forms of irony, such as situational and verbal irony, has led us to narrow the scope of this project from irony in general to verbal irony. Surveying contemporary accounts of verbal irony has also defined the approach to verbal irony that I will be adopting throughout this study. We have seen the deficiencies of semantic accounts, which see verbal irony as inhering in meaning inversion. While counterfactuality can function as a signal of verbal irony, not all ironic statements negate or invert their literal meaning. Indeed, as we saw with CS, the literal interpretation of an utterance does not have priority over the ironic, as all relevant signals are processed simultaneously. Shifting from semantic to pragmatic approaches is an important methodological step that will impact exegesis.

Beyond arguing for the utility of pragmatic approaches over semantics, I have not taken a strong position on the validity of the echoic and pretence accounts of verbal irony. While perhaps neither paradigm provides a complete account, both mechanisms are operative in much verbal irony. Both accounts can thereby make a methodological contribution to this study by functioning as interpretive frameworks for exegeting specific examples of sarcasm in the chapters to come.

Having now defined our approach to verbal irony, it remains to narrow our scope again and construct a working definition of sarcasm that will become the foundation of our analysis. Here we will take the overlap between the two pragmatic accounts surveyed as our starting point. Both the echoic and pretence accounts highlight

---

181–205; Gibbs 1986, 3–15; Katz and Pexman 1997, 19–41; Kovaz, Kreuz, and Riordan 2013, 598–615; Kreuz and Roberts 1995, 21–31; Rockwell 2007, 361–69; Woodland and Voyer 2011, 227–39. For work on other languages, see Adachi 1996, 1–36; Colston 2019, 109–31; Escandell-Vidal and Leonetti 2014, 309–42; Okamoto 2002, 119–39; Yao, Song, and Singh 2013, 195–209.

the importance of evaluation in verbal irony. The ironist's aim is not to be informative but to provide an affective commentary on their utterance.

Bailin's recent definition of verbal irony helpfully captures the importance of evaluation, by emphasizing attitude rather than meaning. I do not suggest that Bailin's is a perfect description of verbal irony, and some theorists may disagree with it. What is important is that, with its balance of specificity and breadth, it is complete enough to provide the foundation for a working definition of sarcasm that will hold up in all the cases treated in this study.

Bailin sees two conditions as necessary to produce verbal irony: inconsistency and implicitness. Inconsistency requires that 'we assume the utterance normatively or typically to imply a certain attitude on the part of the speaker, but assume as well that the speaker producing the utterance has an actual attitude inconsistent with what is normally or typically implied'.[86] Notice that this condition does not supply the mechanism by which inconsistent evaluation is communicated. This allows for the presence of echoic mention, pretence, or sundry other signals to explain how we get from attitude A to attitude B.

Implicitness means that 'the speaker's actual attitude is not directly stated by the speaker in the immediate context'.[87] I prefer a generous interpretation of implicitness. I do not regard statements that are explicitly signalled as ironic or sarcastic after the fact to thereby cease to be so. For example, in the utterance: 'Nice haircut! [pause] Not!' I consider the phrase 'Nice haircut!' an instance of sarcasm, despite its being obviously signalled as such.[88] Sarcasm can be subtle or obvious, but the sarcastic statement itself always conveys the speaker's attitude implicitly.

But how do we get from here to sarcasm? We have already, following the ancients, defined sarcasm as a subspecies of verbal irony. Bailin's definition will therefore only require slight alteration. I define sarcasm as a subset of verbal irony in which an utterance that would normally communicate a positive attitude or evaluation implies a negative attitude or evaluation.[89]

---

[86] Bailin 2015, 112.
[87] Ibid.
[88] Cf. Haiman 1998, 53–55.
[89] By reversing the evaluations (a negative statement implying a positive attitude) we arrive at 'affectionate insults' (see n.29), and by making these self-referential

The Parable of the Disgruntled Undergraduate from §1.2.2, despite the difficulty it presents to semantic accounts, provides an excellent illustration of this definition of sarcasm. With the utterance, 'My, aren't you clever!' – an ostensible compliment and therefore a statement that would normally express positive evaluation – our student implies (through her tone of exasperation) a negative attitude toward the other student's intellectual grandstanding.

1.3 Irony and Sarcasm in Pauline Scholarship

In organizing this review, it will be helpful to follow the progression of scholarship on Pauline irony chronologically, setting these works alongside significant developments in irony studies proper. This structure will enable us to gauge the extent to which Pauline scholars have interacted with the research on irony available to them. Overall, Pauline scholarship has been significantly out of date when it comes to modern scholarship on irony and has not always addressed a sufficient breadth of ancient discussions. Lacking this theoretical grounding can limit the utility of certain observations.

1.3.1 The First Quest for the Nature of Irony

It is difficult to find irony research that still cites work written before 1975, as around this time a shift to pragmatic models renders much earlier scholarship obsolete. However, because the monographs that most Pauline scholars draw on predate this advance in irony studies, we must trace our history back further.

There is little development of note within the semantic tradition between Kierkegaard's 1841 thesis *The Concept of Irony: With Constant Reference to Socrates* and Muecke's *The Compass of Irony* in 1969. Although such works were important contributions for their times, certain conceptual issues render them problematic as accounts of irony (see §§1.2.1–2.2, 1.2.5). Muecke's work and Booth's *A Rhetoric of Irony* represent the pinnacle of the semantic approach to irony. To borrow a principle of organization from elsewhere in New Testament studies, it will be helpful to think of these three monographs as a sort of First Quest for the Nature of Irony.

(a negative statement about oneself implying a positive attitude) we create *asteismos* (see §1.1.2).

During this first-quest period, few authors take up the subject of irony in the letters of Paul. Reumann published 'St Paul's Use of Irony' in 1955. This short paper does not get caught up in discussion of ancient or modern theory on irony. At only five pages long, there is also little time for exegesis. The work consists primarily of brief identifications of different sorts of irony – including litotes, understatement, allegory, and others – following which Reumann concludes that Paul's use of irony in Second Corinthians is intended as 'a teaching device'.[90] For our purposes, the value of this piece lies in its presentation of a list of passages that a scholar has considered ironic and are thereby worth a second look.[91]

Still years before Muecke, Jónsson published *Humour and Irony in the New Testament*. For its time, Jónsson's work is noteworthy for its use of literary theory in addition to ancient discussion of irony and humour.[92] Jónsson focuses primarily on humour, considering irony a secondary interest that is difficult to disentangle from humour itself.[93] Jónsson defines humour as 'always sympathetic' in some way, while he considers sarcasm inherently unsympathetic.[94] He therefore seeks explicitly to study humour and irony to the exclusion of sarcasm. This fact significantly limits the utility of Jónsson's work for our discussion of Pauline sarcasm, but his identification of isolated ironic statements within Paul's letters will merit some reference.[95]

1.3.2   The Pragmatic Revolution: 1975–1984

Although subsequent research would find fault with his paradigm, Grice's pragmatic definition of irony, published in 1975, would begin a shift in irony studies away from semantic approaches.[96] The echoic

[90] Reumann 1955, 141–44.
[91] Linss's paper on humour in Paul, which touches briefly on sarcasm and irony, is similarly more helpful for identification than exegesis (see 1998, 196–97; see also Schütz 1958, 13–17).
[92] See Jónsson 1965, 16–34, 35–40, 41–89.
[93] For disambiguation, see ibid. 22–23.
[94] Ibid. 18–9, 23–4, 26.
[95] See ibid. 223–42.
[96] For reprints of Grice's influential 1975 and 1978 essays, see Grice 1989, 22–57. Grice considers irony as the intentional flouting of the expectation that a speaker in conversation should tell the truth. For example, if a professor who catches a student in clear plagiarism comments, 'I'm impressed by the originality of your argument', the obviousness of the falsehood signals that the statement, 'must be trying to get across some other proposition than the one [it] purports to be putting forward" (ibid. 34,

account follows soon after (1978; §1.2.3) and by 1984, pretence theory joins the conversation (§1.2.4). By this point, we have three competing pragmatic accounts of irony, which have rightly shown the deficiencies of earlier semantic paradigms (§1.2.2).

During this decade of sweeping change within irony studies, we find little work on irony in Paul. In 1981, Spencer published a study on irony in Second Corinthians' 'fool's speech'. Although it is reasonable that this paper should be unaware of a revolution in irony studies still very much in process at the time, Spencer's work also bypasses many of the 'first-quest' texts on irony, drawing primarily on Kierkegaard.[97]

Like Jónsson, Spencer wishes to avoid the term sarcasm in describing Paul's irony in 2 Cor 11:16–12:13, preferring the designation 'sardonic'. For both authors, this seems to be partly methodological; Spencer appears to consider sarcasm to be an element of tone ('in other words, sneering, cutting, caustic, or taunting') rather than a form of irony.[98] There also seems to be an apologetic element in such designations as well, insofar as avoiding the term 'sarcasm' excuses Paul from the use of tendentious rhetoric. Spencer ultimately argues that for Paul, the indirectness of irony functions as a stratagem for winning over a potentially unreceptive audience and ultimately works to 'expertly reinforce his central message'.[99]

1.3.3   The Second Quest: 1985–early 2000s

Over the following years, echo and pretence become greater while Grice becomes less. These former two paradigms expand, develop, and become the basis for hybrid accounts of irony that draw on both.[100] On the whole, the discipline starts shifting towards controlled laboratory experimentation rather than building paradigms on literary examples.[101] We do not reach anything like a consensus

cf. 28). This model, insofar as it requires the ironist to say something that is not true, suffers from the flaw illustrated by The Parable of the Disgruntled Undergraduate (§1.2.2).

[97] Spencer 1981, 349, 360.

[98] Ibid. 351. Cf. Loubser 1992, 509.

[99] Spencer 1981, 349–51, 60.

[100] See §§1.2.3–2.4, n.66. New hypotheses also emerge in this period. For the state of the field at the time, see Attardo 2000b, 797–813.

[101] I have cited several examples of such studies in §1.2.5.

on the nature of irony at this time, but irony studies makes significant gains and there is much insightful, relevant work for Pauline scholars to have drawn on had they chosen to.

Forbes's 1986 article on comparison, self-praise, and irony in 2 Cor 10–12 shows no interest in modern research on irony,[102] but focuses instead on ancient discussions. His citation of ancient authors is broad, including Plato, Demosthenes, Hermogenes, and Quintilian, to name a few.[103] Although I argue that any major study on irony in Paul has much to gain from interaction with both ancient and modern work, Forbes's focus on ancient discussions well suits the article's purpose and scope.

Forbes pushes the importance of Hermogenes for understanding Paul's irony in 2 Cor 10–12 and considers Paul's use of rhetorical techniques, including irony, as providing evidence that he 'may have had a full education in formal Greek rhetoric'.[104] While I am critical of Forbes's ultimate conclusions (see Chapter 7, §7.3.3), I consider his work one of the strongest pieces of scholarship on irony in Paul's letters to date. Forbes will therefore be a significant conversation partner in our chapter on Second Corinthians.

Published a year after Forbes's article, Plank's study of irony in 1 Cor 4:9–13 takes a very different approach to the subject. Like Forbes – though not to the same depth – Plank works through a number of ancient treatments of irony.[105] Unlike Forbes, Plank is convinced by the utility of (relatively) modern scholarship, using Muecke as his starting point for defining irony,[106] and drawing significantly on Kierkegaard and Booth.[107] Plank is thereby the first Pauline scholar to interact with a range of 'first-quest' irony scholarship.

Plank draws three major conclusions about Paul's use of irony. First, for Plank, Paul's irony is apologetic. Paul uses irony to turn the tables in his favour; weakness becomes strength, and thus criticisms of Paul on these lines only support his legitimacy. Second, Paul's irony is homiletic, encouraging the Corinthians to 'view their calling in a new way'. Third, Paul's irony seeks to influence his

---

[102] See Forbes 1986, 1.
[103] See ibid. 10–15.
[104] Ibid. 23, see 12–24.
[105] Plank 1987, 35–36.
[106] Ibid. 34.
[107] Amongst others, see ibid. 35, 42–45.

audience's theological convictions, affirming for his readers God's paradoxical salvific actions.[108]

Plank is concerned with two major forms of irony: dissimulative and paradoxical irony.[109] Plank describes dissimulative irony as 'a technique by which something *appears* to be other than it really is', an effect achieved through the use of exaggeration and pretence.[110] So defined, this form of irony has some affinity to verbal irony, and because I define sarcasm as a form of verbal irony, Plank's work on dissimulative irony in 1 Cor 4:9–13 will be worth some inter-action.[111] However, Plank's greater interest lies in paradoxical irony, where what is said is not what is meant but ultimately turns out to be true on a deeper level.[112] This larger discussion will not figure in our analysis of sarcasm, since the irony of such a paradox would be a product of the situation.

In the early 1990s, Loubser releases a study that draws consider-ably on Plank. Essentially, what Plank does with 1 Cor 4, Loubser does with 2 Cor 10–13. As a result, both works share similar strengths and drawbacks. Compared with Plank, Loubser does cite a greater breadth and depth of modern work on irony,[113] and discusses a greater variety of irony-types.[114]

For Loubser, Paul's 'fool's speech' (*Narrenrede*) is permeated with verbal irony: it is an ironic discourse (dissimulative irony) underlain by the (paradoxical) irony of strength-through-weakness.[115] Loubser uses his analysis of irony in 2 Cor10–13 to argue that these chapters form a *peroratio* to the letter as a whole, thus supporting the integrity of Second Corinthians.[116]

At one point or other in this study I will push back on all these conclusions. As mentioned above, paradoxical irony is better thought

---

[108] Ibid. 92, cf. 33.
[109] See ibid. 38–42.
[110] Ibid. 39.
[111] See ibid. 48–51.
[112] See Plank 1987, 39–42, 51–69. Socrates – who pretends to know nothing, when in reality he is wiser than his contemporaries, precisely because he knows that he truly knows nothing – is the classic example of this form of irony (see ibid. 40). We have already discussed why Socrates' dissembling does not qualify as tropic (verbal) irony (§§1.1.1–1.1.2).
[113] Loubser 1992, 507–11. Loubser draws his definition of irony from an early pragmatic perspective, but not one that would become significant in irony studies. See ibid. 508–9; Warning 1985.
[114] See Loubser 1992, 509–11.
[115] Ibid. 517–18.
[116] Ibid. 518–19.

of as a form of situational irony rather than verbal irony. Partially because of this methodological difference, I will go on to argue that the fool's speech in 2 Cor 10–12 does not contain significant verbal irony or sarcasm. Furthermore, an analysis of Paul's irony in these chapters cannot provide significant evidence for the integrity of Second Corinthians.[117]

1.3.3.1 Glenn Holland's Divine Irony

To date, no one has produced a larger body of work on irony in Paul than Holland. His first paper thereon addresses the fool's speech and his second 1 Cor 1–4.[118] My review will focus on his monograph *Divine Irony*, because it is at once his most complete treatment of irony and also reiterates most of the material from the previous articles.

Holland begins *Divine Irony* with irony's definition. He provides a fuller discussion of contemporary scholarship than he had in his previous papers, although only one of the works cited falls within a decade of his own monograph.[119] The hallmarks of Holland's approach to irony in Paul are that 'Paul uses irony to build solidarity with the members of the church in Corinth by reinforcing their common values' and that Paul's irony invites his audience to consider the situation at hand from the 'divine perspective'.[120] At the same time, within the persuasive task, specific instances can have targeted rhetorical effects and the production of shame stands out as a feature of several cases of Pauline irony.[121] Holland uses Socrates and Paul as his major case studies,[122] concluding that:

> Paul and Socrates are alike in their use of irony as an indirect means of communicating the insights they gained from a revelation of the divine perspective. In both cases

---

[117] See Chapter 8, §8.3.
[118] Holland 1993, 250–64; 1997, 234–48.
[119] Holland begins with Muecke and Booth (Holland 2000, 19, 21–5). He also draws heavily on Kierkegaard (see ibid. 101–16), gets into reader-response theory (ibid. 25–32), but does not make it to the Pragmatic Revolution. He takes the semantic tradition as his starting point (ibid. 20; see also 79, 160; cf. 1993, 250n.4; 1997, 236n.8, 237n.13, 238n.14–16). To Holland's credit, his discussion of ancient irony is considerable (2000, 82–97).
[120] Holland 2000, 131, 148–49.
[121] Ibid. 136–37, 148.
[122] See ibid. 82–118, 119–56, respectively.

their irony was meant to educate, to be recognized as irony, and appropriated by their audiences as a means for discovering divine truth.[123]

Because for Holland 'all irony is at root divine irony',[124] we will explore his concept of divine irony briefly. The basics of this outlook can be described as follows: In being ironic, the ironist adopts a detached perspective, much like that of an omniscient narrator. The divine perspective is also a detached perspective. Therefore, the ironist shares in the divine perspective.[125] Holland grounds his divine irony in a sort of ironic detachment discussed in Kierkegaard,[126] though divine irony is itself a novel paradigm rather than a mere distillation of Kierkegaard.

While there is no space to mount a thorough critique, divine irony suffers from conceptual problems. The jump from the detachment of the ironist to the detachment of the divine is not logically necessary. One's outlook can ascend high indeed without entering the realm of the gods. More significantly, I argue that the ironic perspective is not always detached. A Paul who sarcastically mocks 'very-super apostles' or ironically begs the Corinthians to forgive him the 'injustice' (ἀδικία) of not being a financial burden on them is very much a participant in the conflicts he responds to ironically (2 Cor 11:5,12:11, 13; see Chapter 7, §§7.2.2.2, 7.2.4.2). Furthermore, as we shall see in the next chapter, both Job and his interlocutors employ irony throughout the dialogues of *Job*, and it takes the appearance of God himself to reveal that none of them adequately expressed the divine perspective.[127]

Although we will not go further with divine irony, Holland's exegetical conclusions regarding irony in First and Second Corinthians will merit interaction in our treatment of the Corinthian correspondence.

---

[123] Holland 2000, 156.

[124] Ibid. 149.

[125] See ibid. 59–60. Of course, this summary is somewhat simplified.

[126] See ibid. 105–16. Holland dedicates significant space to discussing Kierkegaard (ibid. 101–18).

[127] Interestingly, Holland addresses God's use of irony in *Job*, but not the irony employed by Job and his friends (2000, 75–79). Lucian's character assassinations provide further examples of a more emotionally invested ironic perspective, although Lucian is more detached than Paul (see Chapter 3, §3.3.3).

1.3.3.2   Scholarship on Galatians

Nanos's *The Irony of Galatians: Paul's Letter in First-Century Context* is not primarily a book about irony. Nanos's interest in irony is taken as far as necessary to characterize Galatians as a letter of ironic rebuke.[128] This characterization forms the foundation of his later argument, where he provides a rethinking of the identity of Paul's opponents and the nature of the situation in Galatia.[129] Although Nanos's discussion of modern theory on irony does not run much deeper than the First Quest, he cites a reasonable breadth of ancient discussions.[130] Because our interests lie solely in irony, we may limit our interaction to the relevant parts of Nanos's study in our treatment of sarcasm in Galatians.

Nikolakopoulos published a dedicated study on irony in Galatians in 2001. He begins with ancient authors in defining irony – Aristophanes, Plato, and Aristotle – and is also influenced by First Quest scholarship.[131] His main focus is rhetorical irony (*rhetorische Ironie*), which he defines after the semantic tradition as inhering in meaning inversion.[132] Additionally, Nikolakopoulos sees this rhetorical irony as always having a didactic element. Irony does not intend to hurt those on the receiving end, and because sarcasm does, Nikolakopoulos does not consider sarcasm a form of irony: '[Irony], in contrast to sarcasm, attempts to bring about pedagogical success in an indirect way.'[133] This exclusion of tendentious rhetoric from rhetorical irony seems to suit Nikolakopoulos's exegetical aims, as he ultimately concludes that Paul's goal in using irony is didactic and non-polemical.[134]

Nikolakopoulos goes on to treat three cases of potential rhetorical irony in Galatians (1:6, 2:6, 5:12).[135] I will discuss all these passages in my chapter in Galatians, where in contrast to Nikolakopoulos I will argue for the presence of sarcasm – although not in all cases.

---

[128]   Nanos 2002, 49–56, 60–61.

[129]   See ibid. 73–322.

[130]   For his use of ancient authors and Muecke, see ibid. 34–39. For citation of Booth and Kierkegaard, see ibid. 305–9, 311.

[131]   Nikolakopoulos 2001, 195–96, 196n.17.

[132]   Although not in those words, see ibid. 197.

[133]   '[Ironie] versucht, im Gegensatz zum Sarkasmus, auf indirektem Weg pädagogischen Erfolg zu erlangen' (Nikolakopoulos 2001, 196).

[134]   Ibid. 207–8.

[135]   Ibid. 199–206.

1.3.4   Recent Scholarship

I will not at this time attempt to demarcate a 'third quest' period in irony studies. More time and distance will be required to determine what the next significant movement in the field might be. The next steps could involve synthesizing different accounts of irony into a unified whole, or perhaps advances in neuroscience will shed light on how the brain processes irony.[136] Colston's recent survey argues that an important step for the field will involve weighing the conclusions of past scholarship, which has been largely Anglocentric, against the different systems for communicating verbal irony across languages.[137] Within this research agenda, the results of our study, especially related to the typical means ancient Greek speakers use to express sarcasm (Chapter 3, §3.1–3.2), can hope to be relevant not only to Pauline scholarship, but to the study of verbal irony as well.

Once we get into the 2010s, we start to see new developments in Pauline scholarship.[138] Schellenberg devotes a chapter to irony in his 2013 study of Paul's rhetorical education. Like the book as a whole, this chapter is an essentially negative project, which argues that Paul's fool's speech is not ironic[139] – although Paul does make 'isolated ironic statements' in 2 Cor 10–13.[140] Schellenberg is critical of Holland's work,[141] and his assertion that Paul's boasting is actual self-promotion delivered without irony is an interesting foil to interpreters such as Loubser and Spencer.[142]

---

[136] For this latter direction, see Akimoto et al. 2017, 42–46; Spotorno et al. 2013, 1–10.

[137] Colston 2019, 109, 124, 127–28.

[138] Duling treats the subject of irony in the fool's speech in a 2008 article. Not engaging with irony research beyond earlier Pauline scholarship, this paper adds little to the work of authors such as Forbes and Holland. Like previous exegetes, Duling conflates a number of phenomena under the umbrella term irony, characterizing Paul's appropriation of the fool's persona as ironic, while also pointing out a few isolated ironic statements in the fool's speech itself (see Duling 2008, 819, 826–28, 839).

[139] See Schellenberg 2013, 169–79. Heckel also considers the association of irony with Paul's appropriation of 'the role and mask of a fool' ('der Rolle und Maske eines Narren') problematic, considering this instead an example of parody (1993, 20–22). Lichtenberger's 2017 article on humour in the New Testament, which devotes about a page to sarcasm and irony in Paul, lists the fool's speech as an example of Pauline irony. Lichtenberger also considers Phil 3:2 and Gal 5:12 instances of sarcasm, though he does not dedicate space to defining sarcasm or irony (2017, 104–5).

[140] Schellenberg 2013, 170.

[141] Ibid. 170–75.

[142] See ibid. 170, 175–79.

Sim's work on verbal irony marks a significant moment in scholarship on irony in Paul. Approaching verbal irony from the standpoint of relevance theory, Sim brings ideas from the Pragmatic Revolution into the conversation.[143] Her discussion moves through both (largely) accepted and (more) contentious examples of irony in the Pauline corpus.[144] Sim then compares Paul's use of irony to that of Jesus and of Epictetus,[145] and also points out prophetic irony in the Hebrew bible.[146]

In line with Sperber and Wilson, Sim defines irony as '*an echoic utterance from which the speaker distances himself*'.[147] Unfortunately, the way that she simplifies the paradigm – perhaps for the benefit of her non-specialist audience – ends up creating a historical problem. Sim's interpretation of echoic mention assumes that irony involves re-presenting the speech or perspectives of another. As part of the process for identifying verbal irony, she recommends asking, 'Can we identify whose thought or utterance the speaker is echoing?'[148] While a more nuanced form of this hypothesis allows for more indistinct forms of mention (§1.2.3), this assumption leads Sim to consistently claim access to the actual perspectives of Paul's interlocutors by means of irony's echo.[149] Making these kinds of historical claims assumes too much about Paul's opponents and congregations, and does not account for the distorting influence of hyperbole and misrepresentation, which are absolutely common in verbal irony.

Despite this caveat, Sim's exegesis of verbal irony in Paul remains helpful, and her work deserves commendation as a first step in bringing the discipline up to date on developments in irony studies since 1975.

1.4   Conclusions

Scholars of Paul have never been scholars of irony. My somewhat tongue-in-cheek choice of 'quest' terminology from historical Jesus

---

[143] See Sim 2016, 53–70.
[144] Ibid. 56–65.
[145] Ibid. 67–68.
[146] Ibid. 65–66.
[147] Sim markets this approach as a new one, which, as we have seen, is not correct (ibid. 5–6, 54). To be fair, it was new to New Testament studies at the time.
[148] Ibid. 55.
[149] See ibid. 56, 58, 61–62.

studies to discuss stages in irony research has been an intentional way of communicating this methodological shortcoming. Most Pauline work stays fixedly in the First Quest period, that is, within the major monographs of the semantic tradition. Only in recent years has Sim broken into early pragmatic approaches. By treating the monographs of Kierkegaard, Muecke, and Booth as if they were the definitive works on irony, scholars of Paul's letters have made a methodological decision akin to reading only Schweitzer as preparation for writing on the historical Jesus.

Partially because Pauline scholarship on irony has been so out of date, there has been little consistency in terms of irony's definition. Some scholars do not consider sarcasm to be a form of irony (Jónsson, Spencer, Loubser, Nikolakopoulos). There is also an overall lack of clarity and consistency regarding how different terms, such as sarcasm, irony, verbal irony, dissimulative irony, and paradoxical irony, relate to one another. Furthermore, in drawing conclusions about Paul's use of irony in a given text, scholars have made generalizations about different forms of irony that, as we saw in §1.2.1, are not formed in the same way and have different rhetorical functions.

Sections 1.1 and 1.2 of this chapter have sought to address these problems. We extended the work of previous Pauline scholarship by creating a more detailed survey of ancient treatments of irony with an especial focus on σαρκασμός. Although there has not been space to be fully systematic with modern research, our survey in §1.2 provides biblical scholars with the resources to become up to date on theoretical discussions of verbal irony, in addition to elucidating some of the more important concepts within the field. We have also sought greater specificity in defining the relationships between different forms of irony. We drew distinctions between situational irony, verbal irony, and sarcasm (§1.2.1), and by focusing primarily on sarcasm, a single form of verbal irony, we will avoid making generalizations about Paul's use of irony that do not hold true for all forms of irony.

We are now equipped with a working definition of sarcasm and several paradigms for explaining how specific examples may be considered sarcastic, such as echoic mention and pretence. This will enable us to begin addressing sarcasm in ancient texts, but it will not be our final word on method. In discussing constraint satisfaction, I emphasized the importance of being able to recognize a diverse range of signals that indicate sarcasm to facilitate accurate identification.

With so little previous work done on sarcasm in ancient texts, it will be necessary to develop our understanding of how ancient Greek speakers communicated sarcasm as we go along. This will begin in the next chapter and will be a major focus of Chapter 3, which will bring together hundreds of examples to elucidate the common linguistic and contextual signals of sarcasm in ancient Greek.

We are also yet to address the rhetorical functions of sarcasm in an ancient context. Determining the situations in which sarcasm is typically appropriate or inappropriate, who may use it with whom and to what end will be an integral part of this project. One of the central aims of the next chapter will be to establish the normal rhetorical functions of sarcasm and also to begin describing less typical, more subversive uses. This work will continue through Chapter 3. By the time we come to discuss Paul, we will have a broad understanding of sarcasm's pragmatic functions within an ancient context as a baseline for comparison.

2

SARCASM IN THE SEPTUAGINT: WITH SPECIAL REFERENCE TO *JOB* AND THE PROPHETS

This chapter will proceed with two case studies analyzing the most sarcasm-dense corpora in the Old Testament: *Job*[1] and the prophets. Here our primary task will be to describe sarcasm's most common rhetorical functions. Although it means saving a strong majority of the sarcastic utterances surveyed in this study for the next chapter, two factors commend the utility of beginning with the Septuagint.

First, the LXX is a major component of Paul's cultural inheritance and had a profound influence on his life and thought. The impact of LXX Greek on Paul's also makes this corpus a valid tool for linguistic comparison.[2] While attempting to demonstrate that Paul's sarcasm is intentionally modelled on or directly influenced by these texts would be too speculative, strong linguistic and cultural overlap will enable the best possible analogical comparisons between corpora. The Septuagint also has the advantage of having a relatively high density of sarcasm compared with other Jewish texts relevant to Paul's historical and religious context. For reasons of scope and because our goal is to establish the use of sarcasm in ancient Greek, we will only refer to the Hebrew versions of the texts in question when doing so is necessary to explain the Greek.

Second, starting with the LXX enables us to answer the question 'what does sarcasm do?' in a logical sequence over this and the following chapter. *Job* magnifies sarcastic interactions to a literary scale, making patterns stand out more boldly. It enables us to observe considerable variation in the use of sarcasm across several different character relationships in a single literary work.[3] By putting

---

[1] I use italics to differentiate *Job* the book from Job the character.
[2] Tim McLay argues that Paul not only read his scriptures in Greek, but that his use of the text in this language impacted his theology (2003, 145, 150–53).
[3] Although Paul makes far more references to the Prophets throughout his letters, he is not unfamiliar with Greek *Job*. Cox suggests that Paul quotes Greek Job 5:12 from memory in 1 Cor 3:19, and Phil 1:19 may allude to Job 13:16 (2017, 1–3).

an analysis of sarcasm in Old Greek (OG) *Job* into conversation with previous scholarship on sarcasm in classics, we will be able to make some preliminary hypotheses about the rhetorical functions of sarcasm, which will set the baseline for our understanding of how sarcasm normally works. We will then further hone and develop these hypotheses throughout the study with reference to texts across several genres and historical situations.

The LXX prophets also engage in frequent sarcasm, making their writings an excellent point of comparison for both reinforcing and refining the conclusions of our work on *Job*. In this case study we will consider both the writings of the prophets themselves, and stories about prophets in narrative works, which contain longer descriptions of sarcastic exchanges that can be helpful for illustrating certain points.[4] The way that the prophets' perceived divine mandate impacts their use of sarcasm will provide an important exception to the normal use of sarcasm defined in our analysis of *Job*. By way of analogy, the prophets will also be important for comparison with Paul, whose apostolic vocation colours the way he interacts with his congregations.

The case study on Lucian in the following chapter (Chapter 3, §3.3) will then build from our work on *Job* and the prophets by laying out further exceptional and subversive uses of sarcasm.

Although the present chapter is primarily concerned with answering the question 'what does sarcasm do?', we will also address in part the communication and identification of sarcasm. As we exegete *Job* and the prophets, we will begin to identify patterns in how speakers communicate sarcasm both linguistically and through context. Establishing common signals of sarcasm in ancient Greek will play an essential role in identifying sarcasm in Paul in Part II of the study. We will continue this work to a higher level of detail in the next chapter, which will focus primarily on answering the question 'how is sarcasm expressed?'

2.1   *Job*: Sarcasm as Implicit Challenge

As a translation, LXX *Job*'s relationship to its Hebrew parent text is complicated. The translator of the OG is well known as the 'freest' Septuagint translator, skilled in the use of Greek and inclined

---

[4] I will refer to this broader grouping of texts as 'the prophets' and reserve the capitalized 'the Prophets' for referring specifically to the major prophets + the XII.

towards paraphrase and epitomization.[5] This results in a text that is not only one-sixth shorter, but a literary work in its own right, advancing a certain interpretation of Job's story.[6] I will treat the text as such. This will allow us to bypass complex debates over the composition history and interpretation of the Hebrew. LXX *Job* is also a composite text, as later translators fill in the gaps, so to speak, left by OG's epitomization.[7] In order to deal with more of a literary unity, and because the later, asterisked portions of LXX *Job* do not contain significant sarcasm, I will focus on the OG for this case study.

We join the narrative at the conflict between Job and his friends,[8] which begins as they react to Job's irreverent curse of his own birthday.[9] We will explore the ways in which each character or group of characters uses sarcasm against their interlocutors within the polemical interactions of *Job* as the basis for our observations about sarcasm's rhetorical functions.[10]

2.1.1   Friends vs Job

By a logical necessity stemming from their theology, Job's friends consider his affliction to be some sort of judgement for wrong-doing.[11] In the face of Job's unrepentance, their criticism focuses on his innocence (Job 4:6–9, 17–21; 8:2–3; 11:2–11; 15:5–6; 22:4–10; 25:2–6). As the discussion moves forward and Job refuses to accept a loss of face, they must also discredit his wisdom in order to call his arguments into question (4:21; 11:7–12;15:2–3, 9–10). Of all Job's friends, Eliphaz is the only one to engage in clear sarcasm, which functions to support the broader challenges to Job's innocence and wisdom raised throughout the friends' speeches.

---

[5] Kepper and Witte 2011, 2054–55. For detailed discussion of translation technique, see Dhont 2018, 18–40, 332–34.

[6] Kepper and Witte 2011, 2046; Cox 2015, 385–88.

[7] See Cox 2007, 668–69; 2015, 396–98.

[8] I will refer to Job's interlocutors as his 'friends', not because they behave in a friendly manner towards him – they usually do not – but because the text designates them as such (φίλοι, Job 2:11).

[9] Robertson, writing on the MT, argues that in cursing the day of his birth, Job has essentially cursed God (1973, 449–51), though Good considers the text ambiguous (1973, 476). Regardless, Job's initial speech 'must have seemed to border on blasphemy' (Driver and Gray 1958, 40; cf. Robertson 1973, 452).

[10] While acknowledging his place in OG's narrative, I will ignore Elihu for reasons of scope.

[11] See Hartley 1991, 44.

In Eliphaz's first speech, after more generally questioning Job's innocence (4:6–9, 17–21), Eliphaz invites Job to 'Call out, then, to see whether anyone will listen to you or whether you will see any of the holy angels' (ἐπικάλεσαι δέ, εἴ τίς σοι ὑπακούσεται, ἢ εἴ τινα ἀγγέλων ἁγίων ὄψῃ, 5:1). The ostensible encouragement of Eliphaz's imperative can be readily explained as a case of sarcastic pretence.[12] 'Call out, then' (ἐπικάλεσαι δέ) suggests momentarily that Job's call for vindication could be efficacious and 'encourages' him to proceed. Because the reader already knows that Eliphaz does not consider Job innocent, and thereby worthy of divine vindication, his pretence is thin enough that Job cannot fail to catch its critical implications.[13]

How we translate *ei* (εἰ), here translated 'whether', in the latter clauses of 5:1 changes how we read Eliphaz's sarcasm. Different ways of reading *ei* will also feature in several other instances of LXX sarcasm, so it will be worth discussing a few potential readings here. NETS takes 5:1b–c as conditionals: 'But call, if [*ei*] anyone will respond...'[14] I do not consider this the most plausible option. *ei* is a common way of indicating indirect questions in Greek.[15] The MT explicitly marks the two latter clauses of 5:1 as questions, with an interrogative *hê* (-ה), and *mî* (מי), respectively. Assuming the translator's *Vorlage* was close to the MT,[16] it seems likely that they have here produced a rendering that retains a question-like element from the Hebrew, and which would appear to a reader with only the Greek in front of them as a series of indirect questions. On this reading – 'Call out, then, to see whether anyone will listen to you or whether you will see any of the holy angels' – the imperative conveys sarcastic encouragement, while the indirect questions communicate the unlikelihood of Job's call for aid being efficacious. In his afflicted position, it is ever so clear that none of the holy angels are rushing to help him.

Another possibility is to take *ei* as dubitative. The dubitative modality expresses uncertainty or doubt – 'maybe' and 'perhaps' are dubitative markers in English – and here it is uncertainty

---

[12] See Chapter 1, §1.2.4.
[13] Cox notes several emphatic elements in the OG ([Forthcoming], 5.1). On hyperbole and emphasis in sarcasm, see Chapter 3, §3.1.2.
[14] Cf. Cox [Forthcoming], 5.1.
[15] LSJ, s.v. 'εἰ'; Boas et al. 2019, §42.3; Smyth 1959, §2671.
[16] An assumption Cox, too, makes here (see [Forthcoming], 5.1).

specifically to which I refer.[17] This reading is close to certain elliptical uses of *ei*, where it can mean 'supposing that',[18] or even 'perhaps'.[19] Categorizing the dubitative use of *ei* is simply a recognition
that this meaning can occur outside of elliptical constructions. We
see this most strongly in Isa 47:12, which we will discuss in §2.2.1,
where *ei* translates the Hebrew dubitative marker אולי ('maybe').

On a dubitative reading of Job 5:1, both the initial imperative
'Call out, then!' and the following clause 'Maybe someone will listen
to you, or perhaps you will see one of the holy angels!' would be
sarcastic. With feigned uncertainty, Eliphaz pretends that Job might
be heard if he calls for help, but ultimately implies that he will not.[20]

I prefer taking *ei* as indicating indirect questions here over a
dubitative interpretation, as I think this best describes how the
translator attempts to convey the sense of their *Vorlage*. However,
we may still note a subtle dubitative element in these indirect questions, insofar as they raise the possibility of Job succeeding in applying to divine aid. Here too one may detect a note of sarcasm.

Eliphaz engages in sarcastic pretence again at the outset of his
second speech, in response to Job's claims that God has over-judged
him (13:22–14:22). Since Job's complaint would have sounded
impious to his friends, the first clause of Eliphaz's reply seems
surprising, capable of being read: 'Will the wise man (i.e. Job) give
an answer of spiritual knowledge?' (Πότερον σοφὸς ἀπόκρισιν δώσει
συνέσεως πνεύματος, 15:2). For a moment, Eliphaz appears to associate Job with wisdom (σοφός) and pneumatic understanding (συνέσεως
πνεύματος).[21] This is even more curious considering Eliphaz's depiction of himself as a recipient of spiritual revelation in 4:15 (καὶ
πνεῦμα ἐπὶ πρόσωπόν μου ἐπῆλθεν). However, in the next clause
the image of the spiritual sage is undercut and replaced by one of
Job attempting to sate himself on hot air: 'Will a wise man give
an answer of windy insight, and did he satisfy the ache in his

---

[17] On the dubitative in sarcasm, see Haiman 1998, 55–56.

[18] See LSJ, s.v. 'εἰ', VII.1.

[19] Cf. Barrett on Acts 8:22 (1994, 1:415–16).

[20] It is reasonable to read an element of indirect questioning in this interpretation,
especially considering that this is a normal function of εἰ and that we have questions
in Hebrew. One can reflect this nuance by adding a question mark to the above
translation.

[21] πνεῦμα (*pneuma*, spirit/wind) is used throughout LXX *Job* with both positive
(4:15; 10:12; 12:10; 27:3) and negative (1:19; 7:7; 30:15) connotations, leaving both
options easily in play during a first-pass reading of 15:2.

belly – [reproving others] with statements that are beside the point, with words that are of no benefit?' (15:2–3 [modified] NETS).

Although the full statement is obviously critical, the ambiguity of the first clause allows for *double entendre* and creates scope for sarcasm. The fact that the whole first clause can be read positively creates a moment of pretence that extends the time between ostensible praise and literal evaluation, in which it seems like Eliphaz is complementing Job. An element of surprise emerges when, following the obvious negativity of what comes, the reader must reassess and reinterpret the statement as a whole. This process of reinterpretation requires inverting the positive qualities of spiritual knowledge and wisdom applied to Job. To Eliphaz, Job is only wise in his own estimation and his insight is vacuous.

2.1.2   Job vs Friends

Job is at once more loquacious and more sarcastic than his friends. His responses to their critiques include several sarcastic statements that implicitly challenge their ability to judge his character.

After bemoaning the fact that, 'Those who held me in respect have now fallen on me like snow or like solid ice' (6:16 NETS), Job refers to his comforters as 'you who see so clearly' (οἱ διορῶντες, 6:19 NETS). In light of the speech as a whole and the fact that Job will characterize them as speaking 'mercilessly' shortly after (ἀνελεημόνως, 6:21), Job means the epithet 'you who see so clearly' (οἱ διορῶντες) sarcastically.[22] Job's friends have turned on him precisely because they have failed to correctly assess the situation.

At the close of the first round of speeches, Job refers to his friends with biting rhetorical questions: 'So are you really human, then? Is it with you that wisdom will die?' (εἶτα ὑμεῖς ἐστε ἄνθρωποι; ἢ μεθ' ὑμῶν τελευτήσει σοφία; 12:2). It is best to read synonymous parallelism here, with both questions based on the same pretence.[23] Job's questions pretend that his friends might have some exclusive claim to superhuman wisdom such that their death would put an end to all wisdom (μεθ' ὑμῶν τελευτήσει σοφία;). Maybe they are not mere

---

[22] Cox recognizes it as a taunt (see [Forthcoming], 6.19).
[23] The parallelism in 12:2 MT is also synonymous, and the verse is clearly sarcastic. For scholars who see 12:2 MT as sarcastic or ironic, see Whedbee 1977, 12; Good 1981, 214; Janzen 1985, 102; Parsons 1992, 40; Geeraerts 2003, 40–41; Luciani 2009, 389; Lauber 2017, 158–59.

mortals after all (εἶτα ὑμεῖς ἐστε ἄνθρωποι;). However, the following verse emphasizes that the friends are just human beings and no better than Job: 'My heart too is just like yours' (12:3). This makes it clear that the pretence of 12:2 was sarcastic, and Job never was in any danger of considering the friends superior.

Later in the same speech, Job challenges his friends to 'Go ahead; become judges yourselves!' (ὑμεῖς δὲ αὐτοὶ κριταὶ γένεσθε, 13:8 NETS). Here the emphatic redundancy of Job's pronoun use (literally 'you yourselves', ὑμεῖς + αὐτοί) signals insincerity. One would typically expect an invitation to become a judge to imply that its object is competent and worthy of the honour. However, in what follows it becomes clear that Job only wishes to see his friends step into a position where they would be under more rigorous divine scrutiny. No matter how faithfully the friends would seek to fulfil their vocation, God's accusations will hound them and expose them as faithless (13:9–12). Job's imperative is therefore sarcastic, like Eliphaz's 'encouragement' in 5:1. To draw a more modern parallel, Job's remark is a bit like telling someone to assert his rights as a nobleman during the French Revolution.[24]

2.1.3 Job vs God

Robertson identifies Job 7:16–18 MT as a parody of Psalm 8, aiming to show that 'God's assaults on [Job] are unjustified.'[25] Parody is also present in the OG, and we see the translator's imitation of the psalmist most clearly in Job 7:17:[26]

> τί ἐστιν ἄνθρωπος, ὅτι μιμνήσκῃ αὐτοῦ ('what is the human that you remember him?'), ἢ υἱὸς ἀνθρώπου, ὅτι ἐπισκέπτῃ αὐτόν; (Ps 8:5).

> τί γάρ ἐστιν ἄνθρωπος, ὅτι ἐμεγάλυνας αὐτὸν ('for what is the human that you have made him great?') ἢ ὅτι προσέχεις τὸν νοῦν εἰς αὐτόν; (Job 7:17).[27]

---

[24] In Hebrew, Job 26:2–3, which I mentioned in the introduction of this study, is a deeply sarcastic critique of Job's false comforters (see Whedbee 1977, 12; Good 1981, 214–15; Janzen 1985, 177; Jackson 2010, 156; Ingram 2017, 55; Lauber 2017, 159). We will not treat it here, however, because the OG version is not sarcastic.

[25] Robertson 1973, 453; cf. Kynes 2012, 63–71; Lauber 2017, 160–61.

[26] Cf. Cox [Forthcoming], 7.17–18.

[27] Note the linguistic similarity of the first clause, even in the translator retaining the μ-sound in the verb.

This parody is also sarcastic. Like we saw with 15:2 (§2.1.1), Job's psalm parody begins with positive-sounding language that can be read as sincere praise: 'What is the human that you have made him great or that you consider him in your mind? Or that you watch over him until morning and until he rests, you judge him (ἢ ἐπισκοπὴν αὐτοῦ ποιήσῃ ἕως τὸ πρωὶ καὶ εἰς ἀνάπαυσιν αὐτὸν κρινεῖς;)?' (7:17–18). *krineis* (κρινεῖς, 'you judge'), the last word of 7:18, is the first clear indication that Job does not consider God's watching over him as benevolent divine protection, but as unwelcome scrutiny. This shift from language that can be read as praise to clear complaint continues in 7:19: 'How long are you not going to let me be and not let go of me, until I swallow my spittle in pain?' (Cox). The point here is that constant divine surveillance leaves Job not even a chance to swallow his own spit.[28] 7:17–19 therefore begins with mock-praise in imitation of Psalm 8, which carries on for almost two verses before finally being clarified as sarcastic by the sincere negative evaluation that begins at the last word of 7:18 and carries through 7:19.

This depiction of God's dogged surveillance is well summarized in 7:20, where Job calls God 'you knower of the mind of humans' (ὁ ἐπιστάμενος τὸν νοῦν τῶν ἀνθρώπων, NETS). As before, this is not meant as an expression of praise, but is a sarcastic epithet. 'A person cannot even retreat into their mind to get away from the Lord, to find peace.'[29]

Robertson maintains that in 12:13, Job seemingly accepts Zophar's argument that God is wise (cf. 11:6–12, esp. 11.6), only to imply God's foolishness in his mismanagement of creation (12:14–25).[30] This contrast is an example of situational irony at the very least,[31] and could suggest that Job originally intended the words 'With [God] are wisdom and power; counsel and understanding are his' (12:13 NETS) as a sarcastic echo of Zophar's assertion.[32] Job repeats a modified version of this line in 12:16. The full passage reads:

---

[28] See Cox [Forthcoming], 7.19.
[29] Cox [Forthcoming], 7.20.
[30] Robertson 1973, 457. Cf. Williams 1971, 245. Although these scholars are discussing the MT, their observations hold for the LXX.
[31] Insofar as it is ironic that a God so described in 12:13 would behave as described in 12:17–24.
[32] Cf. Chapter 1, §1.2.3. On irony here in the MT, see Janzen 1985, 103; Good 1981, 218.

¹³ παρ' αὐτῷ σοφία καὶ δύναμις, αὐτῷ βουλὴ καὶ σύνεσις.
¹⁴ ἐὰν καταβάλῃ, τίς οἰκοδομήσει; ἐὰν κλείσῃ κατὰ ἀνθρώπων, τίς ἀνοίξει;
¹⁵ ἐὰν κωλύσῃ τὸ ὕδωρ, ξηρανεῖ τὴν γῆν· ἐὰν δὲ ἐπαφῇ, ἀπώλεσεν αὐτὴν καταστρέψας.
¹⁶ παρ' αὐτῷ κράτος καὶ ἰσχύς, αὐτῷ ἐπιστήμη καὶ σύνεσις (12:13–16).

¹³ With him are wisdom and power; counsel and understanding are his.
¹⁴ If he tears down, who can rebuild? If he shuts out people, who can open?
¹⁵ If he withholds the water, he will dry up the earth, but if he lets it loose, he has destroyed it completely.
¹⁶ With him are strength and power; knowledge and understanding are his (NETS).

The repetition of 'with him' (παρ' αὐτῷ) followed by four attributes (12:13, 16) – wisdom, counsel, strength etc.³³ – forms a pseudo-doxological *inclusio* that contrasts sharply with the four ἐάν (*ean*) clauses that lie between (12:14–15). This juxtaposition highlights the use of divine power in ways that harm humanity and against which humans are powerless. Furthermore, 12:17–24 depict additional divine injustice,³⁴ making it more difficult to read 12:13, 16 as straightforward praise. Cox's comment on the Greek is apt: 'the Lord is a powerful, disruptive, irritating force in the world'.³⁵ Here we do well to recall from the previous chapter that sarcastic statements need not be counterfactual (Chapter 1, §1.2.2). Job highlights the reality of divine power (δύναμις, κράτος, ἰσχύς) but resents how it works against humanity.³⁶ In light of the negative sentiments communicated in its context, we have good evidence for reading 12:13, 16 as non-counterfactual sarcasm that acknowledges God's power but implies a negative evaluation of its use. With sarcasm in addition to situational irony in 12:13, 16, we can agree that, '[c]hapter 12 shows unmistakably that what began in the folktale as a test of Job has become a test of God'.³⁷

³³ On the use of multiple adjectives separated by καί ('and') in ancient Greek sarcasm, see Chapter 3, §3.1.2.1.
³⁴ Except for 12:21, which mentions God 'heal[ing] the humble' (NETS).
³⁵ Cox [Forthcoming], 13.1.
³⁶ Compare Clines 1989, 1:296.
³⁷ Robertson 1973, 457.

2.1.4   God vs Job

Job has questioned, challenged, and accused the Almighty. In Chapter 38, God enters with no intention of answering but tells Job to steel himself for interrogation (38:3).[38]

Ritter-Müller provides an overview of scholarship that touches on irony in God's first speech. She sees it as symptomatic of such studies to neither define clearly what they mean by irony nor which specific passages they consider ironic.[39] Consonant with this trend, without any further discussion Pfeiffer advances the tantalizing thesis that God's first speech consists of 'a series of sarcastic questions'.[40] To approach the issue with greater specificity, I will argue that God's first speech is sustained sarcasm that provides the counter-challenge to Job's accusations and seeks to put him in his place.[41] While we shall focus primarily on the first divine speech, many of our observations will be applicable to the second.

As God begins to question Job, he interjects sarcastic comments that are suggestive of the tone he will take throughout the speech. God interrupts his first two questions to encourage Job to reply, suggesting sarcastically that Job must know their answers: 'Where were you when I set the earth's foundations? Tell me, if you comprehend insight! Who set its measures? Perhaps you know!' (ποῦ ἦς ἐν τῷ θεμελιοῦν με τὴν γῆν; ἀπάγγειλον δέ μοι, εἰ ἐπίστῃ σύνεσιν. τίς ἔθετο τὰ μέτρα αὐτῆς; εἰ οἶδας,[42] 38:4–5). The imperative 'Tell me!' (ἀπάγγειλον) in 38:4 conveys the same taunting, sarcastic encouragement that we saw in 5:1 and 13:8. NETS takes both *ei* (εἰ) clauses in 38:4–5 as conditionals ('if you have understanding'; 'if you know'). This is uncontroversial in the first instance (38:4), being an isomorphic rendering of the Hebrew (אם־ידעת בינה). But the final clause of 38:5 is a sarcastic assertion in Hebrew, rather than a conditional: 'Who determined [earth's] measurements– surely you know! [כי תדע]' (NRSV). For this reason, I prefer a dubitative reading of *ei* in 38:5 LXX (recall §2.1.1). The feigned uncertainty of 'Perhaps you know!' in the OG is close to the pretence of the Hebrew where God acts like Job must know the answers to his questions.

---

[38] Cf. Job 40:7.
[39] Ritter-Müller 2000, 623–24; for a more recent study, see Lauber 2017, 165–66.
[40] Pfeiffer 1953, 691.
[41] Geeraerts astutely notes that God responds to Job's pragmatic flouting of hierarchy rather than Job's specific accusations or questions (2003, 45–48).
[42] Greek punctuated to reflect dubitative reading (see as follows).

Later in the speech, God asks, 'Again, have you been advised of the breadth of what is under heaven?' before remarking, 'Do tell me how much it is' (ἀνάγγειλον δή μοι πόση τίς ἐστιν, 38:18 NETS). God knows as well as Job that Job cannot answer, but the *faux* sincerity of God's request supplies the ostensible positivity necessary for sarcasm. The pretence underlying this sarcastic request is signalled linguistically with the emphatic particle *dē* (δή)[43] which occurs frequently in ironic statements by virtue of its ability to show exaggeration.[44]

The next question concerns the dwelling places of light and darkness (38:19 LXX), to which Job obviously does not know the answer. But God asks nonetheless, 'Would that you might lead me to their borders! And perhaps too you know their paths?' (εἰ ἀγάγοις με εἰς ὅρια αὐτῶν; εἰ δὲ καὶ ἐπίστασαι τρίβους αὐτῶν; 38:20).[45] Cox sees *ei* as indicating direct questions in both clauses.[46] *ei* + optative is a common way to indicate wishes,[47] which I argue better explains the first instance than a direct question. Smyth notes that this volitive use of *ei* is poetical.[48] The translator may thereby be adding a tone of archaic formality to God's wish that heightens its sarcasm.[49] The second *ei* is probably dubitative ('perhaps'; 'presuming'). With this sequence, neither clause is a direct question, but God's wish for Job to lead him is an implicit request. The image created by this instance of divine sarcasm is quite humorous, as we see the Almighty speaking 'through a whirlwind and clouds' (38:1 NETS) to ask a mortal for directions.

God follows his sarcastic wish in 38:20 by claiming to be convinced that Job's knowledge of the cosmos indicates that his origins are of old: 'Thereby I know that you were born then, and the number of your years is great!' (οἶδα ἄρα ὅτι τότε γεγέννησαι, ἀριθμὸς δὲ ἐτῶν σου πολύς, 38:21 NETS). Ritter-Müller's designation of this verse as a major crux of God's irony ('ein ironischer Höhepunkt') in the MT suits the LXX here as well.[50]

---

[43] Which NETS translates well with the over-polite 'Do tell me...'
[44] See Denniston 1954, 229–36; Pawlak 2019, 557–58.
[45] Translation adapted from NETS.
[46] Cox [forthcoming], 38.20.
[47] LSJ, s.v. 'εἰ', A.2.
[48] Smyth 1959, §1815.
[49] Which I have sought to convey in my translation, and which NETS communicates well. Cf. Minchin 2010a, 394–95.
[50] Ritter-Müller 2000, 274. See also Cox [forthcoming], 38.21.

The concept of pretence provides the best inroad for understanding how these isolated instances of more obvious sarcasm set the tone for the whole (cf. Chapter 1, §1.2.4). The irony of the verses discussed plays on the idea that Job really does have the wisdom and intellect to answer God's questions (38:4–5; 38:18, 20–21), and can even impart knowledge to God (38:4–5, 18)! God performs his speech as if he is either Job's equal or subordinate. MacKenzie's envisages this pretence as one of equality:

> [The author] presents Yahweh as pretending to believe that such criticism and challenge as Job has uttered can come only from a rival God. It must be that this fault-finder is himself, in reality, the One who operates the universe and knows all its secrets![51]

This performance, however, is not trompe l'oeil. Throughout the questioning, we the audience – as much as Job himself – are fully aware that Job cannot answer God's questions, and thus cannot fail to catch the mocking sarcasm that carries on all the way from 38:4–39:30.[52] There is an extreme contrast between God's pretence of ignorance and deference, and the reality that Job is confronted with: an omnipotent being speaking from a raging storm. Compared with the petty squabbling between Job and his friends, God shows himself to be the sarcast par excellence.[53]

2.1.5   Conclusion: Expression and Function of Sarcasm in OG *Job*

2.1.5.1   *Expression*

Surveying the use of sarcasm across OG *Job* has begun to reveal patterns in the communication of sarcastic utterances. The imperative

---

[51] MacKenzie 1959, 441.

[52] Except for 38:7–11; 39:6–7, 21–25, 29–30, where the rhetorical questioning breaks off in favour of statements concerning God or nature.

[53] While space has not permitted discussion of God's second speech, the same sarcastic pretence can be seen throughout much of its rhetorical questioning as well. In the same manner as the first speech, the second too is punctuated with more obvious uses of sarcasm. The most outstanding of these occurs when God dramatically invites Job to display the qualities of divinity, to 'Go ahead take on loftiness and power, and put on glory and honour...' (ἀνάλαβε δὴ ὕψος καὶ δύναμιν, δόξαν δὲ καὶ τιμὴν ἀμφίεσαι... 40:10–13 NETS). For scholars who see irony or sarcasm in these verses (MT), see Dhorme 1926, 562–64; Clines 1989, 3:1181–83; Hoffman 1996, 214; Geeraerts 2003, 41–42; esp. Geiger 2018, 39–42.

featured significantly in several sarcastic commands and requests (5:1; 13:8; 38:4; 38:18), and we also saw various uses of *ei* (εἰ, 5:1; 38:4–5; 38:20). We will hold off discussing these patterns until after we have completed our work on the prophets, since both features recur there as well.

On several occasions sarcastic statements are followed by literal statements that explicitly express negative evaluation (7:17–19; 12:2–3; 13–24; 15:2). This juxtaposition clarifies the presence of more subtle sarcasm that would otherwise have been difficult to detect (esp. 7:17–19; 12:13–24; 15:2). The literal, negative evaluations presented in these passages confirm for the reader what tone the speaker's sarcasm implies. For example, 7:19 makes it clear that, 'What is the human that you have made him great or that you consider him in your mind?' (7:17), sarcastically conveys the subtext, 'What is the human that you consider scrutinizing him so important?'

We also observed two different ways of expressing sarcastic politeness, with God's pseudo-deferential requests featuring the imperative + the particle *dē* (δή) as well as the optative of wish (38:18–19).[54] This mocking over-formality is an excellent tool for deflating the status claims of others, as it implies that its target does not deserve the politeness with which they are being treated.

The friends (6:19), Job (15:2), and God (7:20) are all targets of different sarcastic epithets, positive appellations turned to ironic use, at one point or another. Even more frequent is the use of repetition and parallelism as a means of adding emphasis to sarcastic statements (5:1; 12:13, 16; 38:20, 21). The prevalence of this feature is a likely by-product of dealing with Hebrew poetry in translation. The pinnacle of this sarcastic repetition comes in the divine speeches where a torrent of rhetorical questions forms the longest sustained act of sarcasm in *Job*. God's pretending to require instruction from a near-divine Job creates the insincerity necessary to recognize the sarcasm in this scene, contrasting sharply with the reality of God's manifestation (38:1) and Job's affliction (2:8). Pretence plays an important role throughout our analysis of *Job*, as characters temporarily assume a version of their interlocutors' positions so as to better trash them sarcastically.

---

[54] On particle use in sarcasm, cf. Chapter 3, §3.1.2.3.

2.1.5.2   *Function: Implicit Challenge and Social Hierarchy*

Tracing the use of sarcasm through a single literary work has enabled the observation of its use across diverse character relationships. This will enable us to make some preliminary hypotheses about the pragmatic functions of sarcasm in an ancient Greek-speaking context that we may continue to refine throughout this study on the basis of examples drawn from both literary and more 'real-life' texts.

I argue that sarcasm normally functions as an implicit challenge to what the speaker perceives as a claim to some positive quality made by another party. This has been the case throughout the book of Job. The friends use sarcasm to challenge Job's innocence and wisdom, Job in turn questions their wisdom and ability to judge him, and also challenges God's justice. God uses sarcasm to challenge Job to display divine intelligence, to expose Job's ignorance and unworthiness to call God to account.

The way sarcasm works as a speech act makes it aptly suited to conveying this implicit challenge. As we defined it in the previous chapter, sarcasm always involves an utterance that would normally communicate positive evaluation. This ostensible positivity presents a (possibly exaggerated) version of the positive quality the sarcast sees their target as claiming. For example, the epithet 'You Who See Clearly' (οἱ διορῶντες, 6:19) indicates that Job considers his friends to perceive themselves as insightful. Sarcasm also always implies negative evaluation.[55] This negative evaluation communicates that the sarcast does not accord their interlocutor the positive quality they might wish to possess. Job's sarcastic epithet therefore implicitly denies that his friends see things clearly at all.

Social hierarchy often plays a role in these exchanges because the claim to a positive quality or qualities that sarcasm implicitly challenges is often bound up with status. For example, if Job is really blameless, his friends ought to treat him with greater respect. In using sarcasm to challenge Job's innocence, his friends imply that he is their inferior, while Job's counter-sarcasm challenges his friends' attempt to situate themselves as his superior.

In her excellent work on sarcasm in Homer, which is to my knowledge the only dedicated research on sarcasm in ancient

---

[55] Cf. the roll of implicitness in our definition of sarcasm (Chapter 1, §1.2.6).

Greek texts prior to this study, Minchin makes further observations about sarcasm and social hierarchy:

> Sarcasm responds to—and reinforces—status and rank: it is acceptable for a superior or elder to be sarcastic to a subordinate or junior; equals may trade sarcasm; a subordinate or a junior should not be sarcastic to a superior or elder. In Homer these rules are occasionally broken; and Homer always is careful to observe what happens next: those who speak out of turn will always be reproved.[56]

This pattern also plays out in *Job*. God's second discourse leaves Job thoroughly humbled; he calls himself dust (γῆν καὶ σποδόν, 42:6), the stuff of creation (cf. Gen 3:19), which is a recognition and acceptance of his mortality.[57] God also rebukes Job's friends (42:7). The fact that Job must intercede for them (42:8–10)[58] establishes a clear final hierarchy: God, then Job, then the friends. Just as Minchin describes, those who have challenged this hierarchy are humiliated and must repent, while those who have challenged others below them are vindicated.

As such, I will accept as a further working hypothesis that this is a 'normal' or at least inoffensive use of sarcasm. As long as hierarchies are not upset, sarcasm is appropriate. But when Job or his friends attempt to use sarcasm to assert themselves over those they belong in subordination to, they will be put in their place. Having established this 'rule', we will now turn to some notable exceptions within the prophets as well as in our subsequent work on Lucian. While these more subversive uses of sarcasm are interesting and will be important for comparison with Paul later on, we would do well to remember that they are a clear minority (see Chapter 3, §3.3).

---

[56] Minchin 2010b, 554. Cf. Minchin 2010a, 399.

[57] Cox [forthcoming], 40.6. Some scholars have advanced subversive readings of the Hebrew in which Job's repentance is less than genuine and God comes off as an unsympathetic character (see Robertson 1973, 466–69; Pelham 2010, 105–9; for an overview of and argument against subversive readings, see Newell 1992, 441–56). We will not deal with these interpretations here, as they are foreign to the thought world of the LXX, which ends by blessing Job (42:10–16) and guaranteeing his resurrection (γέγραπται δὲ αὐτὸν πάλιν ἀναστήσεσθαι μεθ᾽ ὧν ὁ κύριος ἀνίστησιν, 42:17aα), the latter especially suggesting lifelong piety (cf. Häner 2019, 41–42, 46, 48–49).

[58] Driver and Gray point out that the friends are made to offer 'an exceptionally large burnt-offering' (1958, 374; see also Hartley 1991, 539). Clines notes that Job remains in his afflicted state when he must intercede for his friends (1989, 3:1234). The friends, who are kings and tyrants (2:11; 42:17eα), must submit to Job at his lowest.

2.2   The Prophets

We now move to another sarcasm-dense corpus: the prophets –
including both the writings of the prophets and stories about
prophets in narrative texts. As before, we are interested in identifying
patterns in sarcastic expression on both linguistic and contextual
levels. We will also explore sarcasm in the prophetic literature as a
means of nuancing our understanding of its pragmatic functions.
Translation tendencies vary widely across the LXX Prophets.
Isomorphism is more common across books such as Ezekiel,
Jeremiah, and the minor prophets – although each translation has
its own particular features.[59] While we shall cite instances of sarcasm
from all these works, partially by coincidence and partially for
expedience, we draw most of the cases for sustained discussion from
Isaiah. More comparable to OG *Job*, LXX Isaiah's translator is both
apt and keen to paraphrase.[60] In light of the complex relationship
between translation and source text in Isaiah and the prophets more
generally, we will again focus on the LXX as a literary production
in its own right, using the MT only where necessary to explain
the Greek.

2.2.1   The Sarcastic Taunt

The story is well known. All Israel is gathered for a spectacle pitting
Elijah against hundreds of Baal's and Asherah's prophets in a contest of life or death. Elijah allows the opposition the first chance at
calling down fire from heaven, ostensibly because of their greater
numbers (3 Kgdms 18:25), but based on what follows one wonders if
it were not for the sake of exposing them to humiliation. Having
allowed Baal's prophets to call on their god for hours to no effect,
Elijah finally speaks out, mocking (ἐμυκτήρισεν), 'Call in a loud
voice! For he is a god, for prating occupies him, and at the same
time he is perhaps giving an oracle, or perhaps he is asleep and will
get up' (ἐπικαλεῖσθε ἐν φωνῇ μεγάλῃ, ὅτι θεός ἐστιν, ὅτι ἀδολεσχία
αὐτῷ ἐστιν, καὶ ἅμα μήποτε χρηματίζει αὐτός, ἢ μήποτε καθεύδει αὐτός,
καὶ ἐξαναστήσεται, 3 Kgdms 18:27 NETS).

---

[59] On Ezekiel, see Olley 2009, 12–14; Hammerstaedt-Löhr et al. 2011, 2850–51;
Lust 2016, 622. On Jeremiah, see Cox 2007, 876–77; Shead 2015, 469–83; Bogaert
2016, 584. On the XII, see Dines 2015, 442, 440–44.
[60] See van der Kooij and Wilk 2011, 2489–91; van der Kooij 2016, 562–64; Ngunga
and Schaper 2015, 457–62, 464–65.

Here Elijah signals his insincerity using exaggeration. Baal's prophets must not only call upon their god, they must cry louder (ἐν φωνῇ μεγάλῃ)! Then comes a threefold repetition of activities from which the god may need to be beckoned. As sarcasm, this list is insincerely affiliative insofar as Elijah pretends to make excuses for the deity. At the same time, the activities suggested belittle Baal for being too weak or preoccupied to notice the summons of hundreds of his prophets.[61] The ostensible uncertainty in the passage is also sarcastically affiliative, as Elijah suggests that Baal might just respond when every outward indication has made it clear that he will not: 'Maybe he is sleeping and will wake up!'

Elijah gives an exaggerated imitation of someone who might support the prophets of Baal. It is an act of pretence, a performance given before a literal crowd. The subtext of this sarcastic encouragement communicates to the people the nonentity of Baal and absurd uselessness of his prophets.

This chapter of Elijah's story is worth telling because it so well captures much of prophetic sarcasm. Sarcastic taunts like Elijah's are the most common form of sarcasm that we see throughout the prophets. In these acts of pseudo-encouragement, the prophet urges his victim(s) to persist in some useless or immoral action. This ostensible encouragement implies that the requested actions may be efficacious, but with a heavy irony undercutting the whole.

Isaiah 47:12–13 provides another clear example of this phenomenon.[62] After proclaiming doom on Babylon (47:11), the prophet 'encourages' the Chaldean diviners:

> στῆθι νῦν ἐν ταῖς ἐπαοιδαῖς σου καὶ τῇ πολλῇ φαρμακείᾳ σου, ἃ ἐμάνθανες ἐκ νεότητός σου, εἰ δυνήσῃ ὠφεληθῆναι.

> Now, stand firm in your charms and your great sorcery, things which you were trained in from your youth! Maybe you will be able to be helped by them (47:12).

Like Elijah's taunt, we have an imperative (στῆθι), here underlined with an emphatic particle (νῦν),[63] encouraging Babylon's diviners in

---

[61] E.g. DeVries notes that Elijah suggests Baal is sleeping while it is still the afternoon (1985, 229).

[62] For scholars who note elements of mockery, irony and/or sarcasm in 47:12–13, see Berges 2008, 498–500; Koole 1997, 1:543–47; Oswalt 1998, 253–54.

[63] I take νῦν here as emphatic since it is rendering the particle נָא rather than a temporal particle. Ancient evidence suggests that the LXX's *Vorlage* was very like the

immoral behaviour that we already know will not benefit them (47:11). This pretence of encouragement is also present in the final clause which suggests (sarcastically) that the Babylonian diviners may be successful (εἰ δυνήσῃ ὠφεληθῆναι).[64] Isaiah's sarcasm continues in the next verse:

> κεκοπίακας ἐν ταῖς βουλαῖς σου· στήτωσαν καὶ σωσάτωσάν σε οἱ ἀστρολόγοι τοῦ οὐρανοῦ, οἱ ὁρῶντες τοὺς ἀστέρας, ἀναγγειλάτωσάν σοι τί μέλλει ἐπὶ σὲ ἔρχεσθαι.

You have become weary with your counsels; let the astrologers of heaven stand up and save you, those who look at the stars; let them declare to you what is about to come upon you (47:13 NETS).

Here we have a series of three imperatives that all function as sarcastic taunts. The first two occur together, calling on the Chaldean astrologers: 'Let them stand and save you! (στήτωσαν καὶ σωσάτωσάν σε). These astrologers are then described with the epithet 'those who look at the stars' (NETS), which can be read either as a sarcastic or neutral reference. Isaiah then encourages them again in the imperative, this time to tell the future (ἀναγγειλάτωσάν σοι τί μέλλει ἐπὶ σὲ ἔρχεσθαι). The repetition of imperatives creates a sense of parallelism, emphasizing Isaiah's taunt.

We find such sarcastic taunts throughout the LXX Prophets (Isa 41:21–23; Jer 2:28; 7:21; 46:11; Mal 1:8),[65] in addition to some that are sarcastic only in the MT (Amos 4:4–5; Jer 44:25 [51:25 LXX]).[66] These taunts are characterized by two significant features. First, with their ostensible encouragement they emphasize the utter uselessness of the actions they satirize.[67] Time and time again we have seen the prophets call on their victims to cry out to gods that cannot save

---

MT in Isa 47:10–13. See 1QIsaᵃ [Col. XXXIX–XL]; 1QIsaᵇ [Col. XX]; Watts 1987, 170; Oswalt 1998, 251n.42; Baltzer et al. 2011, 2653.

[64] Here again, contra NETS, I take the *ei* (εἰ) construction as dubitative. This reading is supported by the fact that the translator probably has 'maybe' (אולי) in his *Vorlage* (see n.63), and has translated the rest of the phrase isomorphically (compare: εἰ δυνήσῃ ὠφεληθῆναι; אולי תוכלי הועיל). Malachi 1:8 also contains a sarcastic taunt and comparable (probably dubitative) *ei* constructions.

[65] Cf. Isa 5:19 (see Good 1981, 136) and Jer 17:15. Here the prophets report the taunts of others.

[66] In both cases where we find sarcastic taunts in Hebrew ('Do X!' / 'May you do X!'), the LXX has unironic criticism in the aorist indicative ('You did X').

[67] Not all taunts are sarcastic. Consider a Pauline example: 'Where, O Death, is your victory? Where, O Death, is your sting?' (1 Cor 15:55 NRSV). While both the

(3 Kgdms 18:27; Isa 41:21–3; Jer 2:28), or to otherwise persist in actions that will not help them in the slightest (Amos 4:4–5 [MT]; Isa 47:12–3; Jer 7:21; 44:25 [MT]; 26:11).

The second major feature of the prophetic taunt is its role in emphasizing divine judgement. Very often, these statements are contextualized by more literal declarations of the outcomes that may be expected from the 'recommended' actions. After Isa 41:21–23 invites hand-made gods to prove their divinity – 'Declare the things that are coming at the end, and we will know that you are gods' (41:23 NETS) – the prophet calls these gods an abomination (41:24).[68] The oracle then turns to judgement, as Babylon brings destruction from the north (41:25), a doom that no false god can predict (41:26).[69] This combination of sarcasm and plain speech functions to make the irony of the ostensible encouragement clear. The sarcastic taunt points to the uselessness of the recommended action while its context expresses the inevitability of judgement. It is a double-edged rhetorical move that mockingly holds up false hope before snatching it away.

2.2.2   Prophetic Sarcasm as Implicit Challenge

In terms of pragmatics, the sarcastic taunts observed throughout the prophets function in much the same way as the sarcasm of *Job*. The element of challenge in these cases is at the forefront, as the prophets call upon their opposition to perform a specific action. They ironically imply that such deeds could be efficacious, 'perhaps you will be able to be helped (by your magic)!' (Isa 47:12; cf. μήποτε καθεύδει αὐτός, καὶ ἐξαναστήσεται, 3 Kgdms 18:27). The inability of the victim(s) to complete the requested action calls their legitimacy – as astrologers and prophets in these examples – into question. One may paraphrase the substance of these speech acts (and their subtexts [and further implications]) as follows: 'you think you are a powerful astrologer (but you're not [and therefore you're a fraud])' (Isa 47:12–13), 'you think you are a true prophet of Baal (but he is not a true god [and therefore you're a fraud])' (1 Kgs 18:27).

---

sarcastic taunts of the prophets and this non-ironic taunt emphasize the impotence of their victims, this example lacks the ostensible encouragement of sarcasm.

[68] On the LXX translation, see Vonach 2011, 2649.

[69] For other instances of this phenomenon, see Amos 4:1–5 (MT); Isa 47:8–15; Jer 26:11–12; 3 Kgdms 22:15–23.

There is more to the use of sarcasm in the Prophets than the sarcastic taunt. Isaiah's ironic lament over the King of Babylon is an excellent example of the way the prophets turn other sorts of sarcasm to the task of challenging another party's status.[70] This song of mourning (θρῆνος, Isa 14:4) is not intended sincerely. Here Isaiah invokes and inverts the category of lament, using a genre of mourning to mock and indict.

Most of Isaiah's 'lament' is not properly sarcastic, but an intense castigation of Babylon's king delivered without irony. There is one point, however, where the prophet shifts to more ostensibly positive language to carry his critique forward:

> πῶς ἐξέπεσεν ἐκ τοῦ οὐρανοῦ ὁ ἑωσφόρος ὁ πρωὶ ἀνατέλλων.[71]
> συνετρίβη εἰς τὴν γῆν ὁ ἀποστέλλων πρὸς πάντα τὰ ἔθνη.

How The Morning Star, the One Who Rises Early, has fallen from the sky! The One Who Sends forth (Light) to All Peoples has crashed into the earth! (Isa 14:12).

Isaiah uses a series of three epithets, 'The Morning Star' (ὁ ἑωσφόρος), the One Who Rises Early (ὁ πρωὶ ἀνατέλλων), and The One Who Sends Forth (Light) to All Peoples (ὁ ἀποστέλλων πρὸς πάντα τὰ ἔθνη), to exaggerate Babylon's glory, self-importance, and divine aspirations (cf. 14:13–14). The use of repetition here and the way these epithets get longer and longer create an effective parody of Babylon's pretention. The way these positive appellations are juxtaposed with a description of Babylon's demise signals that they are intended sarcastically 14:12 (πῶς ἐξέπεσεν / συνετρίβη εἰς τὴν γῆν, cf. 14:15). Instead of mourning Babylon's fall from glory as in a true lament, the prophet glories in its demise (14:7–8). His sarcastic epithets raise his victim up only to give them further to fall. Thus Isaiah's sarcasm becomes one of several ways in which he seeks to challenge and diminish Babylon's status in a mocking lament that ends in portraying its utter decimation (14:21–27).

2.2.3   Prophetic Sarcasm as Insubordination

We have hitherto observed a basic consistency concerning what sarcasm does. But the prophets also attest to a pattern in the way

---

[70] Ezek 28:3–5 (MT) has a comparable case of sarcasm.
[71] Despite the question mark in VTG, I agree with NETS in reading *pōs* (πῶς) as exclamatory rather than interrogative (cf. Chapter 3, §3.1.2.4).

sarcasm-use interacts with social dynamics that confounds the norms established on our reading of *Job* and in Minchin's work on Homer. Here, another narrative about another prophet's sarcastic taunt will serve to illustrate.

In 3 Kgdms 22:13–28, King Ahab grudgingly summons the prophet Micaiah, whom he hates (22:8), to weigh in on the upcoming battle against Ramoth-Gilead (22:1–9). Although Micaiah's response does not appear to contain any overt signals of sarcasm, the narrative presumes that there must have been something in his tone to indicate the insincerity of the pronouncement, 'Go up, and you will succeed, and the Lord will give it into the hand of the king' (22:15 NETS). Ahab's reply, 'How many times must I make you swear that you tell me the truth in the name of the Lord?' (22:16 NETS), makes it clear that Micaiah was only giving a mocking imitation of the other prophetic yes-men who predicted the campaign's success (22:6; 11–12).[72]

Ignoring rank, Micaiah is malicious, even arrogant in the face of peers and superiors alike. When one of the court prophets seeks to reprimand him, Micaiah lashes back by declaring his doom (22:24–25), and even when consigned to prison for the duration of the upcoming battle, Micaiah cannot resist a parting threat against the king: 'If returning you return in peace, the Lord has not spoken by me' (22:28 NETS).

This story well illustrates the tendency of the prophets to use sarcasm as a means of transgressing rank. Where sarcasm was used against the grain of rank in *Job* – such as Job's sarcastic references to God – the insubordinate sarcast was always eventually reproved, and their punishment restored the proper hierarchy (§2.1.5.2).

Not only do the prophets often engage in insubordinate sarcasm, they persist in their insubordination in spite of punishment. Just as Micaiah is sarcastic with Ahab to his face, the prophetic sarcast often pronounces his doom on victims of significantly higher social standing. Foreign powers receive considerable sarcasm (Ezek 28:3–5 [MT]; Isa 14:12; 41:21–23; 47:12–13; Jer 26:11), although this would no doubt play favourably to a domestic audience. However, the extent to which the prophets employ sarcasm to criticize their own people and rulers is significant (Amos 4:4–5 [MT]; Jer 2:28; 7:21; 41:17; 44:25 [MT]; Mal 1:8). Despite their lower rank, they employ

---

[72] See Sim 2016, 65; cf. Montgomery 1951, 336, 338. Micaiah is made aware of the other prophecies in 22:13.

sarcasm like a superior to a subordinate, seeking to expose their victims to shame – often publicly. In the Elijah narrative, this shaming is conceived as a spectacle before the masses. The book of Jeremiah too conceives of a public audience for Jeremiah's oracles (Jer 7:2; 17:19; 25:2; 43:1–26),[73] including the parties criticized (see Jer 43:21). Micaiah's prophecies (22:15, 17, 19–23) are given before everyone they insult, both the king and his prophets (22:10, 24).

The justification for prophetic sarcasm so often transgressing social boundaries lies close at hand. Like so much prophetic speech, the sarcasm of the prophets is frequently contextualized by some version of 'Thus saith the Lord' (Amos 4:5 [MT]; Ezek 28:1–2, 6, 11–12 [MT]; Isa 41:21; Jer 2:29, 31; 7:21; 41:17; 44:25 [MT]; Mal 1:8). By speaking for God, the prophets appropriate a level of status above their interlocutors, which they reflect in the boldness of their criticism.

Claiming to speak for God does not guarantee that the prophet will get away with flouting hierarchy. In our narrative texts, although Elijah ultimately triumphs and Micaiah's prophecy is vindicated (3 Kgdms 22:34–37), both prophets face significant resistance, with the latter struck and imprisoned (3 Kgdms 22:24–27). It appears that the extent to which prophets might expect pushback on their insubordination is proportional to the extent to which their audience accepts their claim to speak for God.[74]

While we lack testimony to the original reception of much of the prophets' writings, the evidence we do have suggests that those who collected and edited these texts were aware of a degree of danger in the prophetic vocation. Jeremiah receives a beating and imprisonment, to which he responds with a Micaiah-esque counter-prophecy (Jer 20:1–6), in addition to significant further hardships (20:7–8, 10; 33:7–11; 43:21–26; 44:11–16; 45:1–13). Unlike in *Job*, here the punishment of the sarcast does not restore the balance of the original social hierarchy. As long as the prophet remains convinced of their divine mandate, one may expect conflict to continue.

---

[73] This includes the sarcastic taunts of 2:28 and 7:21 in addition to other sarcastic comments critical of Israel and Judah (2:33 [MT]; 4:22; 41:17).

[74] The Elijah narrative provides a literary illustration of the way shifting public opinion about the gods in question can have a dramatic impact on the safety of their respective prophets.

2.3   Conclusions

The Septuagint has enabled us to engage with many instances of sarcasm across texts with which Paul would have been intimately familiar. Observing the sarcasm of the prophets can nuance our work on *Job* in important ways. As far as the expression of sarcasm is concerned, there were many similarities. Clarifying the presence of sarcasm by following it with statements of literal negative evaluation was significant in *Job* (§2.1.5.1) and occurred in Isa 41:21–26. As we will see in the next chapter, this is an important signal of sarcasm in ancient Greek texts (Chapter 3, §3.1.1.4). Ways of creating emphasis and exaggeration were used to communicate sarcasm in both corpora. These include repetition (3 Kgdms 18:27; Isa 14:12; 47:13; Job 5:1; 12:13, 16; 38:20, 21), the use of adverbial phrases (3 Kgdms 18:27), and emphatic particle use (Isa 47:12; Job 38:18; 40:10; Mal 1:8). The use of sarcastic epithets was also significant in *Job* (6:19; 7:20; 15:2), and occurs in Isa 14:12.

The most significant pattern in prophetic sarcasm is the prevalence of what I have called sarcastic taunts. These employ the imperative to command or request that the target perform some foolish, useless, or immoral action. While they are most prevalent in the prophets, several sarcastic taunts occur in *Job* (5:1; 13:8; 38:4). They are sarcastic insofar as they ostensibly encourage the other party, engaging in a pretence that the recommended actions could be efficacious. The primary function of these taunts in both the prophets and *Job* is to imply the uselessness of the recommended actions. In the prophets specifically, they also function to emphasize the inevitability of divine judgement.

On a linguistic level, ways of expressing mock uncertainty – that is, when the sarcast pretends to be unsure whether a situation will turn out to the benefit of their victim when it clearly will not – have been an important feature of sarcastic taunts. This is most explicit in 3 Kgdms 18:27 with Elijah's use of the dubitative marker 'maybe' (μήποτε): 'Call out!… maybe Baal's sleeping and will wake up!' We have also observed diverse uses of *ei* (εἰ), including its use to indicate indirect questions (Job 5:1), express wishes with the optative (Job 38:20a), and to form conditional (38:4) or dubitative constructions (Job 38:5, 20b; Isa 47:12; Mal 1:8).[75] Dubitative use, which depending on the context can be translated as 'maybe',

---

[75] A dubitative reading was also a possibility for Job 5:1.

'presumably', or 'perhaps', also adds an air of mock uncertainty to sarcastic taunts.

In terms of rhetorical function both Job and the prophets support the working hypothesis that, in the ancient contexts hitherto surveyed, sarcasm's primary function is to communicate an implicit challenge. The sarcast's negative evaluation calls into question their victim's perceived claim to some positive quality. This often has implications for social hierarchy, communicating that the sarcast's victim does not merit the standing and honour that they believe they deserve. My work on *Job* also agrees with Minchin's observations about the use of sarcasm in Homer: that sarcasm is appropriate when used with the grain of social hierarchy. Superiors may use sarcasm to keep their subordinates in line, but those who break rank are liable to reprisal.

Although it is an exception rather than the rule, the prophets subvert this pattern in an interesting manner. By claiming to speak for God and thereby appropriating a level of status above their normal rank, the prophets take the liberty of criticizing parties of higher status. This flouting of hierarchy presents a danger to the prophet, but here negative consequences do not re-establish the original hierarchy. The prophets continue their insubordination regardless of punishment so long as it fits their perceived divine mandate. These dynamics will be interesting to compare with Paul's letters, as Paul at times speaks as an accepted leader and elsewhere must appeal to divine backing to support an apostolic authority that has been called into question.

3

SARCASM IN ANCIENT GREEK TEXTS: WITH SPECIAL REFERENCE TO LUCIAN

The previous chapter focused primarily on the rhetorical functions of sarcasm, while also providing a partial answer to the question 'how is sarcasm expressed?' The major focus of the present chapter will be addressing the issue of how sarcasm is communicated in ancient Greek. Cross-cultural studies have shown that, while there are many similarities between languages in terms of how speakers communicate sarcasm, different languages have their own particular nuances.[1] Therefore, while it is an important first step, understanding how verbal irony works in modern English does not adequately prepare the exegete for identifying sarcasm in ancient Greek. Minchin's work, which analyses sixty-one examples of Homeric sarcasm,[2] is a helpful starting point. There is however considerable distance in register and dialect between the dactylic hexameter of Homeric Greek and Paul's Koine. Further comparative material is needed. With close to thirty examples of sarcasm assessed as the foundation for our work on the Septuagint, there is still much ground to cover to determine how to be sarcastic in ancient Greek.

The Lucianic corpus is one of the ancient world's most prolific stores of sarcasm. To date I have catalogued well over 200 examples of sarcasm in Lucian. This more than doubles the number of cases surveyed in Minchin and our work on the LXX combined. To Lucian I will also add several other texts and corpora, including the New Testament (excluding Paul), Aristophanes, the satirical epigrams of the Greek Anthology, our previous examples from the LXX, and an eclectic selection of other texts, for a total of 400 examples of sarcasm. Texts have been selected either for their likelihood of containing sarcasm or their relevance to Paul's historical or cultural context.

---

[1] See Colston 2019, 124–28.
[2] By my count, see Minchin 2010a, 540; 2010b, 396n.42.

The chart below breaks down our dataset, showing the total instances of sarcasm analyzed in each author or work.[3] Some examples have been marked as uncertain. When proportions of specific features of sarcasm are given throughout this chapter, they will be given as an average of the percentages including and excluding the uncertain examples. 'Likely examples' refers to instances of sarcasm where I believe there is, at least, a strong argument to be made for a sarcastic reading.

Author/Work	Uncertain Examples	Likely Examples	Total
Lucian	55	215	270
Septuagint	11	22	33
Aristophanes	4	27	31
New Testament[4]	9	17	26
Rhetoricians and Grammarians[5]	0	12	12
Greek Anthology	0	9	9
Pseudo-Lucian	0	7	7
Josephus	0	3	3
Testament of Job	0	2	2
Euripides	0	1	1
Clement of Alexandria	0	1	1
Gospel of Peter	0	1	1
Letter of Aristeas	0	1	1
4 Maccabees	0	1	1
Philo	0	1	1
Tobit	1	0	1
Total	**80**	**320**	**400**

This dataset is large enough to allow us to begin parsing out the contextual and linguistic signals by which ancient Greek speakers typically indicated sarcasm (§3.1). These will be foundational in supporting the identification of sarcasm in Paul. The second section

---

[3] There will be some variation between the findings of this chapter and Pawlak 2019, which uses a dataset consisting only of Lucian and the NT (Paul included); see Pawlak 2019, 547.

[4] Mostly the Gospels and Acts, one example from James.

[5] Such as those cited in Chapter 1, §1.1.2.

of this chapter will identify patterns in the use of sarcasm across our dataset that can both assist in the identification of sarcasm and further our understanding of its pragmatic functions in different contexts.

After addressing the expression of sarcasm, we will return to the question 'what does sarcasm do?' (§3.3). Here we will use Lucian as a case study for furthering the work begun on the rhetorical functions of sarcasm in the previous chapter. Although Lucian is far from Paul in terms of context and genre, sarcasm finds use in both corpora for common rhetorical ends, such as discrediting one's opponents and influencing the sympathies of one's audience. Lucianic sarcasm can therefore further our understanding of the rhetorical advantages and pitfalls of sarcasm in different contexts. Applied analogically, these findings can be helpful in evaluating the role of sarcasm in Pauline rhetoric.

3.1   Signals of Sarcasm

In this section we will identify signals of sarcasm that occur with significant frequency across our dataset. This will bring into sharper focus observations made in the previous chapter concerning linguistic and contextual cues of sarcasm in ancient Greek. Any of the following features, whether alone or in combination with others, can in certain contexts be sufficient for indicating the presence of sarcasm. However, even the occurrence of several signals at once does not guarantee a sarcastic reading, and a best-fit interpretation based on all available evidence must always be sought (Chapter 1, §1.2.5).

3.1.1   Contextual Signals

We begin with signals that are context dependent. These do not involve the linguistic elements of the sarcastic utterance itself but are derived from the surrounding discourse. We will first explore signals peculiar to narrative, which are created by the author as a third-party, and are therefore generally more explicit (§§3.1.1.1–3.1.1.2). We then move on to contextual cues given by sarcasts themselves (§§3.1.1.3–3.1.1.6). Incongruity plays a major role in many of these latter cases, as speakers communicate their insincerity through literal negative evaluations that clash with their sarcasm.

3.1.1.1 Narration

In her work on *The Odyssey*, Minchin discusses the use of narrative devices to signal sarcasm. She found that introductory verbs expressing negative affect such as νεικέω 'to taunt' and κερτομέω[6] 'to mock' often introduce sarcastic dialogue.[7] We saw this in the last chapter: 'Eliou the Thesbite mocked them [*emyktērisen*, ἐμυκτήρισεν] and said, "Call in a loud voice! For he is a god..."' (3 Kgdms 18:27 NETS). Here the LXX translator's verb choice is especially apt considering the close relationship between *myktērismos* (μυκτηρισμός) and *sarkasmos* (σαρκασμός) in ancient discussions of irony (Chapter 1, §1.1.2).

Lucian does not use much narrative, so we the lack the necessary data to determine how prevalent introductory verbs are as signals of sarcasm across ancient Greek texts generally.[8] But Gospel authors use them significantly (ἐνέπαιξαν, Matt 27:29; ἐμπαίζοντες, Mark 15:31; ἐξεμυκτήριζον, Luke 23:35, ἐβλασφήμει, Luke 23:39; cf. Homer *Il.* 16.740–50; *Od.* 22.194–200; Pseudo-Lucian, *Ass*, 24).[9]

3.1.1.2 Victim Recognition

Minchin also shows how the reactions of characters to sarcastic statements can function as a signal of sarcasm.[10] Lucian's comic dialogues lend themselves more to this signal, providing us with more reliable data. Having a character, usually the victim, recognize the implied insult of their interlocutor makes it clear to the text's audience that the previous utterance was meant sarcastically. This occurs in 7 per cent of our examples. *Dialogues of the Sea Gods* provides a helpful illustration. The scene begins with Doris mocking Galatea's cyclopean paramour: 'A good-looking lover they say you have, Galatea, in this Sicilian shepherd who's so mad about you!' (*DMar.* 1.1 [MacLeod]).[11] Galatea returns, 'None of your jokes (Μὴ

---

[6] See n.90.

[7] Minchin 2010b, 539–42, 553.

[8] They occur in 6 per cent of the full dataset. Interestingly, when we ignore Lucian, this jumps to 15 per cent. Further research on narrative texts is necessary to draw meaningful conclusions.

[9] In Lucian, see *Demon.* 44; *Lex.* 23. Clement of Alexandria uses signs of mourning and regret to introduce an instance of self-sarcasm in *quis dives salvetur* (42:10).

[10] Minchin 2010b, 540–43, 553; cf. Minchin 2010a, 399.

[11] Citations of *DDeor.*, *DMar.*, *DMeretr.*, and *DMort.* follow the numbering of MacLeod's Loeb edition. All translations of Lucian, aside from my own, are from the LCL.

σκῶπτε), Doris. He's Poseidon's son, whatever he looks like' (*DMar.* 1.1 [MacLeod]).

This narrative device can help one's audience keep up with subtler uses of sarcasm. In the early part of Lucian's *Lexiphanes*, most of what Lexiphanes' friend Lycinus says is some sort of teasing.[12] However, Lycinus' dissembling makes it difficult to be sure whether his compliments are sincere, until Lexiphanes asks Lycinus to 'throw the irony on the ground' before they move on in the discussion (Τὸν μὲν εἴρωνα πεδοῖ κατάβαλε, *Lex.* 1; cf. *JTr.* 52).[13] We saw a similar case in the last chapter, where Ahab's remark was the only hint that Micaiah's prophecy was sarcastic: 'How many times must I make you swear that you tell me the truth in the name of the Lord?' (3 Kgdms 22:16 NETS, See Chapter 2, §2.2.3).

3.1.1.3 Explicit Echoes

The echoic account of verbal irony considers ironic statements inherently referential, echoing the words or perspectives of others in order to communicate the speaker's evaluation thereof (Chapter 1, §1.2.3).[14] While I have not taken a position on whether all sarcasm is inherently echoic, it is certainly the case that explicit echoes of another's words can signal the presence of sarcasm (present in 15 per cent of our examples).

Lucian's satire on power, status, and the transience of life, *Dialogues of the Dead*, illustrates the use of explicit echoing to indicate sarcasm. Set in Hades, one dialogue finds the late Alexander the Great facing constant mockery from the late Cynic Diogenes. Though dead, Alexander still hopes for apotheosis into the Egyptian pantheon. Echoing the hope expressed in Alexander's words, Diogenes parodies this desire for divinity in the epithet he chooses for his sarcastic reply, 'Anyway, for all that, O Most Divine [Alexander], don't get your hopes up!' (*DMort.* 13.3). The echo here

---

[12] *Lexiphanes* is a discussion between a pompous sophist (Lexiphanes) with a love of archaic terminology, and a concerned friend (Lycinus) who attempts to cure him.

[13] This cue indicates that when Lycinus calls Lexiphanes 'the good guy' (ὁ καλός) and refers to his work as a 'feast', he is being sarcastic (*Lex.* 1 [Harmon]). On Lycinus as a character, see 3.3.2. Other instances of this cue include *Cat.* 2; *DDeor* 2.1; *Icar.* 2; Aristophanes, *Nub.* 293–96.

[14] Markers of direct quotation, despite their relationship to echoic mention and commonality as a signal of verbal irony in English, are not typical cues of sarcasm in Lucian or the New Testament (Pawlak 2019, 548–49, 560–61).

is also linguistic, as 'O Most Divine' (ō *theotate*, ὦ θειότατε) draws on Alexander's use of the word 'god' (*theos*, θεός).[15] Another example occurs in Aristophanes's *Birds*, where one of the protagonists sarcastically refers to an irritating poet as 'this clever poet' (τῷ ποιητῇ τῷ σοφῷ, 934). This sarcastic comment harks back to the poet's self-description, which bombastically appropriates Homer: '"I am he that launches a song of honey-tongued verses, / the Muses' eager vassal", / to quote Homer.' (*Av.* 908–10 [Henderson]).[16] In these examples, by referring to their interlocutors' self-perception, the sarcasts imply that they do not consider their victims to merit the esteem that they accord themselves.

3.1.1.4 Explicit Evaluation

Incongruity is an important signal of sarcasm.[17] A contrast or contradiction between the literal meaning of the sarcastic statement and its context indicates that the utterance has not been meant sincerely and helps express its implicit negative evaluation.[18] There is little more incongruous than immediately negating an assertion. Haiman coins the term 'utterance deflater' to describe this very phenomenon, the use of '...Not!' to explicitly indicate sarcasm – as in: 'What an excellent example ... Not!'[19] I suggest that the concept of utterance deflation ought to be extended to other forms of negation. We find a range of deflative effects in Lucian where ostensibly positive messages are followed by the author or character's literal negative evaluations, making it clear what was really meant all along. We find an example in Lucian's *The Ignorant Book-Collector*, which satirizes a man of many books but little learning:

> Ah yes, already you have been improved beyond measure by their purchase [i.e. the purchase of the books], when you

---

[15] The line reads: 'I've been lying in Babylon for a whole thirty days now, but my guardsman Ptolemy promises that ... he'll take me away to Egypt and bury me there, so that I may become one of the gods [*theōn*] of the Egyptians [ὡς γενοίμην εἰς τῶν Αἰγυπτίων θεῶν]' (*DMort.* 13.3 [MacLeod]). Sarcastic echoing continues in *DMort.* 13.4–5 (see Pawlak 2019, 550).

[16] Further examples include: Aristophanes, *Av.*, 911–14; *Eq.* 175, 703; Lucian, *DDeor.* 2.1; *DMar.* 1.1; *DMort.* 29.2; *Peregr.* 1; *Philops.* 32; *Tim.* 1; 3 Kgdms 22:15; Mark 15:31–32.

[17] Haiman 1990, 192–99.

[18] Cf. Attardo 2000a, 9.

[19] 1998, 53–54; cf. Attardo 2000a, 10–11.

talk as you do – but no [μᾶλλον δέ], you are more dumb than any fish! (*Ind.* 16 [Harmon]; further examples include: *DMort.* 20.7; *Philops.* 32; Aristophanes, *Nub.* 1366–67; *Ran.* 178).

It can be occasionally difficult to determine what should qualify as an 'utterance deflater' in the strict sense that Haiman describes. Even if there is no abrupt negation, speakers often follow their sarcastic utterances with a contrasting and explicitly negative evaluation of their victim (recall Chapter 2, §§2.1.5.1, 2.3). Medea's sarcastic complaint against Jason is an excellent example of juxtaposing sarcasm with literal negative evaluation:

> That, doubtless, is why you have made me so happy in the eyes of many Greek women, in return for these favors [sarcasm]. I, poor wretch [literal negative evaluation], have in you a wonderful and faithful husband [sarcasm] if I am to flee the country, sent into exile, deprived of friends, abandoned with my abandoned children [negative evaluation] (Kovacs).[20]

> τοιγάρ με πολλαῖς μακαρίαν Ἑλληνίδων
> ἔθηκας ἀντὶ τῶνδε· θαυμαστὸν δέ σε
> ἔχω πόσιν καὶ πιστὸν ἡ τάλαιν' ἐγώ,
> εἰ φεύξομαί γε γαῖαν ἐκβεβλημένη,
> φίλων ἔρημος, σὺν τέκνοις μόνη μόνοις (Euripides, *Med.*
> 509–13).[21]

Sharply disjunctive utterance deflaters that clearly negate the affect of the previous utterance, such as our example above from *Ind.* 16, occur in only 5 per cent of the total dataset. The broader trend, such as we see in *Medea*, whereby speakers clarify their sarcasm with statements of literal negative evaluation occurs in 25 per cent of our examples. This use of explicit negative evaluation that confirms the implicit negative evaluation of the sarcastic utterance is, therefore, one of the most prevalent signals of sarcasm in our dataset. Its significance is further underlined by the fact that epistolary

---

[20] Alexander Numenius cites this passage as an example of *eirōneia* (εἰρωνεία, *Fig.* 18).
[21] Cf. Lucian, *DMeretr.* 7.1; *DMort.* 13.5; *Hes.* 7; *Hist. Conscr.* 31; *Tim.* 1; Aristophanes, *Ach.* 71–72; *Eq.* 703; *Nub.* 8–10; *Thesm.* 19–24; *Anth. Gr.* xi.155; Jas 2:19.

theorist Pseudo-Libanius refers to the phenomenon in his definition of the ironic letter: 'The ironic style is that in which we feign praise of someone at the beginning (περὶ τὴν ἀρχήν), but at the end (ἐπὶ τέλει) display our real aim, inasmuch as we had made our earlier statements in pretense' (*Epist. Styl.* 9 [Malherbe]; cf. *Epist. Styl.* 56).

3.1.1.5   Contrasting Evaluative Terms: 'Scare-Quotes' Sarcasm

An entire statement is not always necessary to generate clashing evaluations. Speakers can create incongruity by placing a word with typically positive resonances into a negative context. Consider the following epitaph:

> My murderer buried me, hiding his crime: since he gives me a tomb, may he meet with the same kindness as he shewed me (*Anth. Gr.* vii.310 [Paton, LCL]).[22]

Here the negative associations surrounding being murdered indicate that the writer is being sarcastic when he wishes his murderer to come upon the like 'kindness' (χάρις) that he has received – that is, being buried in a shallow grave by a murderer.

Conversely, a single negative term within a list of positive ones can indicate that the latter are meant sarcastically. For example, in Lucian's *Timon*, Zeus complains that it is difficult for him to hear the Athenians' prayers over the noise of their endless philosophizing about 'some sort of "virtue", and "incorporeal things", and nonsense' (ἀρετήν τινα καὶ ἀσώματα καὶ λήρους, *Tim.* 9).

These ways of sarcastically inverting positive concepts are most naturally expressed in written English with scare quotes or inverted commas.[23] While accurate translation may involve the use of quotation marks, in Greek it is the contrast between the evaluations natural to the different terms' connotations that makes the sarcastic elements stand out. This is a context-dependent means of indicating sarcasm that accomplishes what we do with inverted commas, but through means linguistically distinct from quotation. The prevalence of this signal in our dataset, occurring in 15 per cent of our examples, provides further testimony to the importance of contextual cues of sarcasm in ancient Greek writing.

---

[22] Cf. *Anth. Gr.* xi.86; Lucian, *DMort.* 13.5, 20.8, 20.11; *Fug.* 10; *Hist. Conscr.* 31.
[23] Which are two idioms for the same thing.

3.1.1.6 Counterfactuality and Absurdity

Speakers may also express insincerity through contradictions in matters of fact, and research shows that clear counterfactual messages are identified as sarcastic with significantly greater frequency than factual statements.[24] This use of counterfactuality to create incongruity is common in ancient Greek texts, where the surface meaning of the sarcastic statement contradicts the actual state of affairs. This can be observed in Lucian's *Phalaris*, where the tyrant Phalaris has a craftsman torturously burned inside a hollow, metallic bull that he has just presented to Phalaris as a gift.[25] As the craftsman burns, Phalaris taunts: 'Take the reward you deserve for your wonderful invention' (Ἀπολάμβανε ... τὸν ἄξιον μισθὸν τῆς θαυμαστῆς σου τέχνους, *Phal.I.* 12 [Harmon]; cf. Job 38:21; *Letter of Aristeas*, 19; Tryphon, *Trop.* 19/Homer, *Od.* 17.396–99,[26] 22.194–200).[27] Obviously, sadistic torture is not a reward.

As a signal of sarcasm, absurdity works in much the same way. Here the sarcastic statement is so ridiculous that it cannot be taken literally. Zeus creates absurdity in an argument with Hera in Lucian's *Dialogues of the Gods*. The two are arguing over Ganymede, whom Hera is jealous of for obvious reasons. Zeus defends his choice in cupbearer with sustained sarcasm: 'I suppose we ought to have our wine from your son, Hephaestus, hobbling about, straight from the forge, still filthy from the sparks, having just put down his tongs...' (*DDeor.* 8.4 [MacLeod]; cf. *Anach.* 10; *Anth.* Gr. xi.112; Isa 36:8; Job 38:18, 20; Luke 23:39). Zeus carries on a while in this vein, painting a ridiculous picture of Hephaestus as a cupbearer that makes it obvious that he considers the lame god of the forge to be a poor replacement for Ganymede.

3.1.2 Linguistic Signals

Linguistic signals of sarcasm, those cues proper to the language and phrasing of the sarcastic statement itself, are both diverse and

---

[24] Kreuz and Glucksberg 1989, 382; see also Kreuz and Roberts 1995, 27. See Chapter 1, §1.2.2.

[25] The craftsman intended the bull – heated from below with a person inside – for use as a torture device but did not expect to be its first victim (see *Phal.I.* 11–12).

[26] See Minchin 2010a, 542–44.

[27] Both μισθός (*misthos*, 'reward/payment') and θαυμαστός (*thaumastos*, 'wonderful/shocking') can have positive and negative connotations in Greek that allow for *double entendre* here that does not come across in translation.

essential to its communication. Our discussion of these cues will focus largely on different ways of conveying emphasis and hyperbole, although other signals will come into play as well. Exaggeration is highly significant to the expression of sarcasm.[28] In both speech and writing, hyperbole is used extensively to generate the incongruity necessary to communicate insincerity and also increases the likelihood that a statement will be interpreted as ironic.[29] Our most recent example from §3.1.1.6 is a clear case of hyperbole in ancient Greek sarcasm. The length at which Zeus describes Hephaestus's 'skill' at waiting tables is well beyond what is necessary to grasp his point. Indeed, emphasis and hyperbole are so common in our dataset that I cannot claim to have quantified them reliably. Our focus will therefore not be on hyperbole in general, but on identifying different ways that emphasis is deployed to communicate sarcasm in ancient Greek.

3.1.2.1   Adjective Use: X kai Y, Repetition, and Chunking

The repetition of adjectives is a common way of using emphasis to indicate sarcasm. Lucian has an especial love of pairing ostensibly positive adjectives in the form *x kai y* (15 per cent of examples in our dataset).[30] This formula generates redundancy and emphasis. In Lucian's *Prometheus*, Hermes chats with Prometheus while Hephaestus crucifies him. Hermes teases, 'That's good. The eagle will soon fly down to eat away your liver, so that you may have full return for your beautiful and clever handiwork in clay [ὡς πάντα ἔχοις ἀντὶ τῆς καλῆς καὶ εὐμηχάνου πλαστικῆς]' (*Prom.*[31] 2 [Harmon]; cf. *Icar.* 2, 10; *Alex.* 25; *Cat.* 21; Hermogenes, *Style*, 1.10).[32] Here Hermes' sarcastic double adjectives 'beautiful and clever' (καλῆς καὶ εὐμηχάνου) poke fun at both Prometheus and humanity, his creation.

---

[28] See Haiman 1990, 193–97; Kreuz and Roberts 1995, 21–29; Braester 2009, 75–85.
[29] See Kreuz and Roberts 1995, 24–28.
[30] *kai* (καί) = 'and'. The use of adjectives more generally to generate sarcastic hyperbole is itself far more common. I will focus on more specialized uses of the adjective that stand out as clearer indicators of sarcasm.
[31] To disambiguate, I abbreviate *Prometheus* as *Prom.* and *A Literary Prometheus* as *Prom. Verb.*
[32] For Latin examples, see Apuleius, *Met.* 1.8; Cicero, *Fam.* 2.8; *Cael.* xxvi.63. A similar effect can be accomplished with the *x kai y* repetition of nouns that normally communicate positive affect (see Herodian, *Fig. Epit.* 16–17; Job 12:13, 16). The percentage given above includes *x kai y* adjectives and nouns.

We also find the *x kai y* formula in Pseudo-Lucian's novel *The Ass*, where a group of bandits sarcastically appropriate the common epithet *kalos kagathos* (κάλος κἄγαθος) to refer to a captured girl as 'You beautiful and goodly virgin' ('Ὦ καλὴ κἀγαθὴ σὺ παρθένος, *Ass* 24; cf. Lucian, *Cat.* 1).[33] The emphatic repetition of sarcastic adjectives need not always follow this formula.[34] Lucian's Timon takes sarcastic adjective use to an excessive degree, as the misanthrope sarcastically lauds Zeus' lightning bolt, and so symbolically criticizes Zeus' inactivity in carrying out justice on earth:

> Where is your blasting lightning and loud-roaring thunder and your burning and flashing and frightful thunderbolt now? ... I'm at a loss to describe just how completely extinguished and cold your renowned and far-shooting and ever-at-hand weapon is! (ποῦ σοι νῦν ἡ ἐρισμάραγος ἀστραπὴ καὶ ἡ βαρύβρομος βροντὴ καὶ ὁ αἰθαλόεις καὶ ἀργήεις καὶ σμερδαλέος κεραυνός; ... τὸ δὲ ἀοίδιμόν σοι καὶ ἐκηβόλον ὅπλον καὶ πρόχειρον οὐκ οἶδ' ὅπως τελέως ἀπέσβη καὶ ψυχρόν ἐστι... (*Tim.* 1).

Here, the unnecessary repetition of adjectives hammers home the exaggeration used to convey Timon's sarcasm.[35] The plodding repetition of *kai* (καί) also creates the sense that the standard list of epithets that describe Zeus's power is boringly long.[36] In addition to their quantity, the 'epic' quality of these adjectives further heightens the hyperbole (cf. 3.2.2), as does the use of alliteration (*barybromos brontē*, βαρύβρομος βροντή ['loud-roaring thunder']).[37]

Lucianic sarcasm also attests to a special form of adjectival modification. In several cases, modifiers attach to their nouns, creating sarcastic compound words. This is close to a feature of English sarcasm that Haiman refers to as 'chunking': running words together to create an ironic effect. One can express annoyance – with

---

[33] See Meier 2006.

[34] Beyond adjectives specifically, we have also seen how other forms of repetition can signal sarcasm by communicating emphasis and exaggeration (Chapter 2, §§2.1.5.1, 2.3).

[35] Compare Aristophanes, *Peace*, 50–54.

[36] On Lucian's 'heavy use' of *kai* (καί), both here and elsewhere, see Mackie 1892, 93. This passage is also an excellent example of juxtaposing explicit negative evaluation with sarcasm (§3.1.1.4).

[37] See Hopkinson 2008, 165.

automated telephone customer service, for example – by uttering or writing a cliché as if it were a single word: 'Oh great. Another *your-call-is-important-to-us-and-is-being-held-in-a-queue.*'[38] I will use the term chunking more broadly than Haiman, to refer to the addition of emphatic modifiers to other words to create sarcastic compounds. Lucianic examples include: μεγαλοδωρεᾷ ('great-gift', *Anach.* 9); πάνσεμνα ('totally-clever', *Anach.* 9); καλλιρρημοσύνη (*DDeor* 1.2);[39] and πανδαμάτορος ('all-conquering', *Tim.* 2 [Harmon]).[40] Although such chunking is not a common feature of ancient Greek sarcasm, occurring in only 3 per cent of our dataset, it is worth mentioning for its similarity to the English idiom.

3.1.2.2 Adverbs

Like adjectives, adverbs can play an important role in communicating sarcasm. Late in *Timon*, Timon describes a gluttonous, intemperate philosopher (*Tim.* 54). At the end of this unflattering exposition, Timon concludes sarcastically, 'and he is *all-in-all* a sort of totally-clever thing and accurate *in every way* and *intricately* perfect'. (καὶ ὅλως πάνσοφόν τι χρῆμα καὶ πανταχόθεν ἀκριβὲς καὶ ποικίλως ἐντελές, *Tim.* 55 [adverbs italicized]). This example combines several features we have discussed. Repetitive adjective use following Lucian's standard x *kai* y (*kai* z) cadence combines with triple sarcastic adverbs (ὅλως, πανταχόθεν, ποικίλως) to create emphasis and exaggeration.[41] There is also chunking ('totally-clever', πάνσοφον) and alliteration (*pansophon, pantachothen, poikilōs*; πάνσοφον, πανταχόθεν, ποικίλως).

The sarcastic use of adverbs occurs in 10 per cent of our dataset (cf. *Hist.Conscr.* 15, 29; *DMeretr.* 7.1; Aristophanes, *Ach.* 71; *Av.* 362–63; *Ran.* 1261; Josephus, *Ap.* 2.11.125[42]) and Lucian's fondness for the sarcastic use of πάνυ is worth specific mention (*Deor.Conc.*

---

[38] Haiman 1998, 52.

[39] Levy: "etymologically 'beautiful language'; here 'braggadocio'" (1976, 260).

[40] Cf. βαρύβρομος βροντὴ ('loud-roaring thunder'), *Tim* 1 p.79. See also Aristophanes, *Nub.* 293: πολυτίμητοι ('much-honoured-ones'). *Anth. Gr.* xi.354 juxtaposes the sarcastic ἰσοπλάτωνα 'equal-to-Plato' with the negative σκινδαλαμοφράστην 'straw-splitter' (LSJ, s.v. 'σκινδαλαμοφράστης').

[41] For adjective/adverb combination in English sarcasm, see Kovaz, Kreuz, and Riordan 2013, 600–01, 611; Kreuz and Roberts 1995, 24–25.

[42] 'Apion is therefore *so very* (Σφόδρα) worthy of admiration (θαυμάζειν ἄξιον) for his abundant insight in what is about to be said...' Josephus then cites and refutes Apion's argument (2.11.125–28).

11; *Herm.* 12–13; *Hes.* 7; *Hist. Conscr.* 26; *Ind.* 16; *Pseudol.* 30).
Mark's Jesus uses the adverb *kalōs* (καλῶς) sarcastically, giving it
first position for added emphasis: 'You have a fine way of rejecting
the commandment of God [*Kalōs*/Καλῶς ἀθετεῖτε τὴν ἐντολὴν τοῦ
θεοῦ] in order to keep your tradition!' (Mark 7:9 NRSV; cf. Lucian,
DMeretr. 12.1).

3.1.2.3 Particles

Ancient Greek is rich in the variety of its particles, allowing for
subtleties in expression that are often difficult to render in English.[43]
A subset of Greek particles are emphatic in function and, through
their ability to show exaggeration, occur frequently as a means of
signalling sarcasm – 22 per cent of our examples. *ge* (γε) is the most
common in Lucian and Aristophanes, either on its own or elided to
goun (γοῦν, see Lucian, *Abd.* 14; *Deor.Conc.* 11; *DMeretr.* 14.4;
DMort. 6.5, 29.2; *Herm.* 2; *Ind.* 16; Aristophanes, *Ach.* 71; *Av.*
176–77, 362–63; *Eccl.* 190–91, 422–26; *Nub.* 1064; *Ran.* 491;
Thesm. 20–21; cf. 3.2.1 for *eu ge* [εὖ γε]),[44] but others occur as well,
including *men* (μέν, Lucian, *Icar.* 10), *mēn* (μήν, *Herm.* 2),[45] and *-per*
(-περ, *Alex.* 35).

dē (δή) can also play a significant role in sarcasm (*Abd.* 14; *Peregr.*
33).[46] We saw this in the Septuagint, where it was used in sarcastic
requests and taunts (Job 38:18; 40:10; Mal 1:8).[47] In Lucian's *The
Passing of Peregrinus* – a satire on a sage whose philosophical career
led from Cynicism to Christianity to self-immolation – we find a case
where the identification of sarcasm hinges on the presence of an
emphatic *dē* (δή). After Peregrinus declares his intention to ascend
the pyre alive,[48] the voices calling on him to go on living are soon
overwhelmed by those who would rather see him self-immolate,
much to Peregrinus' chagrin. Harmon's translation of the passage
ends with a sarcastic flourish in which Lucian pretends to believe

---

[43] See Smyth 1959, 631–71.
[44] Cf. Josephus, *Ap.* 2.34.246 (καλά γε [*ge*] ταῦτα); *Letter of Aristeas*, 19.
[45] Here we find three distinct particles – *ge* (γε), *men* (μέν), and *mēn* (μήν) – over two
sarcastic statements.
[46] See Denniston 1954, 229–36.
[47] Cf. *Od.* 22.194–200 (3.2.5).
[48] Apparently, Peregrinus chooses to die in this manner to teach others to 'despise
death and endure what is fearsome' (*Peregr.* 23 [Harmon]). Lucian disagrees (see
Peregr. 22) and intends to prove the man a fame-seeking fraud.

that Peregrinus' motives are sincere: 'he hoped that all would cling to him and not give him over to the fire, but retain him in life – against his will, naturally [*akonta dē*, ἄκοντα δή]!' (*Peregr.* 33 [Harmon]). This translation aptly renders Lucian's use of the emphatic particle *dē* (here translated 'naturally') to indicate insincerity.

3.1.2.4 *Interjections and the Exclamatory* hōs *(ὡς)*

Interjections are also used for emphasis, making it unsurprising that they feature in modern English sarcasm.[49] Although they do not occur as frequently as other signals in our dataset (7 per cent of examples), interjections remain significant as cues of sarcasm in ancient Greek. In Lucian, 'Heracles!' and 'By Zeus!' are common interjections in both literal and sarcastic speech (for sarcasm, see *Im.* 1; *Symp.* 30; *Hist. Conscr.* 25; and *DDeor.* 2.1, respectively). We also find expressions of surprise or distress in sarcasm, such as *babai* (βαβαί) and *papai* (παπαί).[50] Interjection is used to communicate sarcasm in Mark's passion account, where those crucified along with Jesus mock him: '[Wow!][51] You who would destroy the temple and build it in three days, save yourself...!' (Οὐὰ ὁ καταλύων τὸν ναὸν ... σῶσον σεαυτὸν, Mark 15:29–30 [NRSV, with modified interjection]).

Within the broad range of its semantic use, *hōs* (ὡς) can function as an exclamation, an emphatic 'how/so', such as we see in Rom 11:33, which is an unambiguously positive use: 'O the depth of the riches and wisdom and knowledge of God! How [*hōs*] unsearchable are his judgments and how inscrutable his ways!' (NRSV).[52] Speakers use this exclamatory *hōs* sarcastically with enough regularity to suggest a degree of formalization – 6 per cent of examples in our dataset. For example, in *The Wisdom of Nigrinus*, a speaker mocks his friend who has just come back from his study of philosophy: 'How [*hōs*] very clever and lofty have you returned to us!' (Ὡς σεμνὸς ἡμῖν σφόδρα καὶ μετέωρος ἐπανελήλυθας, Lucian, *Nigr.* 1).[53]

---

[49] Kovaz, Kreuz, and Riordan 2013, 601–02, 608, 611.
[50] *Pseudol.* 27 and *Herm.* 5, 55, respectively. Cf. Nordgren 2015, 216–17, 236–37. For interjections in sarcasm outside Lucian, see Aristophanes *Ach.* 64; *Av.* 176–77; *Thes.* 20–21; Homer, *Il.* 16.745–50.
[51] For other, non-sarcastic examples of *oua* (οὐά), an 'exclamation of admiration or of astonishment', see LSJ, s.v. 'οὐά'.
[52] On *hōs* (ὡς), see Smyth 1959, 101–2; for the exclamatory *hōs*, see Smyth 1959, 606–7.
[53] Note the use of multiple adjectives (σεμνὸς ... καὶ μετέωρος) and adverbial emphasis (σφόδρα; §§3.1.2.1–3.1.2.2).

Another example occurs in Aristophanes' *Birds*, where Euelpides teases his companion for behaving in a cowardly manner: 'How manly you are!' (*hōs andreios ei*; ὡς ἀνδρεῖος εἶ, *Av.* 91; cf. *Ran.* 178; see also Lucian, *DMeretr.* 12.2; *Herm.* 55, 82; *Hist.Conscr.* 14, 19; *Nigr.* 1, 10; *Sacr.* 14). *pōs* (πῶς) and *hopōs* (ὅπως) can function in a similar way (see Lucian, *JTr.* 29; *Symp.* 30).

3.1.2.5 Dismissives

All the linguistic signals discussed so far in §3.1.2 have centred on hyperbole and emphasis, especially the exaggeration of positive language to communicate insincerity, but other means of conveying sarcasm are possible. Functioning similarly to the use of contrasting evaluative language (§§3.1.1.4–3.1.1.5), speakers may subtly communicate negative appraisal within sarcastic statements. Using a vague term of reference such as *tis* (τις, 'someone/thing') can function to devalue and dismiss the ideas of others. We saw this in *Tim.* 9 with the dismissal of pedantic philosophical discourse on '*some sort of* "virtue"' (ἀρετήν τινα [§3.1.1.5]).

When used of persons, such markers can be ways of stripping individual identity by avoiding the use of proper names (*DMort.* 20.7; *Hist.Conscr.* 30; *Tim.* 55 [§3.1.2.2]), or otherwise diminishing another's importance. In *Dialogues of the Dead*, the cynic philosopher Menippus mocks Pythagoras sarcastically for his belief in transmigration, cheerfully addressing him by his alleged past lives when he is obviously properly dead: 'Hail Euphorbus, or Apollo or whatever [*tis*] else you like calling yourself!' (Χαῖρε, ὦ Εὔφορβε ἢ Ἄπολλον ἢ ὅ τι ἂν θέλῃς,[54] *DMort.* 6.3; cf. *Luct.* 20; *Im.* 1; *Tim.* 1). While *tis* (τις) is the most common dismissive in Lucianic sarcasm, 'this' (*houtos*/οὗτος, Lucian, *Peregr.* 30 [§3.2.4]; Aristophanes, *Nub.* 8; Hermogenes, *Style*, 1.10;[55] Pseudo-Lucian, *Ass*, 25), 'that' (*ekeinos*/ἐκεῖνος, Lucian, *DMar.* 1.4; *DMort.* 13.5[56]), and 'such' (*toioutos*/τοιοῦτος (*DMar.* 1.5) can function in a similar fashion.[57]

---

[54] The use of ἄν + subjunctive here also contributes to the tone of dismissiveness.
[55] See Chapter 7, §7.3.3.2.
[56] See Pawlak 2019, 550.
[57] For dismissive use of *iste* ('that') in Latin sarcasm, see Cicero, *Cael.* xxvi.63. The use of dismissives in ancient sarcasm represents an avenue for further research, as at this time I do not have reliable statistics for its frequency in our dataset.

3.1.3   Conclusions

With the foregoing discussion of contextual and linguistic signals, we have already gone a long way in facilitating the identification of sarcasm in ancient Greek. The chart below summarizes the findings of this section.

Signal	Likely Examples	Total Examples	Per cent of Dataset
Narration (§3.1.1.1)	21	25	6%
Victim Recognition (§3.1.1.2)	22	26	7%
Explicit Echoes (§3.1.1.3)	48	59	15%
Explicit Evaluation (§3.1.1.4)	83	96	25%
Utterance Deflater (§3.1.1.4)	16	17	5%
Contrasting Evaluative Terms (§3.1.1.5)	46	62	15%
X *kai* Y (§3.1.2.1)	51	59	15%[58]
Chunking (§3.1.2.1)	11	13	3%
Adverbs (§3.1.2.2)	31	38	10%
Particles (§3.1.2.3)	71	84	22%
Interjections (§3.1.2.4)	25	28	7%
Exclamatory *hōs* (§3.1.2.4)	18	22	6%

Summary to §3. 1 – 'Total Examples' includes both likely and uncertain instances of sarcasm. Percentage given is the average of the percentages including and excluding the uncertain examples. Percentages do not sum to 100 per cent, since any given example of sarcasm may be indicated by several cues – or even none of those listed, as this list is not exhaustive.

The contextual cues surveyed reveal that there is more to the identification of sarcasm than the sarcastic statement itself. While signals peculiar to third parties and narrative texts appear to be important, they do not feature in Lucian, or Paul, and will therefore not take a significant place in this study. The echoic approach to irony, however, showed its utility through the prevalence of explicit echoing in our dataset. But the most significant contextual cue was incongruity, manifested in the expression of the speaker's literal evaluation to underline the implicit negative evaluation of sarcasm. The use of conflicting evaluations in the context of sarcastic

---

[58] This cue is probably over-represented in our dataset due to its prevalence in Lucian.

statements clarifies the presence of sarcasm in written texts and makes up for an absence of tonal cues.

We have also collected a number of linguistic features that correlate with the use of sarcasm. These are nearly all ways of creating hyperbole and emphasis, which is unsurprising. Exaggeration is a common way for speakers to indicate that they do not mean what they say (§3.1.2). The repetition of positive adjectives and the use of emphatic particles were the most significant linguistic cues surveyed. The former fits well with the importance of repetition in LXX sarcasm (Chapter 2, §§2.1.5.1, 2.3). The high frequency of emphatic particles is also of particular interest, showing a way in which the idiomatic features of the Greek language itself can contribute to the communication of sarcasm.

Other signals – including adverbs, exclamations, and dismissives – although somewhat less frequent, remain significant cues of sarcasm likely to recur across ancient Greek texts. Furthermore, although we lack frequency data, we have also observed several cases of alliteration as a means of creating emphasis in sarcastic statements. Both analogy and direct comparison to the linguistic and contextual cues discussed will play an important role in the identification of sarcastic statements as we turn to Paul's letters.

3.2   Patterns in Sarcasm Use

We will now identify recurring patterns in ancient sarcasm. As we saw with the sarcastic taunts of the prophets, certain related sarcastic utterances share specific features or are used in analogous situations, occurring with enough regularity to suggest common pragmatic functions. These include speech acts that can be repurposed sarcastically (e.g. §§3.2.1, 3.2.3) and specific situations in which speakers employ sarcasm (§3.2.5). At times there will be overlap between these patterns and signals of sarcasm, especially where indicators of hyperformality are concerned (§3.2.2). This is not a problem, and indeed the recognition of any pattern can be helpful in facilitating the identification of sarcasm. At the same time, exploring common ways in which sarcasm is used can also extend our understanding of its pragmatic functions.

3.2.1   Sarcastic Encouragement

Sarcastic encouragement is present in 15 per cent of our examples. Here the sarcast gives an ostensibly supportive request for their victim to engage in some action or offers their mock encouragement after the fact. The action endorsed is often something foolish, absurd, or otherwise unlikely to turn out well. The sarcastic taunts of the prophets represent a specific subset of sarcastic encouragement, which gesture both to the inevitably of their objects' failure and to divine judgement (Chapter 2, §2.2.1).[59]

But not all sarcastic encouragement is so intense. In Lucian, we find several offhand comments that qualify as sarcastic encouragement. In the trial scenes of *The Double Indictment*, having been thoroughly defeated in court, Stoa appeals to Zeus – despite the improbability of winning the case and the likelihood of further embarrassment. Justice simply replies: 'Good luck to you!' (Τύχῃ τῇ ἀγαθῇ, *Bis.Acc.* 22 [Harmon]; cf. *DMeretr.* 14.4; *DMort.* 3.2; *Philops.* 39). Lucian's go-to means of sarcastic congratulations involves a curt combination of an adverb and emphatic particle: *eu ge* (εὖ γε, see *JTr.* 32, 42; *Pisc.* 45; *DMort.* 3.2; *DMort.* 6.6; *DDeor.* 12.1; cf. Aristophanes, *Av.* 362).[60] As a sarcastic 'well done!' the use of *eu ge* that we find in Lucian is analogous to Jesus' sarcastic *kalōs* (καλῶς) in Mark 7:9 (§3.1.2.2; cf. Jas 2:19).

3.2.2   Hyperformality

Discussed by several scholars of irony, hyperformality is a form of hyperbole that involves showing greater 'respect' than is due in a given social situation.[61] For example, the royal address form in 'Shall I play his majesty a sad, sad song on the violin?' would be a sarcastic way to respond to one's complaining child. Unnecessary politeness can function as an indicator of sarcasm. However, because there are many mechanisms for communicating hyperfomality, including several of those addressed in §§3.1.1 and 3.1.2, I will group all forms of sarcastic politeness as a pattern in sarcasm use.

---

[59] For NT sarcastic encouragement/taunts, see Mark 15:30–32; Matt 27:39–40, 41–42. In Hellenistic Jewish texts, see 4 Macc 5:32 and the exchange in *T.Job*, 37:10–38:6 (Appendix C). See also Homer, *Il.* 3.432–36 (Minchin 2010a, 392–93). Sarcastic encouragement is often given in the imperative. Cf. Quintilian, *Inst.* 9.2.48: 'It is Irony when we pretend to be giving orders or permissions' (Εἰρωνεία *est cum similes imperantibus vel permittentibus sumus* [Russell, LCL].

[60] This exclamation is an ironic version of a common positive expression (for sincere examples, see Lucian, *Pisc.* 28; *Nec.* 15; *Vit.Auct.* 8).

[61] Haiman 1990, 199–202; 1998, 41–44; cf. Sperber and Wilson 1981, 311–12; Kreuz and Glucksberg 1989, 383; Kumon-Nakamura, Glucksberg, and Brown 1995, 3, 20; Minchin 2010a, 394; Minchin 2010b, 554.

Ancient Greek provided speakers with several means of showing respect or familiarity that could be appropriated sarcastically. This makes exaggerated politeness an excellent way to challenge another's status. The over-polite utterance communicates 'This is the status you may think you have', while its sarcastic undertone implies 'but you don't deserve it.' Hyperformality is one of the most prevalent features of sarcasm in the literature surveyed (36 per cent of examples).

The use of ancient Greek address forms related to friendship (φίλε, ἀγαθέ, βέλτιστε, etc.) is complicated. Dickey writes that there is a 'mass of conflicting evidence' in Attic texts concerning the use of friendship terms as vocative forms of address, and that this diversity in use carries forward into later Greek.[62] They can be used positively following their etymological sense, but are often – especially in Plato – used 'with slightly patronizing connotations' by the dominant speaker in an exchange.[63] Dickey argues that this condescending use, though negative, is not sarcastic.[64] She sees Lucian's use of friendship terms as mixed, at times following Plato, and at times not.[65] While I agree to an extent, I argue that Lucian's use of friendship terms is far more likely to be sarcastic than Plato's, even when Lucian imitates Plato. Lucian self-consciously writes comic dialogue, a genre he lays a claim to having invented, rather than philosophical dialogue.[66] Even where he imitates Plato, it is with a comic twist,[67] and so we should expect that where we find subtle condescension in address forms in Plato, we are more likely to find outright sarcasm in Lucian.

Friendship terms are most obviously sarcastic in Lucian when they are combined with other forms of address that clearly do not suit their referents. In *The Cock* for example, a rooster who happens to

[62] Dickey 1996, 121, 127–33. On the social functions of address forms in general, see Dickey 1996, 12–17.
[63] Dickey 1996, 133, 107–33.
[64] Dickey 1996, 118; cf. Lane 2010, 249–50. The distinction between unironic, condescending use of friendship terms and sarcastic, condescending use of friendship terms is a fine one. If the negative use of the friendship term has become so well-worn and clichéd that the user/audience no longer recognizes the original, positive resonance (as is the case with the English phrase 'yeah, right'), it may be used condescendingly without sarcasm (on the impact of repetition on meaning, see Haiman 1998, 128–37, 147–72, 190).
[65] Dickey 1996, 131–33.
[66] On Lucian's invention of comic dialogue, see *Prom. Verb.* 1–7; *Bis. Acc.* 33–35 (cf. 3.3.1).
[67] See especially Lucian's *Symposium*.

be an incarnation of Pythagoras says to a cobbler who has just related a dream about riches: 'Stop it, O Most Excellent Midas (ὦ Μίδα βέλτιστε), with all this gold-chat!' (*Gall.* 7; cf. *DDeor.* 8.2; *DMeretr.* 13.4; *DMort.* 6.4; *JTr.* 41; *Pisc.* 48; *Tim.* 4). Combining the appellation 'Midas', which is clearly hyperbolic when used to address a poor cobbler, with the common friendship term *beltiste* (βέλτιστε) makes the whole address clearly sarcastic. Sarcasm is also likely where friendship terms are employed in statements that have sarcastic elements beyond the address form, such as in *Pisc.* 45 where Philosophy sarcastically congratulates a phony Cynic with 'well done, good sir' (Εὖ γε, ὦ γενναῖε), combining sarcastic encouragement (*eu ge,* §3.2.1 p.86) with a sarcastic friendship term (*ō gennaie,* cf. *Hes.* 7; Aristophanes, *Av.* 91, 362–63). The most common sarcastic friendship terms in Lucian include *ō beltiste* (ὦ βέλτιστε, 'best'),[68] *ō gennaiotate* (ὦ γενναιότατε, 'most noble'),[69] and *ō thaumasie* (ὦ θαυμάσιε, 'wonderful').[70] Friendship terms are not the only forms of address used sarcastically. Royal terms work just as well, as in the famous, 'Hail! King of the Jews!' (χαῖρε, βασιλεῦ τῶν Ἰουδαίων, Mark 15:18).[71]

Epithets can also be used to create sarcastic hyperformality. Many such epithets are simply the adjectival forms of common sarcastic vocatives (see n.68–70), such as when Josephus refers to Apion as 'the noble Apion' (*ho ... gennaios Apiōn*; ὁ ... γενναῖος Ἀπίων, *Ap.* 2.3.32; cf. Aristophanes, *Ach.* 575, 578; *Ran.* 1154; *Anth.Gr.* xi.354; Pseudo-Lucian, *Ass,* 28).[72] While sarcastic vocatives and epithets are

---

[68] See *Deor.Conc.* 10; *DMort.* 2.3, 6.4, 9.3, 29.2; *Gall.* 7; *Prometheus* 6; *Vit.Auct.* 3; *Pseudol.* 14. Dickey does not seem to consider *beltiste* (βέλτιστε) sarcastic in Lucian. I of course disagree. She does note that it is often sarcastic in other authors (Dickey 1996, 139). For the sarcastic use of the adjectival form *beltistos* (βέλτιστος), see *Herm.* 12; *Nav.* 46; *Peregr.* 1, 12.

[69] See *DDeor.* 8.2; *JTr.*41; *Pisc.* 48; *Tim.* 4 (cf. Dickey 1996, 140–41). For *gennaie* (γενναῖε), see *DDeor.* 4.2; *Nav.* 14; *Pisc.* 7, 45. Related forms include *gennaios* (γενναῖος, *Tim.* 22, 47; *Peregr.* 19) and *gennadas* (γεννάδας, *Cat.* 1; *Peregr.* 1).

[70] See *Tim.* 4; *JTr.* 30, 49; *Tox.* 5. For the ironic use of the superlative *thaumasiōtate* (θαυμασιώτατε), see Dickey 1996, 141. For sarcastic use of *thaumastos* (θαυμάστος) and other adjectival *thauma*-terms, see *Hist.Conscr.* 24, 28, 31; *Peregr.* 43; *Symp.* 30, 35; *Anach.* 11; *Peregr.* 11, 30; *Phal.I,* 12; *Prom.* 20; *Pseudol.* 21; *Symp.* 23. For θαυμάζω as a verb, see Josephus, *Ap.* 2.11.125 (n.42).

[71] Cf. Matt 27:29; John 19:3. For further discussion, see Halliwell 2008, 471–74; cf. Haiman 1998, 43. For another, albeit more playfully sarcastic use of 'O king' (βασιλεῦ), see Lucian, *Nav.* 30. For miscellaneous sarcastic vocatives, see Lucian, *Icar.* 2; *JTr.* 47, 49; *Tim.* 1; Aristophanes, *Nub.* 293–95; *Ran.* 491.

[72] For LXX sarcastic epithets, see Job 6:19; 7:20; 15:2; Isa 14:12.

relatively easy to quantify, occurring in 15 per cent[73] and 18 per cent of our dataset, respectively, there are several other ways of manipulating language to express unnecessary formality. Drawing language from an unnecessarily high register for the situation can also signal insincerity. We already noted unnecessarily formal, sarcastic requests in Job, employing emphatic particles and the optative of wish (38:18–19; Chapter 2, §§2.1.4, 2.1.5.1).[74] Lucian enjoys the sarcastic use of poetic and Homeric epithets, such as in *Icaromenippus*, where certain philosophers are referred to as 'High thundering and well-bearded gentlemen' (ὑψιβρεμέταις τε καὶ ἠϋγενείοις ἀνδράσιν, *Icar.* 10 [adapted from Harmon])[75] – the former appellation is typically reserved for Zeus (cf. *Tim.* 4).[76] Here 'well-bearded' (*ēygeneiois*, ἠϋγενείοις has the initial vowel lengthened from *eugeneios* (εὐγένειος) such that it fits with epic metre, signalling further its inappropriately high register. *Timon* 1[77] similarly overuses poetic address forms and epithets for Zeus to convey its sarcasm. But one need not compose Homeric verse to engage in hyperformality. The use of unnecessarily complicated terminology or phrasing, archaic language, and verbosity can all function in this manner.[78]

3.2.3   Sarcastic Concessions

Sarcastic concessions occur when a speaker pretends to concede some point to their interlocutor, usually about a disputed matter. These are common in our dataset (13 per cent), especially in Lucian,[79] although Quintilian recognizes the pattern as well (*Inst.*

---

[73] Note that the sarcastic use of address forms is probably over-represented in Lucian compared to other texts (see the discussion of Dickey p.87).

[74] Cf. Homer *Il.* 24.263–64 (Minchin 2010a, 394–95).

[75] Note x *kai* y (§3.1.2.1).

[76] Cf. the Homeric *pandamatoros* (πανδαμάτορος, *Tim.* 2; §3.1.2.1; LSJ, s.v. 'πανδαμάτωρ'). See Cicero, *Cael.* xxviii.67 for further sarcastic epic language.

[77] Cited partially in §3.1.2.1.

[78] See *Anth.Gr.* xi.11, 17, 155, 354, 410. Job's Psalm parody (Job 7:17–19; Chapter 2, §2.1.3) is a good example of sarcastically appropriating a poetic register. For Lucian's satire on the pretentious use of Atticism, see *Rh.Pr.* 16–17; *Lex*; cf. Plutarch, *De Recta*, 9. For further discussion of Lucian and Atticism, see Adams 2010, 595–97.

[79] Lucian, which makes up 67 per cent of our dataset, contains 80 per cent of the examples of sarcastic concessions. This pattern may therefore appear somewhat more widespread in our dataset than it is in other authors.

9.2.48–49).[80] We find a clear example in Lucian's satire on cultic practices, where he pokes fun at Cretan religious customs by pretending they are correct:

> As for the Cretans, they not only say that Zeus was born and brought up among them, but even point out his tomb. We were mistaken all this while, then, in thinking that thunder and rain and everything else comes from Zeus; if we had but known it, he has been dead and buried in Crete this long time! (*Sacr.* 10 [Harmon]; cf. *Alex.* 35; *Anach.* 9, 10; *DMar.* 1.5; *JTr.* 30, 45, 52).

Mark 15:32 contains sarcastic encouragement and is also a sarcastic concession that ostensibly accepts the *titulus* 'The King of the Jews' (ὁ βασιλεὺς τῶν Ἰουδαίων, Mark 15:26 NRSV) at face value: 'Let now the Christ, the King of Israel [ὁ χριστὸς ὁ βασιλεὺς Ἰσραὴλ] descend the cross, so we might see and believe!' (cf. §3.1.1.3).

In such concessions the speaker is overtly condescending and implies that the position referenced is ridiculous. As we will see in §3.3.1, this tactic can be infuriating for those on its receiving end, who would rather their perspective be taken seriously.

3.2.4   Mock-Astonishment: *thauma*-Sarcasm

The use of *thaumazō* (θαυμάζω) and its derivatives are significant in sarcasm, not only for their commonality (8 per cent of dataset), but also for the interpretive difficulty they create.[81] *thaumazō* is a versatile term that can be used to indicate astonishment in a positive sense ('I am amazed/awed') or negatively ('I am shocked/appalled').[82] As such, it can often be difficult to disentangle straightforwardly negative cases from sarcastic use, where positive resonances are invoked and inverted. We will experience this problem more fully in the next

---

[80] 'It is Irony ... when we concede that our opponents have qualities which we do not want them to seem to have' (Εἰρωνεία *est ... cum ea quae nolumus videri in adversariis esse concedimus eis* [Russell, LCL]). Quintilian provides an example from Virgil (*Inst.* 9.2.49; cf. Virgil, *Aeneid*, 11.383–395).

[81] Because of its frequency in sarcasm, the presence of *thauma*-terminology can aid the identification of sarcasm. I include it as a pattern, however, rather than as a signal because it is only in specific contexts that *thauma*-terminology indicates hyperbolic or mock astonishment and is sarcastic.

[82] See Chapter 4, §4.1.1, n.18. It can also be both positive and negative at once; recall the *double entendre* in *Phal.I.* 12 (§3.1.1.6).

chapter when treating Gal 1:6, which itself contains an ambiguous use of *thaumazō*. Ambiguities aside, Lucian furnishes us with many clear cases of *thauma*-sarcasm. In *The Passing of Peregrinus*, Lucian describes Peregrinus as having 'mastered the Christians' amazing [*thaumastēn*] wisdom' (τὴν θαυμαστὴν σοφίαν τῶν Χριστιανῶν ἐξέμαθεν, *Peregr.* 11). This comment is clearly insincere. Lucian goes on to characterize these Christians as gullible, and Peregrinus' relationship with them as exploitive (*Peregr.* 11–13). Lucian also makes sarcastic remarks about Peregrinus' non-Christian disciples, whom he styles, 'these wondrous [*thaumastois*] followers of Proteus'[83] (τοῖς θαυμαστοῖς τούτοις ὁμιληταῖς τοῦ Πρωτέως, *Peregr.* 30 [Harmon]; cf. Aristophanes, *Ran.* 1261; Euripides, *Med.* 509–13; Pseudo-Lucian, *Cynic*, 14).[84] Beyond these examples, we have already cited many instances of *thauma*-terms as recurrent sarcastic vocatives, epithets, and otherwise (see n.70).

3.2.5   Insult to Injury

Sarcasm occurs with some frequency in situations of torture or otherwise brutal violence. We saw this with Phalaris' bull (*Phal.I.* 12, 3.1.1.6),[85] and with the crucifixions of Prometheus and Jesus (§§3.1.2.1[86] and 3.2.2–3.2.3, respectively). Such sarcasm adds further insult to an already degrading situation.[87]

What is most interesting about this pattern is not necessarily its frequency – it only occurs in 6 per cent of Lucianic examples[88] – but its close relationship to ancient definitions of sarcasm. Tryphon draws on *Od.* 22.170–200 to illustrate the term sarcasm (σαρκασμός, [Greg. Cor.] *Trop.* 16). The scene depicts Odysseus retaking his

---

[83] On the nickname 'Proteus' to refer to Peregrinus, see §3.3.3.

[84] See also Chapter 4, n.14.

[85] For other, less violent situations where the misfortunes of certain characters are sarcastically referred to as 'rewards', see *Abd.* 14; *DDeor.* 11.4; *Tox.* 22; *Anth.Gr.* vii.310; Aristophanes, *Nub.* 1064 (such [Lucianic] examples are also included in the percentage given in this section).

[86] Compare Philo, *Flaccus* 6.36–40, where a sarcastic homage is paid to a 'madman' (τις μεμηνώς) as an act of political satire. See also the *Gospel of Peter*, 6.

[87] On the use of sarcasm to increase the severity of insults, see Colston 2007, 319–38.

[88] 11 per cent of total dataset. The prevalence of this pattern in the Gospels makes it appear more common in our dataset than I suspect we would normally find in other texts.

house by the destruction of Penelope's suitors. Having come upon an enemy accomplice, the goatherd Melantheus, Odysseus orders him to be put to death. While Melantheus is being hung by his limbs, awaiting a slow and painful end, one of Odysseus' companions jeers: 'Now indeed Melantheus, you will keep watch the whole night long, lying on a soft bed.'[89] In these examples the sarcastic utterance plays on the massive incongruity between the physical situation and the literal meaning of the sarcastic statement.[90] A night of death by hanging is far from a soft bed (cf. §3.1.1.6).

In terms of pragmatic function there are also significant differences among the examples we have cited. In Homer, sympathetic characters are the sarcasts and perpetrators of violence alike, while in the Gospels, the brutality of the Romans is meant to increase our sympathy for Jesus. Lucian is often just trying to be funny, and all characters involved are fodder for comedy. The connection to ancient definitions of sarcasm and the variety of its rhetorical functions suggests that the use of sarcasm to add insult to injury in ancient texts would be a fruitful avenue for further research.

3.2.6   Other Patterns in Verbal Irony: *asteismos*

This section explores the pragmatic functions of *asteismos* in Lucian. This form of verbal irony will play an important role in our chapter on Second Corinthians. I have previously defined *asteismos* as the mirror image of sarcasm. While the sarcast expresses something ostensibly positive that implies negative affect, in *asteismos*, insult is used to express positive evaluation. While sarcasm tends to target a third party, *asteismos* is self-deprecating (Chapter 1, §1.1.2). Although Lucian employs far more sarcasm than *asteismos*, his use of the latter is by no means insignificant.

In Lucian *asteismos* features most significantly in apologetic situations. We have already met Lucian's Prometheus, whom we left crucified on a mountain. As Prometheus' story progresses, he sets up a makeshift trial in which he defends his actions against the

---

[89] Minchin notes the presence of 'lofty diction' in lines 197–98 (Minchin 2010b, 551–52; cf. 3.2.2).

[90] Cf. Homer, *Od.* 20.296–300; 22.290 (Minchin 2010b, 547, 552). A comparable scene is used in Tryphon as an example of *epikertomēsis* (ἐπικερτόμησις) – which is a near cognate of *sarkasmos* (σαρκασμός) that combines *allēgoria* (ἀλληγορία) and *chleuasmos* (χλευασμός, *Trop.* 23; cf. *Il.* 16.740–50). For discussion of *kertomeō* (κερτομέω), see Minchin 2010b, 545, 545n.43.

accusations of Hermes (*Prom.* 3–6). Within this apologetic context Prometheus leans heavily on *asteismos* to make Hermes' charges appear unfounded.

After describing his creation of humanity, Prometheus declares, 'Therein lies the great wrong I have done the gods' (ἃ μεγάλα ἐγὼ τοὺς θεοὺς ἠδίκηκα),[91] and then to highlight the absurdity of the divine response to his actions, which were no 'great wrong' whatsoever, he gestures to his own crucified form: 'and you see what the penalty is for making creatures out of mud... (*Prom.* 13 [Harmon]). Prometheus goes on to describe how his creation of humanity benefits the gods, providing them temples and worshippers – although he himself has no temple. Following this description, his *asteismos* comes out strongly, 'You see how I look out for my own interests but betray and injure those of the community!' (*Prom.* 14 [Harmon]). Just as we have seen sarcasm's ability to both reflect and deny the claims of other parties, these self-deprecating ironic comments simultaneously raise and reject the accusations made against him, making Prometheus appear a victim unjustly used.

We find a further example this sort of *asteismos* in *Disowned*, another mock forensic speech in which the defendant, a physician, runs the risk of being disowned by his father for a second time.[92] Having just described, in reasonable terms, the course of actions he has adopted and must defend, the doctor describes himself: 'I who am so difficult and disobedient, who so disgraced my father and act so unworthily of my family...' (*Abd.* 3 [Harmon]). In this case, the physician clearly means the opposite of what he says.

This apologetic function of *asteismos* is highly prevalent (cf. *Anach.* 40; *Herm.* 63, 81; Quintilian, *Inst.* 8.6.55 [Chapter 1, §1.1.2]), and probably one of its primary rhetorical functions.[93] In contrast to sarcasm's implicit challenge, here *asteismos* becomes a defensive tool for those whose status has been challenged. The speaker pretends to accept a version of their opponent's accusation in order to imply its absurdity. It is entirely appropriate that the function of *asteismos* should be a mirror image of sarcasm, since the former is, as a speech act, the inverse of the latter.

---

[91] Prometheus' description of stealing fire from the gods – 'that reprehensible theft' (καὶ τὴν ἐπονείδιστον ταύτην κλοπήν, *Prom.* 18 [Harmon]) – is similarly ironic.
[92] For the humorous backstory, see *Abd.* 1–8.
[93] This apologetic use of *asteismos* is not wholly uniform. We also find cases where self-deprecating irony combines with sarcasm to emphasize mockery (*Herm.* 5; *Sacr.* 10).

3.2.7   Conclusions

A larger dataset has enabled us to greatly expand the work begun with our discussion of sarcastic taunts in the prophets, revealing several new patterns in the use of ancient sarcasm – summarized in the chart below.

Pattern	Likely Examples	Total Examples	Per cent of Dataset
Sarcastic Encouragement (§3.2.1)	47	59	15%
Hyperformality (§3.2.2)	119	138	36%
Sarcastic Address Forms (§3.2.2)	48	60	15%[1]
Sarcastic Epithets (§3.2.2)	62	70	18%
Sarcastic Concessions (§3.2.3)	43	50	13%
Mock-Astonishment (§3.2.4)	26	35	8%
Insult to Injury (§3.2.5)	36	42	11%[2]

Summary to 3.2 – 'Total Examples' includes both likely and uncertain instances of sarcasm. Percentage given is the average of the percentages including and excluding the uncertain examples. Percentages do not sum to 100 per cent since any given example of sarcasm may include several of these patterns – or even none of those listed, as this list is not exhaustive.
[1]Sarcastic address forms are possibly over-represented in our dataset due to their prevalence in Lucian (see §3.2.2).
[2]'Insult to Injury' is probably over-represented in our dataset due to its prevalence in Gospel passion narratives.

These patterns will not only assist in the recognition of comparable sarcasm in other ancient texts, but also extend our understanding of the common functions of sarcasm and of the situations in which sarcasm typically occurs.

Hyperformality was by far the most frequently attested pattern, consisting of inappropriately polite terms of address or otherwise unnecessarily high-register language. A strong, developed honour culture is a likely cause of this prevalence, as the presence of culturally and linguistically encoded means of showing respect lend themselves to sarcastic appropriation.

Other forms of sarcasm will also be significant in our work on Paul. Both sarcastic encouragement and concessions will feature in the Corinthian correspondence, and the examples cited under mock astonishment will be important for comparison with Gal 1:6. Recognizing the apologetic function of *asteismos* is also significant, as this form of verbal irony will play a major role in our treatment of sarcasm in 2 Cor 10–13.

3.3   Rhetorical Functions of Sarcasm in Lucian

Having identified signals that often indicate sarcasm in ancient Greek, along with some patterns in how sarcasm is used, we will now continue the work on sarcasm's rhetorical functions begun in the last chapter, using Lucian as a case study. We have hitherto established the general hypothesis that sarcasm typically functions as an implicit challenge to some positive quality that the sarcast perceives their victim as laying claim to. It is appropriate when used on those of lower or equal status and can be effective for putting upstart subordinates back in line. A quick glance at Lucianic sarcasm reinforces what we have seen so far. A full 46 per cent of sarcastic utterances in Lucian are spoken by persons of higher status compared with their victims, and 30 per cent of sarcasm is traded between equals. This leaves only about a quarter of sarcastic statements subverting social hierarchy.[94]

The prophets revealed one way that sarcasm may be employed subversively, as the prophet's appropriation of the divine voice emboldens him to satirize those of higher rank. This often-brash approach can create difficulty and even physical danger for the prophet, leaving one to wonder whether there might be more subtle ways of being sarcastic at the expense of one's superiors.

With so much sarcasm delivered by a variety of characters across texts ranging from the fantastic to more 'real-life' rhetorical situations, Lucian is well situated to nuance this picture. In the following discussion we will follow Lucian's most common sarcasts, paying special attention to the ways in which characters of lower status use sarcasm to undermine their superiors. Beginning with historical and mythic characters, our observations of Lucian's sarcasts will lead us progressively closer to their author's own narrative persona. This investigation will not only further our understanding of the advantages and dangers of sarcasm use in an ancient context but will shed light on the way Lucian employs sarcasm and narrative voice to accomplish his satire.

---

[94] While proportionally small, this still provides over fifty examples to work with.

Surveying the ends to which speakers employ sarcasm across our case studies will provide several points of comparison for assessing Paul's use of sarcasm in the coming chapters. Lucian portrays the use of sarcasm in interactions between actors across a variety of social relationship, as do *Job* and the Prophets. Analogical comparison to these examples will be a helpful tool for assessing what Paul's use of sarcasm can tell us about his relationships with different early Christian communities.

3.3.1   Lucian's Sarcasts: from Dogs to Gods

This section explores the ways in which major characters in Lucian use sarcasm against their superiors. We begin with one of Lucian's favourite sarcasts, whom we have met once or twice already, the Cynic philosopher and satirist Menippus. Since the works of Menippus are now lost, it is difficult to ascertain the specifics of Lucian's literary relationship to him.[95] Lucian openly claims Menippean influence,[96] and is pleased not only to draw on his work, but also to feature him as a recurring character. A true Cynic, Menippus is fearless in using sarcasm on anyone, regardless of their social standing.

Menippus shows up repeatedly throughout *Dialogues of the Dead*. Not only does he use sarcasm on those who in life were richer and more powerful than himself (*DMort.* 3.2), Menippus also takes shots at more famous philosophers.[97] Meeting Pythagoras and Empedocles in Hades, Menippus pokes fun at their frustrated post-mortem expectations. We have already discussed his hyperformal greeting of Pythagoras (§3.1.2.5). Empedocles, who had hoped for divinization upon throwing himself into a volcano, is met by a sarcastic vocative: 'O brazen-foot most excellent [Ὦ χαλκόπου βέλτιστε],[98] what came over you that you jumped into the crater?' (*DMort.* 6.4 [MacLeod,]). Despite breaking rank, Menippus gets away with his sarcasm and general mockery, as his targets simply seem too dead to care.

When Menippus chances upon Socrates himself, he prides himself on the fact that he at least believed that Socrates truly knew nothing

---

[95] See Hall 1981, 64–66, 74–150.

[96] See Hall 1981, 64; *Bis.Acc.* 33; *Pisc.* 26.

[97] Menippus is even unafraid to be sarcastic with immortals (see *DMort.* 2.3).

[98] The use of χαλκόπους parodies its Homeric meaning, which is to refer to the strength or speed of horses. Here, the term draws attention to how the crater's spewing out of Empedocles' sandal was clear evidence that he was not taken up to the realm of the gods (Levy 1976, 190).

(*DMort.* 6.5). Menippus then asks about those attending the phil-osopher. Socrates replies 'Charmides, my good fellow, and Phaedrus and Clinias' son.' Menippus exclaims, 'Bravo, Socrates! Still following your own special line here! Still with an eye for beauty!' (Εὖ γε, ὦ Σώκρατες, ὅτι κἀνταῦθα μέτει τὴν σεαυτοῦ τέχνην καὶ οὐκ ὀλιγωρεῖς τῶν καλῶν, *DMort.* 6.6 [MacLeod]). Levy notes a possible *double entendre* here. *technēn* (τέχνην)[99] and 'beauty' (τῶν καλῶν) could refer to Socrates work as a philosopher and his pursuit of The Good, or a practice of pursuing pretty boys.[100] But the audience is already aware of Menippus' penchant for mockery and, coupled with the fact that those cited as being in Socrates' company were known to be attractive,[101] it is hard to miss the sarcasm. The way Socrates then goes on to miss the joke (*DMort.* 6.6) shows that he, as Menippus suggested, truly knows nothing.[102]

There is overlap between typical Cynic traits and characters who engage in considerable sarcasm and mockery.[103] Cynic brashness and free speech (παρρησία) are visible in characters who use sarcasm without regard for their victim's social position. Through the mouth of a hostile character, Lucian describes Menippus as 'a really dread-ful dog who bites unexpectedly because he grins when he bites' (*Bis. Acc.* 33 [Harmon]).[104] The similarity between this description of Menippus and Tryphon's definition of sarcasm ('Sarcasm is showing the teeth while grinning.' *Trop.* 20) further strengthens the connec-tion between Cynic and sarcast.[105] At the same time, we cannot draw a one-to-one comparison between Cynic traits and those of Lucian's major sarcasts, as Lucian writes several characters of different back-grounds who use significant sarcasm.

Zeus Rants, which consists of the gods watching helplessly as mortals debate their existence, contains excellent examples. Much of this text's sarcasm is spoken by Momus, the deification of mock-ery and criticism. Momus has plenty of sarcasm for Apollo and takes especial delight at teasing his prophetic (in)abilities (*JTr.* 30–31, 43).

---

[99] 'Craft' or 'art', here translated 'special line'.
[100] Levy 1976, 192.
[101] Ibid. 191.
[102] For further Menippean sarcasm, see *Icar.* 2, 10, 34.
[103] Menippus is not the only sarcastic Cynic in Lucian; Diogenes, whom we encountered in §3.1.1.3, follows essentially the same pattern.
[104] 'Dog' was a colloquial way of referring to Cynics. Note the etymological relationship in Greek.
[105] Futhermore, *sarkasmos* (σαρκασμός) comes from *sarkazō* (σαρκάζω), which literally means 'to tear flesh'.

Even Zeus himself cannot escape censure. As the debate over the gods' existence carries on, Zeus begins to express concern that their side is faring poorly. Momus 'reassures' him sarcastically and in epic style by quoting Homer: 'But whenever you like, Zeus, you can let down a cord of gold and "sway them aloft, with the earth and the sea, too, into the bargain"' (*JTr.* 45 [Harmon]).[106] Unlike in *Dialogues of the Dead* where one might argue that the brashness of our Cynics stems from the fact that they are already dead and cannot be further harmed, Momus gets away with picking on higher ranking gods.

While Momus may be the patron god of sarcasm,[107] Damis – an Epicurean whose debate over the gods' existence against the Stoic philosopher Timocles drives the plot of *Zeus Rants* – does his work on earth. Damis is constantly sarcastic with his opponent. He uses many hyperformal address-forms, insincerely referring to his opponent as: 'Timocles, most noble of philosophers' (ὦ γενναιότατε φιλοσόφων Τιμόκλεις, *JTr.* 41); 'O best of men' (ὦ ἄριστε, 43); 'My good Timocles' (ὦ καλὲ Τιμόκλεις, 42); 'Timocles, best-friend-of-the-gods' (ὦ θεοφιλέστατε Τιμόκλεις, 47, an example of chunking [§3.1.2.1]); 'O wisest (Timocles)' (ὦ σοφώτατε, 49), 'O wonderful (Timocles)' (ὦ θαυμάσιε, 49).[108] Damis goes so far as to ironically concede the entire debate to Timocles (*JTr.* 52), who, when it comes to things divine, 'no doubt know[s] best' (σὺ ἄμεινον ἂν εἰδείης, *JTr.* 45 [Harmon]; cf. §3.2.3). Timocles finds this constant stream of sarcasm masquerading as good manners infuriating and becomes more and more frustrated throughout the debate. The dialogue ends with him storming off in a frenzy of rage, leaving Damis appearing the calm, collected victor who has won the approval of the crowd (*JTr.* 52–53).

Sketching out these sarcastic characters helps further hone our picture of the traits associated with sarcasm in Lucian. Both Momus and Menippus use sarcasm subversively on their relative superiors. Momus lacks something of the Cynic's boldness and unconstrained

---

[106] The sarcasm comes from the fact that both Momus and the audience know that Zeus will not, or cannot, do so – making the comment an example of sarcastic encouragement (§3.2.1).

[107] Momus turns up again in *The Parliament of the Gods*, where he is again full of mockery, and criticism, and is also not without sarcasm (for the latter, see *Deor. Conc.* 11).

[108] Note the use of the superlative in adding further hyperbole in several of these examples.

speech (παρρησία), being overall more subtle and more polite. This enables him to avoid the censure of more powerful gods. He receives no more pushback from Zeus than, 'You are boring us to extinction, Momus, with your untimely criticism' (*JTr.* 43 [Harmon]).[109] Momus' sarcasm also successfully flies under the radar with Apollo, who does not seem to realize that he is being mocked (*JTr.* 29–30). Damis finds himself in a different rhetorical situation. He begins the debate on roughly equal footing with his opponent and both must contest the philosophical standing of the other, aiming to win the crowd to their side with argument and rhetoric. On the rhetorical end, here sarcasm works much as it did with our other sarcasts. Damis' hyperformal insincerity erodes the credibility of his opponent whom the fictitious audience, as well as actual audience, take less and less seriously as the debate progresses, until there is a clear winner and the loser is laughed off stage.

These traits are common across all of our sarcasts so far. The use of sarcasm shows the character to be more clever, collected, and lucid than their victims. Their dry wit and insincere comments undercut their targets with mockery that remains subtle enough to go unpunished, and occasionally undetected.[110] The result is comic, and renders the sarcast a sympathetic character.

However, there is also variation among Lucian's sarcasts that show them to be composites of different influences. Some Cynic elements are common, especially a willingness to criticize without regard for social position. However, our exemplar sarcasts accomplish this with different levels of subtlety, using ostensible politeness to mask offence to varying degrees, at least superficially. In contrast to the brashness of Menippus, Damis' relative calm and polite demeanour has notes of self-deprecating *eirōneia* as Aristotle conceives of it, although Damis' sarcasm is too overt to reach the unbroken pretence of humility and ignorance often associated with Socrates (see Chapter 1, §1.1.1). Doubtless, comic elements influence these characters as well, the ways in which they are always ready with a jocular quip or retort having parallels in Aristophanes.[111]

---

[109] More literally: 'You are slaughtering us...' (Σὺ ἡμᾶς ἐπισφάττεις) or as the LSJ suggests, 'You are talking us to death' (LSJ, s.v. 'ἐπισφάζω'). The point is that Momus is not helping the divine cause.

[110] Undetected by the target, not the audience.

[111] Compare Dicaeopolis in Aristophanes' *Acharnians*, who like our Lucianic sarcasts is always ready with a quip and is at times sarcastic but lacks something of the wit and subtlety of Lucian's characters (e.g. *Ach.* 64–93).

This patchwork of influences probably has its source in Lucian's own composite writing style. In *The Double Indictment*, this style is described through an accusation against Lucian made by the personification of Dialogue, who claims that The Syrian has 'unceremoniously penned me up with Jest and Satire and Cynicism and Eupolis and Aristophanes' (Dialogue also adds Menippus into the mix, *Bis. Acc.* 33 [Harmon]). It is unsurprising that some of Lucian's recurring characters would exhibit these traits characteristic of his style. As we will see presently, the sarcasts surveyed have similarities with the persona that Lucian takes when he writes himself into the narrative.

3.3.2   Lucian as Lucian: the Sarcasm of Lucian's Alter-Egos

Lucian also writes versions of himself into several of his dialogues. These characters engage frequently in sarcasm and share several features with Lucian's other sarcasts. However, important differences in characterization are still present. With only the faintest pretence, Lucian (*Lykianos*, Λυκιανός) appears as the character Lycinus (*Lykinos*, Λύκινος) in several stories. Obviously, Lucian cannot hope to hide under a dropped *alpha*, so it is safe to say that he expects his audience to see a fictionalized version of himself in these narratives.[112]

Generally speaking, Lycinus is characterized in much the same way as other Lucianic sarcasts –the dialogue *Hermotimus* can provide an illustrative example. In this dialogue, Lycinus attempts to convince Hermotimus that his twenty-year study of philosophy has been a waste of time. Lycinus' rhetoric follows essentially the same pattern we have already observed. He is constantly teasing and mocking, confounding, and outwitting his opponent, in addition to using significant sarcasm (see *Herm.* 5, 10, 12, 42, 81, 82). His sarcastic concessions remind one of Damis. Lycinus suggests that Hermotimus' inability to construct a plausible argument must be a deliberate attempt to keep Lycinus from becoming a true philosopher as Hermotimus himself so clearly is (*Herm.* 21; another sarcastic concession occurs in *Herm.* 20).[113]

---

[112] It is important to distinguish between Lucian himself and Lucian's narrative persona. One cannot assume continuity between an author's personal perspective and the perspective of the narrator. This distinction is even more significant in Lucian, who delights in taking almost nothing seriously, himself included.

[113] For Lycinus' sarcasm elsewhere, see *Hes.* 7; *Lex.* 1, 23; *Symp.* 35.

Despite these similarities, Lucian's avatars differ from his other sarcasts in being overall more subtle and more cautious. Lucian enters the narrative of *The Fisherman* as Free-Speech (Παρρησιάδης). This dialogue was written in response to criticism that Lucian received for *Philosophies for Sale*, in which he puts representatives of different philosophical schools up for auction using the market-place as a vehicle for comedy and satire. *The Fisherman* 11 is an excellent example of the way Lucian subtly winks to the audience throughout his apology. The great philosophers of yore have risen from the dead to wreak vengeance on Free-Speech for the outrage of *Philosophies for Sale* (*Pisc.* 1–4). After finally convincing the mob, headed by Socrates, to grant him a trial before execution, Lycinus exclaims, 'Well done [*eu ge*], most learned sirs [Εὖ γε, ὦ σοφώτατοι]; this course is better and more legal' (*Pisc.* 11 [Harmon]). Both *eu ge* and superlative, ostensibly complementary vocatives, are typical of Lucianic sarcasm (§§3.2.1, 3.2.2, 3.3.1).[114] However, it is essential to Lucian's defence at this point that Free-Speech flatter his opposition, and so the line is delivered sincerely, and received as such. It is only beneath the surface where one may recognize that Free-Speech is complimenting his opponents more highly than he actually thinks of them – especially considering that hitherto the behaviour of the philosophic mob has been hardly characteristic of the model sage. Thus there remains an element of irony for those who know the character well enough to detect it.[115] In her article on *The Fisherman*, Marília Pinheiro argues that 'in this dialogue Lucian accentuates the satirical tone of the previous dialogue [i.e. *Philosophies for Sale*], and that this is yet another striking instance of his irreverent, sarcas-tic, and corrosive sophisticate vein'.[116]

In broad strokes, both Lycinus and Free-Speech share several traits with Lucian's other sarcasts (§3.3.1). They are ready wits whose frequent sarcasm undermines their opponents and renders them sympathetic to the audience. They also manage to escape serious censure and come out on top of the exchanges in which they find themselves. This is as clear in *Hermotimus* where Lycinus con-

---

[114] Dickey notes that σοφώτατοι (here translated 'most learned') is 'usually ironic (1996, 143).

[115] For further examples of the exaggerated tone underlying Lycinus' speech in this dialogue, see *Pisc.* 4, 6.

[116] Pinheiro 2012, 296.

vinces his interlocutor to abandon philosophy as it is in Lucian's apologies in which Free-Speech is literally acquitted before a divine court (*Pisc.* 38–39; *Bis.Acc.*[117] 32, 35).

Lucian's avatars do, however, differ from Lucian's other sarcasts in several ways. First, there is a greater degree of levity and playfulness to Lycinus' character compared with the biting wit of Menippus. An excellent example of this difference is *The Ship*, in which Lycinus, though often sarcastic (*Nav.* 29, 30, 37, 39) is much more jocular in teasing his friends (see *Nav.* 14–15, 45). Second, Lycinus' satire is more modest in its objects. He does not directly target Socrates or Zeus but saves his criticism for those of his own rank (*Herm.*; *Lex.*; *Nav.*). When Lucian's avatars satirize philosophy, it is always done indirectly. Free-Speech's defence in *The Fishermen* is based on the argument that he has been criticizing contemporary representatives of philosophical schools, rather than their founders, whom he respects (*Pisc.* 5–6, 29–37). The same indirect critique of philosophy is made in *Hermotimus*. Contemporary philosophy is satirized in its myriad forms, but Lycinus' sarcasm is mostly directed at Hermotimus himself. In these ways, Lucian's avatars accomplish their satire more subtly and indirectly than his literary sarcasts.

3.3.3   Lucian Unmasked: Character Assassinations

We have been moving slowly inwards from significant Lucianic characters, to avatars for Lucian's persona, and now finally we come as close to Lucian as the written word permits. In some works, Lucian does not hide behind even a semi-pseudonym – although it is still important to recognize Lucian's authorial voice as a persona even when he writes as himself.[118] Among these texts, we find several personal attacks. These are absolute character assassinations within which Lucian tends more towards the use of straightforward insult and invective than irony. However, when Lucian employs sarcasm, one experiences it at its full rhetorical force.

Lucian's *The Passing of Peregrinus* consists of a bitterly satirical attempt to discredit a man whose career, which Lucian characterizes as fuelled by insincere and self-serving ambition, transitioned across several philosophical positions, included a stint as a Christian, and

---

[117] Lucian's avatar in this dialogue is "'The Syrian'" – a reference to his native land.
[118] See n.112.

ended in self-immolation.[119] Lucian is not shy of telling his audience exactly what he thinks of Peregrinus, engaging in myriad polemic throughout, both sarcastic and otherwise. Lucian begins his disparagement with stock sarcastic epithets (βέλτιος, γεννάδας, *Peregr.* 1), before styling Peregrinus' life a series of 'spectacular performances ... outdoing Sophocles and Aeschylus' (*Peregr.* 3 [Harmon]). Lucian is always quick to contrast his sarcastic praise with the realities of Peregrinus' character, reminding his audience that 'this creation and masterpiece of nature, this Polyclitan canon, as soon he came of age, was taken in adultery...' (*Peregr.* 9 [Harmon]; cf. §3.1.1.4).

In this sustained work of polemic, Lucian is not above resorting to simple name-calling. Playing on connections between self-immolation and sacrifice, Lucian refers to Peregrinus as a 'holy image' (ἄγαλμα, *Peregr.* 8, 10 [Harmon]). We are also informed that Peregrinus was in the habit of calling himself Proteus (*Peregr.* 1).[120] Lucian echoes this appellation, sarcastically appropriating it as a means of mocking Peregrinus' vainglorious career changes (*Peregr.* 1; cf. §3.1.1.3).[121]

Lucian also shows his capacity for *double entendre* in *The Passing of Peregrinus*, referring to Peregrinus' self-cremation as his greatest work (τὸ κάλλιστον τοῦτο ἔργον, *Peregr.* 36). Considering how little love Lucian has for Peregrinus and his deeds, this statement is straightforwardly sarcastic. However, it is also doubtless true that Lucian is not at all displeased to watch the old philosopher burn, so in some sense Lucian does consider this deed to be Peregrinus' greatest work (κάλλιστον ἔργον).

Lucian's use of sarcasm in *The Passing of Peregrinus* is certainly unrestrained. Its sheer quantity, not to mention all the straightforward insults that occur alongside it, are testament to the fact that Lucian really could not stand the person about whom he was writing. Though the grievances are different, we find the same patterns in Lucian's other character assassinations. For instances of

---

[119] Cf. §§ 3.1.2.3, 3.2.4.

[120] Proteus, as described by Homer, was a sea-god who had the ability to transform himself into various creatures, water, or, more pertinently to this piece, fire (MacLeod 1991, 271).

[121] Lucian does not see 'Proteus', used in a positive sense, as a worthy appellation for man whom he considers a fraud, so it is quite possible that in several other cases where Lucian refers to Peregrinus as Proteus, there is some degree of sarcasm, either poking fun at his changeability or flammability (e.g. *Peregr.* 12, 30, 36).

sarcasm in these works, see *Alex.* 25, 35, 60; *Ind.* 1, 16, 22; *Pseudol.* 6, 14, 21, 23, 27, 29, 30, 31.

The use of sarcasm in Lucian's character assassinations is markedly different from what we observed in the previous sections. We have left far behind the subtle undermining of the opposition by the clever underdog sarcast. The polemic and sarcasm of the character assassinations is direct and vehement. In these works of polemic, sarcasm functions as a satirical device to expose and discredit. It is one of several tactics used to annihilate the reputation of its victim and, blended with other elements of Lucian's sense of humour, turn them into an object of ridicule. There is a persuasive element to this rhetoric as well. The overall weight of Lucian's polemic is such that his audience cannot avoid becoming aware of the fact that should they dissent at all from Lucian's appraisal of Peregrinus – or any of the others he seeks to tear down – they too would soon fall under the same ridicule and shame to which Lucian subjects his victims.[122]

The considerable difference between Lucian's sarcasm in his character assassinations compared with that of his other typical sarcasts is readily explainable. In the assassinations, Lucian's targets are unable to create significant reprisal, being either dead – Peregrinus and Alexander – or of lower social standing. Furthermore, where we have evidence, Lucian appears to be writing the assassinations primarily for a more limited, sympathetic audience (*Alex.* 1–2, 61; *Peregr.* 1–2). These factors enable Lucian to be unrestrained in his polemic and sarcasm without offending anyone who can cause him trouble.

It is important to recall that the sort of sarcasm we find in Lucian's character assassinations is closer to the rule than the exception. Almost half (46 per cent) of Lucian's sarcasm is spoken by characters of higher status. The assassinations may be more tendentious than average, but overall, the freedom with which Lucian uses sarcasm to damage the reputation of his victims is not atypical. Indeed, while it is helpful to explore the more subversive uses of sarcasm that we discussed in §§3.3.1–3.3.2, they are the minority cases.

---

[122] Despite differences in form, *On Sacrifices*, which has affinities to diatribe (MacLeod 1991, 276), a Cynic favourite, is another excellent example of the rhetorical use of sarcasm to beat down the positions or practices of others to the extent that only a fool would raise them again. See *Sacr.* 4, 10, 12–14.

3.3.4   Conclusions

Surveying sarcastic characters throughout Lucian's writings both confirms our general observations about ancient sarcasm-use and nuances our understanding of how sarcasm may be turned to subversive effect. Although they are extreme cases, Lucian's character assassinations fit within the paradigm of majority, appropriate sarcasm. Dealing with victims either unable to do him harm, or beneath him in status, Lucian uses sarcasm as one polemical tool among many to dismantle the reputations of his victims. These cases are also the closest we get to Lucian's own narrative voice, or at least the voice that Lucian wishes his audience to accept as his own.

The other sarcasts analyzed exist at varying degrees removed from their author's persona and take different approaches to using sarcasm against the grain of social status. On the far end of the continuum we find Lucian's recurring Cynics, including Menippus and Diogenes. In line with the reputation of Cynics at the time, these sarcasts are bold and unfiltered in their use of sarcasm and mockery on their victims, whether kings, famous philosophers, or gods. These Cynics are perhaps closest to the prophets of the LXX, insofar as both presume the freedom to criticize whomever they deem necessary with impunity. Of course, the Cynics do so as a matter of philosophical principle, while the prophets are limited by their perception of their divine mandate.

As we move from Menippus toward Lucian's avatars, we begin to see increasing subtlety in the use of insubordinate sarcasm. While Momus and Damis still succeed in turning their sarcasm against those of higher rank, they do so more carefully, employing different degrees of ostensible formality to keep their comments flying either under the radar or over the heads of their victims. Like the Cynics, they manage this flawlessly, undermining their victims and winning over the audience with their wit and humour.

When Lucian writes a version of himself into his dialogues, as characters such as Lycinus and Free-Speech, his avatars use sarcasm to similar effect, despite being more modest in their targets. Lycinus usually saves his sarcasm for characters of his own rank and does not directly take on the likes of Zeus or Socrates. To an even higher degree than Damis or Momus, he uses techniques such as insincere politeness and sarcastic concessions to undermine the positions of his interlocutors and is likewise ever successful.

We thus have three distinct types of Lucianic sarcasts, existing at three degrees of separation from Lucian's narrative persona. What is most interesting is the way that these characters correlate with different uses of sarcasm. Lucian's more literary characters, who at least in name are entirely removed from their author's personality, engage in the most inappropriate, insubordinate sarcasm. As we move inward, Lucian's doppelgängers remain subversive, but choose more appropriate targets commensurate with their social rank, whereas Lucian attacks targets that cannot fight back when writing as himself. I suggest that this correlation between degree of separation from authorial voice and degree of appropriateness in sarcasm-use is not incidental and can extend our understanding of strategies for using insubordinate sarcasm in an ancient context.

The first major strategy is subtlety. Unless you are a Cynic, adjusting one's level of ostensible politeness – or similar tactics such as sarcastic concessions and encouragement – appears to keep one's victim either unable to recognize the speaker's sarcasm or at least less inclined to punish it. The utility of this tactic probably stems from the fact that the sarcast continues to pay lip service to the degree of politeness or deference required by the situation. So long as they do not a make a clear break from the social script, they retain a measure of deniability. This tactic is, however, problematic at least because it depends on one's interlocutor not being savvy enough to get the joke, and also for further reasons we shall discuss presently.

Perhaps the most important evidence for the effect and reception of Lucianic sarcasm comes from beyond the level of the narrative. We have already mentioned two of Lucian's apologies, and these are not the only occasions on which he must respond to significant criticism (see also *Apol.*). These apologies show Lucian to have received serious censure for his satire on multiple occasions. This evidence of pushback is a good reminder that the profile of the sarcasts we have been sketching is in certain aspects a literary fiction. The ease with which Lucian's sarcasts evade censure for being critical of their superiors is a better representation of the way Lucian would like things to be than the way things actually are. It would therefore be fallacious to say that an imitation of Momus or Menippus would be a viable strategy for an ancient person to succeed in insubordinate sarcasm. Lucian himself has much more difficulty getting away with his sarcasm and satire than his characters do. In real life, offending the wrong people is dangerous.

This danger, however, does not stop Lucian from satirizing religious or philosophical positions. As we have seen, Lucian employs different degrees of distance from his own persona depending on the targets of his satire. When he wants to be sarcastic about the gods or make jokes at the expense of Socrates and other famous philosophers, Lucian writes characters fully distinct from himself such as Mennipus or Momus to use as vehicles for his satire. Less controversial or lower status victims do not require so great a distance between author and character, and Lucian is happy to write a version of himself into the narrative. I argue that this is Lucian's most significant strategy for succeeding in insubordinate sarcasm and satire. By adjusting the degree of removal between himself and the satirical voice, Lucian creates the measure of deniability necessary for him to feel comfortable subverting rank. Menippus may mock and insult Socrates, but Lucian has every respect for him!

This disassociation of the self from the critical voice lies at the heart of the strategies for using sarcasm against those of higher rank that we have seen this far. In the prophets, this is the distinction between the divine voice and that of the prophet, whereas Lucian can accomplish varying degrees of distance by manipulating the dramatis personae across his narratives. In both cases, there is evidence that this does not always work as well as the sarcast hopes, and they must be prepared to deal with the fallout of their social transgressions.

3.4   Conclusions

With a dataset of 400 examples, this chapter is by far the largest scale analysis of sarcasm in ancient Greek texts to date. These data have enabled the identification of many common contextual and linguistic signals of sarcasm in ancient Greek, summarized on the chart in §3.1.3. These signals will become essential evidence for identifying sarcasm in Paul throughout the rest of the study. The patterns in sarcasm use discussed in §3.2 – summarized on the chart in §3.2.7 – will also facilitate sarcasm recognition in addition to providing material for comparison when thinking about the rhetorical functions of cases where Paul's sarcasm follows the same patterns.

The means of signalling sarcasm presented in §§3.1 and 3.2 also have implications for modern research on verbal irony. This study presents new linguistic data removed from English both historically and linguistically that can be used to hone our understanding of how sarcasm is expressed across languages and cultures.[123]

Our case study of Lucian's sarcasts in §3.3 has expanded the work begun on the pragmatic functions of sarcasm in the previous chapter. Both case studies confirm the hypothesis that sarcasm normally functions as an implicit means of challenging another party's perceived claim to some positive quality, and that it is most appropriate and most often used by superiors on subordinates or between equals. Our case studies also provide examples of several strategies for using sarcasm against the grain of social hierarchy, such as we saw with the prophets and Lucian's Cynics. The most significant pattern here, however, was the way that Lucian manipulates voice, using characters at different degrees of removal from his authorial persona depending on the prestige of the victims he wishes to satirize.

Voice will become a major theme in our chapter on Romans as we deal with the possibility of sarcasm in the dialogical passages of the text. Here comparison with voice in Lucianic dialogues will be instructive. Analogical comparison with our case studies will also be helpful for thinking about how Paul's use of sarcasm reflects his relationship with different early Christian congregations. Will Paul use sarcasm with the confidence and aggression of Lucian's character assassinations? With the brashness of a Cynic or prophet? Or perhaps with the subtlety of Lycinus?

SUMMARY TO PART 1: THE STATE OF OUR THREE QUESTIONS

The first chapter addressed the question 'What is sarcasm?' Based on ancient and modern discussions, I defined sarcasm as a subtype of verbal irony in which an utterance that would normally communicate a positive attitude or evaluation implies a negative attitude or evaluation.

The next chapter on the Septuagint began to address the question 'How is sarcasm expressed?' Several cues appeared throughout *Job* and the prophets, including repetition, sarcastic politeness, and the sarcastic use of the dubitative. Sarcastic taunts were also prevalent in the prophets. The question of expression was the major focus of the chapter 'Sarcasm in Ancient Greek Texts'. This study analyzed 400 examples of sarcasm across Lucian and other sources to produce

---

[123] See Pawlak 2019, 545–48, 560–63.

the first large-scale study of sarcasm in ancient Greek (cf. the charts in §§3.1.3 and 3.2.7).

The most common signal of sarcasm identified was the use of contrastive evaluation: clarifying the presence of sarcasm by following it with statements of literal negative evaluation (§3.1.1.4). Ways of conveying emphasis and exaggeration were also important, especially the use of emphatic particles and the repetition of adjectives. Hyperformality, or exaggerated politeness, also occurred in a large proportion of the sarcastic utterances surveyed.

Work on the question 'What does sarcasm do?' began with our analysis of *Job* and has since been refined by our case studies on the prophets and Lucian. I hypothesize that sarcasm normally functions as an implicit challenge to what the sarcast perceives as some claim to a positive quality made by another party. Social hierarchy often plays a role in these exchanges because the claim to a positive quality or qualities that sarcasm implicitly challenges is often interconnected with social status. Sarcasm is appropriate when it is used with the grain of social hierarchy: speakers of high rank may use sarcasm on subordinates without censure.

Beyond these more common uses of sarcasm, our case studies in the prophets and Lucian provided several examples where sarcasm was used against parties of higher rank. The prophets appropriate the divine voice to give them the authority to engage in sarcasm with targets of higher status. Lucian's Cynics also use sarcasm boldly and without regard for social hierarchy, while other Lucianic characters employ greater subtlety and ostensible politeness. But Lucian's most significant strategy for engaging in sarcasm and satire against the grain of social hierarchy is to adjust his use of voice and persona. Lucian uses characters far removed from his own voice when satirising higher-status victims, saving more modest targets for characters meant to represent a version of his own persona.

The findings of Part I will provide the tools necessary for identifying and analyzing sarcasm in Paul's letters throughout Part II of this study. Here, beginning with Galatians, we will exegete sarcastic passages throughout all the undisputed Pauline epistles in which sarcasm occurs, and discuss the role of sarcasm in Paul's argumentation and rhetoric across each letter. Our theoretical work on sarcasm and study of its expression in ancient Greek will be essential for identifying Pauline sarcasm. Our case studies on *Job*, the prophets, and Lucian will also provide paradigms against which it will be fruitful to compare the rhetorical functions of Paul's sarcasm in different situations.

PART II

Sarcasm in Paul's Letters

4

SARCASM IN GALATIANS

The rest of the study will explore Paul's use of sarcasm across each of the letters where it occurs. Both the linguistic gains made regarding sarcasm recognition and work done on the pragmatic functions of sarcasm over the previous chapters will provide helpful analogies for furthering our interpretation of Paul.[1]

Not only for chronological reasons but also for the prevalence of conflict therein, Galatians will be an excellent starting point for this investigation. Surveying Paul's rhetoric in passages across this letter will provide insight into the ways he employs sarcasm as a tool for navigating his relationships with Galatian Christians and Jerusalem apostles alike.

We will analyze three passages that have been considered ironic or sarcastic in previous scholarship to determine whether they qualify as instances of sarcasm as we have defined it: an utterance that would normally communicate positive evaluation but implies negative evaluation. We begin with the opening of the letter, where Paul expresses astonishment with the Galatians for their apparent rejection of the gospel (Gal 1:6–7a). We will assess evidence for this opening expressing 'ironic rebuke', which some have argued for based on comparison with ancient papyrus letters. We will then consider whether the δοκέω epithets that Paul uses to refer to the 'pillar' apostles in 2:2, 6, and 9 can be classified as sarcastic, and how their use serves Paul's rhetorical aims across the broader passage. Finally, I will push back on a common misidentification of sarcasm in 5:12.

---

[1] Some material in this chapter overlaps with the open-access article 'Is Galatians an Ironic Letter? Θαυμάζω, Ancient Letter Writing Handbooks, and Galatians 1.6' (Matthew Pawlak, *Novum Testamentum* [2021]: 63: 249–70). For the full attribution and copyright notice, see the note in the preface.

4.1   Galatians 1:6–7 and 'Ironic Rebuke'

The fact that Paul does not open Galatians with his usual thanksgiving but an expression of frustration at his congregation for turning aside from their calling has been much remarked on in scholarship.[2] While the Galatians would not have had other Pauline letters for comparison – and would probably not have been expecting a thanksgiving section in the first place[3] – by the end of 1:6 they could not have missed the intensity of Paul's tone.

A number of scholars have argued that this intense opening in Gal 1:6 is also ironic.[4] Comparison with other ancient letters has played a central role in this argument. Nanos argues that Gal 1:6 contains an epistolary formula for expressing 'ironic rebuke'.[5] The coinage 'ironic rebuke' comes from Mullins's work, which undertakes an analysis of epistolary formulae in the New Testament based on previous scholarship conducted by White on non-literary papyri. Linguistically speaking, the form consists of *thaumazō* (θαυμάζω) plus the 'the object of astonishment', indicated by *hoti* (ὅτι) or *pōs* (πῶς) – i.e. 'I am astonished that. . .' (*thaumazō hoti*) or 'I am astonished how. . .' (*thaumazō pōs*).[6]

Kremendahl's survey of *thaumazō hoti/pōs/ei* in the papyri is the most systematic to date, overviewing thirty instances occurring in the introductions of papyrus letters. For Kremendahl, *thaumazō hoti/pōs/ei* is a way of signalling rebuke, but not direct rebuke. The speaker's comment about their wonder or confusion in the first person implies a second person complaint ('*I* am astonished that' → implies → '*You* did wrong in regards to the thing in question').[7] The indirectness of this expression of wonder can make the speaker's concern or complaint read more politely than open rebuke, creating an overall softening effect.[8] Of course, the actual level of politeness would depend on the situation, and speakers can adjust how thinly

---

[2] For a summary, see Van Voorst 2010, 154–59.
[3] Ibid. 160–66.
[4] Betz 1979, 46. See also as follows.
[5] Nanos 2002, 32–61.
[6] Mullins 1972, 385; White 1971, 96. Dahl adds that these rebuke clauses may also be signalled by 'if', *ei* (εἰ) or *eiper* (εἴπερ, 2002, 118–19).
[7] '*Ich wundere mich, daß* → implies → '*Du hast in der und der Sache gefehlt*' (Kremendahl 2000, 102–3).
[8] Ibid. 103; cf. Dahl 2002, 119.

they wish their complaint to be veiled.⁹ 'In einigen Fällen ist unsere Briefformel sogar nur noch der letzte höfliche Auftakt zu offener Konfrontation und derber Beschimpfung.'¹⁰ Concerning irony, Kremendahl, agreeing with previous work done by Roberts, does not see *thaumazō hoti/pōs/ei* as inherently ironic. Instead, the possibility of irony in such expressions must be determined from context.¹¹ Access to a larger dataset of *thaumazō hoti/ pōs/ei* in letter openings has made this observation clear. There is nothing ironic about concerned, yet polite requests for information such as *P.Mich.* VIII 500:

θα[υ]μ[ά]ζω πῶς ἐπισόλιον ἡμεῖν οὐκ ἔπεμψας / δι' οὗ ἡμεῖν φανερὸν ποιήσῃς [ε]ἰ κατὰ τὰς / εὐχὰς ἡμῶν διεσώθης κα[ὶ] τί ἄρτι πρά[σσ]ε[ις], / ἵν' εἰδῶμεν πῶς τὰ πραγμάτιά σου φέρα[ι-] / ται.

I'm surprised that you haven't sent us a short letter through which you could make it clear to us whether, in answer to our prayers, you've made it through alright and whether you are doing well, so we might know how things are going with you.¹²

The overdone formality of *P.Oxy.* I 123, on the other hand, makes irony much more likely:¹³

κυρίῳ μου υἱῷ Διονυσοθέωνι / ὁ πατὴρ χαίρειν. /... / πάνυ θαυμάζω, υἱέ μου, μέχρις σήμερον γράμ- / ματά σου οὐκ ἔλαβον τὰ δηλοῦντά μοι τὰ περὶ τῆς / ὁλοκληρίας ὑμῶν. κἂν ὥς, δέσποτά μοι, ἀντί- / γραψόν μοι ἐν τάχει· πάνυ γὰρ θλείβομαι διότι / οὐκ ἐδεξάμην σου γράμματα.

The father sends his greetings to my lord and son Dionysotheonos... I am sorely amazed, my son, until today I have not received any letters from you concerning your well-being. And kindly do, my lord, write me back as soon

⁹ For polite use, see *P.Mich.* VIII 479, VIII 500; XV 751. For impolite: *P.Bad.* II 35; *P.Freib.* IV 69.
¹⁰ Kremendahl 2000, 103.
¹¹ Ibid. 103–4; cf. Roberts 1991, 111–13, 116–17, 119; Hansen 1989, 33.
¹² For further unironic examples, see n.9.
¹³ See Chapter 3, §3.2.2.

as possible, for I am woefully afflicted on account of not having received your letter!¹⁴

With *thaumazō hoti/pōs/ei* sometimes ironic but more often unironic in the papyri, we cannot make a one-to-one connection between the use of *thaumazō hoti/pōs/ei* and irony. We must therefore decide whether Gal 1:6 is sarcastic on the basis of the text itself rather than on comparison with the papyri. Before moving on, however, I will push back on an assumption underlying scholarship on *thaumazō hoti/pōs/ei* to promote further critical thinking about the relationship between Gal 1:6 and the papyri.

4.1.1   How Formulaic is the *thaumazō* 'Formula'?

Kremendahl argues that the Galatians would recognize in Paul's *thaumazō hoti* (θαυμάζω ὅτι) an epistolary formula, which 'was familiar to them from their own day to day correspondence'.¹⁵ But there are reasons to doubt that the Galatians would be familiar with this expression as an epistolary convention. Of the thirty examples that Kremendahl cites, several are quite late. Letters written centuries after Paul should be used cautiously in influencing our impression of what would have been typical in the correspondence of Paul and his congregation. If we, still allowing a considerable window, constrict our search only to the first two centuries BCE and CE, we are left with eight to eleven instantiations of this so-called epistolary formula.¹⁶

---

¹⁴ Of the thirty+ examples of *thaumazō* + conjunction cited in scholarship, the following have been identified as ironic: *P.Oxy.* xxxvi 2783, x 1348, xlii 3063 (Kremendahl 2000, 104n.29). *P.Oxy.* ix 1223 (Mullins 1972, 386; Roberts 1991, 117). *P.Cairo.Zen.* 59060/59061 (Roberts 1991, 117).

¹⁵ 'die ihnen aus ihrer eigenen Alltagskorrespondenz geläufig war' (Kremendahl 2000, 99; cf. Longenecker 1990, 11). For others who argue that Gal 1:6 may be interpreted in light of the *thaumazō* formula in the papyri, see Dahl 2002, 118–19, 129–30; Hansen 1989, 33, 43; Nanos 2002, 32–3, 39–46, 304; Roberts 1992, 330–32, 337.

¹⁶ Nine letters date to the first and second centuries CE, and three could be second or third century CE – for a maximum of twelve examples of high relevance –while Kremendahl's other eighteen examples date anywhere from the third to the fifth century CE, except *P.Zen.Pestm.* 56, which is third century BCE (see 2000, 101–2). *BGU* iii 850 should not be counted among the relevant examples despite its early date. It is missing the necessary context to determine the letter's subject and the tone of its θαυμάζω clause. Therefore, nine within the date-range – one missing context (+ up to three that may or may not date within the date-range) = eight to eleven examples.

Comparison with greeting formulae, which perhaps more than any other feature deserve the title epistolary formulae, can help refine our understanding of how strong the evidence for *thaumazō hoti/pōs/ei* as an actual convention is. Between 200 BCE and 200 CE, there are thousands of ancient papyrus letters extant.[17] A ratio of circa ten instantiations of *thaumazō hoti/pōs/ei* out of 3,747 letters should already suggest caution in using the technical designation 'epistolary formula' to refer to an indicative verb + conjunction occurring so infrequently. To add further perspective, a papyrus.info search for the common greeting *chairein* (χαίρειν) between these dates turns up 4,854 hits. These are not all letters, but include contracts, receipts, and other types of writing. The verb for 'to greet' (ἀσπάζομαι/ἀσπάζεται) occurs 364 times within this date-range and, unlike *chairein*, occurs predominantly in letters.

Of course, one must expect greeting formulae to be more prevalent than other conventions that deserve the designation epistolary formulae. However, only about ten examples within the four centuries most relevant to Paul are too few to suggest that the use of *thaumazō hoti/pōs/ei* in letter writing was formalized enough to merit reference as an 'epistolary formula'. We therefore cannot assume that it would be recognizable to an audience as a common letter-writing convention with stereotyped features – that Galatian Christians would hear *thaumazō hoti* (θαυμάζω ὅτι) and immediately recognize Paul as expressing perplexity, rebuke, or whatever. This does not mean that Galatian Christians would hear *thaumazō hoti* with no preconceptions at all. *thaumazō* is a common, versatile verb capable of being used positively, neutrally, and negatively,[18] literally and ironically.[19] Doubtless Paul's audience in Galatians would have used or heard *thaumazō* used in all of these ways.

It is therefore exegetically inappropriate to use the papyri as an interpretive key for understanding Gal 1:6. Without sufficient evidence for *thaumazō hoti/pōs/ei* as an epistolary formula, we cannot assert that Paul's audience would be biased towards a specific interpretation of *thaumazō* in Gal 1:6 just because Paul uses the verb in the context of a letter. This is not to say that comparison between

---

[17] A papyrus.info metadata search for "'letter' OR 'lettre' OR 'Brief'" between 200 BCE and 200 CE (inclusive) returns 3,747 hits.
[18] Kremendahl 2000, 103. Cf. LSJ s.v. 'θαυμάζω'.
[19] See Chapter 3, §3.2.4.

Paul and the papyri is not worth making, only that Paul's use of *thaumazō* must be established in its own right.

4.1.2   Galatians 1:6

Multiple lines of evidence support a sarcastic reading of Gal 1:6, although Paul's use of ambiguous language makes this interpretation ultimately uncertain.[20]

4.1.2.1   A Sarcastic Reading

We have established indices of exaggeration as some of the most prevalent signals of sarcasm in ancient Greek (Chapter 3, §3.1.2). Galatians 1:6 is certainly emphatic. Paul begins: *Thaumazō hoti houtōs tacheōs* (Θαυμάζω ὅτι οὕτως ταχέως). *thaumazō* can indicate amazement, fascination, and awe at something wonderful that has just transpired.[21] The double adverbs *houtōs tacheōs* ('so quickly', οὕτως ταχέως) also create a sense of emphasis, which is underlined by their placement early in the clause, just after the *hoti* (ὅτι).[22] Paul expresses amazement at the Galatians celerity,[23] and when he goes on to describe this as nothing less than the blinding speed with which they have turned from God, it is certainly plausible to read a measure of sarcasm in Paul's expression of awe.

The strongest evidence for a sarcastic reading of Gal 1:6 lies in the element of pretence in the verse as a whole (Chapter 1, §1.2.4). Jesus's sarcastic encouragement, which we saw in the previous chapter, can provide a helpful illustration (Chapter 3, §§3.1.2.2, 3.2.1): 'You do a good job of rejecting God's command so you can hold onto your tradition!' (καλῶς ἀθετεῖτε τὴν ἐντολὴν τοῦ θεοῦ, ἵνα τὴν παράδοσιν ὑμῶν στήσητε, Mark 7:9). Although the audience knows almost

---

[20] We will begin our exegesis with 1:6, as I do not see Paul as having provided significant indication of his tone in 1:1–5. Contra Van Voorst, who argues that in 1:1–5: 'Paul has been implicitly but clearly critical of the Galatians in this prescript' (2010, 171, 166–72). Paul's apostolic self-description in 1:1 does not imply that the Galatians have done anything wrong. Likewise, the benediction and doxological aside in 1:3–4 are mildly positive where they touch on the Galatians at all. There is no reason why the Galatians should have been biased to expect criticism in 1:6, or praise for that matter.

[21] TLG, s.v. 'θαυμάζω', esp. 2b. Note the use of *thaumazō* in describing reactions to miracles in the gospels (Mark 5:20; Matt 8:27, 9:33, 21:20).

[22] Cf. Pawlak 2019, 555.

[23] See Lightfoot 1876, 219; Bonnard 1953, 22–23.

instantly that Jesus does not mean to praise his opponents, his comment is still clearly sarcastic. With his ostensibly positive congratulations ('good job', καλῶς), Jesus creates the sort of 'counterfeited praise' discussed in Quintilian (*Inst.* 8.6.55 [Butler, LCL]; Chapter 1, §1.1.2). This contrasts sharply with the obvious dispraise he means to communicate for 'rejecting God's command' (ἀθετεῖτε τὴν ἐντολὴν τοῦ θεοῦ). The absurdity of this juxtaposition makes his sarcasm obvious; in a discussion about keeping the law, Jesus tells others that they have done well in breaking it!

The same sort of feigned congratulations for doing something obviously wrong would also be present in a sarcastic reading of Gal 1:6. Here Paul pretends to compliment the Galatians, 'amazed' by how quickly they have defected from their calling to a different gospel: 'I marvel at just how quickly you've managed to abandon the one who called you in the grace of Christ for a different gospel!' This pretence would be very thin, the dispraise and rebuke implied being far and away the dominant sentiments communicated.

In addition to such sarcastic congratulations, there may be further sarcasm later in the verse. Paul writes that the Galatians are turning to 'a different gospel, which is not another' (εἰς ἕτερον εὐαγγέλιον, ὃ οὐκ ἔστιν ἄλλο, Gal 1:6–7a). Some scholars argue that Paul uses 'gospel' ironically here, an inversion of its normal positive sense.[24]

We have shown that following an ostensibly positive message with a conflicting statement that expresses the speaker's real attitude is one of the most common signals of sarcasm in ancient Greek texts (Chapter 3, §3.1.1.4). This is precisely what we see in Gal 1:6–7a. 'Which is not another' (*ho ouk estin allo*, ὃ οὐκ ἔστιν ἄλλο) immediately undercuts 'a different gospel' (*heteron euangelion*, ἕτερον εὐαγγέλιον), clarifying that Paul does not mean 'gospel' in a positive sense, but intends to communicate a negative evaluation of his opponents' message, which distorts the gospel (1:7) and is worthy of anathema (1:8–9). To imply such strong negative affect through the positive term 'gospel' is textbook ancient sarcasm.[25]

---

[24] Reumann 1955, 142; Kremendahl 2000, 104; Nikolakopoulos 2001, 200–1; Nanos 2002, 298–300.

[25] Kremendahl writes that for Paul, his opponents' message 'is precisely the opposite of a gospel' ('gerade das Gegenteil eines Evangeliums ist'), and therefore Paul's 'which is not another' (ὃ οὐκ ἔστιν ἄλλο) makes it clear that, 'the term "gospel" [*euangelion*] in 1:6 cannot have been meant in its normal sense' ('der Terminus εὐαγγέλιον in 1,6 nicht im eigentlichen Wortsinn gemeint gewesen sein kann', 2000,

Recognizing this typical means of communicating sarcasm supports the exegesis of scholars who see 'different' (*heteron*, ἕτερον) and 'another' (*allo*, ἄλλο) here as essentially synonymous.[26] Schröter objects, arguing that if *heteron* and *allo* are synonymous, *allo* becomes unnecessary. He also sees it as a problem that they 'stand in syntactical opposition to each other here', and that with the *allo* clause Paul immediately retracts his initial statement that his opponents' message is a gospel.[27] Such repetition and opposition do not, however, indicate inconsistency on Paul's part or create an exegetical problem. Instead, they constitute the common signal of sarcasm discussed above in which the sarcastic statement is juxtaposed with a literal, negative message.

4.1.2.2 A Non-Sarcastic Reading

Although multiple lines of evidence support the plausibility of a sarcastic reading of 1:6, we must also acknowledge a level of ambiguity. *thaumazō* (θαυμάζω) is a polyvalent term, and it is often difficult to determine whether its positive sense is being inverted ironically, or whether it is being used literally in a negative sense. A literal, negative reading of *thaumazō* remains a possibility, communicating emphatic rebuke rather than sarcastic congratulations: 'I'm shocked that you have so quickly abandoned...' It is also possible that Paul's addition of 'different' (*heteron*, ἕτερον) to 'gospel' (*euangelion*, εὐαγγέλιον) is itself meant to convey negative evaluation, leaving no positive affect or 'counterfeited praise' to invert ironically.

At the same time, a straightforwardly negative, non-sarcastic reading of 1:6 leaves little reason for Paul to qualify what he says so immediately ('...different gospel, which is not another', ἕτερον εὐαγγέλιον, ὃ οὐκ ἔστιν ἄλλο, 1:7a). As we have seen, this sort of immediately contrastive statement is common in ancient sarcasm and would be somewhat out of place here if there was no element of ostensible praise or positive affect to undercut in either Paul's

104). This is close to what I have argued, but with one important distinction. Since, as we saw in Chapter 1, §1.2.2, verbal irony inverts ostensible affect rather than meaning, an ironic reading of *euangelion* does not commit the interpreter to a stance on whether Paul admits the possibility of other legitimate gospels (so Schröter 2013, 152–53) – or whether Paul's opponents referred to their message as a gospel (so Nanos 2002, 299).

[26] Moo 2013, 1:79. Contra Longenecker 1990, 15.
[27] Schröter 2013, 140–41.

thaumazō hoti opening or use of *euangelion*. Ultimately, the difference between the sarcastic 'I marvel that...' and the straightforwardly negative 'I am shocked that...' – as well whether 'gospel' belongs in inverted commas – would come down to tone and delivery. Without access to these elements, we must speak in terms of plausibility rather than certainty.

4.1.3 Galatians 1:6 and Paul's Rhetoric

Regardless of whether Paul is being sarcastic, Gal 1:6 certainly communicates a strong, vehement criticism in a highly emotive passage that crescendos through Paul's pronunciation of anathema on anyone who would preach a contrary gospel (1:8–9). As deSilva observes: 'Paul's opening is well calculated to arouse feelings of shame among the hearers.'[28]

Our analysis of Paul's opening also provides insight into the rhetorical register of Galatians. Paul does not select *thaumazō hoti* from a list of established letter-writing conventions. Instead, the vehemence of Paul's tone contrasts sharply with the use of *thaumazō hoti/pōs/ei* in many of the papyri, where this expression softens criticism and seeks to avoid conflict.[29] Paul is therefore not swapping one formula for another in expressing rebuke instead of thanksgiving at this point in the letter.[30] Furthermore, I have shown elsewhere that the potential sarcasm of Gal 1:6 does not support the thesis that Paul crafted the opening of Galatians following conventions for ironic letters found in ancient letter-writing handbooks.[31]

Previous scholarship has made significant use of ancient epistolary conventions and theory in describing the opening of Galatians. These determinations colour expectations of the tone, structure, and argument of the entire letter. Our work on Galatians' opening, however, demonstrates that Gal 1:6 betrays no evidence of such formal rhetorical apparatus. What we find in the text appears to be more like everyday communication than technical rhetoric.

---

[28] deSilva 2018, 125.
[29] See n.8.
[30] Contra Dahl 2002, 118.
[31] See Pawlak 2021, 263–70; contra Nanos 2002, 51; Dahl 2002, 118.

4.2   Galatians 2:1–9: Pillar Apostles

In Galatians 2, Paul narrates his interactions with the leaders of the Jerusalem church in an attempt to defend the divine origin of his gospel (1:11–12). Here he must simultaneously depict his ministry as accepted by the Jerusalem apostles and also demonstrate that their approval is inconsequential compared with his divine commission and empowerment. Within this context, the means Paul employs to refer to these leaders is ambiguous. When obedience to a revelation finds Paul in Jerusalem, he lays out his message before *tois dokousin* (τοῖς δοκοῦσιν), which one can only infer refers to the apostles leading the Jerusalem church (2:2). This epithet snowballs in 2:6, expanding to *tōn dokountōn einai ti* (τῶν δοκούντων εἶναί τι) and reaches its most explicit form at 2:9, where we learn that James, Peter, and John are 'those reputed/who seem to be "pillars"' (*hoi dokountes styloi einai*, οἱ δοκοῦντες στῦλοι εἶναι). Considering the subtlety of Paul's rhetorical aims in this passage, it is difficult to read his tone. Are these references to the Jerusalem apostles sincere acknowledgment of their authority, or a sarcastic undercutting of that authority?

Early Christian interpreters did not recognize irony in this passage; however, since those in question are apostles, one should expect theological biases to come into play. Clement refers to the apostles – Paul included – as 'the greatest and most righteous pillars of the church' (οἱ μέγιστοι καὶ δικαιότατοι στῦλοι, 1 Clem 5:2–3, 5 [Lightfoot]). Chrysostom cites 1 Cor 7:40 to defend the non-pejorative nature of *tois dokousin* (τοῖς δοκοῦσιν) in Gal 2:2, and considers the epithet of 2:9 encomiastic.[32] But the fact that Chrysostom must argue for a sincere reading of these epithets attests to the fact that the Greek can be taken otherwise.

This tendency to take Paul's references to the Jerusalem apostles as expressing positive evaluation has also persisted in modern commentaries. Ernest de Witt Burton writes that for all three of the verses in question: 'There is nothing in the present passage or in the usage of the words to indicate that they are used with irony.'[33] Bruce provides somewhat more discussion to support his assertion that Gal 2:2, 6, and 9 contain neither irony nor sarcasm, citing

[32] Chrysostom, *Comm. Gal.* (NPNF vol. 13, pp. 32, 37; see also Jerome, *Comm. Gal.* bk.1, §2.6a, §2.7–9.
[33] Burton 1921, 71.

instances in Josephus where a similar construction is used positively to refer to 'those of them who seem/were [*dokountes*] considered to be esteemed' (οἱ προύχειν αὐτῶν δοκοῦντες, Josephus, *BJ*, 4.159).[34] Despite this long tradition, a few interpreters advance an ironic reading. Betz cites a number of instances where *hoi dokountes* (οἱ δοκοῦντες) is used both positively and negatively, before leaning towards irony.[35] Longenecker suggests that the repetition of *hoi dokountes*, coupled with a similar use of the verb in Phil 3:4, supports an ironic reading.[36] Although he does not mention sarcasm or irony, Lightfoot sees evidence for 'a tinge of disparagement' in this repetition, as well as in the use of 'to be pillars' (*styloi einai*, στῦλοι εἶναι) and, especially, 'to be something' (*einai ti*, εἶναί τι). To these he also adds 'the contrast implied in the whole passage between the estimation in which [the Jerusalem apostles] were held and the actual services they rendered to [Paul]'.[37]

While interpreters have come away from 2:2, 6, and 9 with different impressions, neither side has marshalled much evidence to support an argument one way or another, and those in favour of irony will not usually push beyond a 'maybe' in terms of the likelihood of this interpretation. It is, then, worth setting out in full the evidence for a sarcastic reading of these epithets, in addition to clarifying where the interpretive difficulties lie.

Parallels do not take us far. Interpreters on both sides have brought examples to either support or reject viewing *hoi dokountes* (οἱ δοκοῦντες) as ironic. These demonstrate that *hoi dokountes* can be read positively, negatively, or ironically. We must therefore move beyond semantics. The Galatians did not have a lexicon in front of them from which they could select the meaning of *dokeō* (δοκέω) most in line with comparable passages from their linguistic milieu. Instead, both Paul and the Galatians would have experienced the term *hoi dokountes* with all its ambiguous resonances – including

---

[34] Bruce 1982, 109; see Josephus, *BJ* 3.453; 4.141, 159. DeSilva adds several ironic uses from Plato to this list (2018, 173n.131; see Plato, *Ap.* 21b, c–e; 221–b; 29a; 36d; 41e). Franz Mußner rejects an ironic reading (1974, 104–5, 120–21).

[35] Betz 1979, 87. Barrett too gives a soft yes to the presence of irony here (1953, 3–4). Jónsson takes 2:9 as ironic (1965, 237). Nikolakopoulos sees a sort of 'double irony' ('doppelten Ironie') in 2:6 whereby Paul's words are tinged with irony but not meant to disrespect the Jerusalem apostles (2001, 202–3).

[36] Longenecker does not seem to be fully committed to this reading, ultimately describing Paul's tone as 'ironic or dismissive' (1990, 57).

[37] Lightfoot 1876, 231.

both the ideas of appearance and reputation (LSJ s.v. 'δοκέω', I.4, II.5) – potentially in play.

The clearest evidence for a degree of negative evaluation in Paul's δοκέω epithets lies in elements that point to his being dismissive of the Jerusalem apostles. Longenecker's assertion that Paul's use of repetition here supports an ironic reading is a good starting point, though the way Paul uses repetition has more to say than its mere presence. It is curious that Paul does not begin with the more unambiguous description in 2:9: 'James and Peter and John, those reputed/ who seem to be "pillars"' (Ἰάκωβος καὶ Κηφᾶς καὶ Ἰωάννης, οἱ δοκοῦντες στῦλοι εἶναι, 2:9). While in 2:2 one may assume from context that the men in question are the leaders of the Jerusalem church, Paul first introduces them with only *autois* (αὐτοῖς, 'them') and *tois dokousin*. In doing so Paul provides only the most generic level of identification and identity. The reader must wait until 2:6 to receive more than superficial information about *hoi dokountes*, and until 2:9 for their names.

Paul's clearest dismissal of *hoi dokountes* comes in 2:6, in the reference to the still-unnamed Jerusalem apostles being reputed and/or seeming 'to be something' – the *einai ti* (εἶναί τι) Lightfoot gestures to. Different forms of *tis* (τις) are frequently used to add a level of dismissiveness to sarcastic statements – communicating a subtle degree of negative evaluation that contrasts with the ostensible positivity of the sarcastic statement (Chapter 3, §3.1.2.5). *ti* (τι) very likely has the same function here.[38] Paul is vague and non-committal about the status attributed to the Jerusalem apostles, implying that he does not esteem them as highly as they 'are reputed' or 'seem' to be.

Both the way Paul makes only cursory reference to the Jerusalem apostles in 2:2, avoiding their names, and the vague use of τι function to indicate dismissiveness, imply some degree of negative evaluation. We therefore have two options for reading the δοκέω epithets in 2:2, 6, depending on their connotations. First, if Paul, as in the passages from Josephus cited above,[39] refers to reputation, then the epithets

---

[38] Dunn states that *tis* is a typical Pauline 'somewhat diminishing allusion', although he does not cite Gal 2:6 here, reserving Paul's 'diminishing' *tis* for 'known opponents' (1996, 146). Paul uses *hoitines* (οἵτινες) in a dismissive fashion also in 2:4, where he gives no identity to his opponents beyond the sharply negative 'false brothers and sisters secretly brought in' (τοὺς παρεισάκτους ψευδαδέλφους, NRSV). Cf. 6:3, which is similar to 2:6, though not directed at the Jerusalem apostles.
[39] See n.34.

are sarcastically dismissive of the status ascribed to the Jerusalem apostles: 'Those Men of Repute' (2:2, 2:6c) and 'those-renowned-for-being-something' (2:6). This reading explains Paul's aside in 2:6b, where his implicit dismissal becomes explicit. Immediately following the epithet, Paul states, 'whatever they were at one time or other doesn't at all matter to me; God does not play favourites' (ὁποῖοί ποτε ἦσαν οὐδέν μοι διαφέρει· πρόσωπον [ὁ] θεὸς ἀνθρώπου οὐ λαμβάνει, 2:6). The use of two nondescript terms of reference here 'whatever' and 'whenever' (ὁποῖοί ποτε) fit with Paul's dismissive tone as observed so far, as does 'it doesn't at all matter to me' (οὐδέν μοι διαφέρει). Juxtaposing explicit negative evaluation with sarcasm was one of the most common signals of sarcasm that we identified in the previous chapter (Chapter 3, §3.1.1.4), and which we saw in Gal 1:6–7a. If this is what Paul is doing with the juxtaposition of 2:6a and 2:6b, then 2:6b provides the literal evaluation that Paul implies with his sarcastic epithets throughout Galatians 2. Though the Jerusalem apostles may be reputed to be 'something', Paul does not care about their ascribed status, nor does it win them any favours with God. It is not that the Jerusalem apostles are not legitimate authority figures, only that their standing is inconsequential.[40]

Second, if however *hoi dokountes* refers to appearance instead of and in contrast to reality, these dismissals are mildly disparaging, but unironic. Here 2:2 and 2:6c would essentially be shorthand for the longer epithet in 2:6a,[41] with all three meaning: 'those who (only) *seem* to be something (but whose status is inconsequential)'.

In 2:9 we have Paul's most elaborated epithet for James, Peter, and John: 'those reputed/who seem to be "pillars"' (*hoi dokountes styloi einai*, οἱ δοκοῦντες στῦλοι εἶναι). Following 2:2, 6, we should be expecting something dismissive, and while we cannot be sure about direct quotation, there is good evidence to suggest that here we are dealing with an echoic and (mildly) sarcastic appellation. Several commentators agree that Paul's use of the term 'pillars' is not his own designation, but stems from the parlance of the Jerusalem

---

[40] Although implied indifference is not negative evaluation *per se*, there remains scope for sarcasm insofar as Paul's implied indifference suggests that the Jerusalem apostles' status is unimportant, making the implicit evaluation negative relative to the ostensible positivity of sarcasm.

[41] See Martyn 1997, 191.

church.[42] Generally, one ought not mirror-read too far into echoic sarcasm, as sarcasts are often uninterested in accurate portrayal.[43] However, the attributive nuance of *dokountes* (δοκοῦντες),[44] brought across by translations such as 'reputed', provides reasonable evidence that Paul means to communicate that he is referring to the designation of others.[45] His implied evaluation here is likely to be the same as it was with previous versions of the same appellation: 'whatever they were at one time or other doesn't at all matter to me; God does not play favourites' (2:6b). To imply such indifference through positive words echoed from another source is clear sarcasm as described by the echoic account of verbal irony (Chapter 1, §1.2.3).

Between the echoic reference in 2:9 and the juxtaposition of dismissive epithet with literal evaluation in 2:6, I suggest that on balance there is more evidence for a sarcastic reading of these appellations in 2:2, 6, and 9 than a literal, negative interpretation. Paul is keen to show that no human can be credited as the source of his gospel, and so he does not go up to Jerusalem following his conversion for many years, and then only at God's summons (2:1–2). He does not name the 'Men of Repute', on recounting his first visit (2:2), then in 2:6 his more disparaging and more dismissive reference to 'those-renowned-for-being-something' emphasizes the fact that 'those Men of Renown added nothing (to my Gospel)'. Instead, 'James and Peter and John, those reputed to be "pillars", gave myself and Barnabas the right hand of fellowship' (2:9).

While I consider there to be more evidence for a sarcastic reading, I do not consider a sarcastic reading and a straightforwardly dismissive interpretation as mutually exclusive options. *dokeō* (δοκέω) encapsulates both 'to seem' and 'to be considered', and there is no reason why Paul should not have meant for both resonances to show through; to convey simultaneously that the Jerusalem apostles *seem* to be something and *are considered* to be of high status.[46] In either case, what Paul implies is the same (2:6b).

Paul's use of ambiguous, polyvalent language in 2:2, 6, and 9 (*dokeō*/δοκέω, *tis*/τις) may be an intentional choice that enables him

---

[42] Lietzmann 1923, 13; Bruce 1982, 122; Longenecker 1990, 57–58; Martyn 1997, 204–5.

[43] See Chapter 1, §1.3.4; Nanos 2002, 60–61; Sperber and Wilson 1998, 284.

[44] See LSJ s.v. 'δοκέω', II.5.

[45] On the origin and implications of the designation 'pillars' within the Jerusalem church, see Lightfoot 1876, 237; Bruce 1982, 122–23; Longenecker 1990, 57.

[46] Recall the *double entendre* in Lucian, *Phal. I*. 12; Chapter 3, §3.1.1.6.

to balance his desire to distance his gospel from human influence with his recognition that the support of the Jerusalem apostles strengthens his overall argument. As we have discussed, Paul's implied, indifferent evaluation accomplishes this first end, but it is also important that Paul does not overtly disrespect the apostles who did not force Titus to be circumcized (2:3) and who offered him their support (2:9). The fact that Paul's language can be read positively, as many later interpreters have done, enables Paul to show a surface level of respect for the Jerusalem apostles while distancing himself from their influence and dismissing their importance off the record. As Haiman writes: 'Part of what I consider the aesthetic appeal of sarcasm, in fact, lies in its ambiguity, and its potential deniability.'[47] For Paul, using ambiguous language enables him to tread the fine line he aims to follow in the autobiographical section of Galatians, where he at once wants to deny human influence on his gospel, but still use the endorsement of other apostles.

4.3   Galatians 5:12: Cutting Language

In 5:12 Paul expresses a wish that his circumcision-promoting opponents would cut off significant portions of their genitalia. Dahl asserts: '(5:12) is sarcasm'.[48] Longenecker calls this verse 'caustic sarcasm' that is 'meant to caricature and discredit [Paul's] opponents'.[49] While the latter point is clearly true, the verse itself is not sarcastic.

I have defined sarcasm as occurring when an utterance that would normally express a positive evaluation implies negative evaluation (Chapter 1, §1.2.6). There is no room for affected positivity in the sentiment 'go cut yourself'. Reading 5:12 as sarcasm betrays a certain colloquial understanding of the term that essentially views sarcasm as cutting language.

Von Campenhausen was on the right track when he called the passage a 'grausigen' or '"blutigen" Witz' ('gruesome' or '"bloody" joke').[50] Longenecker is correct that Paul is not seriously suggesting

---

[47] Haiman 1990, 203.
[48] Dahl 2002, 129.
[49] Longenecker 1990, cxix, 234. Lietzmann sees 'Schärfster Sarkasmus [sharpest sarcasm]' (1923, 36; cf. Lightfoot 1876, 288; Bonnard 1953, 107; Betz 1979, 270; Dunn 1993, 282; Moo 2013, 2:337; Lichtenberger 2017, 104). Nikolakopoulos: 'harte Ironie [harsh irony]' (2001, 205–6).
[50] von Campenhausen 1963, 104.

that anyone castrate themselves.[51] Paul's comment is therefore insincere, hyperbolic, and sharply polemical. I am not sure we can rightly call it a joke; I find it unlikely that Paul is trying to get a laugh here.[52] Considering the ancient connotations of emasculation, Paul's opponents certainly would not have appreciated it.

This verse is not the only point in Galatians where Paul employs strong language regarding his opponents (1:8–9; 2:4; 6:12–13) or his congregation (3:1–5; 4:8–11, 16; 5:4, 15). The vehemence in Paul's tone speaks to his assessment of the urgency and importance of the problem of circumcision in Galatia. Paul knows the Galatians well and knows at one time they 'would have torn out [their] eyes and given them to [him]' (4:15 NRSV). It is perhaps the strength of this prior relationship that enables Paul to employ strong language without feeling like he runs the risk of alienating his audience.

4.4   Conclusions

Although his language is ambiguous in both cases, Paul uses sarcasm in Galatians 1 and 2 to very different effects. I have argued that Paul's use of *thaumazō hoti* (θαυμάζω ὅτι) in 1:6 is not an epistolary convention for expressing 'ironic rebuke', and would not immediately signal a specific interpretation to Paul's audience. There is, however, evidence for sarcasm in 1:6 itself. On this reading, there is an element of sarcastic congratulations in Paul's expression of amazement that his congregation has so quickly run off to find a new gospel. However, the ambiguity of *thaumazō* (θαυμάζω) makes it difficult to be certain about a sarcastic interpretation. It remains possible that Gal 1:6 is a straightforward rebuke conveying only negative evaluation without any ostensible positivity.

Regardless of whether this rebuke is sarcastic, it is representative of the tendentious tone Paul adopts throughout the letter. In our discussion of 5:12, we saw that strong, vehement language is used without irony throughout Galatians with respect to both Paul's opponents and the Galatians themselves. Galatians 5:12 itself is an excellent example, consisting of hyperbolic, insincere polemic at the expense of Paul's opponents but lacking the ostensible positivity of sarcasm. I suggest that it is Paul's close relationship with the

---

[51] So too Dunn 1993, 283.

[52] See Lichtenberger 2017, 104 – although he misidentifies 5:12 as sarcasm. For jokes about circumcision, see Aristophanes, *Ach.* 156–63; *Eq.* 963–64.

Galatians, coupled with his assessment of the import and urgency of the circumcision issue, that emboldens him to take a hard line in persuading the Galatian church to accept his views. In contrast to Paul's behaviour with his congregation and opponents, his use of sarcasm on the Jerusalem apostles is much more subtle. I have argued that the primary characteristic underlying the *dokeō* (δοκέω) epithets in Gal 2:2, 6, and 9 is dismissiveness. Paul's lack of description and use of vague terms of reference (e.g. *tis*/τις) implicitly dismisses the status accorded to the 'pillar' apostles as inconsequential. Paul does not deny their authority, but deflates its importance, emphasizing that whatever others consider them to be is immaterial to him and unimportant to God (2:6).

Paul's language is ambiguous in these epithets, allowing simultaneously for sarcastic resonances (dismissive of status 'reputed') and the idea that the Jerusalem apostles only 'seem' to be something. We have seen ambiguity and ostensible politeness put to use in the previous chapter by some of Lucian's subtler sarcasts, Lycinus especially (Chapter 3, §§3.3.2, 3.3.4). These give the sarcast an advantageous measure of deniability when being sarcastic at the expense of parties of high status.[53] Paul's epithets in Gal 2:2, 6, and 9 take similar advantage of ambiguity, implying dismissiveness without breaking from language that avoids disrespect on a surface level.

Paul's sarcasm in 2:2, 6, and 9 is nowhere near as tendentious as the tone he adopts with his congregation and opponents at different points throughout Galatians. Instead, Paul's use of ambiguous, polyvalent language attests to the complicated nature of his relationship with the Jerusalem apostles and their approval that we see throughout the autobiographical section of Galatians. Here Paul must strike a balance between his desire to establish the divine origin of his gospel as the sole legitimation of his apostleship and the pragmatic reality that the acceptance of other apostles strengthens his position. The epithets in 2:2, 6, and 9 maintain this tension, being mildly dismissive of the Jerusalem apostles' importance without nullifying the fact that Paul still respects them as apostles and recognizes that their approval supports his ministry.

---

[53] Cf. Haiman 1990, 203.

5

SARCASM IN ROMANS: WITH SPECIAL REFERENCE TO DIATRIBE AND VOICE

Previous scholarship has recognized dialogical elements throughout much of Romans reminiscent of ancient diatribe, as Paul engages in a rhetorical back-and-forth with hypothetical interlocutors. Much of Paul's sarcasm in Romans occurs in such exchanges, creating two major interpretive problems. The first problem is the issue of voice; we cannot determine whether a given passage is sarcastic without first knowing who the speaker is.

We will begin, therefore, by nuancing previous scholarship on diatribe in Romans, with reference to Romans and Epictetus's *Discourses* (5.1). Without space to engage in a systematic overview of all texts considered examples of diatribe, Epictetus will be helpful for comparison insofar as his work has the most relevant stylistic parallels with Romans, especially in the use of rhetorical questions answered by *mē genoito* (μὴ γένοιτο, 'absolutely not!') – a feature only he and Paul share.[1]

Previous scholarship has gone too far in separating Paul's voice from the voice of his hypothetical interlocutor, making sections of Romans appear more like dialogue proper than diatribe. I will argue that Romans is closer to a one-man show than a conversation, insofar as the voices of Paul and his interlocutors are never fully separate. Romans contains dialogical elements, but not dialogue.

The second interpretive difficulty is created by the use of rhetorical questions in Romans. For example, in Rom 6:1–2, we have, 'What then shall we say? Should we keep on sinning so we can get even more grace? ... NO!' The question is intentionally absurd and is immediately shut down with the sort of utterance deflater that Haiman identifies as a signal of sarcasm in English – which we have also confirmed as not uncommon in ancient Greek (see Chapter 3,

---

[1] See Malherbe 1980, 231–40.

§3.1.1.4). To determine whether such questions – Rom 3:8; 6:1, 15 – can be considered sarcastic, we will first address the relationship between sarcasm and rhetorical questions in general, in addition to which features suggest the presence of sarcasm in these particular questions. We shall then apply the revised understanding of voice advanced in 5.1 to these questions, which will serve as the interpretive key for understanding how they can be considered instances of sarcasm.

Following this discussion, we will turn to other passages where Paul is sarcastic with his hypothetical interlocutor (2:17–19; 11:19–20). We will discuss the implications of these verses for the identity and characterization of Paul's hypothetical interlocutor. In both cases, attending to the relationship between sarcasm and counterfactuality will be important for avoiding problematic assumptions that could be drawn from a sarcastic reading (Chapter 1, §1.2.2). Finally, we will comment on subversive and ironic readings of Paul's discussion of governmental authority in Rom 13:1–7 and assess whether there is any firm evidence of sarcasm and insubordination therein.

After determining how sarcasm functions within the dialogical back-and-forth of Paul's argument in Romans, we will be able to draw more general conclusions about the pragmatic functions of sarcasm throughout the letter in light of the patterns we have observed in other authors.

5.1   Whose Line Is It Anyway? The Distinction between Dialogue and Dialogical Writing

The contention that Romans should be read in light of diatribe has been influential in scholarship. Epictetus' discourses make up one of the most significant examples of diatribe; and when one lays Romans alongside these texts, considerable stylistic similarities become evident. One of the major impacts of understanding Romans as a diatribe has been the recognition of dialogical elements in the letter. Stowers considers dialogical exchanges to be 'the most distinctive feature of diatribe style', and finds such exchanges to be prevalent throughout Romans.[2] Paul bounces comments and questions off a

---

[2] Stowers 1981, 2, 174–84. Thorsteinsson helpfully emphasizes the importance of dialogical elements in diatribe epistolography as comparative literature (2003, 128–30, 134–44). For a summary of New Testament scholarship on diatribe, see King 2018, 103–23.

hypothetical interlocutor to drive his argument forward. The purpose of this section will be to clarify how voice works in these exchanges.

5.1.1   Diatribe, Dialogue, and Voice

While the discovery of Paul's dialogue partner has produced much exegetical fruit, it has become all too easy to lose track of the interlocutor's hypothetical-ness in terms of narrative voice. The way Stowers lays out dialogical passages in Paul and Epictetus makes the text read like fully fledged dialogue, with clear distinctions between speaking parts:

G. Int.	Do we then overthrow the law through faith?	
H. Paul.	By no means! On the contrary we uphold the law.	
I. Int.	What then shall we say that Abraham our forefather according to the flesh found?[3]	

While some scholars have more nuanced understandings of voice in such passages, it is still common to see language implying sharp distinctions in speaker and characterization slip in.[4] King's recent study is perhaps the superlative example of treating dialogical passages in diatribe texts as scripted dialogues.[5] I argue that such division implies a sharper demarcation between speakers than can be safely assumed from diatribe style.

One may expect fully realized characters who speak with their own voices in Platonic dialogue, or even tragedy and comedy, but not here. Diatribe does not belong to any one of these genera. We must be cautious of thinking about diatribe as a strictly defined genre.[6] Without space to develop a critical definition of diatribe, I will take a minimalist approach, considering it a constellation of stylistic

---

[3] Stowers 1981, 165; cf. 158–65, 172. King summarizes the dialogical divisions of Rom 3:1–9 offered by various scholars, before providing his own (2018, 269–70). Campbell divides the whole of Rom 1:16–3:20 into the voices of Paul and 'The Teacher' (2009, 587–90).

[4] For more nuanced language, see Stowers 1981, 73–74, 128–29, 134–35; Thorsteinsson 2003, 126–30, 145. For treatments of dialogical exchanges as essentially fully fledged dialogues in terms of speaker or characterization, see n.3 above; Stowers 1984, 710–16; 1994, 159–66; Thorsteinsson 2003, 125–26, 148–50, 194–96, 244–46 [see 5.3.1.1].

[5] See King 2018, 157–59, 252–74, 292–98.

[6] See Schmeller 1987, 1–54, 428; Stowers 1981, 75–78; Thorsteinsson 2003, 124; for an argument in favour of diatribe as a genre, see Porter 1991, 655–61.

features common to comparable texts identified by scholars as dia-tribe.[7] What matters most for the present purpose is what diatribe is not. Diatribe is not dialogue. The dialogical exchanges that we find in diatribe may have stylistic features analogous to dialogue, but we cannot assume that the back-and-forth between the speaker of the 'diatribe' and the hypothetical interlocutor will be the same as the interactions between characters in dialogue. We cannot import wholesale the features of the latter into the former.

To respect this distinction, I will lay out an alternative proposal for conceptualizing voice in Romans, and diatribe more broadly.[8] Then, after indicating what lines of evidence lead in this direction, I will go on to discuss how this conception of voice impacts our interpretation of sarcasm in rhetorical questions throughout Romans, such as Rom 3:8; 6:1–2, 15.

5.1.2   Diatribe as a One-man Show

Rather than a dialogue, as a rhetorical performance, diatribe is a one-man show. Whether the audience is Epictetus' classroom or the Roman church, it is clear from this vantage point that there is only one speaker.[9] Thus, the voice of the hypothetical interlocutor cannot be fully separated from the voice of the author.[10] The role of Paul's dialogue partner in Romans would, then, be better billed Paul-as-hypothetical-interlocutor. There is a level of self-consciousness to the performance such that both Paul and his audience remain aware that even when the 'interlocutor' speaks, there is a sense in which it is still Paul.

Five lines of evidence support this conception of voice in the dialogical passages of Romans. First, the use of the first-person plural *ti (oun) eroumen* (τί [οὖν] ἐροῦμεν, 'what [then] shall we say') to introduce potential objections creates overlap between Paul's voice and the voice of his interlocutor (Rom 3:5; 6:1; 7:7; 9:14).

---

[7] For typical features of diatribe, see King 2018, 124–27.

[8] I am operating on the assumption that Paul – regardless of where he learned it, or how intentional his use of the style is – is doing something like other texts that have been collected as representatives of diatribe. At minimum, I will lay out an under-standing of voice that describes Paul in Romans, that works for Epictetus, and that may also work for other texts that share similar stylistic features.

[9] There are instances where Epictetus might be answering actual questions from his audience, but this does not apply to Paul.

[10] Compare Hays 1985, 79n.13.

Scholars have variously attributed some questions introduced by *ti* (*oun*) *eroumen* to Paul (3:5)[11] and others to the hypothetical interlocutor (6:1; 7:7; 9:14).[12] The use of the first-person plural, whether ascribed to Paul or the 'interlocutor', has the effect of drawing all parties into the discussion, including Paul, his audience, and the hypothetical interlocutor.[13] The point is that anyone might draw the false inference represented by the following rhetorical question should they misinterpret Paul's argument. It is therefore better to read multiple potential voices – Paul, interlocutor, and audience – in the cohortative 'we-ness' of questions prefaced by *ti* (*oun*) *eroumen*, rather than the voice of only Paul or only the interlocutor.[14]

The next two pieces of evidence for this imprecision in distinguishing speakers in diatribe – numbered (2) and (3) – are best observed in Epictetus, *Diss.* 2.23. We will describe them there first before drawing parallels with Paul.

(2) *Discourses* 2.23 discusses the superiority of the will (προαίρεσις) over rhetorical expression. Epictetus begins with a series of rhetorical questions and answers such as the following: 'What is the faculty that opens and closes the eyes. . .? The faculty of sight? No, but the faculty of [the will]' (*Diss.* 2.23.9 [Oldfather, LCL], see 2.23.5–19). Stowers considers it typical in diatribe for the hypothetical interlocutor to provide quick responses to the speaker's questions. He cites a question-and-answer string from Epictetus *Diss.* 4.1.1–2 beginning with: 'Who, then, wishes to live in error? -No one [hyphen used to mark change of speaker].'[15] In both of these examples, one can just as easily see a single speaker answering their own questions as two distinct speaking parts. Indeed, Epictetus conducting a back-and-forth with himself is exactly what his students would have observed. At the same time, answering one's own questions still creates a second voice,[16] but

---

[11] Stowers 1984, 715; King 2018, 269; Campbell 2009, 589.

[12] On 6:1; 7:7 as spoken by the interlocutor, see Rodríguez 2016, 110–11, 124–25. On 9:14 as the interlocutor, see Jewett 2007, 581.

[13] '[*eroumen*] makes it sometimes difficult to identify the one speaking because of its inclusive potentials' (Thorsteinsson 2003, 145).

[14] We should view *ti* (*oun*) *eroumen* and *ti oun* (τί οὖν) in Paul as essentially interchangeable. The same blurriness and imprecision apply in all cases. *ti oun* is significant in both Paul (Rom 3:1, 9; 6:15; 11:7), and Epictetus (occurring 295 times; *ti oun eroumen* does not occur at all).

[15] Stowers 1981, 159, for citations across Epictetus and other texts, see 239n.31.

[16] One questioning, which engages in a pretence that an answer is required, and one answering, which engages in a pretence that the speaker must inform themselves as to the answer to their own question.

not necessarily a second persona or distinct character. Thus, we have two voices, at times imprecisely distinguished and at times blurring and overlapping, being performed by a single speaker.

(3) Epictetus' 'interlocutor' can also convey content that Epictetus wishes to teach, showing further overlap between speakers. Consider another passage from *Diss.* 2.23:

> What then? Does a person dishonour the other faculties? *Absolutely not!* Does a person claim there is no use or progress outside of the faculty of the will? *Absolutely not! That would be thoughtless, impious, and thankless towards god. Rather he gives to each its value. For, there is a use for a donkey, but not as much as for an ox.... There is a value for the power of speaking, but not as much as for the power of will* (*Diss.* 2.23.23–25).

King ascribes the text above in italics to Epictetus' interlocutor and the plain text to Epictetus.[17] He argues that following the second question, the interlocutor speaks to the end of 2.23.25, since the whole section provides an answer to the question. King therefore sees the interlocutor as having been won over to Epictetus' position.[18]

If what we have here is an interlocutor who responds to Epictetus' questions by answering at length with a response Epictetus agrees with that also contains the information Epictetus wishes to convey to his students, it is no great leap to see Epictetus' voice in the voice of his 'interlocutor'. Indeed, in the next sentence, Epictetus says, 'When, therefore, I say this [ὅταν οὖν ταῦτα λέγω], let no one suppose that I am bidding you neglect speech, any more than I bid you to neglect eyes, or ears...' (2.23.26 [Oldfather, LCL]). Epictetus clearly considers himself to be the speaker of the above discourse, despite having engaged in rhetorical questioning and answering in a way that creates multiple voices.

Both of these features can also be observed in Romans. (2) Scholars ascribe *mē genoito* negation of rhetorical questions (μὴ γένοιτο, 'absolutely not!') to both Paul (3:31; 6:2; 6:15)[19] and his interlocutor (3:4; 3:6)[20] in different cases. The commonality of μὴ γένοιτο as a means of negating rhetorical questions in Romans

---

[17] King 2018, 152–53; cf. Stowers 1984, 712. I am using King's translation, but have changed the formatting, and added italics to indicate how he parses the passage.
[18] King 2018, 153.
[19] On 3:31, see Stowers 1994, 234. Paul is implied as the speaker of 6:2, 15 in Rodríguez 2016, 110–11, 119.
[20] Stowers 1984, 715; Campbell 2009, 589; King 2018, 269.

creates the same hazy distinction between speakers that we saw in Epictetus: there is a sense in which one voice questions and another responds, but also a sense in which Paul both asks and reacts to his own questions.[21]

(3) There are also cases where, as in Epictetus, speech ascribed to Paul's interlocutor expresses opinions with which Paul agrees and contains information that Paul wishes to convey to the Romans. When Paul asks, 'what advantage has the Jew?' the 'interlocutor' responds: 'Much, in every way. For in the first place, the Jews were entrusted with the oracles of God' (Rom 3:2 NRSV).[22] Here and elsewhere (3:4, 3:6; 4:1–2a), the interlocutor is essentially Paul's mouthpiece for communicating his own perspective to his audience.[23] The questions of the 'interlocutor' likewise do not emerge simply as a consequence of the interlocutor's personality but are selected by Paul to drive his argument forward. That is, the 'interlocutor' asks, 'What then shall we say that Abraham our forefather according to the flesh found?'[24] to give Paul an opportunity to discuss the relationship between Abraham and faith (4:1–5). In such cases we may observe Paul's voice within the voice of his interlocutor.

The fourth piece of evidence for my conception of voice is stylistic: Paul's style does not change depending on which 'speaker' is talking. As we saw above, both *ti (oun) eroumen* (τί [οὖν] ἐροῦμεν) as a means of introducing rhetorical questions and *mē genoito* (μὴ γένοιτο) as a negation have at times been ascribed to Paul, and at times to the interlocutor. The fact that these two 'speakers' share these stylistic traits provides further evidence that Paul has not created his interlocutor as a distinct character with a voice fully separate from his own.[25] Stylistic distinctions between characters are by contrast very common in dialogue. This is clear in the characterizations of Aristophanes and Socrates in Plato's *Symposium* (see 201D–215A, 189C–94E), and also in Lucian's *Philosophies for Sale*, which includes many speaking parts with distinct personalities and even changes in dialect between characters (e.g., *Vit. Auct.* 1–6).

---

[21] Cf. Wilckens on 3:27–31 (1978, 1:244).

[22] King and Campbell script this response as the interlocutor (King 2018, 269; Campbell 2009, 589). Stowers takes it as Paul (1984, 715).

[23] On 3:4, 6, see Stowers 1984, 715; King 2018, 269; Campbell 2009, 589. On 4:1–2a, see Stowers 1994, 234.

[24] See n.3 p.132.

[25] Cf. Stowers 1981, 128–29.

The fifth piece of evidence for overlap between Paul's persona and that of his 'interlocutor' is the text's reception. To illustrate, I reproduce a chart from King's monograph that lays out which parts of Rom 3:1–9 have been attributed to Paul or his interlocutor by different scholars:[26]

Line in Script	Traditional	Stowers	Elliott	King
3:1	Interlocutor	Interlocutor	Paul	Paul
3:2	Paul	Paul	Interlocutor	Interlocutor
3:3	Interlocutor	Paul	Paul	Paul
3:4	Paul	Interlocutor	Interlocutor	Interlocutor
3:5a	Interlocutor	Paul	Paul	Paul
(3:5b)	Paul; authorial aside			
3:6	Paul	Interlocutor	Interlocutor	Interlocutor
3:7	Interlocutor	Paul	Paul	Paul
3:8a				
(3:8b)	Paul; authorial aside			
3:8c	Interlocutor			
3:8d	Paul		Interlocutor	Interlocutor
3:9a	Interlocutor	Interlocutor	Paul	Paul
3:9b	Paul	Paul	Interlocutor	Interlocutor

This chart demonstrates that almost every line in Rom 3:1–9 has at various points been attributed to both Paul and the interlocutor. The fact that the text can be coherently parsed in so many ways further indicates that distinctions between speakers are not clear. I argue that this lack of distinctions as well as the other lines of evidence for overlap between Paul and his 'interlocutor' discussed above are best explained by there being ultimately only one speaker: Paul, who plays both sides of the dialogical exchanges in Romans without breaking fully from his own persona.

One may object that this conception of diatribe as a one-man-show – with a single speaker playing both parts without fully

---

[26] Reproduced with permission of the copyright holder from King 2018, 269 (with slight formatting differences). For full copyright notice, see the note in the preface. For discussion of the 'traditional' reading, see King 2018, 165–96.

breaking from their own persona – is unnecessarily complicated. It is certainly simpler, from the standpoint of the interpreter, to distinguish sharply between passages where Paul is speaking and passages where his interlocutor is speaking. This is how voice and characterization work in dialogue. But Paul is not writing dialogue. Plato writes dialogue, and we have encountered a great deal of dialogue in Lucian. When one places Romans alongside these texts it is immediately clear that Paul is the outlier in terms of genre. We cannot therefore import a conception of voice from dialogue wholesale into Romans. It is precisely the fact that we have dialogical elements but not dialogue proper that creates the muddy distinctions between personae that I have described.

5.2   Sarcasm in Pauline Rhetorical Questions

This blurring of speakers that occurs when dialogical elements are brought to a single-author style like diatribe, or epistolography for that matter, will provide the interpretive key for elucidating the presence of sarcasm in the rhetorical questions that make up our first case study in Romans.

Rhetorical questions are themselves difficult to conceive of ironically. As such, we must first consider the conditions under which rhetorical questions can be sarcastic. We will then identify the elements that make certain rhetorical questions in Romans more likely candidates for sarcasm than others before finally bringing our conception of voice to bear on their exegesis.

In a recent paper, Wilson rightly argues that several tropes often grouped together as forms of irony in experimental literature are not inherently ironic. These include 'hyperbole, banter, understatement, jokes and rhetorical questions'.[27] Although Wilson does not dedicate significant discussion to rhetorical questions specifically, it is easy to conceive of unironic rhetorical questions. With classic examples such as 'If so-and-so jumped off a bridge, would you?' and 'What's wrong with you?' the speaker's evaluation is straightforwardly negative, and there is therefore no scope for the inversion of positive affect through sarcasm. Conversely, Wilson cites an example drawn from the *Teenage Mutant Ninja Turtles* where a question that would

---

[27] Wilson 2017, 201–17; cf. Wilson 2013, 42, 52–54. For studies that associate rhetorical questions with irony, see Gibbs 2000, 5–25; Hancock 2004, 453.

express positive affect if uttered sincerely is used sarcastically to communicate criticism:

> The turtles try to get a computer expert to show them how he did something on a computer. The computer expert just walks away. One turtle remarks, 'Helpful, isn't he?'[28]

Luke's gospel provides another clear case: 'You're the Christ, right? Save yourself, and us too!' (οὐχὶ σὺ εἶ ὁ χριστός; σῶσον σεαυτὸν καὶ ἡμᾶς, 23:39). Thus, with rhetorical questions, sarcasm is a possibility but not a given. As in other cases, we must be on the lookout for the implicit communication of negative evaluation through ostensibly positive sentiments.

5.2.1 Interrogation, Deliberation, and Exhortation: Questions that Look Like They Might Be Sarcastic

Certain rhetorical questions in Romans are posed with an air of absurdity that may indicate sarcasm. These include:

> Shall we do what is wrong so that good may result? (ποιήσωμεν τὰ κακά, ἵνα ἔλθῃ τὰ ἀγαθά; 3:8),
>
> Should we keep on sinning so grace is multiplied? (ἐπιμένωμεν τῇ ἁμαρτίᾳ, ἵνα ἡ χάρις πλεονάσῃ; 6:1),
>
> Should we sin because we are not under law, but under grace? (ἁμαρτήσωμεν ὅτι οὐκ ἐσμὲν ὑπὸ νόμον ἀλλ' ὑπὸ χάριν; 6:15).

These questions share several elements that will enable us to treat them together to some extent. They all take a first-person subjunctive as their main verb and represent absurd misreadings of Paul's logic. Two are negated with *mē genoito* (μὴ γένοιτο, 6:1, 15). Romans 3:8 is negated with 'they deserve what judgement they get!' (ὧν τὸ κρίμα ἔνδικόν ἐστιν), but both this and *mē genoito* function similarly as utterance deflaters – sharp and immediate contradictions of the preceding utterance (Chapter 3, §3.1.1.4). Finally, 6:1, 15 are both prefaced with the introductory question *ti oun* (*eroumen*) (τί οὖν [ἐροῦμεν]), a staple in Romans and typical of diatribe more generally (§5.1.2). Pragmatically speaking, Rom 3:7–8 functions somewhat differently from our other examples and, as such, we will treat it separately.

What makes these rhetorical questions appear sarcastic is the way that they skirt the boundaries between interrogation and statement, and between deliberation and exhortation. Functionally speaking, the major difference between the deliberative and hortatory subjunctive is whether a given phrase is a question or statement: 'The *Deliberative* Subjunctive is merely the hortatory turned into a question.'[29] This distinction has already been weakened in the case of rhetorical questions, which are 'thinly disguised statement[s]',[30] designed to make a point rather than obtain information.

Furthermore, our examples lack any grammatical indication that they are questions in the first place. Porter proposes that in the absence of formal indicators, we may translate a phrase as a question if, left as a statement, it would contradict the overall position of the author, 'or if it poses a set of alternatives'.[31] None of our examples satisfy the latter criterion, and the first is itself methodologically problematic. A proposition that clearly contradicts the author's thought could just as easily be an ironic statement as a question.

This being the case, there remain reasons for reading our examples as questions. The 'What then?' (*ti oun* [*eroumen*], τί οὖν [ἐροῦμεν]) prefaces in Rom 6:1, 15 suggest that these passages are at least asking: 'Is the following statement valid?' More importantly, several other passages in Romans share similar stylistic features to our examples and are explicitly marked as rhetorical questions with an initial *mē* (μή, 3:3, 5–6; 9:14; 11:1). These features make it likely that Paul intends 6:1, 15 to be read as questions.

While I follow almost all interpreters in translating our examples as rhetorical questions, it is worth observing how the fuzziness of the rhetorical question/statement distinction creates further overlap between the deliberative and hortative senses of the subjunctive verbs in our examples. For most first-century Christians, Paul included, to follow the phrase, 'We should keep on sinning so grace is multiplied.' (ἐπιμένωμεν τῇ ἁμαρτίᾳ, ἵνα ἡ χάρις πλεονάσῃ) with a full stop is to engage in sarcasm; it is a statement so absurd in this context that no one can be expected to take it seriously. As a sarcastic utterance, 'We should sin more so grace can increase!' is similar to the

---

[29] Moule 1953, 22. Cf. Porter 1992, 57–58.
[30] Wallace 1996, 467.
[31] Porter 1992, 276.

examples of sarcastic encouragement that we have discussed in Lucian and other authors, which ostensibly recommend useless or foolish actions (Chapter 3, §3.2.1). By contrast, a question mark renders the same words sincere in some contexts and ironic in others. The interrogative form is more ambiguous than the statement insofar as the exhortation, 'We should sin!' implies a much more (ostensibly) positive evaluation than the deliberative,[32] 'Should we sin?', making the former more clearly sarcastic. Greek, however, lacks the syntactic distinction between these two forms that we find in English, allowing more overlap in resonance. We should therefore read the subjunctive verbs in Rom 3:8; 6:1, 15 as expressing simultaneously elements of both deliberation ('should we?') and exhortation ('we should!').[33]

The positive affect associated with the hortatory subjunctive ('we should do *x*!') coupled with the obvious absurdity of the rhetorical questions in Rom 3:8; 6:1, 15 makes these our most likely candidates for sarcastic rhetorical questions in Romans.

5.2.2   Exegesis: Rom 3:8; 6:1, 15

Having established why Rom 3:8; 6:1, 15 might be sarcastic, we may now apply our modified understanding of voice in dialogical diatribe-like texts to their exegesis to determine whether they qualify as sarcasm indeed. To simplify the process, we begin by addressing how these statements function on the lips of Paul's 'interlocutor', and then, considering this, how we can understand them as instances of Paul-speaking-as-interlocutor. Romans 3:8 will be apt for the first stage of this process, as here Paul creates a starker division of speakers than usual in Romans. He writes:

> But if through my falsehood the truth of God brings about an abundant increase in his glory, why am I still judged as a sinner? And why don't we say, as we are slandered and as some say that we say, 'let us do what is wrong so that good things may result!'? They deserve what judgement they get!
> (. . .καὶ μὴ καθὼς βλασφημούμεθα καὶ καθώς φασίν τινες ἡμᾶς λέγειν ὅτι ποιήσωμεν τὰ κακά, ἵνα ἔλθῃ τὰ ἀγαθά; ὧν τὸ κρίμα ἔνδικόν ἐστιν, Rom. 3:7–8).

---

[32] The plural hortative subjunctive represents an invitation to join the speaker in doing some action. It implies that this course of action is a good idea.
[33] Cf. Fitzmyer 1993, 432; Jewett 2007, 390, 394, 415.

Here Paul creates distance between the utterance 'let us do what is wrong so that good things may result!' (ποιήσωμεν τὰ κακά ἵνα ἔλθῃ τὰ ἀγαθά) and his own authorial voice. He first indicates a negative response to the exhortation with an initial *mē* (μή), and then distances it from his own persona by explicit indications of speech (φάσιν τινες, ὅτι, 3:8). Before the statement is even made, we already know that its logic is false and that it consists of other people's words. Thus, here we are not dealing with the sort of ambiguous distinction between Paul and hypothetical interlocutor that we have been discussing, but with something more like quotation. It may even be the case that Paul is here citing actual criticism of his teaching.[34]

In addition to the message 'these words are not mine', Paul communicates two other pieces of information about the accusation at the end of 3:8. First, he states that such criticism is spoken as an instance of mocking slander or blasphemy (*kathōs blasphēmoumetha*, καθὼς βλασφημούμεθα).[35] Second, this slanderous comment is framed as a parodic appropriation of Paul's voice, 'as some say that we say' (καθώς φασίν τινες ἡμᾶς λέγειν).

Bringing these two factors together, we find firm grounds for reading ποιήσωμεν τὰ κακά ἵνα ἔλθῃ τὰ ἀγαθά ('We should keep on sinning so grace is multiplied') as a sarcastic exhortation rather than a question, in its 'original' form spoken by Paul's opponents.[36] Paul depicts them as mimicking him in their mockery, saying something like, 'Typical Paul: [*imitating Paul's voice*] "Let's do what's wrong so good things may result!"' As spoken by Paul's opponents, this is textbook sarcasm according to the echoic account of verbal irony (see Chapter 1, §1.2.3), being a mocking echo of Paul's actual position.

Ultimately, the mocking exhortation of 3:8 does not come to us directly from Paul's opponents but is refracted through Paul's voice. Paul states it as a rhetorical question that asks, 'is this a valid criticism?' before pronouncing judgement on anyone who would answer 'yes' (3:7–8). In this way, as it stands in Romans, ποιήσωμεν τὰ κακά ἵνα ἔλθῃ τὰ ἀγαθά; ('We should keep on sinning so grace is

---

[34] Barrett 1991, 62; Jewett 2007, 251; Longenecker 2016, 350–51.

[35] For another NT example where this verb is used to introduce sarcasm, see Luke 23:39.

[36] For our reading, it does not matter whether Paul is citing real or imagined opponents.

multiplied') is best described as reported sarcasm. It is a citation of someone else's sarcasm, which Paul has rejected.

The clear distinction that Paul makes between his voice and the voice of his opposition in 3:7–8 has given us the opportunity to see how this sort of critical, sarcastic exhortation functions when spoken in the voice of a third party. We may now apply this insight to 6:1, 15 where there is a more complex interplay between Paul's persona and his hypothetical interlocutor's.

We have already established the similarity between the rhetorical questions in 3:8; 6:1–2, 15. It therefore makes sense to read the latter two in light of the features that Paul applies to the first. Thus, when stated in the voice of the hypothetical interlocutor, 'Let us (remain in) sin...' takes on its full hortatory force as a sarcastic, mocking imitation of Paul (6:1, 15).[37] However, unlike 3:8, these objections do not involve Paul directly quoting an opponent, but the murkier performance of the interlocutor that overlaps with the voice of the speaker, which we laid out in our discussion of 'Whose Line Is It Anyway?'. Therefore, while the sarcastic voice of the interlocutor shows through to an extent, we do not fully break away from Paul's persona. This creates multiple layers in the delivery, such that we have Paul-as-interlocutor-imitating-Paul. This blending of voices accounts for the overlap between the deliberative and hortative, and between interrogative and stative that we observed earlier. As Paul, Paul poses a deliberative question. As his interlocutor (imitating Paul), Paul makes a mocking exhortation.

Before offering a working translation, we must first put these questions back into place as they occur following 'What then (shall we say)?' (*ti oun* [*eroumen*], τί οὖν [ἐροῦμεν];). I am not confident that we can 'script' *ti oun* to either Paul or his interlocutor. In both cases, the question essentially asks whether the following utterance is a logical consequence of the preceding argument: 'What, therefore, shall we say?' From the perspective of the hypothetical interlocutor, the question has an undertone of derisive incredulity. In this case, 'What then?' would imply the subtext, 'Is this *really* what you think?' If this were a dialogue and the interlocutor were a fully fleshed-out character, the line might read: 'What should we say, then? [*begins sarcastically imitating Paul's voice*] "Let's keep on sinning so we can get even more grace!"?' However, as I have

---

[37] Rodríguez ascribes both of these questions to the interlocutor (2016, 110–11, 118–19).

argued, we cannot fully separate out Paul's voice. Coming from Paul, *ti oun* (*eroumen*), coupled with the use of the subjunctive in the following question, add a degree of insincere deliberation to 6:1, 15. By asking whether one ought to accept ridiculous caricatures of his position, Paul affects a greater degree of uncertainty in his argument than he actually has. Like the use of the dubitative in LXX sarcasm (Chapter 2, §2.3), such insincere deliberation implies a more positive assessment of the objection than Paul really means to give.[38] We may therefore detect a note of sarcasm in Paul's voice as well. What makes coming to a single translation difficult is that both voices overlap in Paul's performance of his interlocutor (imitating Paul). I suggest a translation that retains elements of both deliberation and exhortation and where elements of an interlocutor/potential opponent's sarcasm show through in the second of the two rhetorical questions:

> So, what shall we say? Maybe we should just keep on sinning so we can get even more grace? Absolutely not! (6:1–2a).
>
> What then? Maybe we should sin because we are not under law, but under grace? Absolutely not! (6:15).

Without launching into a sustained discussion, I would like to suggest the possibility of this sort of multi-layered sarcasm in other Pauline rhetorical questions. Although lacking the affective positivity of the hortatory subjunctive, and without verbs altogether, Rom 7:7 and Gal 3:21 – '(Is) the law sin?' and '(Is) the law opposed to God's promises?' respectively – share affinities to our other examples.[39] In First Corinthians, it is also possible that Paul uses the question, 'Should I take the parts of Christ and stick them in a prostitute?' (ἄρας οὖν τὰ μέλη τοῦ Χριστοῦ ποιήσω πόρνης μέλη; 1 Cor 6:15) to communicate sarcastically the metamessage 'this absurd, offensive question should never have been asked in the first place'.

A sarcastic reading of the rhetorical questions discussed above may appear to conflict with assessments of Paul's didactic aims in these passages. Stowers argues that Paul's interlocutor in the objection-response sections of Romans is a hypothetical member of

---

[38] On the deliberative subjunctive as expressing uncertainty, see Boas et al. 2019, §34.8. For comparable rhetorical questions negated by *mē genoito* in Epictetus that may also be sarcastic, see *Diss.* 1.2.35–36; 1.5.10; 1.11.23–24; 3.1.44.

[39] Cf. Epictetus, *Diss.* 1.12.10.

his congregation posing legitimate questions and seeking to learn.[40] Moo writes that, 'Paul's question-and-answer style in Romans is pedagogical rather than polemical in orientation'.[41] One must, however, avoid creating a false dichotomy between pedagogy and tendentious rhetoric.

King's citation of a painting from Pompeii that depicts a student 'being stripped, restrained by two other students, and whipped by the schoolmaster' is a good reminder that didactic environments did not solely consist of cordial discussion.[42] Even Jesus was known for calling out the stupidity of his students (e.g. Matt 15:16). For Paul's rhetoric to involve a measure of intensity, a sense of absurdity, and elements of sarcasm and mockery does not therefore suggest that his purpose is not didactic. It is also worth noticing, especially considering the prevalence of strong language directed at the Galatians that we observed in the previous chapter, that Paul's sarcasm in these rhetorical questions is not directed at his audience. The Romans observe Paul being sarcastic with hypothetical opponents,[43] and therefore need not feel personally targeted at any point, especially if they agree with Paul.

5.3   Sarcasm Elsewhere in Diatribe-like Passages

Beyond the rhetorical questions discussed, we find sarcasm elsewhere in Paul's performance of the conversation between himself and his hypothetical interlocutor. While our conception of voice will be less essential to the recognition of sarcasm in these passages, it will still be helpful to keep in mind throughout that Paul is playing both roles.

5.3.1   Romans 2:17–20

Εἰ δὲ σὺ Ἰουδαῖος ἐπονομάζῃ καὶ ἐπαναπαύῃ νόμῳ καὶ καυχᾶσαι ἐν θεῷ καὶ γινώσκεις τὸ θέλημα καὶ δοκιμάζεις τὰ διαφέροντα κατηχούμενος ἐκ τοῦ νόμου, πέποιθάς τε σεαυτὸν ὁδηγὸν εἶναι τυφλῶν, φῶς τῶν ἐν σκότει, παιδευτὴν ἀφρόνων, διδάσκαλον νηπίων, ἔχοντα τὴν μόρφωσιν τῆς γνώσεως καὶ τῆς ἀληθείας ἐν τῷ νόμῳ...

---

[40] Stowers 1981, 152–53. For my caution on making specific reconstructions of 'interlocutor's' identity, see §5.3.1.1.
[41] Moo 1996, 356; cf. Jewett 2007, 25–27, 394–95.
[42] See King 2018, 125–27.
[43] Or, potentially, absent third parties (3:8).

But if you call yourself a Jew and take comfort in the law
and boast in God and know The Will and discern what is
best – being taught direct from the law – and you're convinced that you're a Guide for the blind, a Light for those
in darkness, Educator of the Ignorant, Teacher of Infants,
possessing the essence of knowledge and of truth in the law...

This passage has become a hotbed for debate about the identity of
Paul's hypothetical interlocutor. While understanding how these
verses work as sarcasm will be our primary concern, we will also
have something to bring to this larger discussion.

Ironic interpretations of 2:17–20 are nothing new. Origen writes,
'We need to realize, however, that the Apostle is using irony when he
addresses these things to the Jews [*Sciendum tamen est haec apostolum
per ironiam dicere ad Iudaeos*]. For it is impossible to believe that
those who truly rest in the law ... could do the things which are
enumerated [in 2:21–24].' (*Comm.Rom.* 2.11.12 [Scheck]). Chrysostom
takes Paul as 'indirectly mocking' his interlocutor in 2:17 (ἠρέμα ...
σκώπτειν)[44] and catches the undertones of dispraise throughout 2:19–20
(*Epist.Rom.* pp. 432–33 [homily 6]; cf. NPNF vol.11, p. 666).

Modern commentators too have recognized irony in 2:17–20.
Moo writes, 'There is some measure of irony in the way Paul
presents these privileges as items in which the Jew boasts ... the
irony emerges in the piling up of these distinctives and in the antici-
pation of the point that will be made in vv. 21–24.'[45] However, in
previous scholarship, irony usually receives only brief mention. The
reader is left wondering whether Paul is intentionally, or uninten-
tionally, drawing our attention to an ironic situation, or whether he
may be engaging in a more pointed form of verbal irony.

Paul's description of his interlocutor in 2:17–20 satisfies both the
echoic and pretence accounts of verbal irony (Chapter 1, §§1.2.3,
1.2.4). That Paul is echoing his interlocutor in 2:17–20 is self-evident.
Paul's discussion partner is fictitious; a fiction constructed by the
statements Paul makes about the hypothetical interlocuter – granting
of course that this characterization need not be fully fleshed-out or

[44] ἠρέμα can indicate an aside or 'stage whisper' (LSJ, s.v. 'ἠρέμα') and can be
glossed: '1. gently, 2. indirectly, 3. gradually' (Lampe, s.v. 'ἠρέμα').
[45] Moo 1996, 159. Other exegetes who see irony in 2:17–20 include Gifford 1886,
78; Murray 1967, 81; Cranfield 1975, 1:164; Thorsteinsson 2003, 208; Jewett 2007,
223. Linss designates 2:17–23 as sarcastic, though without supporting argumentation
(1998, 196–97).

always consistent. Thus, if Paul says that the hypothetical interlocutor calls himself a Jew (Ἰουδαῖος ἐπονομάζῃ), or considers himself (πέποιθάς ... σεαυτόν) a guide for the blind, a light to those in darkness, etc., he does, and in characterizing him thus Paul simultaneously creates and makes reference to his perspective. Furthermore, the designations Paul uses in 2:17–20 can be traced back to Jewish literature,[46] and therefore could be appropriated seriously in other contexts. While the echoic element of 2:17–20 is clear, we must turn to evidence of hyperbole to uncover the way Paul disassociates himself from the statements he echoes.

In 2:17–20, Paul's description of his interlocutor is exaggerated both in terms of its content and style. The section is heavy with repetition, as Paul applies no less than ten ostensibly positive appellations to his interlocutor. Between these, Paul's plodding use of καί ('and') four times in 2:17–18 creates an impression of repetitiveness, that his interlocutor's credentials go on and on pretentiously and unnecessarily.[47] He also creates a sense of flow using alliteration and wordplay.[48] The way Paul adjusts his cadence throughout these verses also creates emphasis in different ways. Longer phrases such as 'you discern what is best – being taught direct from the law' (δοκιμάζεις τὰ διαφέροντα κατηχούμενος ἐκ τοῦ νόμου) and 'possessing the essence of knowledge and of truth in the law' (ἔχοντα τὴν μόρφωσιν τῆς γνώσεως καὶ τῆς ἀληθείας ἐν τῷ νόμῳ) convey a sense of wordiness and pretension. These are juxtaposed with denser lists of epithets – 'a Light for those in darkness, Educator of the Ignorant, Teacher of Infants' (φῶς τῶν ἐν σκότει, παιδευτὴν ἀφρόνων, διδάσκαλον νηπίων) – that increase the pace and lend to the impression that Paul's interlocutor's list of qualifications has carried on overlong. These stylistic features coincide well with the means of indicating sarcasm through exaggerated formality previously discussed (Chapter 3, §3.2.2).

Paul's repetitious and exaggerative characterization of his interlocutor also signals the section as sustained pretence. Exaggeration is a common means of indicating insincerity, which is a major component of pretending in general, and sarcastic pretence specifically.[49] Paul also employs terms capable of expressing the message 'you

[46] Dunn 1988, 109–13; Fitzmyer 1993, 316–17.
[47] Cf. Chapter 3, §3.1.2.1.
[48] *eponomazē kai epanapauē vomō kai kauchasai*; *dokimazeis ta diapheronta* (ἐπονομάζῃ καὶ ἐπαναπαύῃ νόμῳ καὶ καυχᾶσαι; δοκιμάζεις τὰ διαφέροντα).
[49] Cf. Haiman 1998, 25–26, 34–35, 45.

consider yourself to be *x*', while allowing the implication, 'however, you are not'. (ἐπονομάζῃ, καυχᾶσαι, πέποιθας ... σεαυτὸν, ἔχοντα τὴν μόρφωσιν). Paul performs praise in an exaggerated manner, and with language flexible enough for him to implicitly communicate the insincerity of his performance – along with a negative evaluation of his interlocutor.

As is the case with much ancient sarcasm, Paul does not leave his sarcastic pretence implicit, but will end his performance by 'breaking the fourth wall', so to speak, and providing his literal evaluation of his interlocutor (cf. Chapter 3, §3.1.1.4). In 2:21–24 Paul uses a series of rhetorical questions to highlight the hypocrisy and situational irony present in the rift between his interlocutor's self-presentation and actions. 'Since you're the one out teaching others, do you teach yourself? You preach, "Thou shalt not steal", but don't *you* steal?' (2:21). This series of rhetorical questions makes the dispraise communicated implicitly through sarcasm in 2:17–20 more explicit.

With Paul's characterization of his interlocutor qualifying as ironic by both the echoic and pretence accounts of irony, there is much to commend a sarcastic reading of Rom 2:17–20. But there is one line of objection worth addressing. Nygren writes that, in 2:17–20, irony 'is not Paul's intention. The special status of the Jews ... he does not consider as something unimportant or paltry about which one might speak ironically.'[50] For Nygren, an ironic interpretation undermines Paul's intention to lay out starkly the 'contrast which he draws between knowing the law and keeping the law'.[51] From this standpoint, irony and a Pauline acceptance of legitimate Jewish advantages are mutually exclusive interpretive options.

We may address this objection by briefly clarifying the implications of a sarcastic reading. As we learned in the Parable of the Disgruntled Undergraduate (Chapter 1, §1.2.2), sarcastic statements are not always factually untrue. Paul's use of sarcasm need not imply that those markers of Jewish 'special status' that he lists in 2:17–20 do not legitimately apply to the Jewish people. Paul's use of sarcasm in 2:17–20 functions as polemic and characterizes his hypothetical interlocutor negatively. It should not be read as a statement of Paul's opinion of Jews in general.[52]

---

[50] Nygren 1952, 131. Followed by Fitzmyer 1993, 315; cf. Longenecker 2016, 303.
[51] Nygren 1952, 131.
[52] Novenson notes significant differences between Paul's characterization of the interlocutor in 2:17–29 and the Jewish people in Romans 9–11 (2016, 160–62).

5.3.1.1   *The Debate over Paul's Interlocutor: a Jew or a So-called Jew?*

Having spoken of the extent to which Paul accepts the 'Jewish advantages' enumerated in 2:17–20, we now discuss a trend in scholarship toward viewing Paul as not addressing Jews here at all, hypothetical or otherwise. Thorsteinsson argues that Paul dialogues with the same interlocutor in 2:1–5 and 2:17–29, and throughout Romans 2–11.[53] He characterizes this interlocutor as a potential Gentile proselyte 'who calls himself, or wants to call himself, a Jew'.[54] Thiessen develops this thesis further, arguing that this Judaizing Gentile interlocutor has undergone circumcision and 'believes that he has become a Jew'.[55] It will not be my aim here to resolve the debate over the identity of Paul's interlocutor, but instead to show areas in which my analysis suggests interpretive caution.

Thorsteinsson highlights the fact that Paul does not explicitly say that he is addressing a Jew, only someone 'who calls himself, or wants to call himself, a Ἰουδαῖος [*Ioudaios*, "Jew"]'.[56] He argues that there were situations in which Gentiles could be referred to as *Ioudaioi* (Ἰουδαῖοι), and that this is the case with Paul's interlocutor in Rom 2:17.[57] Thiessen argues that Paul disputes his Gentile interlocutor's claim to Jewishness, which he sees as a designation that Paul reserves only for ethnic Jews.[58]

I would caution against reading too much into *Ioudaios eponomazē* (Ἰουδαῖος ἐπονομάζῃ). 'If you call yourself a Jew' could refer to an ethnic Jew or to a Gentile who considers himself a Jew. In the sarcastic reading of 2:17–20 argued above, Paul negatively evaluates his hypothetical interlocutor's claim to markers of Jewish advantage, then characterizes him as a hypocrite (2:21–24). But we have also established that a sarcastic interpretation does not necessarily mean that Paul denies his interlocutor the qualities listed. 'You call yourself a Jew' need not imply, 'But you're not a Jew.' Any positive quality can serve as the basis for sarcasm,[59] and Paul certainly considers Jewish identity worth boasting about in certain

---

[53] Thorsteinsson 2003, 145–50, 159–64.
[54] Ibid. 204, see 188–204.
[55] Thiessen 2016, 59, see 54–59.
[56] Thorsteinsson 2003, 198.
[57] See ibid., 197–204.
[58] Thiessen 2016, 55–59, 70–71.
[59] Haiman 1998, 24.

contexts (2 Cor 11:22). There is no reason therefore that Paul cannot be sarcastic about a hypothetical Jewish interlocutor's claim to the positive qualities attached to his ethnic identity and do so without disputing that ethnic identity.[60] At the same time, my reading also does not rule out the possibility of a Judaizing Gentile interlocutor who calls himself a Jew. *Ioudaios eponomazē* leaves both options open.

If, as I argue, the distinction between Paul's voice and his interlocutor's is less clear than scholarship has suggested, we should also expect less certainty in our attempts to characterize this hypothetical interlocutor. The more detailed we are in our characterization, the more we run the risk of creating a more fully fleshed-out interlocutor than Paul himself does. Therefore, in addition to the possibility of a Jewish or Gentile interlocutor, we should also consider the possibility that Paul is not being ethnically specific at all times. In 2:1 Paul is at minimum addressing a human who judges others (ὦ ἄνθρωπε πᾶς ὁ κρίνων). This character may remain the same or be developed further by the time he is referred to as one who calls himself a Jew in 2:17, a designation that could encompass Judaizing Gentile and ethnic Jew alike.[61]

Taking the informality and imprecision of diatribe into account means viewing Paul's interlocutor as an *ad hoc* construction. There is no reason to presume detail or consistency in characterization. This means that the interlocutors described by scholars on both sides of the identity debate are likely to be well fleshed out. A greater breadth of possibilities that allows for the presence of ambiguities and inconsistencies needs to be considered for future scholarship to do justice to the lively performance of ancient diatribe.

5.3.2   Sarcastic Concession: 11:19–20

ἐρεῖς οὖν· ἐξεκλάσθησαν κλάδοι ἵνα ἐγὼ ἐγκεντρισθῶ. καλῶς· τῇ ἀπιστίᾳ ἐξεκλάσθησαν, σὺ δὲ τῇ πίστει ἕστηκας.
So then you'll say: Other branches got cut off so I could be grafted in! Congrats. They were cut off for their unbelief; but you got your place by faith.

---

[60] For example, noting my aversion to cold while visiting my family in Canada, one of my brothers may tease me with a comment like, 'And you call yourself Canadian!' without meaning to contest my citizenship or suggest that I have ceased to be Canadian in any meaningful way.
[61] See King 2018, 238–51, who argues for an ethnically unspecific interlocutor.

Stowers classifies Rom 11:17–24 as diatribe, with Paul's imaginary interlocutor personified as a wild olive branch, and symbolic of the Gentiles.[62] Paul characterizes this conversation partner as arrogant, prone to boasting over those less advantaged.[63] While I agree with this characterization, it should be stressed again that Paul does not create an entirely separate persona. There is no change of speakers, but instead Paul anticipates what his 'interlocutor' is going to say. 'You will say' (ἐρεῖς οὖν), distances Paul from the content of the next phrase – it is not his opinion – but is still spoken by Paul.[64] In this way 11:19–20 well illustrates what I have argued concerning voice in dialogical passages throughout Romans.

The egoistic pride that Paul attributes to his hypothetical interlocutor comes to the forefront in 11:19, as Paul depicts his interlocutor as ready to assert his superiority over the Jews who were 'cut off' so that the Gentiles might take their place among God's chosen. In 11:20 Paul counters this opinion with 'admonishing imperatives',[65] before explaining in more detail the error he has stated as his interlocutor (11:21–22). This short dialogue-like exchange turns on Paul's use of *kalōs* (καλῶς, here translated 'congrats', 11:20), with the exclamation bridging the assertion of Gentile superiority and Paul's rebuttal.

A minority of commentators hear a note of irony in Paul's 'well done'. Unfortunately, this position receives little argumentation beyond assertions such as Michel's: 'Paul's riposte in 11:20 begins with an ironic *kalōs*.'[66] It would be helpful indeed to hear more specifically what Morris means in saying that Paul 'concedes the point, though with some irony'.[67] Is Paul's concession entirely feigned? Sincere? Or only partially so?

The majority of interpreters follow either of these latter two options. Moo characterizes 11:20 as 'qualified agreement', with Paul acknowledging that the absence of the Jews has allowed for the inclusion of the Gentiles, but also keen to stress the point that the

---

[62] Stowers 1981, 99–100.

[63] See ibid. 114–15; Morris 1988, 415–16; Moo 1996, 705.

[64] Paul's use of the future makes this clear. The interlocutor has not spoken yet, therefore it must still be Paul.

[65] Stowers 1981, 99–100.

[66] 'Die Entgegnung des Paulus in **V20** beginnt mit einem ironischen καλῶς.' (Michel 1978, 351). Cf. Zahn 1910, 518; Lagrange 1931, 281; Manson 1962, 949; Schmidt 1963, 196.

[67] Morris 1988, 414.

process of Gentile inclusion is ultimately intended to stimulate the re-ingrafting of the Jews.[68] Still others see Paul's use of *kalōs* as conceding the point to his interlocutor: 'Paul grants the fact; but he denies the inference drawn from it.'[69] Jewett understands Paul as constructing for his interlocutor a clever retort that turns Paul's own language back on him. This makes Paul's concession a witty piece of self-deprecation: 'The audience would enjoy Paul's admission that a sharp riposte was made at his own expense by such an undiscerning Christian blockhead.'[70]

While many have taken sides on whether Paul's response to the assertion, 'Other branches got cut off so I could be grafted in!' includes irony, very little has been said in defence of these positions beyond assertions and brief assessments of the extent to which the objection of Paul's interlocutor could be seen as true in some sense. We shall therefore look more closely at the evidence for a sarcastic reading.

In terms of semantics, one requires little time to collect diverse uses of *kalōs*, both sarcastic and otherwise. Jewett cites several classical texts employing *kalōs* as an unreserved or partial concession.[71] The New Testament furnishes us with relevant sarcastic 'well dones' (Mark 7:9 [see Chapter 3, §3.1.2.2]; Jas 2:19[72]). Paul elsewhere makes sarcastic comments linguistically similar to Rom 11:20 (2 Cor 11:4, 19; Chapter 7, §§7.2.2.1, 7.2.3). While noting Paul's own use is helpful, for our purpose there is little to be gained from citing varied uses of *kalōs*. The term is clearly versatile, and, like any positive statement, can be used sincerely or sarcastically.

When we broaden our search from analogous linguistic use to analogous situations, we find evidence that sarcasm is a common response to the sort of rhetorical context in which Paul places himself in Rom 11:17–24. We have seen the prevalence of sarcastic concessions in ancient Greek texts, as well as the use of a sarcastic 'well done' (*eu ge*, εὖ γε) to mock-encourage one's opponents.[73] It is also telling that here we have the juxtaposition of ostensibly positive

---

[68] Moo 1996, 705. Others from the 'qualified agreement' camp include Dunn 1988, 2:663; Käsemann 1980, 310; Schreiner 1998, 607.

[69] Godet 1883, 407. Cf. Wilckens 1978, 2:247; Siegert 1985, 169; Barrett 1991, 203.

[70] Jewett 2007, 687.

[71] Ibid. 687n.212–13.

[72] James 2:19 is structurally very similar to Rom 11:19–20. Several of the arguments made below for a sarcastic reading of the latter will also apply to the former.

[73] Chapter 3, §§3.2.1, 3.2.3.

language (*kalōs*) with a literal, negative evaluation of the 'interlocutor's' boastful assertion immediately following (τῇ ἀπιστίᾳ ἐξεκλάσθησαν, σύ δὲ τῇ πίστει ἕστηκας). 'They were broken off because they broke faith, but you have your place because of faith' communicates negative evaluation insofar as it denies the validity of the attitude underlying the previous assertion (ἐξεκλάσθησαν κλάδοι ἵνα ἐγὼ ἐγκεντρισθῶ). One may paraphrase as follows: 'You boast X. Great. X is nothing to boast about.' This is one of the most common ways of signalling sarcasm in ancient Greek texts.[74] With the combination of these factors present, it is not difficult to see why Paul might employ a sarcastic concession in Rom 11:19–20. Indeed, If Jewett is correct that Paul hopes to display wit in this exchange, sarcasm would achieve this end nicely.[75]

Much of the reluctance to reading irony or sarcasm in these verses comes from the fact that there is a sense in which the assertion, 'Branches were broken off so that I might be grafted in' is true (11:19 NRSV). Again, as 'The Parable of the Disgruntled Undergraduate' reminds us, sarcastic statements need not be counterfactual (Chapter 1, §1.2.2). Paul can react sarcastically to this assertion independent of its validity. Paul's sarcastic *kalōs* implies a negative evaluation of the arrogance with which he characterizes his interlocutor for claiming privileged status *vis-à-vis* the Jews. He then spends 11:20–24 not only correcting his conversation partner's assessment of the facts – the logistics and rationale for the Jews' standing with respect to the vine metaphor – but also directly warning against the sort of arrogance that he represents in his interlocutor (μὴ ὑψηλὰ φρόνει, ἀλλὰ φοβοῦ, 11:20). In this way, the attitudes underlying different positions on Gentile inclusion take a significant role in the overall discussion. Paul uses sarcasm to make an arrogant self-satisfaction in what appears to be the privileging of Gentile over Jew appear foolish, and in doing so invites his audience to reject this attitude.

5.4 Romans 13:1–7: 'Submit' to 'Authorities'?

We now leave diatribe behind for a moment to discuss the role of irony in scholarship on Romans 13. Paul's seemingly unqualified

---

[74] Chapter 3, §3.1.1.4.
[75] See Jewett 2007, 687.

endorsement of the political powers-that-be in 13:1–7 has sparked many lines of interpretation, leading Moo to remark: 'It is only a slight exaggeration to say that the history of the interpretation of Rom. 13:1–7 is the history of attempts to avoid what seems to be its plain meaning.'[76] Scholarly work-arounds include attempts to dismiss these verses altogether as an interpolation or construals of the pericope's 'authorities' as angelic or demonic powers,[77] although neither of these perspectives has taken hold in contemporary scholarship.

More recently, several scholars have advanced subversive readings of Rom 13:1–7 that marshal elements of resistance hidden beneath Paul's apparently complicit rhetoric. This work draws on theory from post-colonial studies, which distinguishes between the public and hidden 'scripts' found in the discourse of the colonized. From this perspective, Paul's words about the government are designed have a legitimately flattering effect on those in power. However, behind this show of compliance, those within Paul's colonized in-group may detect a 'hidden script' containing a subtle parody of the colonizer. While far from outright rebellion, this covert speech constitutes a form of resistance to imperial domination.[78]

Carter also suggests a subversive reading of Rom 13:1–7, although through the lens of irony rather than post-colonialism. Carter depicts Rom 13:1–7 as a covert critique of Rome in which Paul does not recommend rebellion, but rather presents submission to the authorities as a way to 'overcome evil with good' (as in Rom 12:21).[79] To bring about this ironic reversal in meaning, Carter draws heavily on Quintilian, seeing Paul as 'blaming through apparent praise'.[80] Although Carter himself does not make the connection, Quintilian associates this definition with a specific sort of irony: sarcasm (*Inst.* 8.6.55–57; cf. Chapter.1, §1.1.2). Since Carter's ironic reinterpretation of Romans 13 is made in part with reference to ancient

---

[76] Moo 1996, 806.

[77] For summaries of scholarship on Rom 13:1–7, including these perspectives, see Jewett 2007, 782–88; Marshall 2008, 160–62.

[78] Herzog 1994, 339–42, 351–60; Elliott 2004, 117–22; Wan 2008, 173–84; Lim 2015, 1–9. Employing Bhabha's concept of hybridity, Marshall blurs the lines between subversion and compliance in the 'hidden scripts' perspective, viewing Paul's (legitimate) endorsement of submission in Rom 13:1–7 as part of the flux between affiliation and resistance both typical of the colonized subject and observable throughout Paul (2008, 162–74). For a recent non-subversive reading, see Bertschmann 2014, 126–70.

[79] Carter 2004, 226–28.

[80] Ibid. 213–14; Quintilian, *Inst.* 8.6.55.

discussion of sarcasm, we will assess his arguments in more detail, along with other evidence of a 'hidden script'.[81] Carter reconstructs a historical situation in which Paul's lower-status Roman audience, not to mention Paul himself, would be no strangers to mistreatment at the hands of the Roman authorities. As a result, they would recognize something amiss in Paul's portrayal of the imperial government as succeeding in the righteous execution of justice (Rom 13:3–4).[82] This incongruity between Paul's flattering depiction of the political authorities and the realities of life under Roman rule forms a key signal of irony.[83]

While Paul and the Roman church were clearly subordinates to Rome, Jewett argues that the Roman church would have contained a number of individuals whose professions set them with the greater Roman administrative machine. Thus, the opening verses of Romans 13 'provide a significant sanction for their activities', legitimizing the occupations of some members of the Roman congregation.[84] While Jewett recognizes the distance between Paul's apparently idealistic depiction of Rome and its actual activities, he also grounds Paul's endorsement of submission in missional concerns. Being keen to preach in Spain, Paul is careful not to ruffle any feathers in Rome.[85]

Carter's identification of incongruity between Paul's description of the government's actions and the Roman church's experience of mistreatment as supporting an ironic interpretation of 13:1–7 is therefore dependent on how one reconstructs the underlying historical situation. If Carter's persecution-narrative holds, then the case for irony has a reasonable foundation. If, however, other concerns such as those outlined by Jewett may be found in Paul's rhetoric, irony becomes less likely. Leaving the question of social situation presently unresolved, it will be useful to seek evidence of sarcasm more grounded in the text of Romans itself.

---

[81] Writing independently of Carter, Hurley also argues for irony in Rom 13:1–7. The foundation of Hurley's argument is that θεός in 13:1–7 is an ironic reference to Nero rather than a reference to the God of Israel (2006, 49–53). Because I find this argument unconvincing, as I suspect most exegetes would, we will focus primarily on Carter's work in our analysis of Rom 13:1–7.

[82] Carter 2004, 210–12, 215–17, 219–22; cf. Hurley 2006, 55–59. Carter also notes Paul's own clashes with the authorities, which included imprisonments and beatings (2004, 212).

[83] Ibid. 215–17.

[84] Jewett 2007, 792, 794.

[85] Ibid. 793–94.

Linguistically speaking, the strongest evidence for sarcasm in Rom
13:1–7 lies in potential hyperbole. Paul begins this section with the
epithet *exousiais hyperechousais* (ἐξουσίαις ὑπερεχούσαις, 'governing
authorities', 13:1 NRSV). This particular combination, with its
doubling of terms for authority and *hyper*-prefix, is a bit of an odd
one and at least seems to have an element of redundancy.[86] This
epithet could be explained as hyperbole, reminiscent of Paul's 'very-
super apostles' (*hyperlian apostolōn*, ὑπερλίαν ἀποστόλων, 2 Cor 11:5;
12:11; Chapter 7, §7.2.2.2). Paul goes on to describe these authorities
as 'God's servant(s)' (*theou diakonos*, θεοῦ διάκονος) twice (13:4), the
fore-placement of *theou* emphasizing the divine authorization of
political 'service'. When considered with the description of tax collectors as 'ministers of God' (*leitourgoi theou*, λειτουργοὶ θεοῦ) in
13:6, these appellations could create an air of overstatement, especially if the Romans' experience of these 'ministers' was overwhelm-
ingly negative. While Carter acknowledges that *leitourgoi* can simply
indicate public servants,[87] he argues that the pairing of the term with
theou brings out its cultic resonance, creating a strong, ironic contrast with the dishonest reputations of tax collectors.[88] Furthermore,
the intensity of the commitment and devotion implied by the term
proskarterountes (προσκαρτεροῦντες) could also be hyperbolic (13:6).

As was the case with the political situation, each piece of evidence
for hyperbole can be read in different ways: either as overstatement
or as technical, if somewhat laudatory, statement. Wan sees the use
of terms that allow for double-meaning as providing evidence for
covert subversion.[89] However, when one sets these glimpses of
hyperbole against the seemingly straightforward argumentation of
Rom 13:1–7, it is difficult to recognize hidden intentions on Paul's
part with much confidence.

In addition to contextual and linguistic evidence, there is also a
sense in which Paul's argumentation subverts the basis of imperial
power. Roman rule is limited by the fact that its leaders are

[86] Cf. Jewett 2007, 787–88. Hurley notes a 'tiering effect' ('effet de hiérarchisation')
created by the juxtaposition of *hyper-/hypo-* prefixes in 13:1 (2006, 49).

[87] Jewett notes that the use of λειτουργοὶ θεοῦ is surprising, and: 'In view of the
historical circumstances, it remains a breathtaking claim.' (2007, 799–800). Moo
acknowledges cultic use but also points out that λειτουργοί was often used 'to denote
public officials of various kinds' (1996, 804). For an example of the latter, see
P. Corn. 52.

[88] Carter 2004, 223–26.

[89] Wan 2008, 174.

subordinated to the authority of God.[90] Establishing Paul's God as responsible for the institution of government undermines the standard imperial narrative, especially insofar as divine honours for the emperor are concerned.[91]

While these points must be granted, it is this very positioning of the imperial authorities under divine purview that makes submission to Rome a compelling argument for Paul's audience.[92] This line of reasoning is explicit in 13:1, which can be paraphrased: 'Submit to the authorities, because God established them.' This rhetoric is hardly subversive.

With certain elements leaning in support of a subversive reading, and much of the pericope apparently arguing for submission to governmental authority in a rather straightforward manner, it is difficult to come down on either side with much certainty. Perhaps what makes Rom 13:1–7 so difficult is that any sarcasm, irony, or 'hidden script' therein would have been intentionally occluded. Those belonging to the outgroup, including the Roman authorities and the modern exegete, are not supposed to pick up on subversive elements.

This potential occlusion calls into question whether Carter's characterization of the passage as irony is the best paradigm for thinking about potential subversion in Rom 13:1–7. The ironist seeks to convey a message – the evaluation behind their literal statement – to their audience, if implicitly (Chapter 1, §1.2.6). What Carter classifies as irony in Romans 13 falls closer to what Haiman describes as the 'put-on'. Unlike sarcasm, put-ons include no clear cue that the speaker means anything other than what they say. Instead, only an initiated subsection of the audience is meant to understand the speaker's real intent.[93] Should this be an accurate description of what Paul is doing in Rom 13:1–7, such a put-on would also have trouble fitting into ancient conceptions of irony. While Carter's analysis of Romans 13 makes much of Quintilian's statement that irony 'is made evident to the understanding either by the delivery, the character of the speaker or the nature of the subject', central to this description of ironic cues is the fact that irony is something

[90] Carter 2004, 219.
[91] See Lim 2015, 5–9; Wan 2008, 177–78; Jewett 2007, 789–90.
[92] Cf. ibid. 790.
[93] Haiman 1998, 18.

readily intelligible (*intelligitur*) to the speaker's audience, including the brunt of the joke (*Inst.* 8.6.54 [Butler] LCL).[94]

What Carter describes as irony, if its presence in Romans could be sufficiently demonstrated, may better fit into a different category of ancient allegory, which Quintilian defines as *aenigma*.[95] These riddles are intentionally obscure statements which, although insiders who share relevant cultural background may know their answers, require explanation for those on the outside (Quintilian, *Inst.* 8.6.52–53).

Overall, with the linguistic and contextual evidence readable from different angles, the modern exegete may be situated at too great a distance to resolve the possibility of subversion in Rom 13:1–7.[96] Categorically speaking, a 'hidden script' is too covert for irony or sarcasm, but the question remains whether there is some degree of enigmatic resistance behind Paul's compliant political rhetoric. While answering such riddles is beyond the scope of a study on Pauline sarcasm, both the complete-affiliation and covert-resistance perspectives are probably too extreme to respect the balance of the evidence. I suspect that Marshall rightly places Paul's situation in between these two: 'Paul is both "in and of" that world, working in relation to its centre from its margins, gathering and deploying its resources in the interest of his own programme, whether that means swimming with or against the current of imperial power in any particular moment.'[97]

5.5   Conclusions

Exploring the use of sarcasm in Romans has led to a rethinking of how authorial voice functions in the dialogical exchanges within diatribe. Whether it is Paul or Epictetus who is engaging in a back-and-forth with a hypothetical interlocutor, it is important to draw a distinction between these passages as dialogical and the conventions of dialogue proper. Ancient dialogue involves a conversation

[94] The examples Quintilian gives of the various species of irony are all quite overt (*Inst.* 8.6.55–56). Of course, certain individuals may misunderstand irony, but the assumption that irony seeks to communicate and be understood underlies both ancient and modern descriptions.
[95] For Quintilian, both irony and *aenigma* are species of allegory (*Inst.* 8.6.44–54).
[96] Especially considering that one of Paul's earliest interpreters, the author of 1 Pet 2:13–17, was not sufficiently on the 'inside' to catch Paul's subversive rhetoric.
[97] Marshall 2008, 174, see 170–74.

between fully distinct characters, at least one of whom is completely separate from the author's persona. In both diatribe and (single-author) epistolography, however, there is only one speaker. When dialogical elements turn up in these genera, the result is something of a hybrid. A single speaker plays both sides of the conversation without fully breaking from their own voice. They may distance themselves from perspectives that they place in the mouth of their hypothetical interlocutors, but this distance never reaches the level of a fully realized, separate persona. While this paradigm adds a layer of ambiguity and complexity to the simpler notion of clearly demarcated dialogue, it better illustrates the liveliness and imprecision of diatribe.

This conception of voice has been the key for understanding the extent to which certain rhetorical questions in Romans can be considered sarcastic. I have argued that Rom 3:8 represents an instance of reported sarcasm. Paul cites someone else's sarcastic criticism of his position. In 6:1–2, 15 Paul's rhetorical questions insincerely deliberate the sarcastic criticisms of his hypothetical interlocutor – that is, Paul pretends to entertain the objection without really entertaining the objection – which Paul states on behalf of his hypothetical interlocutor (who, like in 3:8, is mockingly imitating Paul). The element of sarcasm in this insincere deliberation is slight, as there is a sense in which Paul pretends to give more ground to the objection than he really means to. This use of sarcasm has its closest parallels in the sarcastic use of the dubitative identified in our work on the LXX (Chapter 2, §2.3). But the sarcasm of Rom 6:1, 15 comes through most strongly where we hear the voice of the 'interlocutor', mockingly caricaturing Paul's position with the exhortation 'Let's sin!' – in a manner analogous to the reported sarcasm of 3:8. This blurring of Paul's voice with the voice of the 'interlocutor' accounts for the overlap between statement and question and between deliberation and exhortation that we see in these rhetorical questions.

We have also seen sarcasm elsewhere in diatribe-like passages in Romans (2:17–20; 11:19–20). In both cases, Paul's use of sarcasm characterizes the interlocutor as arrogant and pretentious. These uses of sarcasm have not been well recognized in previous scholarship, potentially because they are not necessarily counterfactual. While past interpreters have shied away from ironic readings on the assumption that they would negate the propositional content of the theologically significant statements in these passages, this is not the case. Paul's sarcasm expresses a negative evaluation of the arrogance with which he characterizes his interlocutor but does not mean that Jews lack the advantages enumerated in 2:17–20 or that Gentiles have not been grafted into the people of God.

The conception of voice in dialogical, diatribe-like texts that I have argued for in this chapter also has implications for scholarship on the identity of Paul's interlocutor in Romans. Without clear distinctions between Paul's voice and the voice of his interlocutor, we cannot assume that Paul has created a consistent, well fleshed-out character for his hypothetical interlocutor. I argue that attempts to use 2:17–20 to determine the ethnic identity of Paul's interlocutor run the risk of creating a characterization more specific than Paul intends. A Jewish, Judaizing Gentile, or ethnically unspecific interlocutor must all be considered as options, along with the possibility of imprecision and inconsistency in characterization from one passage to the next. If the debate over Paul's interlocutor is to move forward, a ground-up rethinking of the interlocutor is needed that takes the more informal conception of voice in diatribe described in this chapter into account.

Surveying the evidence for sarcasm in Romans 13:1–7 has proved ultimately inconclusive. Had Paul intended a counter-imperial 'hidden script' to be visible to his audience, the modern exegete could well be too far from the intended in-group to detect it to a reasonable degree of probability. I also argue that even if such a hidden script were present, it would be too clandestine to qualify as sarcasm, being better described by Haiman's 'put-on' or Quintilian's *aenigma*. By contrast, sarcasm is meant to communicate rather than conceal negative evaluation.[98]

Considering Paul's use of sarcasm in Romans altogether, it is also significant that Paul is never directly sarcastic with his audience. Instead, he is only sarcastic with parties who do not exist – his 'interlocutor' – and also uses sarcasm in representing misreadings of his argument. This is certainly not the case in Galatians or, as we shall see, in the Corinthian correspondence, where Paul is sarcastic with his congregations quite frequently.

---

[98] We have discussed ambiguity, deniability, and *double entendre* in sarcasm, especially regarding Galatians 2. While there would be similarity between these and a 'hidden script' in Rom 13:1–7, negative evaluation meant to be undetectable to one party and discernible to another differs from these uses of sarcasm by an important degree.

Familiarity probably plays a role in this difference. Paul has never met the Roman church and is therefore interested in ingratiating himself to them rather than directly criticizing them. The audience is invited to identify with Paul and enjoy watching him unmask the arrogance and deflate the pretension of his hypothetical conversation partner. The use of sarcasm, absurdity, and sweeping negations in Paul's rhetorical questions may likewise work as a means of engaging his audience.[99]

Comparison to Lucian can help us understand how Paul's stylistic decisions enable him to mitigate the possible offence of sarcasm. Lucian seeks to avoid reprisal for his more controversial uses of sarcasm by placing them in the mouths of characters removed from his authorial voice. This creates distance between Lucian and the satirical voice of his characters. Paul too creates a sort of character, albeit an only partially realized one, in his hypothetical interlocutor. Regardless of whether the interlocutor is sarcastic with Paul or Paul is sarcastic with the interlocutor, the interlocutor always gets the worse of the exchange. In this way Paul deflects sarcasm from his audience onto the interlocutor, not distancing himself from the critical voice, but distancing his audience from his criticism.[100] Paul can therefore be a version of the sarcast-as-sympathetic-character that we saw in Lucian (Chapter 3, §§3.3.1–3.3.2), who decisively and wittily undercuts the arguments of his conversation partner, while minimizing the likelihood of offending his audience. The audience is invited to affiliate with Paul in pointing out the absurdity of other positions and enjoy the lively back-and-forth of the dialogical repartee.

---

[99] See also, for example, Jewett 2007, 221, 394–95, 687.

[100] Thorsteinsson argues that Paul's interlocutor is meant to represent his congregation (2003, 134–50, 231–34). While I suggest caution in characterizing the interlocutor too specifically, Thorsteinsson rightly recognizes the use of the hypothetical interlocutor to avoid directly criticizing the audience (2003, 234; cf. Stowers 1994, 103).

6

SARCASM IN FIRST CORINTHIANS

First Corinthians is varied in its themes, as Paul pieces together responses to different questions and reports. So it comes as no surprise that his use of sarcasm in this letter occurs in several distinct rhetorical and contextual situations. We will begin by seeking out sarcasm in Paul's paradoxical discussion of divine foolishness and worldly wisdom in 1 Cor 1:18–2:5, a discourse within which Holland sees much irony. Next, we will consider 4:8–13. Many scholars consider 4:8 ironic and several also see irony in 4:10. In exegeting the pericope as a whole, I shall agree with the former, but diverge from ironic readings of 4:10, although not drastically. Other potential uses of sarcasm in First Corinthians fall within what scholars have termed the letter's 'Corinthian slogans'. Critical thinking on how closely or loosely these slogans represent the Corinthians' actual words or positions will be necessary to determine which slogans may be considered sarcastic. Finally, we will briefly address the so-called 'gods' of 8:5 before dealing with 11:19, one of the letter's interpretive cruxes, which some scholars have attempted to resolve through ironic readings.

6.1   Irony and the Inversion of Worldly 'Wisdom': First Corinthians 1:18–2:5

In 1 Cor 1:25, Paul writes that 'God's foolishness is wiser than human wisdom, and God's weakness is stronger than human strength' (NRSV). Holland sees Paul as employing irony throughout 1 Cor 1:18–25 to create a stark contrast between divine and human standards, presenting God's perspective as that which the Corinthians should adopt. To accomplish this end Paul sets 'Christ crucified' as the controlling norm against which worldly standards clash ironically.[1]

---

[1] Holland 1997, 242–43; 2000, 131–34.

The idea that God's actions can be described as either 'foolishness' or as the result of divine 'weakness' starkly contrasts the standards of heaven and earth. The ironic reversal of human valuations of worth indicates what is true from God's point of view.[2]

There are certainly elements of paradox here. God's wisdom is foolish from a human perspective but is simultaneously true wisdom that transcends human categories. It is unclear what makes this an 'ironic reversal'. Is it the element of contrast between divine and human standards that is ironic? Or perhaps the insincerity that Paul employs in speaking of God's wisdom as 'foolishness'? Holland also does not specify what sort of irony he sees as operative in this passage. I for one do not find evidence of sarcasm or verbal irony in 1:18–25.

Perhaps there is an argument to be made here for some sort of situational irony. Such an argument would require further critical discussion of the relationship between situational irony and paradox and would also need to address the likelihood that these elements are intended by Paul or whether they are simply products of our interpretation.[3] While this analysis would be an interesting avenue for future research, it departs too far from the aims of this study to be dealt with here. My task will be to clarify where sarcasm plays a role in Paul's allegedly ironic discourse on wisdom and foolishness, and weakness and strength. As we shall see, this role is relatively minor.

6.1.1 Implicit vs Explicit Criticism: 2:1–5 (with 1:27–28)

In 2:1–5 Paul uses sarcasm in passing to dismiss worldly standards and rhetorical skill. Proclaiming Christ at Corinth, Paul avoided using 'a superabundance of speech or "wisdom"' (*hyperochēn logou ē sophias*, ὑπεροχὴν λόγου ἢ σοφίας, 2:1). In this context, 'speech' (*logos*) indicates that Paul refers to professional rhetoric specifically.[4] From 1:18–25, we are already aware that the 'wisdom' of 2:1 can be nothing more than 'the wisdom of the world' (*tēn sophian tou kosmou*, τὴν σοφίαν τοῦ κόσμου, 1:20 NRSV), which God has made foolish (cf. 2:5). Paul therefore uses the ostensibly positive term

---

[2] Holland 2000, 133–34.
[3] See Schellenberg 2013, 174.
[4] See Collins 1999, 118; Fitzmyer 2008, 171–72; Thiselton 2000, 208–9.

'wisdom' (*sophia*, σοφία) sarcastically here to communicate the same negative evaluation that he ascribed beforehand to worldly wisdom. Paul's use of *kath' hyperochēn* (καθ' ὑπεροχήν, 'superabundance') also supports a sarcastic reading, as an indication of insincerity through hyperbole. *hyperochē* is a term of intensification. It can denote '*excess*' (comparable to *hyperbolē*/ὑπερβολή) or '*prominence*'. It is often used in relation to social status, and takes on a positive resonance in such cases, indicating people in positions of eminence or authority (LSJ, s.v. 'ὑπεροχή', cf. 1 Tim 2:2). LXX usage follows this pattern, with *hyperochē* carrying positive evaluation when describing the social level of esteemed persons (2 Macc 3:11; 15:13) but expressing negativity when emphasizing a negative quality (2 Macc 13:6). Considering this baseline emphatic function, *hyperochēn logou* (ὑπεροχὴν λόγου) on its own could refer sarcastically to 'impressive rhetoric' or criticize 'excessive rhetoric' by conveying literal negative evaluation. However, the fact that hyperochē modifies both logos and *sophia*,[5] the latter of which is normally a positive term, suggests that a sarcastic reading of the whole is to be preferred. The translation 'superabundance of speech or "wisdom"' captures both the emphatic function of *hyperochē* and conveys the negative evaluation implied in Paul's sarcasm, namely, that such a show of rhetoric is ostentatious.

Overall, Paul's sarcasm in 2:1 is not a sustained critique, but more of a passing dismissal that succinctly implies that the rhetorical aptitude Paul disavowed in Corinth was not worth his time in the first place, being a part of the system of worldly wisdom that God has made foolish (1:20).

As a methodological exercise, it will be helpful to clarify why I consider *hyperochēn logou ē sophias* (ὑπεροχὴν λόγου ἢ σοφίας) to be sarcastic but not 'the wisdom of the world' (*tēn sophian tou kosmou*, τὴν σοφίαν τοῦ κόσμου, 1:20 NRSV). In constructing our working definition of sarcasm, I agreed with Bailin that implicitness is necessary to verbal irony. In verbal irony 'the speaker's actual attitude is not directly stated by the speaker in the immediate context'.[6] I also argued for a generous interpretation of 'immediate context' that allows for examples such as 'Good one! [Pause] Not!' and Rom 6:1–2a to be properly considered sarcastic (Chapter 1, §1.2.6; Chapter 5, §5.2.2). However, *tēn sophian tou kosmou* stretches

---

[5] Cf. Chapter 3, §3.1.2.1.
[6] Bailin 2015, 112.

the boundaries of what may be reasonably termed 'implicit'. Here the genitive and its antecedent form a single semantic unit, and as such the negative evaluation associated with 'the world' applies to the whole.[7] Therefore while both *hyperochēn logou ē sophias* ('a superabundance of speech or "wisdom"') and *tēn sophian tou kosmou* communicate negative evaluation, the former does so implicitly through sarcasm and the latter explicitly.[8]

This understanding of implicitness also suggests that we would be right to read sarcasm in 2:4, but not in 2:5. In 2:4 Paul denies again the use of *peithoi[s] sophias* [*logois*] (πειθοῖ[ς] σοφίας [λόγοις], 'convincing words of "wisdom"') in his preaching. Although the textual difficulties here are considerable, fortunately for our purposes, some sort of 'persuasive wisdom' remains regardless of how the text is sorted out.[9] As in 2:1, this is none other than the so-called 'wisdom' of sophistry,[10] which Paul will term 'human wisdom' (*sophia anthrōpōn*, σοφία ἀνθρώπων) in the next verse (2:5 NRSV). Thus, we have sarcasm in 2:4 in the communication of negative affect through ostensibly positive words. 2:5 however, does not meet Bailin's requirement for implicitness. Paul has already established human wisdom as a negative category (1:17–25, especially 1:25), so here *sophia anthrōpōn* is straightforwardly negative, just like *sophian tou kosmou* (1:20).[11]

Also on the basis of this explicit/implicit distinction, we may detect sarcasm earlier in the passage as well. Paul explains the fact that among the Corinthians there are few counted among the clever or powerful (1:26) by stating, 'but God chose the foolish things of the world to shame the wise (ἵνα καταισχύνῃ τοὺς σοφούς), and God chose the weak things of the world to shame the strong (ἵνα

---

[7] The boundaries between implicit and explicit are subjective and cannot always be drawn along grammatical lines. Syntax can also play a determinative role. For example, something like 'the wonderful and resplendent wisdom of this wicked world' (τὴν σοφίαν θαυμασίαν καὶ λαμπράν τοῦ τούτου τοῦ πονηροῦ κόσμου) would allow for sufficient distance between the positive and negative affective elements of the broader semantic unit to enable sarcastic pretence.

[8] Other constructions that express negative evaluation but fail the implicitness condition include: 'taught by human wisdom' (διδακτοῖς ἀνθρωπίνης σοφίας, 2:13 NRSV); 'the god of this world' (ὁ θεὸς τοῦ αἰῶνος τούτου, 2 Cor 4:4 NRSV).

[9] For text-critical discussion, see Lietzmann 1931, 11; Conzelmann 1975, 54–55; Collins 1999, 119–20; Thiselton 2000, 215–16.

[10] See Collins 1999, 116, 118; Fee 1987, 94.

[11] Certain manuscript traditions include 'human' (ανθρωπινης/ανθρωπινοις) with the various permutations of *peithoi[s] sophias* [*logois*] (πειθοῖ[ς] σοφίας [λόγοις]) in 2:4 (see NA 28 apparatus). These variants show an awareness of Paul's tone and could represent attempts to make Paul's implicit evaluation explicit.

καταισχύνῃ τὰ ἰσχυρά). . .' (1:27). Paul has already upset the standards of the world, showing their wisdom for foolishness and God's foolishness for true wisdom. Here Paul is not indicating this reversal explicitly, as he did in 1:20 (οὐχὶ ἐμώρανεν ὁ θεὸς τὴν σοφίαν τοῦ κόσμου), but we must infer that when he says, 'the wise' (τοὺς σοφούς), 'the strong' (τὰ ἰσχυρά), and 'the things that are' (τὰ ὄντα, 1:27–28), he means their opposite. These references therefore, unlike 1:20, satisfy Bailin's implicitness condition.

6.1.2   Conclusions: Sarcasm as Passing Dismissal

Some sarcastic statements are sustained critiques woven together to entrap and tear down their victims. But for every one of these more targeted remarks there are at least several offhand uses of sarcasm, such as a passing, deadpan 'Awesome. . .' or 'Brilliant', which tersely express a subtext equivalent to an eyeroll and an exasperated 'whatever'.[12] It is this latter sort that we find in 1 Cor 2:1, 4 and 1:27–28. The critique implied in these cases is not the main point. In 2:1–5, Paul's primary focus is on the christocentric nature of his ministry and the way the empowerment of Christ has driven his activity in Corinth. In making this broader point, Paul sarcastically dismisses the rhetorical showiness (*hyperochēn logou*, ὑπεροχὴν λόγου, 2:1; *peithoi*[*s*] [*logois*], πειθοῖ[ς] [λόγοις], 2:4) that he wishes to disassociate himself from in emphasizing the activity of Christ in his ministry. This sophistry is symptomatic of the world's wisdom, and Paul inverts the normally positive term *sophia* (σοφία) sarcastically in 2:1 and 2:4. He also dismisses *sophia anthrōpōn* (σοφίᾳ ἀνθρώπων) in 2:5, although here Paul's negative evaluation is explicit and therefore not sarcastic. These comments throughout 2:1–5, both sarcastic and sincere, amount to passing dismissals of rhetorical skill, suggesting that this ability is not something the Corinthians should value.

While 1:27–28; 2:1–5 by no means contain Paul's most significant instances of sarcasm, our analysis can push back on a trend in scholarly assessments of Paul's critique in these passages. In an article on 2:4, Lim argues that Paul does not seek to discount professional rhetoric, but instead only censures an overdependence thereon in preaching.[13] Schrage too argues that while Paul's mention of persuasion (πείθω) in 2:4 carries a 'negativer Unterton [negative undertone]'

---

[12] For passing sarcasm in Aristophanes, see *Av.* 176–77, 934; *Eq.* 175; *Ran.* 1154.
[13] Lim 1987, 148–49.

Paul only opposes the misuse and overuse of rhetoric by the sophists rather than rhetoric *per se*.[14] Such claims attempt to reconcile what Paul says about professional rhetoric in 1:27–28; 2:1, 4 with a perspective that views him as trained in and making use of the same.[15]

These qualifications do not quite do justice to the force of Paul's dismissals. Although I have argued that Paul's sarcastic comments within 1:17–2:5 are only peripheral to the main thrust of the discussion, they do provide insight into his attitude. His sarcastic dismissals suggest that Paul finds practitioners of rhetoric and philosophy irritating, and he writes off their claims to *sophia*. Rhetoric (2:1, 4) and philosophy (1:22–23, 27) are parts of a worldly system brought to shame by the wisdom of God, a wisdom the world has taken for foolishness (1:18–25, 27–29).[16]

A degree of tension must remain with reconstructions of a rhetorically educated and appreciative Paul and Paul's comments in 1 Cor 1:17–2:5. Such a Paul could see himself as practising the art of rhetoric 'properly' in contrast to others – it is certainly not uncommon for people to seek to distance themselves from groups to which they belong. But even this more generous reading leaves within Paul an element of hypocrisy (or at least situational irony) in disavowing something which he himself practises. Of course, from a historical standpoint there is nothing problematic about asserting that Paul was inconsistent. However, it may also be worth entertaining the possibility that Paul's dislike of rhetors has more to do with the fact that he does not consider himself to be one (2 Cor 11:6; see Chapter 7, §§7.2.2.2, 7.4), and has experienced certain disadvantages as a result of not belonging among this group.

6.2 Sarcasm and 'the Guiltive': First Corinthians 4:8–13

6.2.1 Sarcasm in 4:8

To the same congregation where 'not many... were wise by human standards, not many were powerful, not many were of noble birth'

---

[14] Schrage 1991, 1:225, 232. This is different from arguing that 'Paul is not anti-intellectual' (Fitzmyer 2008, 148). Paul does not address the role of reason and the intellect in the abstract with his sarcastic quips at the expense of professional rhetors and popular philosophers in 1:27–28; 2:1, 4. On the intellect in Paul, see Bornkamm 1969, 29–46.

[15] See Lim 1987, 137, 148–49; Schrage 1991, 1:225.

[16] For ancient satire on philosophy and rhetoric, see Aristophanes' *Clouds* and Lucian's *Hermotimus, Philosophies for Sale*, and *Symposium* (philosophy), as well as *A Professor of Public Speaking* and *Lexiphanes* (rhetoric).

(1 Cor 1:26 NRSV), Paul will later declare 'Already you have all you want! Already you have become rich! Quite apart from us you have become kings!' (4:8 NRSV). Sim describes 4:8a as 'generally regarded as ironic by biblical scholars'.[17] Indeed, other than 2 Corinthians 10–12, 1 Cor 4:7–14 may be the most treated passage in dedicated studies of irony in Paul.[18]

Several lines of evidence support this ironic reading of 4:8. Plank and others argue that the apparent contradiction between 4:8a ('you have become kings') and 4:8b ('if only you had become kings')[19] suggests irony.[20] Furthermore, 4:8 is set within a 'climate of criticism' that biases the reader to expect negative evaluation,[21] and its words also call back and invert Paul's praise of the Corinthians in 1:4–7.[22]

In terms of identification, there is little to add to past scholarship beyond my agreement that 1 Cor 4:8a is clearly ironic, even sarcastic. Paul's exaggerated, lofty depiction of the Corinthians' attainment is meant precisely to bring them back down to earth.

6.2.2   Issues with Ironic Readings of 4:10

Sim, agreeing with Fee and Barrett, also sees irony in 4:10: 'We are fools for the sake of Christ, but you are [wise] in Christ. We are weak, but you are strong. You are honored, but we are dishonored' ([modified] NRSV). The basis of her interpretation is that Paul echoes the Corinthians' assessment of him rather than his own.[23] They see Paul as weak and themselves as strong, Paul as foolish

---

[17] Sim 2016, 55.

[18] See Plank 1987, 44–51; Holland 1997, 243–45; Sim 2016, 56. For commentators who take 4:8 as ironic or sarcastic, see Weiss 1910, 106; Lietzmann 1931, 19; Barrett 1971, 108–9; Conzelmann 1975, 106; Fee 1987, 172; Schrage 1991, 1:338; Witherington 1995, 136–37; Thiselton 2000, 357–59; Arzt-Grabner et al. 2006, 172; Fitzmyer 2008, 217–18; Ciampa and Rosner 2010, 178.

[19] Both NRSV.

[20] Plank 1987, 45. Cf. Fitzmyer 2008, 218; Thiselton 2000, 357; Sim 2016, 56. Interpreters also point out that Paul's *ophelon* (ὄφελον) construction, grammatically speaking, suggests an unattainable wish (Fee 1987, 174n.45; Thiselton 2000, 357; Fitzmyer 2008, 218; cf. BDF §359).

[21] Plank 1987, 45.

[22] Holland 1997, 244; Plank 1987, 45–46. Others note the presence of rhetorical devices, such as asyndeton (Fee 1987, 172) and hyperbole (Plank 1987, 48).

[23] Sim 2016, 57; cf. Fee 1987, 176; Ciampa and Rosner 2010, 182–83. We must be cautious in reconstructing the Corinthians' assessment of Paul on the basis of 4:10. On mirror-reading ironic statements, see Chapter 1, §1.3.4; Chapter 7, §7.3.1.

and themselves as wise, and Paul parrots this arrogance back to them ironically. For Barrett, Paul's ironic assault on the Corinthians is '*ad hominem*', both 'more subtle' and 'more devastating' than the previous verses.[24] Surely Paul does not consider the Corinthians far wiser, stronger, and more honourable than the apostles, at least not in any sense that really matters. Thus irony, with sarcasm couched in the ostensibly positive terminology, and self-deprecating irony, *asteismos*,[25] that is, in the negative, seems a reasonable reading.[26]

While I will argue that 4:10 is close to sarcasm, there are problems with an ironic reading of the text. Because the verse contains two potential forms of verbal irony, sarcasm ('You are wise in Christ, etc.') and *asteismos* ('We are fools for Christ, etc.'), it will be helpful to treat each form of irony separately to show more clearly where the problem lies.

If 'We are fools for Christ... We are weak... We are dishonoured' is *asteismos*, Paul would be using negative language to imply something positive about himself and his co-workers. His discourse would in some way undercut or invert the negativity associated with foolishness, weakness, and dishonour. This is the opposite of what we find in the surrounding context. In 4:9, which we shall discuss in more detail presently, the apostles are decidedly in last place (ὁ θεὸς ἡμᾶς τοὺς ἀποστόλους ἐσχάτους ἀπέδειξεν), while 4:11–13 emphasize their weakness (πεινῶμεν καὶ διψῶμεν, ἀστατοῦμεν) and dishonour (γυμνιτεύομεν καὶ κολαφιζόμεθα, λοιδορούμενοι, διωκόμενοι, δυσφημούμενοι, ὡς περικαθάρματα τοῦ κόσμου ἐγενήθημεν, πάντων περίψημα ἕως ἄρτι). With Paul so highlighting his weakness in 4:9, 11–13, it would be somewhat out of place for him to imply the insincerity of the self-deprecatory statements in 4:10 through *asteismos*.

The same problem underlies a sarcastic reading of 'You are wise in Christ... You are strong; you are honoured...' Here comparison with the clear sarcasm of 4:8 can be illustrative. We have already noted the way Paul clarifies the sarcasm of 4:8a by contradicting it in 4:8b: 'already you are kings!/I really wish you were kings (implies that they are not kings)...' We have seen this means of communicating sarcasm by juxtaposing it with an immediately following,

[24] Barrett 1971, 110–11.
[25] Chapter 1, §1.1.2; Chapter 3, §3.2.6.
[26] For others who take 4:10 as ironic, see Origen, *Comm. 1 Cor.* 20; Lietzmann 1931, 20; Fitzgerald 1988, 137; Schrage 1991, 1:343; Collins 1999, 184.

contrastive, literal statement time and time again. It is one of the most common signals of sarcasm in ancient Greek and is also typical of Paul (Gal 1:6–7a; 2:6; Rom 2:17–23; 3:8; 6:1–2a, 15; 11:19–20).[27] But this is not what Paul does with 4:10–13. Instead, Paul's following discourse in 4:11–13 presumes the sincerity of 4:10, as Paul goes on to relate his hardships, weakness, and dishonour.[28] Now, sincerity does not mean that 4:10 cannot in some way be exaggerated, facetious, or consist of Paul saying something that he does not really mean in one way or another. And the fact that Paul does not use a common signal of sarcasm does not rule out the possibility that he is being sarcastic.

However, read as irony, 4:10 does not fit the surrounding discourse, which earnestly depicts Paul's suffering and upholds rather than inverts the sentiment that, relatively speaking, Paul has been dishonoured and the Corinthians honoured. Because 4:10, set within its context, does not appear to communicate the implicit inversion of affect necessary to sarcasm or *asteismos*, it is well worth pursuing an alternate reading.

6.2.3   Haiman's 'Guiltive' and 4:9–13

To address these problems, I will lay out how we might read 4:10 as a speech act that Haiman describes as the 'guiltive modality', which is closely related to sarcasm but differs in important ways. This reading avoids the problems of an ironic interpretation and better respects the overall flow of Paul's argument and tone throughout 4:9–13.

6.2.3.1 The Guiltive

Haiman coins the term 'guiltive' to describe a common speech act that comes close but is not quite sarcastic. To illustrate, one might imagine a text message from a hypothetical mother to her son:

> Don't worry if you don't have time to call tomorrow, even if it *is* my birthday, I know you're busy with your academic

---

[27] Chapter 3, §3.1.1.4.

[28] Foolishness/intelligence does not appear to come into play in 4:9, 11–13. If the reference to the apostles as 'fools' (μωροί) in 4:10 relates to the proceeding, it could be that they are exposed as fools in the spectacle of 4:9 – 'intelligent' (φρόνιμοι) then, would function as a convenient term of contrast. If Paul does not mention foolishness/intelligence in 4:9, 11–13, he certainly does not invert these assessments there either.

work at Cambridge, and there's the time difference ...
I only want you to be happy, no sense making a fuss about
your old mother.[29]

Unlike sarcasm, where a speaker communicates their insincerity
implicitly through an ostensibly positive statement, in such guilt trips
'the guilter ... has to sound perfectly sincere'. The guilter's subtext
communicates only their great virtue and (long-)suffering, which they
exaggerate but do not undermine. It is hyperbole, but without insincerity. It is their target who must infer for themselves the absurdity of
the original message on the basis of this exaggeration and other cues
and realize that they ought to feel terrible about themselves.[30] We may
further clarify using our example. Here the original, literal message
may be summarized, 'Don't worry about calling your mother.' The
phrasing of this message communicates the metamessage, or subtext,
'Though I suffer unjustly, I endure.' This subtext is not sarcastic
because it does not communicate a negative evaluation of the other
party. The guilted must infer this for themselves. From the exaggeration present in the phrasing of the original message coupled with its
metamessage, the guilted must themselves infer a further metamessage, namely: 'The original message ("Don't worry about calling your
mother") is absurd', along with the implication 'I should feel terrible
about not calling my mother (so I should call my mother).'

Thus, the guiltive comes close to sarcasm insofar as both make use
of implicit communication and ultimately bring about a negative
evaluation of their target, but there are two significant differences.
First, although the guilter exaggerates their selflessness, they express
their sentiments sincerely.[31] It therefore lacks the pretence of sarcasm. Second, the negative evaluation of the guiltive is generated not
by the guilter but by the target, who also produces the guilt.

6.2.3.2 *A Guiltive Reading of 1 Cor 4:9–13*

Approaching 1 Cor 4:9–13 through a guiltive lens situates the antitheses Paul lays out in 4:10 within his overall rhetoric better than an

---

[29] Example adapted from Haiman, who illustrates using scenes from *Portnoy's
Complaint* (1998, 23–25).
[30] Haiman 1998, 23–25.
[31] By 'sincerely', I mean without any perceptible indices of insincerity/pretence.
Whether the guilter might, after a moment of self-reflection, admit to having exaggerated is another matter – and would doubtless vary from person to person.

ironic or sarcastic reading. The guiltive tone begins in 4:9 as Paul describes apostolic suffering on a grand scale. The first signal that Paul is painting an exaggerated picture of his hardships is his use of *dokō* (δοκῶ, 'it seems to me'). He describes things as they appear to be rather than how they necessarily are. The simile Paul uses is literally theatrical; it is as if God has condemned the apostles to death in the arena (ὁ θεὸς ἡμᾶς τοὺς ἀποστόλους ἐσχάτους ἀπέδειξεν ὡς ἐπιθανατίους, ὅτι θέατρον ἐγενήθημεν).[32] We also see emphasis through Paul's repetitious description of the audience for this spectacle, a drama that plays out in view of 'the world and angels and humanity' (τῷ κόσμῳ καὶ ἀγγέλοις καὶ ἀνθρώποις).[33] This emphatic depiction of apostolic suffering fits well with the guiltive as Haiman describes it. Paul exaggerates his suffering but does not express insincerity.

The tone of the guiltive continues into 4:10, as Paul contrasts the foolishness, weakness, and dishonour of the apostles with the wisdom, strength, and honour of the Corinthians. Here again emphasis is signalled through repetition,[34] and Paul makes explicit contrast between the qualities of the apostles and qualities of the Corinthians through his use of pronouns and conjunctions: '*we* are this, but *you* are that' (ἡμεῖς ... ὑμεῖς δέ...). Although his portrayal of both apostolic weakness and the Corinthians' privilege is exaggerated, Paul does not imply a negative assessment of the Corinthians in this verse. Indeed, if there is any subtext, it is the implication that the Corinthians have benefited at Paul's expense. It is from this situation that the Corinthians must infer for themselves that they do not deserve to be exalted above the apostles, and ought to be ashamed of sitting idly by while others suffer for Christ.

The guiltive continues throughout 4:11–13, with its sincerity and emphasis on the speaker's suffering. Paul and the other apostles 'hunger and thirst and are naked and beaten and homeless' (4:11). These sufferings are described vividly in the present tense, depicted as taking place 'up to this very hour' (ἄχρι τῆς ἄρτι ὥρας, 4:11; cf. ἕως ἄρτι, 4:13). In 4:12–13 the focus on suffering continues with an emphasis on the way the apostles behave blamelessly despite

---

[32] On the background of this metaphor as the gladiatorial arena, see Schrage 1991, 1:342; Barrett 1971, 110; Collins 1999, 188. Barrett also mentions death by beasts (1971, 110; cf. Ciampa and Rosner 2010, 181–82).

[33] On hyperbole in 4:9, cf. Plank 1987, 49.

[34] And chiasm, see Collins 1999, 189; Conzelmann 1975, 108.

mistreatment. For every evil suffered the apostles return good: 'insulted, we bless; persecuted, we endure' (4:12). This list of trials concludes with the lowest self-description: 'We have become like the rubbish of the world, the dregs of all things, to this very day' (4:13 NRSV). The emphasis on Paul's blameless endurance of suffering in 4:11–13 is both consistent with and deepens the guiltive tone of the previous verses.[35]

Following Paul's treatment of his sufferings, 4:14 provides further evidence for why the guiltive has been an appropriate category for thinking about Paul's rhetoric in 4:9–13. Here Paul reassures his congregation, 'I'm not writing this to shame you but I'm admonishing you as my beloved children' (Οὐκ ἐντρέπων ὑμᾶς γράφω ταῦτα ἀλλ' ὡς τέκνα μου ἀγαπητὰ νουθετῶ[ν], 4:14). Holland suggests that this verse betrays the fact that shame is precisely Paul's aim.[36] But we should also acknowledge that Paul seems to have no trouble intentionally shaming his congregation in 1 Cor 6:5; 15:34. We may then perhaps give Paul's motives the benefit of the doubt, while recognizing two important implications. First, the fact that Paul denies shaming his church shows that he is aware that guilt is a probable response to the proceeding soliloquy. Second, even if Paul has no conscious desire to shame the Corinthians, framing his 'admonition' in this way still strengthens its guiltive function. Highlighting again the blamelessness of his motives still has the potential to make the Corinthians feel even worse about themselves by comparison.[37]

A guiltive reading of 4:9–13 shows the text to be all of one rhetorical piece. Paul does not invert the sentiments expressed in 4:10 through irony. Instead, the guiltive emphasis on and exaggeration

[35] One school of thought argues that Paul's list of hardships follows ancient conventions for *peristasis* catalogues. 4:9–13 shows Paul to be the ideal sage through his endurance of suffering (Fitzgerald 1988, 145–48; Witherington 1995, 143; Collins 1999, 183). Conversely, Schellenberg argues that features present in what scholars term *peristasis* catalogues are common throughout ancient catalogue-making in general (2013, 125–36). 'We certainly need not posit any one particular stylistic influence to account for Paul's tribulation lists' (Schellenberg 2013, 136). If Paul does not mean to express the sage's indifference toward sufferings, he is, amongst other rhetorical aims, communicating a degree of real frustration with his sufferings and the role that God 'seems' (δοκῶ, 4:9) to be playing in them – or perhaps also the Corinthians' lack of sympathy for them. Both readings fit with the guiltive, the *peristasis*-interpretation emphasizing the endurance and blameless forbearance of the speaker, and the latter reading emphasizing the sufferings themselves.
[36] Holland 1997, 246; cf. Sim 2016, 57.
[37] Any child who has been chided by a parent who is, 'not angry, just disappointed', understands this fact intuitively.

of suffering carries from Paul's depiction of the apostles as the cosmos's spectacle (4:9) all the way through his vivid list of hardships in 4:11–13. This description, 4:10 included, is hyperbolic, but not insincere. Paul does not imply that the Corinthians should feel guilty for experiencing relative privilege as he suffers for Christ (4:14), but – as Haiman describes – the Corinthians must infer for themselves that they ought to feel ashamed.

6.2.4   Conclusions

Many scholars have weighed in on the presence of irony in 1 Cor 4:8, 10. I agree with ironic readings of 4:8 and consider it a clear example of sarcasm. Paul's reference to the Corinthians as already reigning as kings is an implicit critique of what Paul perceives as their arrogance. This criticism is, however, tempered with humour as Paul jokes about the possibility of really reigning as kings along with his congregation in the latter half of the verse.

This fanciful image of kingship contrasts sharply with the depiction of apostolic suffering that Paul begins in 4:9 and carries through 4:13. Here I have departed from ironic readings of 4:10 in arguing that the whole of 4:9–13 is best described by Haiman's 'guiltive'. This reading shows the passage to be all of one rhetorical piece, as opposed to Paul interrupting his attempt to gain his audience's sympathies in 4:9 and 4:11–13 with a sarcastic insult in 4:10.

A guiltive reading is not far from a sarcastic interpretation; there are areas of overlap between the two categories but also important differences. Unlike the implicit negative evaluation communicated in sarcasm, the guilter's subtext communicates only their own (long-) suffering. The guilter therefore delivers their guilt trip without insincerity. However, when I say that Paul is being sincere in 4:10, I do not mean that he really thinks that the Corinthians are wiser, stronger, and ultimately more honourable than the apostles. Haiman writes that in the guiltive, 'the speaker ... suppresses his or her own emotions, is known to be suppressing them, and still manages to sound sincere'.[38] Paul is not being sarcastic, but he is still not saying what he really thinks. Paul's actual assessment of his congregation's social standing is doubtless better represented in places such as 1 Cor 1:26.

---

[38] Haiman 1998, 24. Cf. n.31.

The guilter also does not imply a negative assessment of their target, but the guilted must infer their culpability in the sufferings of the guilter and consequently feel bad about themselves. The way Paul emphasizes the hardships he has endured blamelessly while the Corinthians have been experiencing relative privilege throughout 4:9–13 fits nicely within this model. Thus, in 4:14, Paul need not write to shame the Corinthians. At this point, they should already be shaming themselves.

6.3   Corinthian Slogans: Direct Quotation vs Loose Resemblance

'"All things are permitted for me", but not all things are beneficial. "All things are permitted for me", but I will not be dominated by anything' (1 Cor 6:12 NRSV). These antitheses suggest the possibility of sarcasm, as Paul mentions the speech of another group – with no indicators of direct quotation in Greek – before clearly distancing himself from their position. This description sounds close to the echoic definition of irony (Chapter 1, §1.2.3). Considering also the prevalence of feigned concessions in sarcastic speech and the tendency of ancient-Greek speakers to follow sarcastic comments with a straightforward declaration of negative evaluation, an ironic reading seems to be a real interpretive possibility for statements such as the above (Chapter 3, §§3.1.1.4, 3.2.3).[39] This sort of re-presented speech[40] is worth further investigation, as 6:12 is not the only point at which Paul 'cites' the Corinthians' perspective. Omanson lists nineteen such 'Corinthian slogans' identified by previous scholars.[41] Before looking at specific examples, I will make some general comments on these slogans and the likelihood of their being sarcastic.

Generally speaking, Corinthian slogans are more thoroughly discussed than defined. It is common to find scholars assessing Paul's presentation of these 'slogans' with language relating to citation or quotation, without addressing the issue of how literally or loosely Paul has recast the language of others.[42] Such word choice implies

---

[39] On these features, see Siebenmann, who writes that Paul presents 'All things are lawful for me' (*Panta moi exestin*, Πάντα μοι ἔξεστιν) 'as if he agreed with it' (1997, 166). Cf. Fee: 'in both cases [6:12; 10:23] [Paul] qualifies [*Panta moi exestin*] so sharply as to negate it—at least as a theological absolute' (1987, 251–52).

[40] To borrow Sim's language (2016, 29–51).

[41] Omanson 1992, 203–12. Smith helpfully breaks these down in charts according to which major commentators and translators support each reading (see 2010, 87–88).

[42] E.g., Naselli 2017, 974, 979, 981, 987; Fee 1987, 251, 262, 365.

an essentially word-for-word reproduction of the Corinthians' positions.[43]

Murphy-O'Connor conceives of these slogans as more or less direct citations, arguing that Paul's rhetorical training was too advanced for him to weaken his position by misrepresenting his opposition.[44] Tentatively critical of this position, Smith sees it as reasonable for Paul to have adjusted the wording of the Corinthians while still maintaining a fair representation of their viewpoints.[45] Synthesizing the work of Siebenmann and Stowers, Smith goes on to define the Corinthian slogan as 'a motto [or similar expression that captures the spirit, purpose, or guiding principles] of a particular group or point of view at Corinth, or at least a motto that Paul was using to represent their position or attitudes'.[46] Smith's broader definition is to be preferred. Regardless of the actual level of Paul's rhetorical training, one may conceive of many situations in which reframing the words of one's interlocutors would present some rhetorical advantage. While both Murphy-O'Connor and Smith see the Corinthian slogans as nothing other than fair representations of the views they cite,[47] I argue that Paul could have intentionally misrepresented or exaggerated certain aspects of the Corinthians' positions for various reasons, including sarcasm, parody, and mockery.

In terms of how the Corinthian slogans function as reproduced speech, we are faced with a range of possibilities from direct quotations of previous written correspondence to mottos formulated by Paul himself to represent their views.[48] For our purposes, this distinction between direct quotation and looser representation is essential, as it can have a significant impact on whether a statement is sarcastic. In the absence of other indices of evaluation, direct quotation may serve no other function than to indicate the topic under discussion. For example, a slogan such as 7:1, 'Now concerning the

---

[43] The language of direct quotation is pervasive in early studies. See Omanson 1992, 201–13; Hurd 1965, 65–68, 74.

[44] Murphy-O'Connor 2009, 25.

[45] Smith 2010, 83n.51. Cf. Collins 1999, 243–45, 312.

[46] Smith 2010, 82, see 82n.51. See Siebenmann 1997, 54. Part of the wording [in square brackets] appears also to come from the *Random House Webster's College Dictionary*, 1996, s.v. 'motto', which Siebenmann cites (see 1997, 54n.154). For a similar perspective, see Willis 1985, 65–66.

[47] So too Siebenmann 1997, 63–65.

[48] See Smith 2010, 83.

matters about which you wrote: "it is good for a man not to touch a woman"' (NRSV), is a strong candidate for direct quotation indicating the subject to be addressed.[49] As such, it contains no hint of sarcasm.

In other cases where we find greater looseness in representation on Paul's part, especially when combined with signals of negative affect, sarcasm becomes more likely. Consider where Paul claims, 'One of you [Corinthians] says, "I follow Paul"; another, "I follow Apollos"; another, "I follow Cephas"; still another, "I follow Christ"' (1:12 NIV). Mitchell makes a strong case for Paul altering the Corinthians' words in 1:12 by using a genitive of relationship to stress the subservience of the Corinthians to their factions.[50] Paul intends his rephrasing to be 'particularly nettlesome to the Corinthians who prize freedom'.[51] Similarly, Käsemann considers 'I follow Christ' (ἐγὼ δὲ Χριστοῦ) a Pauline invention rather than direct citation; an 'ironic exaggeration of the other slogans being circulated'.[52] While Mitchell and Käsemann rightly note Paul's use of exaggeration, Käsemann's designation of 'I am Christ's' as ironic is imprecise.

While the interpreter may read situational irony in the presence of an ostensible Christ faction at Corinth, parody is a more accurate designation for Paul's imitation of the Corinthians in this verse than any form of verbal irony, sarcasm included. Because this parody is presented as a direct quotation, it contains none of the ostensible positivity necessary to sarcasm. The comment could be made sarcastic if some feigned compliment were added, by placing *kalōs* (καλῶς) between *egō de christou* (ἐγὼ δὲ Χριστοῦ) and *memeristai ho christos* (μεμέρισται ὁ Χριστός), for example: 'One of you says, "I follow Paul"; another, "I follow Apollos" ... still another, "I follow Christ". Well done! Christ is divided.' However, as the text currently stands, 1:12 is not sarcastic, but does provide a helpful illustration of how Paul need not cite the Corinthians directly and how he may, by recasting their positions in his own words, communicate his (negative) assessment of their actions.

---

[49] Thiselton identifies an 'increasing consensus' that 7:1 contains a direct citation of the Corinthians (2000, 498–99; cf. Schrage 1991, 2:59).

[50] Mitchell 1991, 28:83–86.

[51] Ibid. 28:85.

[52] 'ironisierende Überbietung der anderen umlaufenden Parolen' (Käsemann 1963, 1:X). So too Schrage 1991, 1:148.

6.3.1   All Readings Are Permitted: 6:12; 10:23

Where does this leave us with 6:12 – and its parallel in 10:23? With a few notable exceptions,[53] most commentators take these as citations of Corinthian slogans.[54] While I agree that they are some form of re-presented speech, just how directly or loosely Paul 'cites' the Corinthians is unclear. We have no means of verifying the original words or thoughts underlying what Paul represents as *Panta moi exestin* (Πάντα μοι ἔξεστιν, 'All things are permitted for me', 6:12 NRSV) and *Panta exestin* (Πάντα ἔξεστιν, 10:23).[55] Because in this case the sort of 'quotation' Paul employs determines whether the statement is sarcastic, one must retain a certain degree of agnosticism in interpretation. We are left with a range of possibilities, conditions under which 'all things are permitted (for me)' could be stated sarcastically or non-sarcastically.

If, as we discussed with 7:1, Paul is directly quoting the Corinthians in 6:12; 10:23, taking, for example, their exact words from their letter, Paul is most likely not being sarcastic. Paul's audience would simply recognize their own words as indicating the subject under discussion without necessarily indicating agreement or disagreement. Paul's own position would then become evident from the following statements.

It is also possible that Paul has constructed this slogan himself based on his interpretation of the Corinthian position. One could see how Paul, coming across more elaborated statements of the ethical neutrality of bodily actions, such as 'Every sin that a person commits is outside the body' (πᾶν ἁμάρτημα ὃ ἐὰν ποιήσῃ ἄνθρωπος ἐκτὸς τοῦ σώματός ἐστιν, 6:18 NRSV),[56] could summarize their essence with something like *Panta moi exestin* (Πάντα μοι ἔξεστιν). If this or something similar is the case, such a summary would be most recognizable to Paul's audience as sarcastic – in comparison with the other possibilities we have discussed. Paul's formulation could be designed to highlight the arrogance of the Corinthian position, casting what they would consider more sophisticated theology as an arrogant and

---

[53]   Dodd 1999, 78–90; Garland 2003, 225–29.

[54]   See Hurd 1965, 68; Smith 2010, 87.

[55]   Cf. Ciampa and Rosner 2010, 252.

[56]   6:18b is too specifically formulated for Paul to have deliberately (mis)constructed it to imply negative evaluation in and of itself. That evaluation comes in 6:18c. On 6:18b as a Corinthian slogan, see Naselli 2017, 969–87. Cf. Murphy-O'Connor 2009, 20–22, 26–31.

unnuanced declaration that one can just do whatever one wants. This option lies closer to 1:12, which contains a parody of the Corinthians in Paul's own words. In the case of 6:12; 10:23, such a parody would be sarcastic: an appropriation of the Corinthians' voice that momentarily feigns acceptance of their position. Without access to more information about what the Corinthians were actually saying, I am doubtful that we can safely narrow these options and determine to a high degree of probability whether Paul meant *Panta (moi) exestin* sarcastically (6:12; 10:23). Within this continuum of possibilities, the fact that Paul follows these slogans with the sort of negations that one frequently finds in sarcasm is interesting. The way Paul repeats this 'slogan' twice each time he references it could also be indicative of hyperbole, but sarcasm is only one of several possible explanations for these features. There is simply not enough evidence extant to determine how directly Paul references the actual words or thoughts of the Corinthians in 6:12; 10:23, or whether in doing so he is being sarcastic.

6.3.2   Knowledge: 8:1–2

Paul begins First Corinthians 8 by citing another of the letter's Corinthian slogans: 'Now concerning food sacrificed to idols: we know that "all of us possess knowledge".' (Περὶ δὲ τῶν εἰδωλοθύτων, οἴδαμεν ὅτι πάντες γνῶσιν ἔχομεν, 8:1 NRSV).[57] In the ensuing discussion of idol-food (8:1–13) we find the highest concentration of sarcastic statements in First Corinthians, which have generally not been identified as sarcasm or irony in scholarship.

On the surface, there appears to be a contradiction between 8:1 'we know that "all of us possess knowledge"' (NRSV) and 8:7 'It is not everyone, however, who has this knowledge' (Ἀλλ᾽ οὐκ ἐν πᾶσιν ἡ γνῶσις, NRSV). Willis sees this contradiction as lying in the fact that Paul apparently claims that all possess knowledge in the first instance and denies it in the latter, and also in the fact that Paul initially appears to agree with those that he will go on to correct.[58] To resolve these discrepancies, Willis proposes extending Paul's quotation to encompass 'we know that' (*oidamen hoti*, οἴδαμεν

---

[57] See Hurd 1965, 68; Smith 2010, 87; Thiselton 2000, 620n.49–50. The issue of how exactly Paul reproduces his congregation's words will not factor into our discussion of 8:1–13, where other cues are sufficient to establish Paul's use of sarcasm.

[58] Willis 1985, 68–69.

ὅτι) – rendering the full slogan: 'we know that all of us possess knowledge' (οἴδαμεν ὅτι πάντες γνῶσιν ἔχομεν) – thus assigning any words that support the sentiment 'all of us possess knowledge' (πάντες γνῶσιν ἔχομεν) to voices other than Paul's.[59]

But this solution leads to an unnatural reading of 8:1. 'The formula οἴδαμεν ὅτι [*oidamen hoti*] is freq. used to introduce a well-known fact that is generally accepted.'[60] We see as much in 8:4, where we have two 'slogans' being referenced, each following after *hoti*: 'we know that (*oidamen hoti*) "no idol in the world really exists", and that (*kai hoti*, καὶ ὅτι) "there is no God but one"'. (NRSV). It is therefore best to see the slogan beginning after *oidamen hoti* in both cases, and to look elsewhere to resolve the apparent contradiction between 8:1 and 8:7.

Several potential solutions have been suggested. Garland argues that the crucial distinction lies in the difference between *gnōsin* (γνῶσιν, 'knowledge', 8:1) and *hē gnōsis* (ἡ γνῶσις, 'this knowledge', 8:7). He cites several other commentators who see Paul as differentiating between intellectual and emotive knowledge, respectively, in these two verses.[61] I propose that a sarcastic reading of 8:1 can do one better. It accounts for the apparent contradiction between 8:1 and 8:7, while still allowing the slogan to fall most naturally after the *hoti* in 8:1. It also does not require the interpreter to supply a substantive difference between the knowledges referred to in these verses that Paul himself does not provide.

In our discussion of 6:12, we have already noted the prevalence of sarcastic concessions and the tendency of sarcasts to follow their comments with statements of literal evaluation (6.3). Both of these factors are present in 8:1, but what makes this instance of sarcasm clearer than 6:12 is the way that Paul begins with a pseudo-affiliative *oidamen* (οἴδαμεν), which we have seen is often 'used to introduce a well-known fact that is generally accepted'.[62] A stock formula for expressing agreement is an excellent means by which to express sarcastic agreement. The ostensible concession 'we know that, "all of us possess knowledge"' (NRSV) contrasts sharply with 'Knowledge puffs up' (ἡ γνῶσις φυσιοῖ, 8:1 NRSV), and later with 8:7, making it clear that Paul never endorsed the slogan in the first

---

[59] Ibid. 67–70.
[60] Cited in Fee 2014, 403n.33.
[61] Garland 2003, 379–80. For further possible solutions, see Willis 1985, 68n.10.
[62] n.60.

place.[63] The apparent contradiction between 8:1 and 8:7 disappears when we recognize Paul's sarcasm in 8:1. The contrast between Paul's (feigned) acceptance of the Corinthian 'meat-party's'[64] position and his own (sincerely stated) views are simply the means by which he indicates insincerity.[65]

Paul's sarcastic use of a quotative formula also contains an element of imitation. Paul mimics the sort of person who would mean 'all of us possess knowledge' (πάντες γνῶσιν ἔχομεν, NRSV) seriously, implying the arrogance of such bold and unnuanced appeals to universal knowledge. Paul then straightforwardly calls out the arrogance of this position (8:1b), before calling into question whether those who make such claims actually have meaningful knowledge (δοκεῖ, 8:2).[66] This is different from negating the content of the message cited, as if Paul were seeking simply to place inverted commas around 'knowledge' in 8:1.[67] Paul may agree with elements of the meat-party's argument (8:4–6), but takes issue with what he perceives as the arrogance and lack of consideration with which such theory is put into practice (cf. Chapter 5, §5.3.2).

Paul's sarcasm in 8:1 also has an impact on how we understand his tone throughout this discussion of idol-food. For Schlatter, Paul's concession in 8:1 seeks to avoid casting aspersions on the Corinthian's 'knowledge'.[68] Thiselton argues that 'Paul adopts a common starting point' with the Corinthians in 8:1, as a means of criticizing their position without causing undue offence.[69] Siebenmann

---

[63] Knox, in passing, cites *oidamen* in 8:1 and 8:4 as meant ironically (1939, 136n.7; cf. Collins 1999, 311 [on 8:1]). Since Paul agrees with the statements, he cites in 8:4, even if he will nuance the perspective (8:5–6), his use of *oidamen* in 8:4 is without sarcasm.

[64] I have chosen a non-standard designation for this group because it avoids the more common 'the strong' and 'the "strong"', both of which are evaluative in different ways (I will only use 'the "strong"' when describing Paul's assessment of the meat-party). The meat-party was also a party that argued for their right to eat (certain kinds of) meat, as well as a group that ate meat at parties.

[65] As such, contra Willis, there is no real reason to read the Corinthian slogan in 8:1 as including anything more than 'all of us possess knowledge' (πάντες γνῶσιν ἔχομεν, NRSV).

[66] See Garland 2003, 369.

[67] Fee rightly notes Paul's emphasis on correcting the Corinthians' attitude (2014, 399, 401).

[68] 'Erkenntnis' (Schlatter, A. 1928, 2:95). For scholars who see Paul as initially conceding 'all of us possess knowledge' (πάντες γνῶσιν ἔχομεν, NRSV), see Weiss 1910, 214; Barrett 1973, 189; Conzelmann 1975, 140.

[69] Thiselton 2000, 621; cf. Collins 1999, 309; Fitzmyer 2008, 338. In Thiselton's assessment, Paul's tendency to 'stand within the projected "world" of [his] addressees'

sees such a rhetorical strategy behind Paul's use of slogans more generally, whereby Paul only shifts from affiliation to pushback slowly and only after presenting sufficient argumentation.[70] Recognizing Paul's sarcasm in 8:1, however, shows Paul's rhetoric to be more tendentious from its outset than these readings suggest. Paul's claim to common ground with the meat-party is an act of short-lived pretence; it looks not to avoid offence, but to produce shame.[71]

But what might prompt this more aggressive approach on Paul's part? As we follow the contours of Paul's sarcastic critique of the meat-party through 8:8–11, Paul reveals more about what he sees at stake in the consumption of idol-food, explaining his more abrasive rhetoric.

6.3.3   'Authority' and That Knowledge of Yours: 8:8–11

After clarifying what has hitherto only been strongly implied, that the 'knowledge' (*gnōsis*, γνῶσις) of the meat-party is not ubiquitous, Paul lays out how acting without due consideration for other Christ-followers could be damaging to their consciences (8:7). Then the opposition gets one more word in, as Paul appears to reference a Corinthian argument about the moral neutrality of food (8:8).[72] Paul's response to what he perceives as a cavalier attitude towards idol-meat consumption and the claim to knowledge it represents will occupy 8:9–13. As Paul counters by depicting an ironic situation, his critique is peppered with sarcasm.

Paul warns the meat-party not to let their 'authority' become a stumbling block (8:9). The syntax of *hē exousia hymōn hautē* (ἡ ἐξουσία ὑμῶν αὕτη), 'this "authority" of yours', is reminiscent the of dismissive use of demonstratives discussed in our work on Lucian.[73] This suggests that Paul is using *exousia* (ἐξουσία) sarcastically to imply that this 'authority' or 'right' to eat idol-food is nothing

---

is for him a 'fundamental rhetorical strategy' (2000, 621; cf. Thiselton 1973, 215–18). Murphy-O'Connor, however, states that, 'It is unfortunately typical of Paul in 1 Cor that he consistently refuses to enter the thought-world of those in the community who disagreed with him' (2009, 31; cf. Murphy-O'Connor 1996, 282–84). I side with Murphy-O'Connor concerning 8:1.

[70] Siebenmann 1997, 63–65.

[71] Cf. Fee's assessment of Paul's response to the idol-food issue as 'combative' (2014, 395–96).

[72] On 8:8 as a Corinthian slogan, see Murphy-O'Connor 2009, 76–86; cf. Thiselton 2000, 647–49; Fitzmyer 2008, 345; Fee 2014, 421–24.

[73] Chapter 3, §3.1.2.5. Fee describes *hē exousia hymōn hautē* as a phrase that Paul 'speaks bitingly' (Fee 2014, 278; cf. Garland 2003, 387).

more than a 'stumbling block' (πρόσκομμα), a term placed in close proximity.

Then, making his critique more personal and sarcastic,[74] Paul describes a situation in which other Christians are scandalized by witnessing the 'strong' exercise their 'freedom' to eat idol-food: 'For if someone sees you, The One-Who-Has-Knowledge, dining at an idol feast, won't their weak conscience be encouraged to eat idol-food?' (ἐὰν γάρ τις ἴδῃ σὲ τὸν ἔχοντα γνῶσιν ἐν εἰδωλείῳ κατακείμενον, οὐχὶ ἡ συνείδησις αὐτοῦ ἀσθενοῦς ὄντος οἰκοδομηθήσεται εἰς τὸ τὰ εἰδωλόθυτα ἐσθίειν; 8:10). The way that Paul juxtaposes the epithet 'The One-Who-Has-Knowledge' (*ton echonta gnōsin*, τὸν ἔχοντα γνῶσιν) with 'dining at an idol feast' (ἐν εἰδωλείῳ κατακείμενον), an activity that proves to be destructive and therefore not a clever choice in the first place, calls into question the claim of the meat-party to meaningful knowledge. *se ton echonta gnōsin* is therefore sarcastic. Paul's sarcasm here also deepens the broader irony of the situation he describes,[75] as those claiming a position of intellectual superiority are doing no more than 'encouraging' their brothers and sisters to engage in practices that will lead to their destruction (8:11).[76] As such, by the end of 8:11, *en tē sē gnōsei* (ἐν τῇ σῇ γνώσει, 'by that knowledge of yours')[77] is terse and sarcastic, implying a sharp negative evaluation of the meat-party's claim to knowledge, which Paul portrays as the downfall of 'the brother for whom Christ died'.

From beginning to end, Paul's discussion of idol-meat in 8:1–13 has no lack of intensity. His use of sarcasm targets the meat-party's claim to knowledge, characterizing it as arrogant (8:1) and meaningless when un-tempered by love (8:1–2). This basic critique carries through Paul's sustained and increasingly sarcastic response to the arguments referenced in 8:8 (see 8:9–11). The eschatological import of the situation Paul lays out in these verses explains his use of more

---

[74] Note the shift from second person plural to singular between 8:9 and 8:10.

[75] While the situation is ironic from an interpretive standpoint, one should not assume that Paul is consciously employing irony as a rhetorical trope. It is, however, clear that Paul intends to show that the actions of the 'knowledgeable' entirely miss the point, do not truly understand the situation, and thus are ultimately foolish.

[76] Fee asserts that Paul is using the typically positive verb οἰκοδομέω ('to encourage') ironically, appropriating the language of a Corinthian argument (2014, 427, 427n.135, 399, 399n.23; cf. Conzelmann 1975, 149; Schrage 1991, 2:265; Garland 2003, 388). If Fee is correct about the imitation, then the expression is a sarcastic critique of the meat-party.

[77] Note the repetition of *gnō*-language in 8:1–13 (nine occurrences).

aggressive rhetoric. As Garland puts it, 'They might wound others eternally and harm themselves eternally.'[78] Because the actions of the strong threaten to destroy the weak (8:11), Paul has no qualms about resorting to tendentious rhetoric. If the meat-party can be stirred to recognize the urgency of the situation and what is really at stake in the consumption of idol-food, perhaps they will stop sinning against Christ (8:12) and adopt the attitude Paul models in verse 13: 'if eating scandalizes my brother, may I never eat meat again!'

6.3.4   Conclusions

Investigating Paul's use of sarcasm across various Corinthian 'slogans' has led to reflection on different means speakers may use to portray the positions of others. I have argued for the acknowledgement of a broader range of possibilities for how closely Paul references the words and perspectives of the Corinthians. This continuum spans from direct quotation of previous correspondence (7:1) all the way to the strategic misrepresentation of their positions (1:12) for reasons that could include parody, mockery, and sarcasm.

I argued that whether the slogan repeated four times across 6:12 and 10:23, *Panta (moi) exestin* (Πάντα [μοι] ἔξεστιν) is sarcastic depends on where it falls on this continuum. If Paul has used his own words to tersely caricature a position that the Corinthians would have articulated with greater nuance, 'All things are permitted for me' (NRSV) could be a sarcastic parody designed to push the Corinthians' logic into absurdity. However, if Paul is directly quoting a phrase the Corinthians were saying, he is less likely to be engaging in sarcasm and more likely to be simply indicating the position to be addressed, before providing his assessment in what follows.

Paul's treatment of idol-food enables more confidence in identifying sarcasm, without having to know how directly Paul cites the Corinthians. Paul begins with the sarcastic concession, 'We know that "we all possess knowledge"', a claim which he explicitly characterizes as arrogant in the latter half of the verse. A sarcastic reading of 8:1 clears up a number of interpretive difficulties, resolving the apparent contradiction between 8:1 and 8:7 without requiring

---

[78] Garland 2003, 386; cf. Schrage 1991, 2:265.

the interpreter to supply different denotations for 'knowledge' (*knōsis*, γνῶσις) in each case. This reading sees Paul taking a hard line throughout his discussion of idol-food rather than beginning by building common ground with the meat-party as some have suggested.

The sarcastic tone that begins Paul's treatment of idol-food is resumed in 8:9 with his sarcastic use of 'authority' (ἐξουσία) and builds through 8:10–11 with the sarcastic epithet 'you-who-has-knowledge' (8:10) and sarcastic reference to 'that "knowledge" of yours' (τῇ σῇ γνώσει, 8:11). These comments are made as Paul depicts an ironic situation in which the 'knowledge' of the meat-party leads to the destruction of a fellow Christian. The more tendentious rhetoric that we see in Paul's use of sarcasm throughout 8:1–13 reflects the eschatological implications that he sees as operative in this situation. Because leading another Christian astray is a sin against Christ (8:12), Paul displays indignation and a sense of urgency as he deals with the issue of idol-food.

6.4   So-Called 'Gods': First Corinthians 8:5

καὶ γὰρ εἴπερ εἰσὶν λεγόμενοι θεοὶ εἴτε ἐν οὐρανῷ εἴτε ἐπὶ γῆς,
ὥσπερ εἰσὶν θεοὶ πολλοὶ καὶ κύριοι πολλοί

Markers of direct reference, including quotation marks and 'so-called', function as common cues of sarcasm in English.[79] For example, one might complain about the 'so-called "service"' at a restaurant. Such markers, however, do not appear to play a significant role in ancient-Greek sarcasm.[80] This fact makes the identification of sarcasm more difficult in 1 Cor 8:5, where Paul refers to 'so-called gods' (*legomenoi theoi*, λεγόμενοι θεοί). Ultimately, determining whether this designation is sarcastic is a question of Paul's world view: what does Paul believe about the existence of the gods referred to? This question is debated and too large to resolve here. Instead, I will briefly lay out three options for understanding Paul's reference to so-called gods depending on how one reconstructs his world view.

First, if Paul is a monotheist, he is being sarcastic. In this case Paul would be using *legomenoi theoi* in 8:5 to imply that such 'so-called "gods"' do not actually exist. Although *legomenos* (λεγόμενος) often

---

[79] Haiman 1998, 49–52.

[80] λεγόμενος and indicators of direct speech seldom occur as signals of sarcasm in the examples surveyed in this project (cf. Pawlak 2019, 548–49, 560–61).

indicates that something is called something else without implying evaluation,[81] this is less likely in 8:5. If Paul does not consider other gods to exist, he is not merely stating that others call them gods, especially in 8:5b which lacks *legomenos* and where the tone of Paul's sarcastic concession is therefore most clear: 'Just as indeed there are many "gods" and many "lords!"' (ὥσπερ εἰσὶν θεοὶ πολλοὶ καὶ κύριοι πολλοί, 8:5b). Also speaking in favour of a sarcastic reading are Paul's emphatic double use of the particle *-per* (-περ, Chapter 3, §3.1.2.3),[82] and the contrast between 8:5 and 8:6 (cf. Chapter 3, §3.1.1.4).

Translations that take this position would do well to put 'gods' in inverted commas, including the references to 'many "gods"' and 'many "lords"' in 8:5b (θεοὶ πολλοί καὶ κύριοι πολλοί).[83] I suggest the following translation for bringing out the tone of Paul's sarcasm: 'So what if there are many so-called "gods" in heaven and earth, just like *of course* there are many "gods" and many "lords", for us...'

Second, if Paul believes in the existence of the gods to which he refers, he may be expressing an unironic concession. Fredriksen argues that, despite his exclusive commitment to Israel's God, Paul would have accepted the existence of other gods, considering them *daimonia* (δαιμόνια).[84] If this reconstruction is correct, Paul would be conceding the existence of other deities in 8:5 before reiterating an exclusive commitment to the God of Israel in 8:6: 'For even if there are many beings known as gods in heaven and earth, just as there are many gods and many lords, for us...'

Third, Paul may still be engaging in sarcasm if he accepts the existence of the gods in question. On this reading, Paul's implied evaluation would disparage other gods rather than deny their existence, highlighting that these 'so-called "gods"' compare unfavourably with Paul's God.[85] This reading would represent another example of non-counterfactual sarcasm (cf. Chapter 1, §1.2.2, Chapter 5, §§5.3.1, 5.3.2).

Without space to resolve the issue of monotheism in early Judaism, I will leave both reconstructions of Paul's world view open,

---

[81] See Arzt-Grabner et al. 2006, 330–31.

[82] Cf. ibid., 329–30.

[83] As in Barrett 1973, 192; Conzelmann 1975, 143; Fee 1987, 372; Thiselton 2000, 632; Ciampa and Rosner 2010, 381–82.

[84] Fredriksen 2017, 12, 68–69, 167–74. Cf. 1 Cor 10:19–21.

[85] Cf. Schrage: 'It is their dignity and divinity that is denied with *legomenoi* rather than their existence and power' ('Mit λεγόμενοι wird ihre Würde und Gottheit, nicht ihre Existenz und Mächtigkeit bestritten', 1991, 2:239–40).

as well as the possibility of sarcastic and non-sarcastic readings in the case of polytheism. If Paul is being sarcastic, he is so in a passing fashion as we observed in 2:1, 4, dismissing offhand the existence of other gods (or their rank *vis-à-vis* his own god) as he carries forward his broader argument about the consumption of idol food.

6.5 On Approval and the Necessity of Division: First Corinthians 11:19

δεῖ γὰρ καὶ αἱρέσεις ἐν ὑμῖν εἶναι, ἵνα [καὶ] οἱ δόκιμοι φανεροὶ γένωνται ἐν ὑμῖν.
For there surely need to be factions among you, so everyone can see which of you will be vindicated.

Several scholars have argued that 11:19 is ironic.[86] This reading offers itself as a solution to a verse that Fee designates 'one of the true puzzles in the letter'.[87] Recourse to irony seeks to explain the apparent contradiction between Paul's following discussion of the Lord's supper with its emphasis on unity – not to mention Paul's argument against factionalism throughout the letter – and the statement that *haireseis* (αἱρέσεις, 'factions') are necessary (δεῖ, 11:19).[88]

Sim also notes this contradiction and further develops the case for verbal irony here. She argues that Paul's use of *hoi dokimoi* (οἱ δόκιμοι, 'approved', above: 'vindicated') is an echo of wealthier Corinthian believers whose behaviour at the Lord's supper was representative of their belief 'that there had to be a separation between those who could show the approval of God in material terms and those who could not'.[89] So described, 11:19 would be an example of sarcasm, communicating implicitly both Paul's distaste for divisions at the Eucharist and his mocking disapproval of those who consider themselves 'approved'. Horsley's translation reflects this reading: 'For of course there must be "discriminations" among you so that it will become clear who among you are the "distinguished ones".'[90]

dokimos (δόκιμος, 'approved') is not an obvious choice for a sarcastic echo of a general report that a group has claimed a higher

---

[86] Horsley 1998, 159; Garland 2003, 538–39; Fitzmyer 2008, 433; Ciampa and Rosner 2010, 544.
[87] Fee 1987, 538.
[88] See Campbell 1991, 63, 69; Garland 2003, 433.
[89] Sim 2016, 61–63; cf. Campbell 1991, 69; Ciampa and Rosner 2010, 544.
[90] Horsley 1998, 159.

social status and its attendant privileges. Campbell only cites one example of the term's use to describe those of high social status (Philo, *de Josepho* 201).[91] This contrasts with Paul's own (positive) *dokimos* use (Rom 14:18; 16:10; 2 Cor 13:7). Elsewhere when Paul is sarcastic about a target's high social standing or privilege, he engages in far more exaggeration and repetition (Rom 2:17–20; 1 Cor 4:8). These factors make it unlikely that Paul's audience would detect sarcasm in his reference to 'the approved' in 11:19.

But could Paul be directly echoing the Corinthians' language in his use of *hoi dokimoi*, indicating his sarcasm in the way that his discourse distances himself from their position? This is even less likely. An improbable set of conditions must be true for Paul's sarcastic echo of something as understated as *hoi dokimoi* to be recognizable to his audience. We must imagine a group of rich Corinthians revelling at the Lord's supper ahead of poorer believers. When criticized, the wealthy defend themselves with (inebriated) theological reasoning about how their greater leisure and wealth is a sign of God's approval. Then, Chloe's people, or another party, present their complaint about this behaviour to Paul not in general terms but citing the vocabulary of these elite to such a degree of specificity that Paul feels the very mention of *hoi dokimoi* will make it clear to his audience that he is referencing their words.[92]

Not only is such a chain of events improbable, an echoic argument for irony here also leads to problematic mirror reading. I see no reason to doubt that, 'when the time comes to eat, each of you proceeds to eat your own supper, and one goes hungry and another becomes drunk' (11:21 NRSV), although there could be a degree of hyperbole in the final clause. However, asserting that those of greater means were constructing theological arguments to justify flaunting their wealth and status over poorer believers overreaches the evidence.

Although a sarcastic reading of *hoi dokimoi* in 11:19 is unlikely, there remain signals of insincerity that should not be ignored. Just before 11:19, having received a report of divisions when the church is assembled, Paul engages in a bit of wry understatement, saying, 'and to some extent I believe it' (καὶ μέρος τι πιστεύω, 11:18 NRSV), when his following discussion makes it clear that he does so wholeheartedly.[93] While 11:19 has none of the hyperbole of the clearly sarcastic 4:8, the adverbial use of *kai* (καί, 'surely') is somewhat emphatic and could hint at insincerity.[94] Finally, the surface contradiction between Paul's criticism of divisions at the Lord's supper and the statement that divisions are necessary remains.

With some evidence that Paul is saying something he does not mean but not enough for a sarcastic reading, I advocate a middle course in interpreting 11:19, arguing that Paul is doing something that overlaps with sarcasm but is ultimately different. Understanding Paul as being facetious in stating that factions are necessary in order to challenge the Corinthians to address a problematic situation best explains the features of the text discussed so far.

Because communicative acts that are simple to perform can often be complicated to describe, an analogy drawn from my childhood will be helpful for explaining what I mean by facetious:

> My two brothers and I go up to my mom and start pestering her while she is trying to read. 'Who's your favourite son?' asks my older brother. 'It's me, right?' 'Yeah mom, who is it? Who is it!' I add ('Pick me!' cries the youngest). My mother, giving us a bemused look, says, 'My favourite child is whoever's not annoying me at the moment.'

My mother does not really have a favourite child, nor does she believe one ought to. She therefore does not mean what she says. She is engaging in a sort of pretence that presumes the premise that her children have presented her, namely, that she does or ought to have a favourite son. It is the assumption of this pretence that I refer to when I speak of 'being facetious'. In this example, this pretence is not sarcastic because it lacks the inversion of affect necessary to sarcasm. 'My favourite child is whoever's not annoying me at the moment' does not imply a negative evaluation of an ostensibly positive message. Instead, it (jokingly) implies an imperative, 'Stop pestering me.'

Reading 1 Cor 11:19 as facetious in this way resolves the contradiction between Paul's apparent acceptance and rejection of factionalism, explains the evidence for pretence in the pericope, and avoids the problems of an ironic interpretation. With 'For there surely need

---

[93] On 11:18 as 'mock disbelief', see Mitchell 1991, 28:263–64; Witherington 1995, 247; Horsley 1998, 158.
[94] Campbell notes the emphatic role of the (potentially) dual *kai*s in 11:19, taking both as original (1991, 69).

to be factions among you' (δεῖ γὰρ καὶ αἱρέσεις ἐν ὑμῖν εἶναι), Paul engages in pretence, pretending to accept that the situation reported to him (11:18, 11:20–21) is the way things ought to be (*dei*, δεῖ). Paul does not really consider such divisions necessary, nor does he support them, but he pretends to do so to turn the situation to his own rhetorical purposes.

This sort of pretence is not sarcastic because it is not clearly evaluative. To say that division is 'necessary' is fairly neutral. It is not ostensibly positive; Paul does not say 'I'm glad there are divisions', which would be sarcastic. It could communicate a resigned acceptance of a bad situation,[95] but the overall pretence is one that takes the given state of affairs as the way things need to be.[96] Instead of the implicit criticism of sarcasm, this facetious statement implies a challenge to the Corinthians' behaviour – which we shall discuss in more detail presently. To be sure, Paul does make his negative evaluation of the Corinthians' divisive behaviour at the Lord's supper clear elsewhere (e.g. 11:17), but the facetious statement itself works on the assumption that division is necessary.

In a similar fashion to how my mother's facetious comment implied an imperative, 'stop being annoying', Paul implicitly challenges the Corinthians to change their behaviour. Carrying on the premise of his facetious assertion that divisions are necessary, Paul states that the purpose of the divisions during the Lord's supper at Corinth is to reveal whose actions merit divine approval (ἵνα [καὶ] οἱ δόκιμοι φανεροὶ γένωνται ἐν ὑμῖν). In the ensuing discussion, however, Paul makes it clear that those responsible for these divisions are not 'approved' (δόκιμος, 11:20–22, 27), but instead must change their behaviour by testing themselves (δοκιμαζέτω δὲ ἄνθρωπος ἑαυτόν, 11:28; cf. 11:31–34) to avoid the consequences of disobedience (11:29–30). My mother's facetious comment, 'My favourite child is whoever's not annoying me at the moment' drew attention to the fact that her children were behaving in a manner that disqualified them

---

[95] Compare Luke 17:1: 'Occasions for sin are bound to come' (ἀνένδεκτόν ἐστιν τοῦ τὰ σκάνδαλα μὴ ἐλθεῖν, NRSV).

[96] *dei* (δεῖ) can be used sarcastically when insincerely expressing that an absurd or unhelpful course of action should be taken. We saw this in *DDeor.* 8.4 when Zeus sarcastically argues that Hephaestus would be a better cupbearer than Ganymede (τὸν Ἥφαιστον ἔδει ... οἰνοχοεῖν ἡμῖν χωλεύοντα; see Chapter 3, §3.1.1.6). We also see the potential for sarcasm when *dei* is used in rhetorical questions expressing insincere deliberation (Epictetus, *Diss.* 1.11.23–24; 3.1.44, see Chapter 5, n.38). Neither of these features apply to 1 Cor 11:19.

from receiving the title 'favourite son', and thereby implied that her boys should stop annoying her. Likewise, Paul draws attention to the fact that the Corinthians' behaviour at the Lord's supper is inappropriate, disqualifying them from meriting the appellation *hoi dokimoi* (οἱ δόκιμοι). The facetious statement 'For there surely need to be factions among you, so everyone can see which of you will be vindicated'[97] is meant to highlight this disjunction between the Corinthians' current behaviour and appropriate observance of the Lord's supper, and thereby challenge them to change their behaviour and become 'approved/vindicated' (*dokimos*, δόκιμος).[98] By pretending to accept the current situation as a necessity, Paul pushes his congregation to eliminate the factions (αἱρέσεις) among them altogether.

6.6   Conclusions

Paul's use of sarcasm in First Corinthians is varied in both form and function. In 2:1, 4, and 1:27–28, Paul's sarcasm amounts to a passing dismissal of Hellenistic rhetoric and 'wisdom', comparable to the dismissive use of sarcasm in Gal 2:2, 6, 9. In 1 Cor 2:1, 4, the critique implied through sarcasm is elliptical to the main thrust of the argument, used in an offhand manner as more of an aside expressing a negative evaluation of sophistry as Paul seeks more broadly to highlight the activity of Christ in his ministry. This passing use of sarcasm may also be present in 8:5–6, although other readings are possible.

I have argued that two verses often considered ironic in scholarship, 4:10 and 11:19, are neither verbal irony nor sarcasm. The whole of 4:9–13 is best described by Haiman's 'guiltive modality'. Paul delivers a hyperbolic depiction of apostolic sufferings and the Corinthians' relative privilege with full sincerity, leaving the Corinthians to work out for themselves that they ought to feel ashamed. I have also argued that 11:19 is better described as 'facetious' than sarcastic. It is a form of pretence that does not imply a negative evaluation, but instead implicitly challenges the Corinthians to change their behaviour at the Lord's supper in order

---

[97] With 'vindicated' I mean to convey the sense of having successfully tested oneself as Paul describes in 11:28–32.

[98] Paul's rhetoric here is similar to 2 Cor 2:9: 'I wrote this so I could determine if your behaviour is acceptable, whether you are obedient in everything' (εἰς τοῦτο γὰρ καὶ ἔγραψα, ἵνα γνῶ τὴν δοκιμὴν ὑμῶν, εἰ εἰς πάντα ὑπήκοοί ἐστε).

to become 'approved/vindicated' (*dokimos*, δόκιμος). In both cases, Paul's rhetoric shows features that overlap with sarcasm, but this overlap is incomplete. Because these examples do not fully qualify as sarcasm or verbal irony, alternative explanations have been necessary to create a fuller description of Paul's rhetoric.

But Paul is sarcastic elsewhere, and in a more pointed fashion than in 2:1, 4. He is sarcastic at the Corinthians' expense in 4:8, implying that they are putting on airs, behaving at a level of status above their station. Here this critique is tempered with humour, but in 8:1, 9–11 we see a more tendentious use of sarcasm on Paul's part. Within Paul's discussion of idol-food, his use of sarcasm criticizes the meat-party's arrogance and aims to show how acting without due consideration for Christians of weaker conscience is foolish and destructive. There is also the possibility of sarcasm in 6:12; 10:23 depending on how closely Paul has reproduced the Corinthians' language in the 'slogan' *Panta (moi) exestin* (Πάντα [μοι] ἔξεστιν, 'All things are permitted for me', 6:12 NRSV). Finally, as discussed in the previous chapter on Romans (5.2.2.), 1 Cor 6:15 may contain a sarcastic rhetorical question.

Taking these more targeted uses of sarcasm together reveals two significant patterns. First, most of Paul's sarcasm in First Corinthians, and all his most tendentious sarcasm, is at the expense of his congregation. There is the strongest overlap here with Galatians where Paul is also sarcastic with his church, and a stark contrast with Romans where Paul is only sarcastic with hypothetical interlocutors. Proximity probably plays a role here. Paul is only sarcastic with churches that he knows personally and with whom he already has a rapport. There is also a relationship between proximity and the presumption of authority. Paul's use of sarcasm with his congregation in First Corinthians reflects what we have seen across the Septuagint, Lucian, and other ancient-Greek texts as the normal use of sarcasm by superiors as a means of reinforcing social hierarchy by challenging their subordinates' perceived claim to some positive quality – such as status (4:8) or knowledge (8:1, 9–11). For Paul to be sarcastic with his congregation as he is throughout First Corinthians shows Paul secure enough in his status as an apostle and his relationship with the community to use sarcasm like an authority figure.

The second pattern lies in the frequency with which Paul uses sarcasm as a means of criticizing perceived arrogance, both in First Corinthians (4:8; 6:12/10:23?; 8:1, 9–11) and elsewhere (Rom

2:17–20; 11:19–20). We shall address the implications of this pattern more fully in this study's final conclusion in order to include Second Corinthians in the discussion as well. Considering both letters side by side will also enable analysis of how Paul's use of sarcasm changes as his relationship with the Corinthians develops over time.

7

SARCASM (AND *ASTEISMOS*)
IN SECOND CORINTHIANS

The Corinthian correspondence has already provided many examples of sarcastic speech. In this regard, Second Corinthians will not disappoint; 2 Cor 10–13 contains considerable sarcasm spread over a relatively short stretch of text. These chapters will make up the focus of the present analysis. This does not presume any particular partition theory, and this chapter's major arguments are meant to be valid regardless of how one reconstructs the composition history of Second Corinthians. I will not be addressing 2 Cor 1–9 simply because I do not consider it to contain any significant instances of sarcasm.

Within the focus on 2 Cor 10–13 itself, the scope of this chapter may also be somewhat surprising. Previous scholarship on irony in 2 Cor 10–13 has dedicated significant discussion to the irony of the fool's speech in 2 Cor 11:21b–12:10.[1] While there is not enough space here to take a position on the extent to which the fool's speech contains other forms of irony, I do not find sarcasm or other forms of verbal irony therein. This finding is itself significant and will be discussed in §7.3.2, but the content of the fool's speech itself will not be a major focus of this chapter.

In previous chapters I have addressed passages considered ironic or sarcastic in scholarship but which do not qualify as sarcasm. This will not be possible with 2 Cor 10–13, as there is too much verbal irony in the text to dedicate space to arguing why certain verses are not sarcastic. For a list of such verses, I refer the reader to Appendix B.

While the above factors narrow the scope of this chapter, our analysis will also broaden. Alongside sarcasm, we will also treat Paul's use of *asteismos*. As discussed previously, *asteismos* is essentially

---

[1] Forbes 1986, 18–22; Loubser 1992, 514–16; Holland 2000, 141–49; Lichtenberger 2017, 104–5.

sarcasm's mirror image: a self-deprecating form of irony that implies a positive evaluation of the speaker through ostensibly negative language and that is often used apologetically (Chapter 1, §1.1.2; Chapter 3, §3.2.6). This form of verbal irony has not occurred significantly elsewhere in Paul's letters but is highly prevalent in 2 Cor 10–13 and essential for understanding Paul's use of sarcasm in these chapters.

Second Corinthians 10–13 has also received the lion's share of scholarly attention when it comes to irony in Paul. We will therefore use previous scholarship as a framing device for our discussion. I will begin by laying out the major conclusions of previous studies (§7.1). This will be a short, preliminary sketch, saving more detailed analysis of past scholarship until after our exegesis of sarcasm and *asteismos* (§7.3.3). This exegesis section will also move quickly for two reasons. First, many examples of verbal irony in in 2 Cor 10–13 are broadly accepted as ironic in scholarship, making identification often uncontentious. Second, we will be able to proceed with more detailed analysis of sarcasm and *asteismos* in Second Corinthians once we have collected all the relevant examples. This analysis will occupy §7.3, which addresses the role of ironic passages in reconstructing the situation at Corinth and the relationship between Paul's use of sarcasm and the fool's speech. Following this, we return to previous scholarship on irony in 2 Cor 10–13 and assess the findings of past studies in light of our data. Here our analysis of sarcasm and *asteismos* will at times reinforce, nuance, or provide pushback on previous scholarship. After this discussion, we will finally draw our own conclusions about the rhetorical functions of sarcasm and *asteismos* in 2 Cor 10–13.

7.1   Previous Scholarship on Irony in Second Corinthians 10–13

Before turning to the text itself, I will sketch out briefly the conclusions of previous scholarship on irony in 2 Cor 10–13. We will assess these findings in more detail in §7.3.3 after completing our exegesis of sarcasm and *asteismos* in 2 Cor 10–13.

Reumann describes Paul's motivation in using irony in Second Corinthians as follows: 'Paul desired to edify, using irony as a teaching device.'[2] More recent studies on irony in 2 Cor 10–13 have

---

[2] Reumann 1955, 144.

considered these two motivations, didacticism and edification, as underlying Paul's use of irony. Holland argues that Paul's ironic discourse in the fool's speech 'invites the reader to look past the surface meaning of the text in order to find its deeper, true meaning',[3] a task that encourages the audience to apply their 'spiritual insight'.[4] Holland portrays Paul's use of irony as inciting a didactic process that seeks to bring the Corinthians to a deeper understanding. This process also has a rhetorical end in mind: 'Paul's use of irony in the Corinthian correspondence has no other intention than to persuade his readers to be reconciled to him by accepting his divinely sanctioned perspective on wisdom and foolishness, strength and weakness.'[5] Persuasion is also central to Spencer's account of irony in 2 Cor 10–12. Here it is irony's indirectness that lends itself to the persuasion of an unsympathetic audience, functioning to 'expertly reinforce [Paul's] central message'.[6]

Continuing the emphasis on persuasion, but taking a different approach to Paul's tone, Forbes considers *barytēs* (βαρύτης, 'indignation'), treated in Hermogenes' *On Types of Style*, as an important concept for elucidating Paul's irony in 2 Cor 10–12. Forbes defines *barytēs* as 'the quality of speech which is appropriate to a strongly reproachful tone' and considers this tone as being most often conveyed through irony.[7] Forbes identifies the effect of *barytēs* throughout his analysis of Paul's irony in 2 Cor 10–12.[8]

We should recognize that these scholars do not all share the same concept of irony, and that their reconstructions of Paul's aims in being ironic will be based on different datasets consisting of varying proportions of verbal, situational, and other ironies. My conclusions after assessing two forms of verbal irony will not therefore intend to overturn what others have said about irony in general, although some degree of pushback will be possible. Instead, the aim in §7.3.3

---

[3] Holland 2000, 138.
[4] Holland 1993, 251, 258, 264. On the fool's speech as ironic, cf. Duling 2008, 826–28, 839. Schellenberg spends his chapter on irony in the fool's speech, where he interacts significantly with Holland, arguing that the discourse is not ironic (2013, 169–81). Here the irony in question would be a sort of literary or situational irony, and therefore does not factor into our discussion. Schellenberg does allow that Paul 'make[s] isolated ironic statements' in 2 Cor 10–13 (2013, 170).
[5] Holland 2000, 160.
[6] Spencer 1981, 349–51, 360; cf. Loubser 1992, 517–18.
[7] Forbes 1986, 12–13.
[8] Forbes recognises *barytēs* in 10:12; 11:1, 5, 11, 21; 12:13 (1986, 16–18, 22).

will be to assess the extent to which observations about irony in general hold true when we narrow our scope to sarcasm and *asteismos*.

7.2 Verbal Irony in Second Corinthians 10–13

We now embark on the identification and exegesis of sarcasm and *asteismos* in specific passages throughout 2 Cor 10–13. These ironic utterances will first be considered in isolation and in relationship to their immediate contexts. We will be able to move quickly through the identification-phase, as several cases are widely accepted as ironic in scholarship. Laying out all of the data at once will enable more detailed analysis in the following sections, where we will address places where ironic passages influence our reconstructions of the situation at Corinth (§7.3.1) and the relationship between Paul's use of verbal irony and the fool's speech (§7.3.2), before putting our findings into conversation with previous studies (§7.3.3).

7.2.1 Self-Deprecating Irony: 10:1

Paul begins by emphatically charging his congregation:[9] 'I myself, Paul (who, face-to-face, behaves timidly with you, but, when away, acts boldly towards you) urge you by the meekness and gentleness of Christ' (Αὐτὸς δὲ ἐγὼ Παῦλος παρακαλῶ ὑμᾶς διὰ τῆς πραΰτητος καὶ ἐπιεικείας τοῦ Χριστοῦ, ὃς κατὰ πρόσωπον μὲν ταπεινὸς ἐν ὑμῖν, ἀπὼν δὲ θαρρῶ εἰς ὑμᾶς, 10:1). The mildness of the exhortation 'by the meekness and gentleness of Christ' contrasts with what follows, as Paul concedes to being humble in person but bold in print (ὃς κατὰ πρόσωπον μὲν ταπεινὸς ἐν ὑμῖν, ἀπὼν δὲ θαρρῶ εἰς ὑμᾶς, 10:1). This tension is resolved a few verses later, where we discover that 10:1b refers to a criticism of Paul by certain persons at Corinth (ὅτι αἱ ἐπιστολαὶ μέν, φησίν, βαρεῖαι καὶ ἰσχυραί, ἡ δὲ παρουσία τοῦ σώματος ἀσθενὴς καὶ ὁ λόγος ἐξουθενημένος, 10:10). The way that Paul plays with this accusation in 10:1–2 displays significant wit. 10:1a flouts the charge of being bold in writing with its mild exhortation, while 10:1b sees Paul apparently accepting the criticism wholesale. Then Paul turns the critique around in 10:2, urging his congregation not to force him to be bold when present in dealing with his critics.

---

[9] *Autos de egō Paulos* (Αὐτὸς δὲ ἐγὼ Παῦλος). Note the emphatic redundancy (*autos + egō + Paulos*). Cf. Loubser 1992, 513; see also Sundermann 1996, 50.

Paul's use of apparent contradiction and the way he echoes the position of others makes 10:1 suggestive of verbal irony, *asteismos* specifically. There is no feigned praise or ostensible positive evaluation as one would expect in sarcasm. Instead, Paul is self-deprecating. In referring to himself as one 'who, face-to-face, behaves timidly with you, but, when away, acts boldly toward you' (10:1), Paul pretends to accept the criticism cited in 10:10 in order to imply its invalidity. 'The ironical tone is . . . manifested in Paul's pretence of appropriating his opponents' representation of him.'[10] This self-irony is the *asteismos* we observed in the rhetorical handbooks and Lucian (Chapter 1, §1.1.2; Chapter 3, §3.2.6). This form of irony becomes closely intertwined with Paul's use of sarcasm in 2 Cor 10–13. The extent to which Paul will go on to combine sarcasm with self-deprecation in these chapters is unique among Paul's letters and important for understanding the way Paul negotiates the difficult developments in his relationship with the Corinthian church.

7.2.2   Paul in Contrast to His Opponents: 11:4–8

7.2.2.1   Tolerating Another Jesus: 11:4

εἰ μὲν γὰρ ὁ ἐρχόμενος ἄλλον Ἰησοῦν κηρύσσει ὃν οὐκ
ἐκηρύξαμεν . . . καλῶς ἀνέχεσθε.
For if someone comes around preaching another Jesus that
we didn't preach . . . you tolerate it well!

With Gal 1:6, I argued that Paul may have used the normally positive term 'gospel' ironically to imply that his opponents' message is not the true gospel, which he states explicitly in 1:7a ('. . .different gospel, which is not another', ἕτερον εὐαγγέλιον, ὃ οὐκ ἔστιν ἄλλο). In a similar fashion, Paul makes reference to 'another Jesus', a 'different spirit', and a 'different gospel' in 2 Cor 10:4 before clarifying that these do not amount to the real Jesus, Spirit, or gospel (ὃν οὐκ ἐκηρύξαμεν . . . ὃ οὐκ ἐλάβετε . . . ὃ οὐκ ἐδέξασθε).[11] 'Another Jesus' (ἄλλον Ἰησοῦν), 'different spirit' (πνεῦμα ἕτερον), and 'different gospel' (εὐαγγέλιον ἕτερον) may therefore convey a touch of dismissive sarcasm implying a critique of Paul's rivals that reinforces the charge he states in the following clause – namely, that theirs is a false

---

[10] Thrall 1994, 2:598; cf. Martin 2014, 483; Sundermann 1996, 51.
[11] Reumann sees irony in both verses (1955, 142).

Jesus/Spirit/gospel. However, it is also possible that Paul intends the modifiers other/different (ἄλλος/ἕτερος) to themselves carry negative evaluation, rendering the statement straightforwardly critical rather than sarcastic.

Regardless of whether this negative assessment of Paul's opponents is sarcastic, the focus of his critique in 11:4 is the Corinthian church, which he delivers with clear sarcasm. With the final clause of 11:4, Paul tersely implies that the Corinthians would gladly tolerate even the grossest false teaching (*kalōs anechesthe*, καλῶς ἀνέχεσθε, 'you tolerate it well'). Paul elsewhere, including in 11:1, uses *anechomai* (ἀνέχομαι, 'to tolerate') positively as expressing generous forbearance (cf. 1 Cor 4:12; Rom 3:26 [*anochē*/ἀνοχή]; also *dechomai* [δέχομαι] in 2 Cor 11:16).[12] With reference to the toleration of a false Jesus, Spirit, and gospel, *anechesthe* is clearly not meant to express praise in 2 Cor 11:4, nor does Paul really mean that the Corinthians do 'well' (*kalōs*).[13] This sarcastic compliment is reminiscent of Mark 7:9 and analogous to Lucian's sarcastic use of *eu ge* (εὖ γε, see Chapter 3, §3.2.1).[14] It is all the more jarring coming in the final clause of the verse, and on the heels of the more positive language used to describe the Corinthians in 11:1–3 (παρθένον ἁγνήν, 11:2; ἁπλότητος, ἁγνότητος, 11:3).

7.2.2.2 Very-Super Apostles and the Untrained Apostle: 11:5–6

Λογίζομαι γὰρ μηδὲν ὑστερηκέναι τῶν ὑπερλίαν ἀποστόλων. εἰ δὲ καὶ ἰδιώτης τῷ λόγῳ, ἀλλ᾽ οὐ τῇ γνώσει. . .
For I don't think I lack anything in comparison to those Very-Super Apostles. But if I am unskilled at rhetoric, I am not so when it comes to knowledge. . .

Across 11:5–6, Paul shifts from sarcasm to self-deprecation. He does not consider himself inferior to *tōn hyperlian apostolōn* (τῶν ὑπερλίαν ἀποστόλων, 'those Very-Super Apostles', 11:5), whom he will go on to call 'false apostles' (*pseudapostoloi*, ψευδαπόστολοι) and 'deceitful workers' (ἐργάται δόλιοι, 11:13 NRSV). Considering these literal negative evaluations and the fact that Paul has implied that

[12] Cf. Eph 4:2; Col 3:13; 2 Thess 1:4 in the disputed letters. See also LSJ, s.v. 'ἀνέχω', C. II.; 'ἀνοχή', II.
[13] Cf. *kalōs* in Rom 11:20 (Chapter 5, §5.3.2).
[14] For scholars who see irony or sarcasm in 11:4, see Zmijewski 1978, 96; Furnish 1984, 500; Loubser 1992, 514; Sundermann 1996, 86–87.

these 'apostles' preach a false gospel (11:4), it is not hard to catch the sarcasm in this hyperbolic epithet, with its redundant compound adjective *hyperlian* (ὑπερλίαν). Compared with the lighter, dismissive sarcasm in Paul's reference to the 'pillar apostles' (Gal 2:9; Chapter 4, §4.2), Paul is here much more sharply critical with his opponents.

Paul's is the earliest extant use of *hyperlian*, and those who employ it over the next millennium are almost all Christian authors. Paul may therefore have invented the word,[15] although this is near impossible to prove. Either way, in describing his opponents as 'Very-Super Apostles' (*hyperlian apostoloi*, ὑπερλίαν ἀπόστολοι), Paul is employing an emphatic expression as a means of communicating insincerity. This compound adjective is an example of both 'chunking' (Chapter 3, §3.1.2.1) and the use of uncommon vocabulary or pretentious-sounding language as a cue of sarcasm (Chapter 3, §3.2.2).

11:6 shifts from sarcasm to self-deprecation, as Paul admits to being untrained in rhetoric (εἰ δὲ καὶ ἰδιώτης τῷ λόγῳ).[16] Forbes considers 11:6 'elegant ἀστεϊσμός [*asteismos*]', analogous to Dio Chrysostom's strategic downplaying of his own rhetorical abilities (cf. Dio Chrysostom, *Or.* 12.15, which Forbes cites).[17] For a professional like Dio Chrysostom to feign a lack of oratorical skill would certainly be *asteismos*, but Paul has already acknowledged criticism of his public speaking (10:10). I therefore agree with Thrall, who argues that Paul was indeed considered 'oratorically incompetent' to some extent at Corinth, and therefore his congregation would not have taken the concession of 11:6 ironically.[18] Here Paul is self-deprecating, but because he does not imply a positive evaluation of his rhetorical skill, there is no *asteismos*. Paul is concerned that he not be thought deficient according to measures he considers important (τῇ γνώσει), but rhetoric does not fall into this category (cf. Chapter 6, §§6.1.1–6.1.2).

---

[15] So Thrall 1994, 2:671; cf. Plummer 1915, 298–99; Grässer 1969, 2:129; contra Hughes 1962, 379n.40. For further discussion of *hyperlian*, see Harris 2005, 746; Héring 1967, 77n.1. On *hyper/hyper*-prefixes in 2 Cor 10–13, see Plummer 1915, 299; Barnett 1984, 5.

[16] For *tō logō* (τῷ λόγῳ) as referring to rhetorical skill, see Barrett 1973, 279; Furnish 1984, 505; Martin 2014, 528; Thrall 1994, 2:676–78; cf. 1 Cor 2:1.

[17] Forbes 1986, 17; cf. Lim 1987, 140. For others who read irony here, see Allo 1937, 279; Barrett 1973, 279; Sundermann 1996, 94.

[18] Thrall 1994, 2:677–78; cf. Bruce 1971, 237; Harris 2005, 748–729.

7.2.2.3 Stealing from Churches: 11:7–8

Paul's concessions become increasingly absurd throughout 11:7–8, reaching *asteismos* in 11:8. With respect to his preaching the gospel free of charge, Paul asks, 'What sin did I commit in humbling myself so you could be exalted?' (Ἢ ἁμαρτίαν ἐποίησα ἐμαυτὸν ταπεινῶν ἵνα ὑμεῖς ὑψωθῆτε; 11:7). Several commentators consider this question ironic.[19] Paul certainly does create absurdity in suggesting that such selfless actions and motives – 'humbling myself to exalt you, in preaching the gospel to you for free' – could be sinful. While the situation that such virtue could be considered vice can be perceived as ironic, we do not reach verbal irony here. The rhetorical question expects a negative answer ('I didn't sin, did I?'),[20] and therefore the perlocutionary force of the whole is the assertion, 'Of course I did not sin!'

Even though Paul has ruled out the possibility of wrongdoing on his part, the (insincere) suggestion of sinfulness that he raises in 11:7 will create the pretence through which the *asteismos* of the following verse operates. That is, Paul pretends he has sinned in 11:8, even though he just made it clear he did not. If Paul has wronged anyone, he has wronged other congregations: 'I stole from *other* churches when I drew my wages, so I could serve you' (ἄλλας ἐκκλησίας ἐσύλησα λαβὼν ὀψώνιον πρὸς τὴν ὑμῶν διακονίαν, 11:8). Resultantly, 11:8 appears to answer 'yes' to the rhetorical question of the previous verse: Paul did sin. He has plundered his converts for the Corinthians' sake![21] Having already brought the idea of sinfulness into the discussion, Paul may adopt the persona of the egregious sinner he denies being in the previous verse. Thus the statement is *asteismos*, insofar as Paul ironically puts himself down, but at the same time avoids suggesting that Paul's actions have ever been done for anything other than the Corinthians' benefit. Paul may be a thief, but only to save their expense (πρὸς τὴν ὑμῶν διακονίαν, 11:8). By pretending to accept the suggestion that he has done wrong, Paul creates an absurd picture of himself robbing his churches that is meant to highlight that he has really committed no sin whatsoever.

---

[19] Furnish 1984, 506; Sundermann 1996, 102; Matera 2003, 249; Gräßer 2005, 2:134; Harris 2005, 754; Martin 2014, 529.
[20] Thrall 1994, 2:682n.187.
[21] On the military resonance of συλάω ('to steal'), see Furnish 1984, 492; Bultmann 1985, 205; cf. Gräßer 2005, 2:136. See also LSJ, s.v. 'συλάω'.

7.2.3   Putting up with Abuse: 11:19–21

> ἡδέως γὰρ ἀνέχεσθε τῶν ἀφρόνων φρόνιμοι ὄντες· ἀνέχεσθε
> γὰρ εἴ τις ὑμᾶς καταδουλοῖ, εἴ τις κατεσθίει, εἴ τις λαμβάνει, εἴ
> τις ἐπαίρεται, εἴ τις εἰς πρόσωπον ὑμᾶς δέρει. κατὰ ἀτιμίαν
> λέγω, ὡς ὅτι ἡμεῖς ἠσθενήκαμεν.
> For you gladly tolerate fools, clever as you are. For you
> tolerate it if someone enslaves you, if someone devours you,
> if someone exploits you, if someone exalts themselves over
> you, if someone strikes you in the face. It's shameful, really;
> seems that we were too weak to treat you that way.

After a not insignificant digression, 2 Cor 11:16–21 sees Paul
return to discussion of his impending foolish boasts. As was the case
earlier in the chapter, this topic again draws out Paul's sense of irony.
'For you gladly tolerate fools, clever as you are' is obviously sarcastic (11:19).[22] *hēdeōs anechesthe* (ἡδέως ἀνέχεσθε, 'you gladly tolerate')
is close to *kalōs anechesthe* (καλῶς ἀνέχεσθε, 'you tolerate it well')
in 11:4, although here the sarcastic adverbial phrase is in an emphatic
first rather than last position,[23] and Paul's play on *aphrōn/phronimos*
(ἄφρων/φρόνιμος, 'fools, clever') neatly signals incongruity.[24]
If any of the Corinthians had failed to catch the sarcasm of 11:19
on oral reading, 11:20 would have made Paul's meaning abundantly
clear.[25] Here hyperbole and repetition drive home the point that
enslavement (καταδουλοῖ), exploitation (κατεσθίει, λαμβάνει), pretention (ἐπαίρεται), and abuse (εἰς πρόσωπον ὑμᾶς δέρει) have been
anything but 'wisely' endured (*anechesthe*, ἀνέχεσθε).[26]
One might expect that because Paul has just been sarcastic at their
expense, that *kata atimian legō* (κατὰ ἀτιμίαν λέγω, here translated
'it's shameful, really') in 11:21 would refer to the dishonour of the

---

[22] Scholars who see irony/sarcasm here include Allo 1937, 291; Hughes 1962,
398–401; Zmijewski 1978, 205–6; Furnish 1984, 511; Bultmann 1985, 211; Loubser
1992, 514; Thrall 1994, 2:715; Matera 2003, 257; Gräßer 2005, 2:154–55; Harris 2005,
783; Sim 2016, 58–59. Holland's argument that the Corinthians' endurance of the
insults of fools displays the perseverance of the sage does not hold (2000, 142–43). Paul
does not depict the Corinthians as wise sufferers, but as party to their own exploitation
through foolish inaction.
[23] See Martin 2014, 550.
[24] See Furnish 1984, 497; see also Harris 2005, 783.
[25] See Thrall 1994, 2:716.
[26] We may take *anechesthe* (ἀνέχεσθε) as sarcastic in 11:20 as well, after the fashion
of 11:4, 19, but the hyperbolic characterization of Paul's opponents in this verse is
unironically negative.

Corinthians.[27] But Paul subverts this expectation in the next clause, which provides the reason for the 'shame' of the previous.[28] Paul and the other apostles were too 'weak' to abuse the Corinthians after the fashion of 11:20 (ἡμεῖς ἠσθενήκαμεν, 11:21). This 'weakness' is the cause for *atimia* (ἀτιμία) in the foregoing clause; Paul is speaking about his own dishonour.[29] This creates an absurd situation in which not mistreating another party is described as a sign of weakness worth being ashamed about. This absurdity communicates the insincerity underlying Paul's *asteismos*. The negative language of shame and weakness that Paul uses about himself ironically (ἀτιμίαν, ἠσθενήκαμεν) implies that his honourable treatment of the Corinthians should be counted to his credit, especially compared with the exploitation he portrays his opponents as engaging in (11:20). The Corinthians need not read hard between the lines to catch the implication that their failure to support the innocent Paul against his abusive opponents is their own weakness and their own dishonour.

Over these three verses (11:19–21) Paul shifts from sarcasm (11:19) to unironic polemic (11:20) to *asteismos* (11:21). We will discuss how 11:21 can also be considered an example of sarcasm in §7.2.4.2.

7.2.4 Paul Reflects on His Foolish Boasting: 12:11–13

7.2.4.1 Paul as Nothing, but Not in Comparison to the Very-Super Apostles: 12:11

Γέγονα ἄφρων, ὑμεῖς με ἠναγκάσατε. ἐγὼ γὰρ ὤφειλον ὑφ' ὑμῶν συνίστασθαι· οὐδὲν γὰρ ὑστέρησα τῶν ὑπερλίαν ἀποστόλων εἰ καὶ οὐδέν εἰμι.

I've become a fool, but you made me do it! For I deserved your commendation, since I lack nothing compared to those Very-Super Apostles, even if I am nothing.

---

[27] So Lietzmann 1949, 149.

[28] On the options for reading *hōs hoti* (ὡς ὅτι) in 11:21, see Harris 2005, 787–88. Harris, I think rightly, takes *hoti* as explicative, indicating the content of Paul's ironic confession: 'I admit . . . that. . .' (2005, 788–89; cf. TCNT; Gräßer 2005, 2:156).

[29] Paul's use of 'we' (ἡμεῖς) 'indicates that the apostle has himself in view' (Thrall 1994, 2:718; cf. Zmijewski 1978, 213). For scholars who see 11:21's *atimia* as Paul's, see Allo 1937, 290; Furnish 1984, 497; Bultmann 1985, 212; Klauck 1986, 87; Harris 2005, 787; Martin 2014, 553. On irony, see Zmijewski 1978, 213; Heckel 1993, 21; Sundermann 1996, 129.

Just as Paul engaged in verbal irony before embarking on his foolish boasts (11:21), he uses sarcasm again just following the fool's speech (12:11), which he also pairs with *asteismos* (12:13). In 12:11, Paul compares himself to the *hyperlian apostolōn* (ὑπερλίαν ἀποστόλων, 'Very-Super Apostles') for a second time (cf. 11:5), and here again the epithet is sarcastic. The more difficult exegetical question this verse raises is whether Paul juxtaposes this sarcasm with *asteismos* when he apparently concedes, 'I am nothing.' Spencer considers this remark an example of ironic understatement,[30] while Schellenberg takes Paul's claim to be 'nothing' sincerely.[31] Drawing on Betz, who sees a relationship between this verse and Socratic rhetoric,[32] Thrall suggests that this passage has both serious and ironic elements: 'It is wholly serious, in that, apart from the power of Christ, [Paul] knows himself to be really "nothing". But at the same time, in relation to his opponents, he speaks ironically and with polemical intent. His concession is "mock-modest."'[33]

I am sceptical that here Paul is engaging in some sort of Socratic irony. Whether Paul is aware of Socrates' habit of claiming to know nothing and the extent to which Paul's use of irony is similar to that of Socrates are questions that need to be answered at greater length than we have space for here. For now, it must suffice to note that what Paul is doing in 12:11 is far from the sort of irony associated with Socrates (Chapter 1, §1.1.1). Socrates' didactic approach begins from a posture of feigned ignorance in which he places himself on a level lower than his interlocutors, asks them to instruct him, and then slowly and calmly dismantles their arguments with his questions.[34] This is quite the opposite of 2 Cor 12:11, where Paul's whole point – which he makes with none of Socrates' calm detachment – is that he is not at all inferior to his rivals (οὐδὲν γὰρ ὑστέρησα τῶν ὑπερλίαν ἀποστόλων).

Laying aside Socrates-like irony as an interpretive option, taking Paul's claim to be 'nothing' either sincerely or as *asteismos* remain as possible readings. Rhetorically speaking, here these two possibilities are not so different. Recall that it is precisely Paul's nothingness that

---

[30] Spencer 1981, 357.
[31] Schellenberg 2013, 173–74.
[32] See Betz 1972, 121–23.
[33] Thrall 1994, 2:836–37; cf. Harris 2005, 873.
[34] E.g. Plato *Grg.* 486D–491E. Cf. Warren 2013, 13–14.

makes him something. His weaknesses are strengths in Christ (12:7–10, esp. 12:10). Therefore, a straightforward reading of 12:11 implies that Paul's recognition of his nothingness sets him a cut above his self-aggrandizing opponents. An ironic reading of 'even if I am nothing' (*ei kai ouden eimi*, εἰ καὶ οὐδέν εἰμι) is, in terms of pragmatics, almost the same. Paraphrasing Paul's statement (with subtext in parentheses) will be helpful to illustrate:

> Sincere: For I lack nothing at all in comparison to those Very-Super Apostles (false apostles), even if I am nothing (because I am thereby strong in Christ).

> *asteismos*: For I lack nothing at all in comparison to those Very-Super Apostles (false apostles), even if I am, apparently, 'nothing' (but I am not nothing).

Both readings of 12:11 find Paul indirectly asserting his superiority over his opponents through a combination of comparison, sarcasm, and self-deprecation. Whether through the paradox of weakness-as-strength or through irony, *ei kai ouden eimi* ultimately works to Paul's commendation. Deciding conclusively between these two interpretations requires a level of insight into authorial intent that I am uncomfortable claiming. I shall therefore remain agnostic, though content that the similarity between the two readings leaves little at stake.

7.2.4.2 Sorry, Not Sorry: 12:13

In 12:13b Paul apologizes to the Corinthians, 'Do forgive me this injustice!' (χαρίσασθέ μοι τὴν ἀδικίαν ταύτην). Here the absurdity of what Paul apologizes for signals that he is not in earnest. He then asks rhetorically: 'In what way were you made worse off than the other churches – except that *I* was never a drain on your resources?' (τί γάρ ἐστιν ὃ ἡσσώθητε ὑπὲρ τὰς λοιπὰς ἐκκλησίας, εἰ μὴ ὅτι αὐτὸς ἐγὼ οὐ κατενάρκησα ὑμῶν; 12:13). This is the 'injustice' (ἀδικία) Paul begs forgiveness for: not being a financial drain on his church.[35] The absurdity of apologizing for something that benefits the other party

---

[35] The standard reading is that both here and in 11:7–8, Paul is responding to criticism for refusing an offer of financial support from the Corinthian church (for a survey of scholarship on Paul's motives for rejecting financial support, see Briones 2013, 2–19). Schellenberg has recently challenged this perspective, arguing that there is no firm evidence that such an offer existed, and that instead Paul is 'appealing to his prior non-pecuniary work among [the Corinthians] as evidence of his sincerity and devotion' – an appeal he makes for apologetic reasons (Schellenberg 2018, 312–30,

makes it clear that Paul does not mean what he says, and Paul's apology contains elements of both *asteismos* and sarcasm. The way Paul insincerely pretends to have wronged the Corinthians qualifies his apology as *asteismos*. Paul's rhetorical question in 12:13a implies that he has made the Corinthians no worse off in any way (τί γάρ ... ἡσσώθητε), but with one exception (εἰ μή). Paul did not burden them (αὐτὸς ἐγὼ οὐ κατενάρκησα ὑμῶν). Paul inflates the gravity of this 'wrong' in 12:13b, using the (exaggerated) language of wickedness (ἀδικία) to describe his conduct and apologizing with the (overdone) humility of a repentant sinner. This pretence is transparent and the implication of Paul's self-deprecating *asteismos*, that Paul has done no wrong, comes through clearly.

A request for forgiveness also normally communicates positive affect, demonstrating a concern for the wronged party's feelings and a desire to make amends. This positive sentiment can be inverted sarcastically to communicate that the speaker has done nothing wrong and that the notion that they ought to apologize is ridiculous. This is precisely what we see here. The exaggerated tone of the apology, asking for gracious forgiveness (χαρίσασθέ μοι) of Paul's 'injustice' (ἀδικία), adds an element of sarcastic hyperformality (Chapter 3, §3.2.2).[36]

Having identified sarcasm in the feigned apology of 12:13 and *asteismos* in its self-deprecation, we may recognize this same dual irony in 11:21, which we have hitherto discussed only as a case of *asteismos*. When Paul says he is ashamed for having been too weak to mistreat the Corinthians, his utterance is an indirect apology. Not all apologies explicitly contain requests for forgiveness or expressions of remorse. For example, many indirect apologies begin with statements such as, 'I feel terrible, I really shouldn't have done *x*.' κατὰ ἀτιμίαν λέγω, ὡς ὅτι ἡμεῖς ἠσθενήκαμεν in 11:21 ('It's shameful, really; seems that we were too weak to treat you that way') follows this pattern – communicating 'I'm ashamed that...' – except its indirect apology is insincere and therefore sarcastic. In this way both 11:21 and 12:13 contain both sarcasm and *asteismos*, the former implying that Paul is not sorry and that he should not have to apologize, and the latter that he has done nothing wrong.

---

quotation from 329). Neither reconstruction significantly impacts or is impacted by our analysis of verbal irony in 11:8 and 12:13.

[36] The sharp, alliterative dental sounds in *tēn adikian tautēn* (τὴν ἀδικίαν ταύτην, 'this injustice') convey something of the biting tone underlying Paul's sarcasm here.

7.2.5   Shifty Paul: 12:16

Although all of Paul's sarcasm in 2 Cor 10–13 is delivered alongside *asteismos*, this self-deprecating form of irony is ultimately more prevalent. After stressing his paternal love and generosity to his church (12:14–15), Paul writes, 'But be that as it may, I have refused to burden you; but since I'm so shifty I must have cheated you somehow' ("Εστω δέ, ἐγὼ οὐ κατεβάρησα ὑμᾶς· ἀλλ᾽ ὑπάρχων πανοῦργος δόλῳ ὑμᾶς ἔλαβον, 12:16). Surrounded as it is by a sincere defence of his actions (12:16a, 17–18), it is difficult to read Paul's claim to be a *panourgos* (πανοῦργος, here: 'shifty') as anything other than *asteismos*, communicating that any suggestion that Paul has behaved dishonestly is ridiculous considering his blameless conduct.[37]

7.3   Analysis

Second Corinthians 10–13 has furnished us with many examples of sarcasm and *asteismos*. These data will enable discussion from multiple angles. We will begin by addressing matters that arise directly from the foregoing exegesis. The first issue is historical. Several of the passages where we have identified verbal irony have been used in historical reconstructions of the situation at Corinth. We will therefore begin by addressing the extent to which the interpreter may safely glean historical information from such ironic statements.

Looking at our examples of sarcasm and *asteismos* in 2 Cor 10–13 *in toto* also reveals an interesting pattern in terms of where verbal irony arises within the overall discourse. Exploring the implications of what subjects bring out Paul's sarcasm and *asteismos* in these chapters will be the second matter arising from the foregoing exegesis to be addressed. Then, finally, we will consider our data in light of previous scholarship on irony in 2 Cor 10–13.

---

[37] On irony here, see also Martin 2014, 641; cf. Sundermann 1996, 200–1. Many consider the statement a response to allegations of financial dishonesty with respect to the Jerusalem collection (Harris 2005, 889; Martin 2014, 641; Plummer 1915, 363–4; Klauck 1986, 98; Sim 2016, 60; Thrall 1994, 2:850). This is not a safe assumption on the basis of an ironic statement alone, and we cannot know if the term *panourgos* was specifically being used in reference to Paul (see 7.3.1). 12:17–18 can also be read as supporting the presence of allegations of dishonesty (so Barrett 1973, 324), but to my mind neither strictly necessitate nor rule out such a reading.

7.3.1   Mirror Reading Ironic Statements

Because much verbal irony echoes or refers to the words or positions of others, Paul's sarcastic statements have become focal points for scholarship seeking to reconstruct the identity and actions of his opponents in Second Corinthians. Käsemann considers 2 Cor 11:4 central to both our understanding of Paul's opponents in Corinth as well as our interpretation of 2 Cor 10–13 on the whole.[38] 11:4 has played a significant role in reconstructions of the theological disagreement between Paul and his opponents. For some, 'Another Jesus' becomes a Christological discrepancy,[39] 'a different Spirit' indicates conflicting ideas about the role of the Spirit,[40] and 'different gospel' indicates a Judaizing message.[41]

The abuses that Paul portrays his opponents as inflicting on the 'tolerant' Corinthians in 11:20 – ranging from assertions of superiority (εἴ τις ἐπαίρεται) to enslavement (καταδουλοῖ) – have also featured in historical reconstructions. While some scholars recommend caution in gleaning historical information about Paul's opponents' behaviour from this description,[42] others consider Paul's characterization of his opponents to be reasonably accurate.[43] Hughes goes so far as to consider 'if someone strikes you in the face' (εἴ τις εἰς πρόσωπον ὑμᾶς δέρει) as most likely 'alluding to instances of actual physical assault'.[44]

Sim's discussion of verbal irony in Second Corinthians also purports to see elements of the Corinthians' perspectives echoed in Paul's ironic statements. On the basis of her interpretation of the echoic approach to verbal irony (see Chapter 1, §§1.2.3, 1.3.4), Sim sees reflections of the Corinthians' criticisms of Paul in 11:20c and 12:13, 16b,[45] and describes 11:20 as 'a series of statements that

---

[38] 'Schlüsselpunkt für das Verständnis der in Korinth auftretenden Gegner und damit zugleich für die Interpretation von c. 10–13 ist 11₄' (Käsemann 1942, 37).

[39] Martin 2014, 521, 523, 527. Walter Schmithals sees 'another Jesus' as evidence of Gnosticism (1971, 132–35; cf. Bultmann 1985, 202–03).

[40] Georgi 1986, 4–5, 229, 272–73.

[41] So Allo 1937, 279; Bruce 1971, 235–36. For further discussion of theological conflict on the basis of 11:4, see Baur 1873, 288; Kee 1980, 76; Thrall 1994, 2:669–70; Gräßer 2005, 2:121–25; Murphy-O'Connor 2010, 247–52.

[42] See Furnish 1984, 511–12; Bultmann 1985, 212.

[43] Allo 1937, 190–91; Hughes 1962, 398–401; Bruce 1971, 240; Matera 2003, 257–58; Harris 2005, 784–87. Others recognize the verse as containing elements of irony or hyperbole but also material of historical value (Martin 2014, 551–54; Thrall 1994, 2:716–18).

[44] Hughes 1962, 400–1.

[45] Sim 2016, 58–61. Cf. Harris's reconstruction of the Corinthians' criticisms of Paul on the basis of 12:11–13 (2005, 870).

almost certainly reflect what had been happening in [the Corinthian] churches'.[46]

In advising caution with such interpretations, I will begin with Sim's work, as it most clearly lays out the assumptions underlying other scholarly reconstructions. Sim's understanding of verbal irony presumes that the interpreter may detect the thoughts or statements of others echoed in ironic speech.[47] However, even at the genesis of the echoic approach to irony, Sperber and Wilson state that ironic echoes 'are not intended to inform anyone of the content of a preceding utterance'.[48] While sarcastic statements may contain a reasonable approximation of what has been said before, they may just as well be loose enough to make reconstructing the original speaker's statement or perspective impossible.[49] For example, 'Very-Super Apostles' (ὑπερλίαν ἀπόστολοι) is perfectly comprehensible as a sarcastic epithet regardless of whether Paul's opponents were actually using the term in reference to themselves,[50] or whether it reflects the Corinthians' estimation of them,[51] or even if they really were not particularly arrogant at all and Paul only perceived them as such and invented the appellation himself. Without knowing how specific or vague a given ironic echo is, we simply cannot reconstruct the words or thoughts alluded to.

We may draw further caution from Pauline studies itself. Barclay argues that intentional distortion is commonplace in polemic, and that caricature and misattribution of motives are not beyond Paul.[52] This warning applies well to sarcasm, which often functions as a specific form of polemic and lends itself to hyperbole and distortion. Exaggeration is present in nearly all the instances of verbal irony we have identified in 2 Cor 10–13, but we cannot be sure of the extent to which Paul is being hyperbolic without knowing the actual conduct of his opponents.

There is, then, a range of possible positions and actions underlying Paul's sarcastic remarks. It is more profitable to work within a continuum of probabilities that respect the fact that the scholar can

---

[46] Sim 2016, 58.
[47] Ibid. 53–55, 61, 70. Cf. Chapter 1, §1.3.4.
[48] Sperber and Wilson 1981, 306. Cf. Chapter 1, §1.2.3.
[49] For discussion and examples, see Sperber and Wilson 1981, 306–8. Cf. Wilson and Sperber 2012, 130; Piskorska 2016, 61–63.
[50] See McClelland 1982, 84–85; Hughes 1962, 397.
[51] See McClelland 1982, 84.
[52] Barclay 1987, 75–76.

only view Corinth through a (potentially) distorted mirror.[53] The interpreter should therefore be wary of making strong claims that ascribe to Paul's opponents the hubris of inventing the term 'very-super apostles' for themselves, or of being in the habit of striking Corinthian Christ-followers in the face (11:5, 20).[54] There also needs to be a greater allowance for a margin of error in reconstructing the theology of Paul's opponents (11:4) and in attempting to identify what the Corinthians had been criticizing Paul for (11:7–8; 12:11–13, 16).

These considerations suggest that scholars who hesitate to make specific historical claims based on Paul's ironic statements in 2 Cor 10–13 have done so for good reason.[55] This caution, however, does not mean total agnosticism. Recognizing the prevalence of hyperbole, distortion, and polemic in sarcasm means acknowledging broader ranges of possibilities and lower levels of certainty.

7.3.2   Where Paul Is Sarcastic and What It Can Tell Us

The examples of sarcasm identified in 2 Cor 10–13 allow further observations about Paul's attitude towards his foolish boasting across the discourse. There is an interesting correlation between Paul's sarcastic statements in 2 Cor 10–13 and their contexts. Paul first engages in sarcasm shortly after raising the subject of his impending foolish boasts (11:1–5). His next sarcastic statement comes just after raising the subject a second time following a digression (11:16–21). When Paul begins boasting like a fool in 11:21b he does not engage in further sarcasm or *asteismos* throughout the fool's speech (11:21b–12:10). It would be easy to conceive of a fool's speech thick with sarcasm amidst its comparison and polemic, but this is not what we find. Instead, Paul is sarcastic next only following the close of the fool's speech, as he reflects on the necessity of the preceding discourse (12:11, 13). Thus, Paul is only ever sarcastic

---

[53] For Barclay's discussion and application of differing levels of probability, see ibid. 85–90.

[54] Concerning 11:20: δέρω ('to strike') finds metaphorical use elsewhere in proverbs, including 'to beat a dog you've already beaten' (κύνα δέρειν δεδαρμένην, Pherecrates, *Fragmenta*, 179) – like the modern 'kicking a dead horse' – and 'the man who has not been beaten doesn't learn' ('Ο μὴ δαρεὶς ἄνθρωπος οὐ παιδεύεται, Menander, *Sententiae*, 173; LSJ, s.v. 'δέρω'). The LSJ also takes 2 Cor 11:20 metaphorically (s.v. 'δέρω').

[55] On 11:4, see Sumney 1990, 170–71; cf. Furnish 1984, 500–2; Matera 2003, 243–44. On 11:20, see n.42.

when in meta-discussion of his foolish boasting; it is only reflection on the necessity of his boastful self-promotion that draws out the sarcastic side of Paul's irony.

I suggest that one may explain this correlation quite simply by taking it as a sign of Paul's frustration. He sees himself as being forced to promote himself in ways that he is not comfortable with,[56] which irritates him, prompting a sarcastic response when the subject of his boasting arises. This level of irritation and discomfort would also explain why Paul spends so long circling around the subject of the fool's speech before getting on with it (11:1–21).

This explanation for the fact that Paul's sarcasm in 2 Cor 10–13 clusters in the meta-discussion of his boasting fits best with Schellenberg's interpretation of the fool's speech as unironic.[57] If Paul's foolish discourse is not a cleverly ironic[58] dismantling of worldly self-promotion but a participation in it – that is to say, if his boasting is indeed boasting[59] – then Paul is most likely to be frustrated by the fact that he finds himself engaging in something he considers problematic (11:17; ἐν ἀφροσύνῃ λέγω, 11:21; παραφρονῶν λαλῶ, 11:23; Γέγονα ἄφρων, 12:11). This frustration brings out his sarcastic ire, which targets those Paul sees as responsible for necessitating his self-praise: his congregation and opponents.

These observations suggest that further work on irony in the fool's speech is required. This scholarship must be critically informed and specifically delineate where and how situational and other forms of irony occur in this discourse, and assess the probability that any form of irony observed by the interpreter is also signalled by Paul himself or exists primarily as a product of our interpretation.

7.3.3   Assessing Previous Scholarship

We will now consider the data in light of previous scholarship on irony in these chapters. While recognizing that scholars treating irony in general have analyzed a broader range of phenomena than the present study, it will still be instructive to consider the extent to

---

[56] On the constraining factors influencing Paul's boasting, see Schellenberg 2016, 512–35. On Paul's discomfort with the boasting of the fool's speech and the ways in which it transgresses his principles concerning self-promotion, see Pawlak 2018, 374–78.

[57] See n.4; Chapter 1, §1.3.4.

[58] Or parodic (so Heckel 1993, 22).

[59] So Schellenberg 2013, 111, 121, 177; Pawlak 2018, 374, 376–378.

which their conclusions about irony hold true for verbal irony. In this section Forbes's work will be treated to the greatest depth, as his use of Hermogenes can further our understanding of sarcasm and *asteismos* alike.

I agree with those who have recognized didactic elements in Paul's irony, insofar as Paul's use of verbal irony clearly intends to persuade his audience to adopt his perspective. There remains, however, a significant trend within this perspective requiring pushback. Spencer claims that while Paul can be 'bitterly ironical', his tone does not approach sarcasm, or 'in other words, sneering, caustic, cutting, or taunting'.[60] While this distinction is partly methodological, indicative of the fact that Spencer considers sarcasm to be a quality of tone rather than a form of verbal irony,[61] it is also symptomatic of a tendency to avoid ascribing tendentious rhetoric to Paul. There is altogether too much niceness and cordiality in a Paul seeking merely 'to edify'[62] or build his congregation's 'spiritual insight' (cf. 7.1)[63] to do justice to the sharpness of Paul's sarcasm and *asteismos*. Paul not only uses frequent sarcasm but is also sarcastic at the expense of his addressees (11:4, 19–21; 12:13), and uses self-deprecating irony to imply that they have badly misjudged him (11:8, 21; 12:13, 16). While it may not be 'sneering' or 'taunting', Paul's sarcasm is clearly cutting and sometimes caustic.

7.3.3.1 Hermogenes as a Tool for Understanding Paul

Forbes's work on irony in 2 Cor 10–12, with its focus on Hermogenes' *barytēs* (βαρύτης, 'indignation'), provides a more accurate assessment of Paul's use of verbal irony in these chapters and will therefore merit more sustained interaction. At the same time, Forbes's work on Hermogenes still requires further nuancing. We will begin with critical discussion of Hermogenes' utility as a tool for understanding Paul's use of verbal irony. From there, we will address Forbes's treatment of Hermogenes, which can be improved and extended by employing a broader reading of Hermogenes' *On Types of Style*. I will argue that Hermogenes does not associate *barytēs* with sarcasm, but instead considers it to be the tone achieved by *asteismos*.

---

[60] Spencer 1981, 351.
[61] Cf. Loubser 1992, 509.
[62] Reumann 1955, 144.
[63] Holland 1993, 251.

This reading of Hermogenes supports the observations made in Chapter 3 (§3.2.6) about *asteismos* as a primarily apologetic form of verbal irony.

Before discussing Forbes's use of Hermogenes, we must consider the role of this mid-second century writer[64] as a tool for reading Paul. For Forbes, the fact that Paul uses irony to create a tone of *barytēs*, 'achieved according to the method recommended by Hermogenes',[65] is part of a cumulative argument that 2 Cor 10–12 provides evidence of Paul's training in Greek rhetoric.[66] While I shall not address this broader argument here, it is important to recognize that there is no evidence that Paul is or could have been familiar with a treatment of *barytēs* like we see in Hermogenes. Forbes has not provided citation of the relationship between irony (εἰρωνεία) and *barytēs* in earlier authors. Furthermore, as a TLG search shows, no inflection of *eirōneia* occurs within fifty words of the lemma *barytēs* in any context relevant to our discussion before Hermogenes. Respecting this absence of evidence, the interpreter should not assume that Paul could have had access to a treatment of *eirōneia* and *barytēs* like that of Hermogenes. It is safer to assume that theoretical work on the relationship between *eirōneia* and *barytēs* had no influence on Paul's use of verbal irony in 2 Cor 10–12.

This does not mean Hermogenes is unhelpful. If he succeeds in describing the nature of irony or providing a paradigm that explains Paul's use of sarcasm and *asteismos* in 2 Cor 10–13, it means that in looking back over the rhetorical tradition, Hermogenes' observation has been keen. Haiman's guiltive, the exaggeration of one's selflessness to make one's interlocutor feel bad about themselves which we discussed in the previous chapter (Chapter 6, §6.2.3),[67] can provide a helpful illustration here. Speakers with and without rhetorical training had been guilt-tripping their friends and relations for years before Haiman ever coined the term 'guiltive modality' to describe it. No one would dream of positing some proto-Haiman literary-theoretical tradition influencing the great guilters of the past. Haiman simply theorized *post hoc* about a common speech act to enable more self-reflexive discussion thereon. In the absence of further evidence,

---

[64] Forbes 1986, 12.
[65] Forbes 1986, 17, cf. 16, 18.
[66] Ibid. 22–24.
[67] See Haiman 1998, 23–25.

we should default to this assumption when considering later rhetoricians such as Hermogenes.

7.3.3.2 *Forbes,* barytēs, *and* asteismos

Now with a more balanced picture of what Hermogenes can do for our understanding of Paul, we will assess his observations about ancient irony. Here we must clarify what exactly Hermogenes says about *barytēs* (βαρύτης, 'indignation') and its relationship to irony. Probably because he is working without the benefit of an English translation, Forbes limits his discussion of irony in Hermogenes to Hermogenes' specific discussion of *barytēs*.[68] But Hermogenes has more to say on both *barytēs* and irony.

When we consider *On Types of Style* as a whole, we discover that the first feature Hermogenes associates with irony is not *barytēs*, but an effect called 'vehemence' (σφοδρότης, Hermog. *Style*, 1.10; cf. 2.3).[69] Vehemence is a stylistic element that involves heavy criticism and is explicitly intended for use on parties of lower social status (Hermog. *Style*, 1.8).[70] Interestingly, the examples of irony Hermogenes associates with vehemence are all sarcastic:

> Ironic statements make it clear that one can reveal character[71] and be vehement at the same time, as in the following examples from Demosthenes: 'How do your affairs stand thanks to these good men?' (3.27) or 'She brought you up to be her pretty puppet, her marvelous bit-part actor' (18.129) (*Style*, 1.10 [Wooten]; cf. 2.3).

Although Hermogenes does not use the word sarcasm (σαρκασμός), both of these examples coincide with ancient definitions of sarcasm as expressing dispraise through ostensible praise ('these good men', 'pretty puppet', 'marvelous bit-part actor'; see Chapter 1, §1.1.2). By associating vehemence with sarcasm, Hermogenes provides further evidence for the thesis I have advanced from the outset: that sarcasm is appropriate when used with the grain of social hierarchy.

---

[68] See Forbes 1986, 12–13, 27n.58. Forbes's translation has several problems. I would instead commend Wooten's translation to the interested reader.

[69] I follow Wooten's translation of Hermogenes' rhetorical terms but remove his capitalization.

[70] Hermogenes contrasts vehemence with 'asperity' (τραχύτης), the milder, less pointed style used to reproach parties of higher status (*Style*, 1.7; cf. 1.8).

[71] See n.72–73 p. 215.

Hermogenes classifies 'indignation' (*barytēs*) as an element of emotive expression that demonstrates what sort of person the speaker is.[72] Basically, it is a quality of tone. The combination of *barytēs* with (mock) modesty (ἐπιείκεια) results in self-deprecating irony:[73]

> Indignant thoughts are created even out of those that seem to be modest [Γίνονται μέντοι βαρύτητες κἀκ τῶν ἐπιεικῶν πως εἶναι δοκουσῶν ἐννοιῶν], whenever they are approached in such a way that the speaker willingly gives up some of his own advantages or agrees to yield an advantage to his opponent or, from what he says in his speech, obviously deems himself or his opponent worthy of deeds or words that are the opposite of those stated. Ironic statements are like this... (Hermog. *Style*, 2.8 [Wooten]).[74]

To put it as simply as possible: mock modesty (ἐπιεικῶν . . . δοκουσῶν ἐννοιῶν) produces *barytēs*.

Although Hermogenes does not use the term, ironic modesty is precisely what other ancient rhetoricians and grammarians describe as *asteismos*. Hermogenes' primary example of *barytēs* – drawn from Demosthenes – qualifies as *asteismos*: 'Perhaps someone wants to think me mad. For it is probably madness to attempt something beyond one's means' (*Style*, 2.8 [Wooten]).[75] Hermogenes describes this example as creating considerable *barytēs*: 'There is remarkable indignation in this passage.' And writes that, 'whenever a speaker uses irony about himself, especially if he is addressing himself to the jurors rather than to his opponent, he creates pure Indignation' (*Style*, 2.8 [Wooten]). Hermogenes also cites an example of sarcasm in his treatment of *barytēs*, but makes it clear that it produces

---

[72] Hermogenes considers *barytēs* and other tonal elements to be means of showing 'character' (*ēthos*/ἦθος, *Style*, 2.2). Vehemence and *ēthos* are the two qualities that Hermogenes primarily associates with irony (*Style*, 1.10; cf. 2.3). *barytēs* is therefore related to irony through its association with *ēthos*. Hermogenes' taxonomy of terms is complicated and often difficult to follow (he shows some awareness of this in *Style*, 2.2). What is important for the present purpose is this: *barytēs* is the tone conveyed by irony – *asteismos*, to be specific, as we shall see.

[73] *barytēs* cannot express *ēthos* (ἦθος) on its own but must combine with another style in order to do so (Hermog. *Style*, 2.2; on *ēthos*, see n.72). It is unclear to me why this is a rule.

[74] For modesty, see Hermogenes, *Style*, 2.6.

[75] The speaker's feigned acceptance of a charge of madness creates the *asteismos* in this example.

minimal *barytēs* (σφόδρα δὲ ὀλίγον τι τὸ τῆς βαρύτητος καὶ ἀμαυρὸν ὑποφαίνεται, Hermog. *Style*, 2.8). Therefore, just as Hermogenes considers sarcasm appropriate to a vehement style, he describes *asteismos* specifically as conveying the tone of *barytēs*. This is where Forbes's treatment of Hermogenes becomes misleading. In his block citation, Forbes passes over Hermogenes' example of *asteismos*, consigning it to ellipses.[76] This truncation leaves only the sarcastic example ('What is your position because of these worthy men?' Herm. *Style*, 2.8 [Wooten]), making it appear that Hermogenes primarily associates sarcasm with *barytēs*, when he explicitly limits *barytēs* to a minor role in this example. Resultantly, Forbes concludes that 'straightforward irony was perhaps the most common method of producing the effect [of *barytēs*]...'[77] However, as we have seen, Hermogenes is more specific in associating *barytēs* with self-deprecating irony rather than irony in general.

Putting everything together, we have now established indignation (*barytēs*) as the tonal or emotive element evoked through *asteismos*, while sarcasm is expressed with a vehement style proper to reproaching subordinates. As an astute ancient observer, Hermogenes provides good evidence that Paul's use of *asteismos* would produce an air of *barytēs*. But we should not therefore conclude that Paul uses *asteismos* primarily to produce indignation. *barytēs* is a means, not an end.

Hermogenes is clear that *barytēs* is appropriate to situations where speakers are denied the status that they believe they deserve: 'Indignation is found in all reproachful thoughts whenever the speaker who is discussing his own benefactions says by way of criticism that he has received little or no gratitude for them...' That honour and status are in question is evident from the next clause, '...or, the opposite when he says that he has in fact been thought worthy of punishment rather than honor' (ὅτι καὶ τιμωρίας ἀντὶ τιμῆς ἠξίωται, Hermog. *Style*, 2.8 [Wooten]).[78] In the face of this perceived slight, statements characterized by a tone of *barytēs* seek to reproach those who have misjudged the speaker (Ἡ βαρύτης ἐννοίας

---

[76] See Forbes 1986, 12.

[77] Forbes 1986, 13. Fortunately, because, as we have seen throughout this chapter, Paul's use of sarcasm and *asteismos* occur in concert throughout 2 Cor 10–13, Forbes's identification of *barytēs* usually still lands on an example of *asteismos* (see ibid. 16–22).

[78] The use of αξιόω ('worthiness') language continues throughout the pericope.

μὲν ἔχει τὰς ὀνειδιστικὰς ἀπάσας, Hermog. *Style*, 2.8). Though not stated explicitly, the aim of such reproaches must be to induce the speaker's audience to accord them the level of status they have been denied. This evidence from Hermogenes accords well with our earlier discussion of *asteismos* where we outlined its primary rhetorical function as apologetic, a way of rejecting a threatened loss of face (Chapter 3, §3.2.6).

7.4   Conclusions: Sarcasm and *asteismos* in Second Corinthians 10–13

In the foregoing discussion we weighed Paul's use of sarcasm and *asteismos* against other treatments of irony in 2 Cor 10–13, finding Paul's rhetoric to be at times more tendentious than previous scholarship has recognized. We also developed a clearer picture of Hermogenes' treatment of irony and its utility for our interpretation of Paul. What remains now is to offer an assessment of how sarcasm and *asteismos* function within Paul's broader rhetoric throughout 2 Cor 10–13.

The situation is well established: Paul's opponents have challenged his authority and his congregation is in danger of shifting their allegiance. Paul's use of sarcasm shows that he does not accept the threatened loss of face, as he responds by presuming the authority that his opponents seek to deny him. We have seen the same pattern played to literary proportions in the book of Job, where Job's use of sarcasm concedes no ground to his interlocutors and seeks to put them in their place (Chapter 2, §§2.1.2, 2.1.5.2). The fact that Paul's sarcasm targets both his congregation and his opponents, then, suggests two things. First, it implies that he seeks to retain the superior, apostolic position from which it is appropriate for him to make sarcastic comments to his churches. Second, Paul's sarcasm aims to challenge his congregation's and rivals' attempts to situate themselves higher than they ought to vis-à-vis himself. These aims are well described in Hermogenes, who associates sarcasm with a vehement style that makes use of strong criticism to reproach one's subordinates.

Of course, sarcasm is only one of several rhetorical moves that Paul makes throughout 2 Cor 10–13. In the broader discourse, much of the argumentative weight comes from the fool's speech itself, which establishes the very weaknesses that appear to disqualify Paul from a position of authority as evidence of his divine empowerment. 'So I will boast all the more gladly of my weaknesses, so that the power of Christ may dwell in me.' (12:9 NRSV, cf. 11:21b–12:10). There is much that can and has been said about this discourse, but for our purposes it explains an interesting phenomenon. We have already noted that Paul responds to a situation in which he cannot reasonably assume authority by doing just that. Paul is by no means unaware of the challenge to his authority and what is at stake in the questioning of his apostleship. His conviction that his apostolic authority is divinely mandated, however, explains his actions. Here the use of sarcasm that we observed in the LXX prophets can provide a helpful parallel. Despite their lower social position, the prophet is often emboldened to criticize their far superiors by the claim 'Thus saith the Lord', the conviction that they are conveying God's message (Chapter 2, §2.2.3). The appropriation of the divine voice enables the use of rhetoric that presumes a greater level of authority than the prophet could normally claim. In the same way, Paul does not budge from his apostolic position. It is not his on the basis of human approval, but comes from God (1 Cor 1:1; 2 Cor 1:1). The argument of the fool's speech establishes even Paul's weaknesses as evidence of his apostolic mandate, a divinely ordained position of authority remaining regardless of whether this authority is properly acknowledged. Paul therefore engages in sarcasm with the vehement tone of a superior, even if the reality of the situation makes his standing with the Corinthian church precarious. Whether Paul's sarcasm will be received as appropriate by his congregation, then, depends on the extent to which they accept his divine mandate. This acceptance is the rhetorical goal throughout the entire discussion.

In concert with the sarcastic side of Paul's rhetoric with its appropriation of authority and challenge to his opponents and congregation, Paul's use of *asteismos* adds another layer to his communication. This speech act is apologetic, implicitly rejecting perceived accusations while – if we accept Hermogenes' assessment – creating a tone of offended indignation. Such *barytēs* should weigh heavily on any conscience that still feels allegiance or sympathy toward Paul, encouraging a recognition that Paul has been shamefully mistreated. While Paul's sarcasm presumes a position of authority, his more defensive use of *asteismos* shows his awareness of the threat to his position. Indeed, the fact that *asteismos* is more prevalent than sarcasm in Second Corinthians 10–13 testifies to the apologetic thrust of the text. The use of sarcasm and *asteismos* together that we see in 11:5–8, 21; 12:13 creates an interesting pattern of rhetorical attack and defence that aims to reject the charges against Paul (*asteismos*) and reassert his apostolic authority with the Corinthian church (sarcasm).[79]

Having analyzed the form and function of Paul's verbal irony in 2 Cor 10–13, I would like to make two brief qualifications to guard against potential misreadings of the data. First, this analysis shows Paul's rhetoric to be multi-layered, as streams of direct argument and different forms of implicit speech, each with their own nuanced expression and effects, all seek to draw Paul's audience in the direction he wishes them to go. On this basis, it would be easy to conclude that the complexity of Paul's rhetoric evinces formal training. It would, however, be fallacious to assume that the interplay between sarcasm and *asteismos* that we find in 2 Cor 10–13 is necessarily the product of studied deliberation. What we find here in Paul may well be no more than the regular complexity of human communication, which we could observe in all sorts of conversation should we be inclined to analyze all our interactions to the same degree of detail that I have done here.[80]

Second, our analysis has focused on elucidating the ways in which ironic speech is used in navigating and reinforcing social hierarchies and as a means of negotiating which speakers may appropriately adopt positions of authority and the speech patterns that go along with them. With everything broken down as questions of status, it becomes easy to read 2 Cor 10–13 as an agonistic power struggle characterized by posturing and manipulation. This is one possible reading, although it does require us to assume the worst of all parties involved. While we must grant that much is on the line for Paul in this exchange, and he certainly has no trouble resorting to tendentious rhetoric, we ought also to recognize that negotiating hierarchies of social status is a common sort of interaction within Paul's cultural context. Therefore, we need not necessarily interpret Paul's repeated protestations of love and affection as disingenuous or manipulative (11:2, 11; 12:14–15, 19).

---

[79] For sarcasm combined with *asteismos* elsewhere, see Chapter 3, §3.2.6n.93.
[80] Cf. Gibbs 2012, 113–14.

8

CONCLUSION

8.1 Answering Our Three Central Questions with Reference to Paul

8.1.1 What is Sarcasm?

The first part of this study focused on answering the three questions: What is sarcasm? How is sarcasm expressed? And what does sarcasm do? The first chapter addressed the first of these questions, producing a working definition of sarcasm on the basis of ancient and modern discussions. This process required bringing Pauline studies up to date on modern scholarship on verbal irony, having found it not to have gone beyond First Quest treatments of irony. As a result of this methodological shortcoming, it has been common for previous Pauline scholarship to conflate different forms of irony, such as sarcasm and other forms of verbal irony with different types of situational irony. This problem is perhaps most visible in scholarship on the 'fool's speech' in Second Corinthians, which several scholars have identified as an ironic discourse, but which I have found not to contain verbal irony (sarcasm or *asteismos*). Here greater methodological clarity is needed to define what sorts of irony are in view, and the extent to which they might be intended by Paul or exist primarily as a matter of the interpreter's perception.

To resolve this methodological problem, I first narrowed the scope of the study from irony in general, to verbal irony, and from verbal irony to sarcasm. I defined sarcasm as a subtype of verbal irony in which an utterance that would normally communicate a positive attitude or evaluation implies a negative attitude or evaluation. One of the important features of this definition is that it takes us beyond semantic accounts of verbal irony, that is, of thinking of sarcasm as saying one thing and meaning the opposite. As illustrated by The Parable of the Disgruntled Undergraduate (Chapter 1, §1.2.2), sarcastic statements can be factually true. This insight has been important for exegeting Paul. Several cases of sarcasm encountered throughout this study involved the expression of implied negative evaluation through sarcasm, but without negating the truth value of the sarcastic utterance (Gal 2:9; Rom 2:17–20; 11:19–20; 1 Cor 8:1).

8.1.2   How Is Sarcasm Expressed?

The next chapter on the Septuagint began to address the question 'How is sarcasm expressed?' Here we saw several cues recur throughout *Job* and the prophets, including repetition, sarcastic politeness, and the sarcastic use of the dubitative – in addition to the prevalence of sarcastic taunts in the prophets. The question of expression was the major focus of the chapter on sarcasm in ancient Greek texts, which brought together 400 examples of sarcasm across Lucian and other authors to produce the first large-scale study of sarcasm in ancient Greek. Here I identified common linguistic and contextual signals for communicating sarcasm as well as several significant patterns in the use of sarcasm across these texts (see the charts in Chapter 3, §§3.1.3 and 3.2.7).

The most common signal of sarcasm identified was the use of contrastive evaluation, that is, following sarcasm with a literal statement expressing negative evaluation that conflicts with a literal reading of the sarcastic utterance and confirms that it was intended sarcastically. Ways of conveying emphasis and exaggeration were also important, especially the use of emphatic particles and the repetition of adjectives. Hyperformality, or exaggerated politeness, was by far the most significant pattern observed in the use of ancient sarcasm. Sarcastic encouragement and sarcastic concessions also occurred with high frequency. This work is relevant to scholars in biblical studies and classics interested in ancient texts containing verbal irony and contributes to modern research on sarcasm by providing a dataset for comparison with previous studies that is removed from modern English both chronologically and culturally.

The cues identified in this chapter played an important role in the exegesis of sarcasm in Paul, and there was much overlap between the way Paul expresses sarcasm and the signals of sarcasm identified in our dataset.[1] The most common cue in Paul was also contrastive evaluation by a significant margin. Repetition and explicit echoic

---

[1] For a full listing of signals of sarcasm in Paul, see Appendix A.

mention were also significant. Paul appears to have a developed sense of absurdity, as absurdity features significantly in Paul's sarcasm as a means of conveying insincerity. In terms of patterns, Paul employed significant sarcastic encouragement and sarcastic concessions, but used less exaggerated politeness than average. Emphatic particles occurred in Pauline sarcasm significantly less than average, corresponding with a lower breadth of particle use in Paul generally compared with authors such as Lucian or Aristophanes. This may be a case where Paul's Greek does not show the same level of fluency as other authors in the subtle use of particles to convey tone.

8.1.3   What Does Sarcasm Do?

Part I also addressed the question 'What does sarcasm do?' On the basis of *Job* and previous scholarship in classics, I hypothesized that sarcasm normally functions as an implicit challenge to what the speaker perceives as a claim to some positive quality made by another party. Social hierarchy often plays a role in sarcastic exchanges because the claim to a positive quality or qualities that sarcasm implicitly challenges is often bound up with social status. Sarcasm is appropriate so long as it is not used against the grain of social hierarchy. That is, persons of high rank may use sarcasm on subordinates without censure. These observations were reinforced in my work on Lucian where 46 per cent of sarcastic utterances were spoken by superiors to subordinates and 30 per cent were traded between equals.

Lucian also provided data for discerning the typical pragmatic functions of *asteismos*, a self-deprecating form of verbal irony that is essentially sarcasm's mirror image. In Lucian *asteismos* is normally used apologetically as a way of implying the invalidity of whatever challenge to their status or position the asteist is facing. My conclusions about the pragmatic functions of both sarcasm and *asteismos* were further supported by an analysis of Hermogenes in the chapter on Second Corinthians. Hermogenes associates sarcasm with a vehement style meant for reproaching subordinates and considers self-deprecating irony to convey a tone of offended indignation proper to the speaker who has not been granted the honour due them.

In addition to these more common uses of sarcasm, the case studies on the prophets and Lucian provided a number of examples where sarcasm was used against the grain of social hierarchy. By appropriating the divine voice, the prophets are emboldened to criticize sarcastically parties of higher status, including nations and kings. Paul's use of sarcasm in 2 Cor 10–13 was analogous to this, insofar as Paul's foolish boasting established his sufferings as credentials in support of his divinely mandated apostolate. From this position of authority, Paul may use sarcasm in rebuking both his addressees and opponents, even when his authority has been significantly called into question. For both Paul and the prophets, the viability of appropriating divine legitimation to validate their use of sarcasm and other forms of criticism depends on their audience accepting their divine mandate.

Lucian writes several characters with different strategies for using sarcasm subversively. These range from the brashness and impunity of his Cynics to the greater subtlety and feigned politeness of other characters. However, Lucian's most significant strategy for engaging in sarcasm and satire against the grain of social hierarchy is to adjust his use of voice and persona. Lucian uses characters far removed from his own voice when being sarcastic about the gods or famous philosophers, while saving more modest targets for characters meant to represent a version of his own persona. We find analogy to this use of voice to mitigate the offence of sarcasm in Romans, although with a significant difference. Paul does not distance himself from the voice engaging in sarcasm, but instead consistently uses a hypothetical interlocutor as his victim. This creates a separation between his audience and the position criticized, inviting them to affiliate with Paul without feeling that their own positions are necessarily being targeted.

8.2 Sarcasm in Paul: a Summary

Part II has focused on the identification and exegesis of sarcasm in Paul's letters, paying specific attention to how Paul expresses sarcasm and its rhetorical functions. With Galatians, Paul's use of ambiguous language complicates the detection of sarcasm and opens up possibilities for polyvalence and *double entendre*. Although Paul's opening in Gal 1:6–7a cannot be considered an epistolary formula for expressing 'ironic rebuke', it may contain sarcasm. Paul's ambiguous references to the 'pillar' apostles in Galatians 2 probably have a sarcastic element dismissive of what Paul perceives as an overemphasis on the Jerusalem apostles' special status by certain parties.

Understanding authorial voice in the dialogical back-and-forth of texts considered examples of ancient diatribe was essential to the identification of sarcasm in Romans. Drawing on Romans and Epictetus' *Discourses*, I laid out a revised understanding of voice in dialogical, diatribe-like texts that accounts for the fact that what we have in Romans is not true dialogue, but a single speaker playing both sides of a conversation without breaking fully from his own voice. This paradigm suggests caution with respect to the debate over the identity of Paul's dialogue partner in Romans, as scholars run the risk of creating a more fleshed out characterization for Paul's hypothetical interlocutor than Paul himself does. My treatment of voice can also explain how some of Paul's rhetorical questions in Romans can be conceived of as sarcastic, such as: 'Maybe we should just keep on sinning so we can get even more grace?' (Rom 6:1). I then investigated how sarcasm functions in its use on Paul's 'interlocutors' in Rom 2:17–20 and 11:19–20 before addressing how Paul's overall use of sarcasm in the letter works as a means of securing the attention and agreement of his audience.

The final two chapters investigated the use of sarcasm in the Corinthian letters. Discussion of First Corinthians focused primarily on 1 Cor 4:8–13 and 8:1–11. In the former case, Paul combines sarcasm with the 'guiltive modality' to deflate what he perceives as the undue pride of his congregation. Although past interpreters have not normally considered the presence of irony in 1 Cor 8:1–11, I argued that sarcasm permeates Paul's discussion of idol-food, which led to a reassessment of Paul's rhetoric in this section. The chapter on Second Corinthians focused on 2 Cor 10–13, where Paul is at his most polemical and sarcastic. In 2 Cor 10–13 Paul combines sarcasm with self-deprecating irony to an extent unparalleled in his other letters. This results in a combination of rhetorical attack and defence that employs *asteismos* to reject the charges against Paul and uses sarcasm to reassert his apostolic authority with the Corinthian church.

Throughout Part II, I also argued that several passages that previous scholars have considered ironic or sarcastic do not qualify as sarcasm. These discussions have highlighted several different speech acts that share some, but not all, features with sarcasm. Galatians 5:12 is a case of hyperbolic and insincere polemic that lacks the inversion of affect necessary to verbal irony. Romans 13:1–7 was a difficult case, where Paul's injunction to civil obedience could have been meant sincerely or left intentionally as an *aenigma*.

Haiman's 'guiltive' better explained 1 Cor 4:10 than ironic readings, and Paul's apparent acceptance of factionalism in 1 Cor 11:19 was facetious, meant to imply a challenge to the Corinthians' behaviour.

8.3 Comparing Paul's Use of Sarcasm across His Letters

In this section I consider Paul's use of sarcasm across his undisputed letters. Differences in sarcasm-use between Galatians and Romans probably have to do with the nature of the situations Paul is addressing and Paul's prior relationships with these congregations. Paul uses sarcasm and other strongly worded forms of rebuke with the church in Galatia, where he is addressing a situation that he considers urgent amongst a community with which he already has a significant prior relationship. Conversely, Paul is never sarcastic at the expense of the Roman church, the members of which he has never met in person. Instead, Paul distances his audience from his criticism by using a hypothetical interlocutor to take the brunt of his sarcasm. Bound up with his diatribe style, Paul's sarcasm in Romans becomes a tool to engage his audience, rather than a means of directly censuring the congregation as we see in other letters. Paul's use of sarcasm in Galatians is therefore more similar to what we find in First Corinthians, both in terms of Paul's prior familiarity with his congregation and his use of sarcasm and other strong forms of reproach with his addressees.

In what follows I will focus primarily on comparison of First and Second Corinthians, as these texts provide an opportunity to assess Paul's use of sarcasm over time with the same congregation in response to a developing situation.

The first significant trend emerges from silence. Although sarcasm occurs in several places throughout First Corinthians and verbal irony is so prevalent in 2 Cor 10–13, I find none in 2 Cor 1–9. This difference may be added to the pieces of evidence in play within the debate over the unity of Second Corinthians. Interested scholars must address the presence of stark overall differences in tone between the two sections,[2] which is also reflected in verbal irony use. I will not, however, attempt to resolve this issue here, since at best my treatment of verbal irony can only represent one datum in a many-faceted conversation.

---

[2] For an overview of the issue of the letter's unity, see Furnish 1984, 30–48.

Moving on to more positive evidence: Paul's sarcastic comments often find their way to specific targets. He very often directs his sarcasm at arrogance (1 Cor 4:8; 6:12/10:23?; 8:1, 9–11; 2 Cor 11:5; 12:11),[3] oratory and its practitioners (1 Cor 1:27–28; 2:1, 4),[4] and those who are arrogant about being skilled at oratory – namely, his opponents (2 Cor 11:5–6). These tendencies are interesting and may give us some insight into Paul's personality, insofar as they could indicate that the Paul had a particular dislike of arrogance and professional rhetoric. Conversely, respecting arrogance, we should consider that the focus on pretention in Paul's sarcasm may also be due to the nature of sarcasm itself. With its ability to challenge and deflate undue claims to status, sarcasm is certainly apt to take the arrogant down a peg. As a result, one would need more evidence to establish arrogance as an especial Pauline pet peeve.

That professional rhetoric is often in the crosshairs of Paul's sarcasm, both as passing dismissals (1 Cor 1:27–28; 2:1, 4) and targeted criticism of his opponents (2 Cor 11:5–6) is more interesting. A Paul with a particular dislike of orators, or at least a tendency to mock the discipline, does not square well with certain reconstructions of the apostle as a highly trained practitioner of rhetoric.[5] While one must acknowledge that this pattern in Paul's sarcasm reconciles most easily with a Paul of little rhetorical training who can in earnestness claim to be an ἰδιώτης τῷ λόγῳ, other interpretive options remain. Lucian himself is an excellent example of an outstanding author and speaker who constantly harangues sophistry and rhetoric (see, for example, *A Professor of Public Speaking*).[6] Paul's annoyance could well be with those of a different degree of training, or who practise rhetoric in ways he considers misleading. While this explanation is sufficient to explain the pattern, it is

---

[3] Cf. Rom 2:17–20; 11:19–20.

[4] Cf. Col 2:4, 8, 23.

[5] We must also consider the possibility that sarcastic quips about sophistry are also influenced by the specific issues Paul must deal with in his letters – namely, that Paul is often sarcastic about oratory because he finds himself compared unfavourably to rhetors (e.g. 2 Cor 10:10). This possibility and the possibility that Paul found practitioners of rhetoric particularly irritating are probably best considered mutually reinforcing rather than mutually exclusive.

[6] Although Lucian, as a Syrian, mocks Greek rhetoric as a cultural outsider to some extent. Regardless, satire targeting sophistry goes back much farther (e.g. Aristophanes, *Clouds*).

difficult not to detect any inconsistency – or even (situational) irony –
in a Paul so simultaneously skilled in and disparaging of rhetoric.[7]

While Paul's frustration with practitioners of rhetoric is clear, his
use of sarcasm cannot settle the question of whether his criticism of
rhetoric is made from the position of an insider or outsider. It would
be fallacious to assume that sarcasm was the purview of an educated
elite in the ancient world. At minimum, Paul need only have had
interactions with other people who use sarcasm throughout his day-
to-day life to have developed a sense for it.

Even Paul's most subtle uses of sarcasm – the δοκέω epithets in
Galatians, the rhetorical questions of Romans, and the combination
of sarcasm and *asteismos* in Second Corinthians – need not be the
product of specific training. Such cases may be complicated to
describe academically, but they are not particularly difficult to perform. Sarcasm and other forms of implicit speech occur frequently in
conversation,[8] and one could multiply examples of people without
formal rhetorical training who use such speech acts at levels of
intricacy comparable to Paul's by simply observing everyday interactions.[9] There is therefore nothing in Paul's use of sarcasm that
provides evidence for or against his having had specific training in
Greek rhetoric.

Moving on from the question of Paul's education, it is also significant that the Corinthians receive the lion's share of Paul's sarcastic
remarks in both letters, even with such a sustained polemical focus
on Paul's opponents in 2 Cor 10–13.[10] As discussed with regard to
Galatians, this pattern is suggestive of both proximity and the nature
of the issues Paul seeks to address. Paul seems to require a certain
prior relationship with a given congregation to feel comfortable
using sarcasm with them. The fact that Paul is so sarcastic with the
Corinthians is also a reflection of the fact that his problems with the
church have to do with obedience and authority. If sarcasm is adept
at challenging the status claims of others and is most appropriate
when used by those of greater authority, as I have argued, it is

---

[7] Cf. Chapter 6, §6.1.2.

[8] See Gibbs 2000, 14–25.

[9] My mother's facetious comment from Chapter 6 (6.5) is an excellent example of
how even offhand examples of implicit speech can appear complex and intricately
constructed when subject to critical analysis.

[10] The Corinthian church is the victim of the apostle's sarcasm in 1 Cor 4:8; (6:12/
10:23?); 8:1, 9–11; 2 Cor 11:4, 19–21; 12:13, compared to his opponents (2 Cor 11:4–5;
12:11).

natural that Paul should employ it when he sees his congregation having pretensions to special knowledge (1 Cor 8:1, 9–11) or entertaining those who challenge his authority (2 Cor 11:4, 19–20).

Finally, I have already discussed a singular feature of Paul's verbal irony in 2 Cor 10–13, the presence of *asteismos*. The prevalence of this defensive form of verbal irony in 2 Cor 10–13 reflects an escalation of the situation at Corinth since Paul wrote First Corinthians. As noted above, problems of obedience primarily occasion Paul's use of sarcasm with his congregation in First Corinthians, and indeed such issues are prevalent throughout the letter (see, for example, 1 Cor 5–6, 12, 14). Paul's response to these situations, both sarcastic and otherwise, presumes a position of authority. While Paul certainly does not concede his apostolic prerogative in 2 Cor 10–13, his use of *asteismos* shows him concerned to defend it. This apologetic shift reflects the fact that Paul's situation has changed for the worse, apparently due to the influence of his opponents. As such, Paul is not only concerned to defend his apostolic authority to his congregation but must also discredit his rivals and so stem their influence.

Changes in the way Paul employs verbal irony, especially in his use of *asteismos*, reflect changes in his relationship with the Corinthians. In 2 Cor 10–13, Paul reacts defensively to his more precarious position and cannot presume the degree of authority he had in First Corinthians. His use of *asteismos* and the boasting of the fool's speech are two means by which Paul seeks to defend and reassert his authority. This position must be re-established to legitimize his use of sarcasm to challenge the status claims of his opponents and reinforce his apostolic authority with the Corinthians. In the end, it appears that all Paul's irony, arguing, pleading, and polemic eventually paid off, as he would go on to write Romans from Corinth not so long after penning what is now 2 Cor 10–13.

8.4   Directions for Future Research

There is much profitable work that can be done to broaden the study of ancient Greek sarcasm, expanding to new authors, texts, and dialects. Further work on sarcasm in the Septuagint could make a novel contribution to our understanding of the translation tendencies of different translators, enabling focused observation of the ways in which implicit speech is carried from Hebrew into Greek. Work on other Jewish texts from the Hellenistic period would well complement work on LXX sarcasm, allowing for exploration of how this form of verbal irony functions in Greek when transposed into a different cultural idiom – and here Appendix C can provide a starting point. As far as Paul is concerned, comparison of sarcasm-use between the undisputed and disputed letters would be especially interesting. *asteismos* represents a fruitful avenue for future research, as subsequent scholarship has more to uncover in terms of how it was typically expressed and in nuancing our understanding of its pragmatic functions – both on its own and in relation to other forms of verbal irony.

This study has focused on the identification of sarcasm in the medium of writing, which is only natural considering the nature of the extant evidence. However, embodied signals such as tone, facial expression, and gesture would doubtless have been as central to the communication of sarcasm in the ancient world as they are today. I have already noted references to insincere smiling in ancient definitions of sarcasm and the importance of delivery to ironic expression in Quintilian.[11] While most of the evidence is probably lost, some reconstruction of the physical and oral signals of ancient sarcasm may still be possible. Interdisciplinary work on the embodied expression of affect in ancient contexts that brings together written sources describing the physical aspects of communication with visual evidence from artwork, inscriptions, and graffiti could produce important results.

Research on the logistics of how ancient letters were delivered and read could also shed light on how Paul's audiences would have experienced his sarcasm. Drawing on performance criticism, Johnson argues that Paul's letters would have been prepared in advance and performed by their letter carriers rather than sight-read from the manuscript. In this setting, the letter carrier's ability to deliver the letter with appropriate emotional expression would have been essential to the success of Paul's exhortation.[12] Further performance-critical research on the delivery of Paul's letters would therefore be fruitful where it can uncover how specific elements of Paul's letters might have been performed.

The conception of voice in diatribe that I advanced in my treatment of Romans creates opportunities for work on texts considered examples of diatribe and for further scholarship on Romans itself. First, further study of diatribe texts – such as Teles and Seneca, as

---

[11] See Chapter 1, §1.1.2, and Chapter 1, n.32, respectively.
[12] Johnson 2017, 62–72, 76. On performance and Paul, see also Oestreich 2012.

well as more systematic treatment of Epictetus – could extend and nuance our understanding of how the speaker of diatribe simultaneously plays both sides of dialogical exchanges, and how these exchanges impact interpretation. A full reading of Romans that acknowledges the extent to which Paul's own voice overlaps with the voice of the 'interlocutor' would represent an important step forward for scholarship on Romans with significant exegetical implications. Such a reading has the potential to change the landscape of the debate over the identity of Paul's interlocutor.

This study has sought to bring much-needed methodological clarity to the concept of irony and demonstrate the importance of drawing distinctions between its various forms. A more critically informed approach to irony can benefit scholarship on Paul and New Testament studies more broadly. For example, I have already mentioned the need for a reassessment of irony in Second Corinthians' 'fool's speech' that specifically delineates what forms of irony, if any, are present and the extent to which such irony is a product of features that Paul seeks to draw his audience's attention to, or whether they are the result of the scholar's interpretation. Comparable work on the Gospels could also produce insight into their authors' rhetorical aims.

Sarcasm is one form of irony among many, and it is my hope that a detailed study of sarcasm in Paul will provide a foundation for methodologically rigorous studies of other forms of irony as well, including its more ancient species such as *myktērismos* in addition to the more recent category of situational irony. Analyzing sarcasm and other forms of verbal irony is one piece of a broader project seeking to understand human communication across historically and culturally distant contexts.

Appendix A

SARCASM IN PAUL WITH SIGNALS
AND TRANSLATIONS

This appendix lays out the examples of sarcasm in Paul discussed in this study, providing translations. A question mark (?) indicates cases where I have argued that a sarcastic reading is plausible, but uncertain. In such cases, the translation provided represents a sarcastic reading.

Beneath each translation, I list which common signals of sarcasm or patterns in sarcasm use identified in Chapter 3 are represented in the example. Abbreviations for these signals are listed below in parentheses. The list is numbered according to the order in which each item appears in Chapter 3. Where no abbreviation is listed, the signal or pattern does not occur in Paul.

Abbreviations

3.1.1.1   Narration **(narr)**
3.1.1.2   Victim Recognition
3.1.1.3   Explicit Echoes **(expl.echo)**
3.1.1.4a   Explicit Evaluation **(expl.eval)**
3.1.1.4b   Utterance Deflater **(udeflate)**
3.1.1.5   Contrasting Evaluative Terms: 'Scare-Quotes' Sarcasm **(CET)**
3.1.1.6a   Counterfactuality **(cfact)**
3.1.1.6b   Absurdity **(absurd)**
3.1.2   Hyperbole/Emphasis[1] **(hyperb)**
3.1.2.1a   X *kai* Y
3.1.2.1b   Repetition **(rep)**
3.1.2.1c   Chunking **(chunk)**
3.1.2.1d   Alliteration **(allit)**
3.1.2.2   Adverbs **(adv)**
3.1.2.3   Particles **(ptc)**
3.1.2.4   Interjections and the Exclamatory *hōs*

---

[1] I will only mark an example with 'hyperb' where it appears to be the case that Paul is using emphasis/exaggeration to communicate his sarcasm, but in a way that does not fit under any of the other headings that indicate specific forms of emphasis/exaggeration (i.e. Chapter 3, §§3.1.2.1b −3.1.2.4, 3.2.2, 3.2.4).

3.1.2.5 Dismissives **(dis)**
3.2.1   Sarcastic Encouragement **(enc)**
3.2.2a Hyperformality **(hypformal)**
3.2.2b Sarcastic Address Forms
3.2.2c Sarcastic Epithets **(epithet)**
3.2.2d Unnecessarily High-Register or Complicated Language **(register)**
3.2.3   Sarcastic Concessions **(concess)**
3.2.4   Mock-Astonishment: *thauma*-Sarcasm **(thaum)**
3.2.5   Insult to Injury
Misc.   Sarcastic Dubitative **(dubit)**[2]

Galatians

(?) 1:6–7a: I marvel at just how quickly you've managed to abandon the one who called you in the grace of Christ for a different gospel! Which is not another...
    expl.eval (ὃ οὐκ ἔστιν ἄλλο, 'Which is not another');[3] CET; adv (οὕτως ταχέως, 'just how quickly'); enc; thaum

2:2: And I went down because of a revelation, and I laid the gospel that I proclaim throughout the nations out before them, but just when I was on my own with those men of repute, so that I shouldn't be running or have run for no reason.
    expl.eval (2:6); dis

2:6: But from those-renowned-for-being-something – whatever they were at one time or other doesn't at all matter to me; God does not play favourites – since those men of repute added nothing to my message...
    expl.eval; dis; rep; epithet

2:9: ...and knowing the grace given to me, James and Peter and John, those reputed to be 'pillars', gave myself and Barnabas the right hand of fellowship...
    expl.echo; expl.eval (2:6); rep; epithet

(?) 3:21 (Chapter 5, §5.2.2): Then is the law opposed to God's promises? Absolutely not!
    expl.eval; udeflate; cfact; absurd; dubit

---

[2] Cf. Chapter 2, §2.3.
[3] A bit of a grey area whether this also qualifies as udeflate.

Romans

2:17–20: But if you call yourself a Jew and take comfort in the law and boast in God and know The Will and discern what is best – being taught direct from the law – and you're convinced that you're a Guide for the blind, a Light for those in darkness, Educator of the Ignorant, Teacher of Infants, possessing the essence of knowledge and of truth in the law...
  expl.echo; expl.eval; absurd; rep; allit; hypformal; register

3:7–8: But if through my falsehood the truth of God brings about an abundant increase in his glory, why am I still judged as a sinner? And why don't we say, as we are slandered and as some say that we say, 'let us do what is wrong so that good things may result!'? They deserve what judgement they get!
  narr (βλασφημούμεθα, 'we are slandered'); expl.echo; expl.eval; udeflate; absurd; enc

6:1–2a: So, what shall we say? Maybe we should just keep on sinning so we can get even more grace? Absolutely not!
  expl.eval; udeflate; absurd; enc; dubit

6:15: What then? Maybe we should sin because we are not under law, but under grace? Absolutely not!
  expl.eval; udeflate; absurd; enc; dubit

(?) 7:7: So, what shall we say? The law is sin? Absolutely not!
  expl.eval; udeflate; cfact; absurd; dubit

11:19–20: So then you'll say: Other branches got cut off so I could be grafted in! Congrats. They were cut off for their unbelief; but you got your place by faith.
  expl.echo; expl.eval; enc; concess

First Corinthians

1:27–28: But God chose the foolish things of the world so that he might shame the 'wise', and God chose the weak things of the world so that he might shame the 'strong', and the lowly things of the world and the things despised, these too God chose; the things that aren't so that he might abolish 'the-things-that-are'.
  CET; rep

2:1: I did not come preaching the mystery of God to you with a super-abundance of speech or 'wisdom'.
  hyperb

2:4: But my speaking and my message were not delivered with convincing words of 'wisdom', but with the clear demonstration of the Spirit and power...
  expl.eval (2:5)

4:8: You're already satisfied, you've already gotten rich, without us you've started to reign as kings! I wish you really were made kings, so we could all reign with you!
cfact; absurd; rep; ptc

(?) 6:12: 'I'm allowed to do anything!' But not everything is helpful. 'I'm allowed to do anything!' But I will not be subjected to the dominion of some external thing.
expl.echo; expl.eval; absurd; rep; concess

(?) 6:15 (Chapter 5, §5.2.2): Should I take the parts of Christ and stick them in a prostitute? Absolutely not!
expl.eval; udeflate; absurd; enc; dubit

8:1: Now, about idol-food; sure, we know that 'we all have knowledge.' Knowledge inflates egos, but love is constructive.
expl.echo; expl.eval; cfact (8:7); rep; concess

(?) 8:5(–6a): 'So what if there are many so-called "gods" in heaven and earth, just like *of course* there are many "gods" and many "lords", for us. . .'
expl.echo; expl.eval; cfact; rep; ptc; concess

8:9: See to it that somehow this 'right' of yours doesn't become a stumbling block to the weak.
expl.echo; CET; diss

8:10: For if someone sees you, The One-Who-Has-Knowledge, dining at an idol feast, won't their weak conscience be encouraged to eat idol-food?
expl.echo; rep; epithet

8:11: So then the weak person gets destroyed by that 'knowledge' of yours; the brother, the one Christ died for.
expl.echo; CET; rep

(?) 10:23: 'Everything is allowed!' But not everything is helpful. 'Everything is allowed!' But not everything is constructive.
expl.echo; expl.eval; absurd; rep; concess

Second Corinthians

In this section, I will differentiate between sarcasm and *asteismos*. Signals will not be provided for *asteismos*, since identifying means of communicating *asteismos* has not been a focus of this study.

10:1 (*asteismos*): I myself, Paul (who, face-to-face, behaves timidly with you, but, when away, acts boldly toward you) urge you by the meekness and gentleness of Christ.

11:4 (sarcasm): For if someone comes around preaching another Jesus that we didn't preach, or you receive a different Spirit that you didn't receive before, or you accept a different gospel that you didn't accept before, you tolerate it well!

expl.eval? CET?; rep?;[4] adv (καλῶς, 'well'); enc

11:5 (sarcasm): For I don't think I lack anything in comparison to those Very-Super Apostles. But if I am unskilled at rhetoric, I am not so when it comes to knowledge. . .

expl.eval (11:13–15); hyperb; chunk; epithet; register

11:8 (*asteismos*): I stole from *other* churches when I drew my wages, so I could serve you.

11:19–20 (sarcasm): For you gladly tolerate fools, clever as you are. For you 'tolerate' it if someone enslaves you, if someone devours you, if someone exploits you, if someone exalts themselves over you, if someone strikes you in the face.

expl.eval; CET; absurd; adv (ἡδέως, 'gladly'); rep

11:21 (sarcasm/*asteismos*): It's shameful, really; seems that we were too weak to treat you that way.

hypformal; concess

12:11 (sarcasm; [*asteismos*?]): I've become a fool, but you made me do it! For I deserved your commendation, since I lack nothing compared to those Very-Super Apostles, even if I am nothing.

hyperb; chunk; epithet; register

12:13 (sarcasm/*asteismos*): In what way were you made worse off than the other churches – except that *I* was never a drain on your resources? Do forgive me this injustice!

absurd; allit; hypformal

12:16 (*asteismos*): But be that as it may, I have refused to burden you; but since I'm so shifty I must have cheated you somehow.

---

[4] Question marks here indicate cues relevant to 'another "Jesus". . . "Spirit". . . "Gospel"', which I have designated as plausibly, but not definitively sarcastic (see Chapter 7, §7.2.2.1).

Appendix B

PASSAGES CONSIDERED IRONIC OR SARCASTIC BY OTHER INTERPRETERS THAT I DO NOT CONSIDER INSTANCES OF SARCASM

This appendix lists passages where interpreters have identified irony or sarcasm in the undisputed Pauline epistles, which I do not consider sarcastic. It is important to emphasize that the passages listed may still contain other forms of irony, although several very probably do not. These lists are not meant to be exhaustive. One to two scholars are cited with each reference. Cases where I deal with a given example elsewhere in the study are listed, and further citations and discussion can be found in those sections.

Galatians

Chapter/Verse	Considered	Reference	Section in Chapter
1:13–16	'irony'	Nanos 2002, 38.	
1:23–24	'irony'	Nanos 2002, 38.	
2:14–18	'irony'	Nanos 2002, 38.	
3:1–5	'irony'	Nanos 2002, 38; cf. Dahl 2002, 129.	
3:2	'a note of irony'	Dahl 2002, 126.	
3:3b	'clearly ironic'	Dahl 2002, 129.	
3:10–14	'irony'	Nanos 2002, 38.	
4:8–20	'irony'	Nanos 2002, 38.	
4:9	'irony'	Dahl 2002, 129.	
4:21–31	'irony'	Nanos 2002, 38.	
4:21	'irony'	Dahl 2002, 129.	
5:1–4	'irony'	Nanos 2002, 38.	
5:11–12	'irony'	Nanos 2002, 38.	
5:12	'caustic sarcasm'	Longenecker 1990, cxix, 234; cf. Lietzmann 1923, 36.	§4.3
5:15	'sarcastic'	Dahl 2002, 129.	
5:23	'irony'	Nanos 2002, 38.	
6:1	'half ironic, half serious'	Dahl 2002, 128.	
6:3–5	'irony'	Nanos 2002, 38.	

(*cont.*)

6:7–10	'irony'	Nanos 2002, 38.
6:11	'irony'	Nanos 2002, 38.
6:12–13	'irony'	Nanos 2002, 38.
6:14	'irony'	Nanos 2002, 38.

Philippians

Chapter/Verse	Considered	Reference	Section in Chapter
3:2	'Sarkasmus'	Lichtenberger 2017, 104.	
3:19	'ironically'	Reumann 1955, 142.	

Romans

Chapter/Verse	Considered	Reference	Section in Chapter
13:1–7	'irony'	Carter 2004.	§5.4

First Corinthians

Chapter/ Verse	Considered	Reference	Section in Chapter
1:12	'ironic exaggeration of the other slogans being circulated'[5]	Käsemann 1963, 1:X; cf. Schrage 1991, 1:148.	§6.3
1:18–25	'irony'	Holland 1997, 242–43; 2000, 131–34.	§6.1
4:10	verbal irony	Sim 2016, 57.	§§6.2.2–6.2.3
8:4	'ironically'	Knox 1939, 136n.7.	§6.3.2
11:18	'ironic understatement'	Pogoloff 1992, 127.	
11:19	verbal irony	Sim 2016, 61–63.	§6.5
14:18, 21	'irony'	Fitzmyer 2008, 518–20.	

Second Corinthians

Chapter/ Verse	Considered	Reference	Section in Chapter
3:1	'Fragen ironischer Art' ('ironic questions')	Schütz 1958, 15.	

[5] 'ironisierende Überbietung der anderen umlaufenden Parolen'.

(*cont.*)

4:4	'ironic'	Reumann 1955, 142.	§6.1.1
8:7	verbal irony	Sim 2016, 63–65.	
10:12	'εἰρωνεία [eirōneia]'	Forbes 1986, 16.	
11:6	'elegant [asteismos]'	Forbes 1986, 17.	§6.2.2.2
11:7	'ironic exaggeration'	Furnish 1984, 506.	§6.2.2.3
11:21b–12:10	irony	*Varia*[6]	§6.3.2

[6] Several scholars consider portions of the fool's speech ironic (e.g. Loubser 1992; Holland 1993; Lichtenberger 2017, 104–5). I will not cite specific verse ranges here.

Appendix C

HELLENISTIC JEWISH TEXTS

This appendix lists Hellenistic Jewish texts that I have surveyed for the presence of sarcasm. Simply to include as many examples as possible, for the purpose of this appendix I consider any ancient Jewish text preserved at least predominantly in Greek as a Hellenistic Jewish text. After the list of works surveyed, examples of sarcasm are then laid out along with translations and explanatory notes. These examples have been included in our overall dataset, and several have been cited in Chapter 3. A question mark (?) indicates cases where a sarcastic reading is plausible, but uncertain. This survey is intended to provide a starting point for further research on sarcasm or verbal irony in Hellenistic Jewish texts. It is not exhaustive, and closer study may still yield examples of sarcasm in the works already listed, as well as in other texts.

Texts surveyed:

Joseph and Aseneth
Josephus, Against Apion
Judith
Letter of Aristeas
2 Maccabees
3 Maccabees
4 Maccabees
Testament of Abraham
Testament of Job
Philo, Flaccus
Tobit

Examples of sarcasm:

Josephus, *Ap.* 2.3.32

> ὁ δὲ γενναῖος Ἀπίων δοκεῖ μὲν τὴν βλασφημίαν τὴν καθ᾽ ἡμῶν ὥσπερ τινὰ μισθὸν ἐθελῆσαι παρασχεῖν Ἀλεξανδρεῦσι τῆς δοθείσης αὐτῷ πολιτείας

The noble Apion's calumny upon us is apparently designed as a sort of return to the Alexandrians for the rights of citizenship which they bestowed upon him (Thackeray, LCL).

Notes: Juxtaposition of normally positive term γενναῖος ('noble') with βλασφημία (here: 'calumny'). Josephus goes on to accuse Apion of 'lying shamefully' (ἀναισχύντως ψευδόμενος) in two clauses' time.

Ap. 2.11.125

Σφόδρα τοίνυν τῆς πολλῆς συνέσεως καὶ ἐπὶ τῷ μέλλοντι ῥηθήσεσθαι θαυμάζειν ἄξιόν ἐστιν Ἀπίωνα·

Apion is therefore so very worthy of admiration for his abundant insight in what is about to be said...

Notes: Josephus then cites and refutes Apion's argument (2.11.125–28). Here Josephus creates hyperbole with an adverb/adjective combination (σφόδρα/πολλή). We also see the use of *thaumazō* (θαυμάζω, here: 'admiration').

Ap. 2.34.245–46

εἶθ' ὁ γενναιότατος καὶ πρῶτος, αὐτὸς ὁ πατὴρ, τὰς ἀπατηθείσας ὑπ' αὐτοῦ καὶ γενομένας ἐγκύους καθειργνυμένας ἢ καταποντιζομένας περιορᾷ, καὶ τοὺς ἐξ αὐτοῦ γεγονότας οὔτε σώζειν δύναται κρατούμενος ὑπὸ τῆς εἱμαρμένης, οὔτ' ἀδακρυτὶ τοὺς θανάτους αὐτῶν ὑπομένειν. Καλά γε ταῦτα καὶ τούτοις ἄλλα ἑπόμενα, μοιχείας μὲν ἐν οὐρανῷ...

Furthermore, the noblest and chief of them all, the Father himself, after seducing women and rendering them pregnant, leaves them to be imprisoned or drowned in the sea; and is so completely at the mercy of Destiny that he cannot either rescue his own offspring or restrain his tears at their death. Fine doings are these, and others that follow, such as adultery in heaven... (Thackeray, LCL).

Notes: The long epithet 'the noblest and chief of them all, the Father himself' (ὁ γενναιότατος καὶ πρῶτος αὐτὸς ὁ πατὴρ) is sarcastic, especially when followed by an indictment of Zeus's behaviour. 'Fine doings are these' (καλά γε ταῦτα), is also sarcastic, as it both follows and precedes literal negative evaluation of Greek religion.

Letter of Aristeas, 19

Ὁ δέ Μικρόν γε, εἶπεν, Ἀριστέας ἡμᾶς ἀξιοῖ πρᾶγμα.

'It is just a small thing,' he said, 'that Aristeas has seen fit to request of us.'

Notes: Here the king responds to Aristeas' request for the freedom of 100,000 Jewish slaves (14–19). Μικρόν γε ('just a small thing') is considerable understatement that ostensibly communicates the (positive) sentiment that this request will be easy to fulfil. Note the use of an emphatic particle (γε) to indicate insincerity. This light, jocular sarcasm implies that Aristeas is asking a lot of the king. Aristeas ultimately succeeds in his petition.

Fourth Maccabees 5:32

πρὸς ταῦτα τροχοὺς εὐτρέπιζε καὶ τὸ πῦρ ἐκφύσα σφοδρότερον.

Therefore get your torture wheels ready and fan the fire more vehemently! (NRSV).

Notes: This sarcastic taunt is spoken by Eleazar, who is facing martyrdom for refusing to eat unclean food (5:1–13). Having just declared that no torture will break his resolve (5:27–31), he 'encourages' his tormenters to try anyway.

Testament of Job[7] 25:1–7

Τίς οὐκ ἐξεπλάγη λέγοντες ὅτι
αὕτη ἐστιν Σίτιδος ἡ γυνὴ τοῦ Ιωβ;
ἥτις εἶχεν σκεπάζοντα αὐτῆς τὸ καθεστήριον βῆλα δεκατέσσαρα
καὶ θύραν ἔνδοθεν θυρῶν
ἕως ἂν ὅλως καταξιωθῇ τις εἰσαχθῆναι πρὸς αὐτήν –
καὶ νυνὶ καταλλάσσει τὴν τρίχα αὐτῆς ἀντὶ ἄρτων.
ἢ ἦσαν κάμηλοι γεμοσμένοι ἀγαθῶν
ἀπεφέροντο εἰς τὰς χώρας <τοῖς> πτωχοῖς –
ὅτι νῦν δίδωσιν τὴν τρίχα αὐτῆς ἀντὶ ἄρτων.
ἴδε ἡ ἔχουσα ἑπτὰ τραπέζας ἀκινήτους <ἐπὶ τῆς> οἰκίας
ἢ ἤσθι<ον> οἱ πτωχοὶ καὶ πᾶς ξένος –
ὅτι νῦν καταπιπράσκει τὴν τρίχα <αὐτῆς> ἀντὶ ἄρτων.
Βλέπε ἥτις εἶχεν τὸν νιπτῆτα τῶν ποδῶν αὐτῆς
χρυσοῦν καὶ ἀργυροῦν –
νυνὶ δὲ ποσὶν βαδίζει ἐπὶ ἐδάφους
ἀλλὰ καὶ τὴν τρίχα <αὐτῆς> ἀντικαταλλάσσει ἀντὶ ἄρτων.
ἴδε τε ὅτι αὕτη ἐστὶν ἥτις εἶχεν τὴν ἔνδυσιν ἐκβύσσου
ὑφασμένην σὺν χρυσῷ –

---

[7] Greek text and versification follow Kraft 1974. Alternate text-critical decisions could impact the presence of sarcasm.

νυνὶ δὲ φορεῖ ῥακκώδη καὶ ἀντικαταλλάσσει τὴν τρίχα
αὐτῆς ἀντὶ ἄρτων.
Βλέπε τὴν τοὺς κραββάτους χρυσιοῦς καὶ ἀργυρέους ἔχουσαν –
νυνὶ δὲ πιπράσκουσαν τὴν τρίχα <αὐτῆς> ἀντὶ ἄρτων.

Who would not express amazement, saying:
Is this Sitidos, the wife of Job?
Who is used to have protecting her chamber
    fourteen draperies and a door within doors,
    until a person was really considered worthy to
    gain entrance to her –
But now she even exchanges her hair for loaves!
Who had camels, loaded with good things,
    that used to carry (them) off to the proper places
    for the indigent –
For now she gives her hair in return for loaves!
See her who used to have seven tables reserved at her house,
    in which the indigent and every stranger used to eat –
For now she sells <her> hair for loaves!
Look at one who used to have gold
    and a silver basin for her feet –
But now goes by foot on the ground,
    But even <her> hair she gives in exchange for loaves!
See that this is she who used to have clothing
    of linen, woven with gold –
But now she bears a ragged garment,
    And gives her hair in exchange for loaves!
Look at her who used to have couches of gold and silver –
But now she sells her hair for loaves! (Kraft).

Notes: This text is at once Sitidos' lament for herself and her perception of the potential sarcastic mockery of others (Τίς οὐκ ἐξεπλάγη
λέγοντες). She has just had her hair shorn off by Satan in the marketplace
in exchange for bread, with the text making it clear that this was a
shameful experience made more shameful by the observation of onlookers (ἀτίμως ἔκειρέν μου τὴν τρίχα ἐν τῇ ἀγορᾷ παρεστῶτος τοῦ ὄχλου καὶ
θαυμάζοντος, 24:10; cf. 23:1–13). We ought not therefore think that
Sitidos would consider the onlookers to be sincerely mourning on her
behalf, but instead taunting her for her fall from grace. This sarcastic
mockery is communicated through the repetitious portrayal of Sitidos'
former wealth and station juxtaposed with the refrain 'But now she sells
her hair for loaves of bread!' The repetition of imperatives of sight (βλέπε,
ἴδε) emphasizes how the shame of the situation is sharpened by the
presence of onlookers.

37:10–38:1

καὶ πάλιν λέγω σοι, εἰ ἐν τῷ καθεστῶτι ὑπάρχεις, δίδαξόν με, εἰ ἔστιν σοι φρόνησις, διὰ τί ἥλιον μὲν ὁρῶμεν ἀνατέλλοντα ἐπὶ ἀνατολὰς, δύνοντα δὲ ἐν τῇ δύσει, καὶ πάλιν ἀνιστάμενοι κατὰ πρωὶ εὑρίσκομεν τὸν αὐτὸν ἐν ἀνατολαῖς ἀνατέλλοντα; νουθέτησον πρὸς ταῦτα.

καὶ εἶπον

νουθέτησόν με πρὸς ταῦτα, εἰ ἐστίν σοι φρόνησις· <ἔστιν μὲν φρόνησις> ἐν ἐμοί, καὶ σύνεσις τῇ καρδίᾳ μου·

And again I [Baldas] say to you, if you are in a stable condition, instruct me – if you have your wits about you, why do we see the sun rising in the east and setting in the west, and again when we get up early we find the same sun rising in the east? Advise <me> concerning these matters.

And I [Job] said:

Advise me concerning these matters, if you have your wits about you! <but I have my wits> about me, and there is understanding in my heart... (Kraft).

Notes: Baldas speaks first. He began his questioning by sincerely trying to ascertain whether Job is mentally stable (36:1–3). As the discussion continues, he becomes increasingly frustrated with Job's answers and has most recently asked Job how he places his hope in God when God is the one who has afflicted him. The question implies that Baldas considers Job to be impiously accusing God of his misfortunes (37:1–9). By the time we reach 37:10, Baldas is irritated with Job to the point that it is clearly not out of concern that Baldas asks Job if he is mentally stable. This insincerity is reflected in the hyperbolic repetition of imperatives (δίδαξόν, νουθέτησον). Baldas' requests to be instructed become sarcastic taunts because his question is unanswerable. Job cannot instruct him; and Baldas implies that Job understands neither the universe nor God. Job's response is also sarcastic, echoing Baldas' insincere request for information. Reading the *ei* (εἰ) clauses following both Baldas' and Job's imperatives as dubitative would further heighten the sarcasm (i.e. 'Teach me! Perhaps you have wisdom' [εἰ ἔστιν σοι φρόνησις]; cf. Chapter 2, §2.1.1). The insincerity of Job's request for instruction is further emphasized by the vulgarity of his question, as he asks Baldas who it is who divides urine from faeces after food and drink become mixed upon entering through the same mouth (38:3–6).

Philo, *Flacc.* 6.36–40

There was a certain lunatic named Carabas, whose madness was not of the fierce and savage kind, which is dangerous both to the madmen themselves and those who approach them, but of the easy-going, gentler style. He spent day and night in the streets naked, shunning neither heat nor cold, made game of by the children and the lads who were idling about. The rioters drove the poor fellow into the gymnasium and set him up on high to be seen of all and put on his head a sheet of byblus spread out wide for a diadem, clothed the rest of his body with a rug for a royal robe, while someone who had noticed a piece of the native papyrus thrown away in the road gave it to him for his sceptre. And when as in some theatrical farce he had received the insignia of kingship and had been tricked out as a king, young men carrying rods on their shoulders as spearmen stood on either side of him in imitation of a bodyguard. Then others approached him, some pretending to salute him, others to sue for justice, others to consult him on state affairs. Then from the multitudes standing round him there rang out a tremendous shout hailing him as Marin, which is said to be the name for 'lord' in Syria. For they knew that Agrippa was both a Syrian by birth and had a great piece of Syria over which he was king (Colson, LCL).

Notes: Most of the sarcasm here lies in actions rather than words. Carabas, the 'madman' (τις μεμηνώς), is meant to be a stand-in for Agrippa, who is ultimately the one satirized by the mob – although Carabas is certainly a victim as well. The actions related to paying homage and the parody of court proceedings are all sarcastic insofar as they would convey positive affect if performed sincerely, but in this case are done in mockery.

Tobit 2:14 (?)

> Καὶ ποῦ εἰσιν αἱ ἐλεημοσύναι σου; ποῦ εἰσιν αἱ δικαιοσύναι σου; ἰδὲ ταῦτα μετὰ σοῦ γνωστά ἐστιν (Sinaiticus).[8]

So where are your merciful deeds? Where are your acts of righteousness? Everyone knows these things about you!

Notes: Here Tobit's wife Anna expresses her frustration with her husband, who has just unjustly accused her of theft. Gruen considers ἰδὲ ταῦτα μετὰ σοῦ γνωστά ἐστιν ('Everyone knows these things about you!') sarcastic, if difficult to render in English.[9] If Anna is referring to Tobit's good reputation as a way of implying that he is not behaving in a way commensurate with that reputation, and therefore does not deserve it, her statement would be sarcastic. I am, however, not confident in a sarcastic reading here, as other interpretations are possible. For example, Anna could be saying something like, 'Everyone knows of your kindness to others; why won't you treat me the same way?' On such a reading, Anna does not undercut Tobit's good reputation, but emphasizes it to convince him to treat her fairly.

---

[8] Cf. Vaticanus + Alexandrinus: Ποῦ εἰσιν αἱ ἐλεημοσύναι σου καὶ αἱ δικαιοσύναι σου; ἰδοὺ γνωστὰ πάντα μετὰ σοῦ.
[9] Gruen 2009, 318n.63.

BIBLIOGRAPHY

Adachi, Takanori. 1996. 'Sarcasm in Japanese.' *Studies in Language* 20.1:1–36.

Adams, Sean. 2010. 'Lucian and the New Testament: An Evaluation of His Life, Work, and Relationship to New Testament Studies.' *The Expository Times* 121.12:594–600.

Akimoto, Yoritaka, Hidetoshi Takahashi, Atsuko Gunji, Yuu Kaneko, Michiko Asano, Junko Matsuo, Miho Ota, et al. 2017. 'Alpha Band Event-Related Desynchronization Underlying Social Situational Context Processing during Irony Comprehension: A Magnetoencephalography Source Localization Study.' *Brain and Language* 175:42–46.

Allo, E.B. 1937. *Saint Paul: Seconde épître aux Corinthiens.* Études Bibliques. Paris: Librairie Lecoffre.

Arzt-Grabner, Peter, Ruth Elisabeth Kritzer, Amphilochios Papathomas, and Franz Winter. 2006. *1. Korinther: Mit zwei Beiträgen von Michael Ernst, unter Mitarbeit von Günther Schwab und Andreas Bammer.* Papyrologische Kommentare zum neuen Testament 2. Göttingen: Vandenhoeck & Ruprecht.

Attardo, Salvatore. 2000a. 'Irony Markers and Functions: Towards a Goal-Oriented Theory of Irony and Its Processing.' *Rask* 12.1:3–20.

——— 2000b. 'Irony as Relevant Inappropriateness.' *Journal of Pragmatics* 32.6:793–826.

Bailin, Alan. 2015. 'On the Characteristics of Verbal Irony.' *Semiotica* 204:101–19.

Baltzer, K., K. Koenen, A. van der Kooij, and F. Wilk. 2011. 'Esaias / Isaias / Das Buch Jesaja.' Pages 2484–695 in *Septuaginta Deutsch: Erläuterungen und Kommentare zum griechischen Alten Testament.* Edited by Martin Karrer and Wolfgang Kraus. Vol. 2. 2 vols. Stuttgart: Deutsche Bibelgesellschaft.

Barclay, John M. G. 1987. 'Mirror-Reading a Polemical Letter: Galatians as a Test Case.' *Journal for the Study of the New Testament* 31:73–93.

Barnett, P.W. 1984. 'Opposition in Corinth.' *Journal for The Study of the New Testament* 22: 3–17.

Barrett, C.K. 1953. 'Paul and the 'Pillar' Apostles.' Pages 1–19 in *Studia Paulina: in honorem Johannis de Zwaan septuagenarii.* Edited by J.N. Sevenster and W.C. Unnik. Haarlem: Bohn.

1971. *The First Epistle to the Corinthians.* 2nd ed. Black's New Testament Commentary. London: A & C Black.

1973. *A Commentary on the Second Epistle to the Corinthians.* Black's New Testament Commentary. London: A & C Black.

1991. *A Commentary on the Epistle to the Romans.* 2nd ed. Black's New Testament Commentary. London: A & C Black.

1994. *The Acts of the Apostles.* 2 vols. International Critical Commentary. London: T & T Clark.

Baur, F.C. 1873. *Paul, The Apostle of Jesus Christ, His Life and Works, His Epistles and Teaching: A Contribution to a Critical History of Primitive Christianity.* Translated by A. P. 2nd ed. London: Williams and Norgate.

Beard, Mary. 2014. *Laughter in Ancient Rome: On Joking, Tickling, and Cracking Up.* Berkeley: University of California Press.

Berges, Ulrich. 2008. *Jesaja 40–48.* Herders Theologischer Kommentar zum Alten Testament. Freiburg: Herder.

Bertschmann, Dorothea. 2014. *Bowing before Christ – Nodding to the State? Reading Paul Politically with Oliver O'Donovan and John Howard Yoder.* Library of New Testament Studies 502. London: Bloomsbury.

Betz, Hans Dieter. 1972. *Der Apostel Paulus und die sokratische Tradition; eine exegetische Untersuchung zu seiner Apologie 2 Korinther 10-13.* Tübingen: Mohr Siebeck.

1979. *Galatians: A Commentary on Paul's Letter to the Churches in Galatia.* Hermeneia. Philadelphia: Fortress.

Boas, Evert van Emde, Albert Rijksbaron, Luuk Huitink, and Mathieu de Bakker. 2019. *The Cambridge Grammar of Classical Greek.* Cambridge: Cambridge University Press.

Bogaert, Pierre Maurice. 2016. 'Jeremias / Ieremias / Jeremia.' Pages 577–95 in *Einleitung in die Septuaginta.* Edited by Siegfried Kreuzer. Handbuch zur Septuaginta 1. Gütersloh: Gütersloher Verlagshaus.

Bonnard, Pierre. 1953. *L'épitre de saint Paul aux Galates. Commentaire du Nouveau Testament.* Neuchatel: Delachaux & Niestlé.

Booth, Wayne. 1974. *A Rhetoric of Irony.* Chicago: Chicago University Press.

Bornkamm, Günther. 1969. *Early Christian Experience.* Translated by Paul Hammer. New Testament Library. London: SCM.

Braester, Marlena. 2009. 'Du 'signe ironique' à l'énonce ironique.' *Semiotica* 92.1–2:75–86.

Briones, David E. 2013. *Paul's Financial Policy: A Socio-Theological Approach.* London: Bloomsbury.

Bruce, F.F. 1971. *1 and 2 Corinthians. New Century Bible.* London: Oliphants.

1982. *The Epistle to the Galatians: A Commentary on the Greek Text.* New International Greek Testament Commentary. Grand Rapids: Eerdmans.

Bruntsch, Richard, and Willibald Ruch. 2017. 'Studying Irony Detection Beyond Ironic Criticism: Let's Include Ironic Praise.' *Frontiers in Psychology* 8.606:1–15.

Bultmann, Rudolf. 1985. *The Second Letter to the Corinthians.* Edited by Erich Dinkler. Translated by Roy Harrisville. Minneapolis: Augsburg.

Burton, Ernest de Witt. 1921. *A Critical and Exegetical Commentary on the Epistle to the Galatians. ICC.* Edinburgh: T & T Clark.

Butler, H.E., ed. 1966. *The Institutio Oratoria of Quintilian.* 4 vols. Loeb Classical Library. Cambridge: Harvard University Press.

Camp, Elisabeth. 2012. 'Sarcasm, Pretense, and The Semantics/Pragmatics Distinction*.' *Noûs* 46.4:587–634.

Campbell, Douglas A. 2009. *The Deliverance of God: An Apocalyptic Rereading of Justification in Paul.* Grand Rapids: Eerdmans.

Campbell, John, and Albert Katz. 2012. 'Are There Necessary Conditions for Inducing a Sense of Sarcastic Irony?' *Discourse Processes* 49.6: 459–80.

Campbell, R. Alastair. 1991. 'Does Paul Acquiesce in Divisions at the Lord's Supper.' *Novum Testamentum* 33.1:61–70.

Campenhausen, Hans von. 1963. *Aus der Frühzeit des Christentums.* Tübingen: Mohr Siebeck.

Carter, Timothy. 2004. 'The Irony of Romans 13.' *Novum Testamentum* 46.3:209–28.

Ciampa, Roy, and Brian Rosner. 2010. *The First Letter to the Corinthians.* Pillar New Testament Commentary. Grand Rapids: Eerdmans.

Clark, Herbert, and Richard Gerrig. 1984. 'On the Pretense Theory of Irony.' *Journal of Experimental Psychology: General* 113.1:121–6.

Clines, David J.A. 1989. *Job 1–20; 21–37; 38–42.* 3 vols. World Biblical Commentary 17–18B. Dallas: Word Books.

Collins, Raymond. 1999. *First Corinthians. Sacra Pagina 7.* Collegeville: Liturgical Press.

Colston, Herbert. 2007. 'Salting a Wound or Sugaring a Pill: The Pragmatic Functions of Irony.' Pages 319–38 in *Irony in Language and Thought: A Cognitive Science Reader.* Edited by Raymond Gibbs and Herbert Colston. New York: Lawrence Erlbaum Associates.

——— 2017. 'Irony Performance and Perception: What Underlies Verbal, Situational and Other Ironies?' Pages 19–42 in *Irony in Language Use and Communication.* Edited by Angeliki Athanasiadou and Herbert Colston. Amsterdam: John Benjamins.

——— 2019. 'Irony as Indirectness Cross-Linguistically: On the Scope of Generic Mechanisms.' Pages 109–31 in *Indirect Reports and Pragmatics in the World Languages.* Edited by Alessandro Capone, Manuel García-Carpintero, and Alessandra Falzone. Perspectives in Pragmatics, Philosophy & Psychology 19. Springer.

Conzelmann, Hans. 1975. *1 Corinthians: A Commentary on the First Epistle to the Corinthains.* Translated by James Leitch. Hermeneia. Philadelphia: Fortress.

Cox, Claude. [Forthcoming]. *Iob.* Society of Biblical Literature Commentary on the Septuagint.

——— 2007. 'To the Reader of Iob.' Pages 667–70 in *A New English Translation of the Septuagint.* Edited by Albert Pietersma and Benjamin Wright. Oxford: Oxford University Press.

2015. "Job." Pages 385–400 in *T&T Clark Companion to the Septuagint.* *Edited by James Aitken.* London: Bloomsbury T&T Clark.

2017. 'The Book of Job in the New Testament.' Available from: <www .academia.edu/33626545/Old_Greek_Job_in_the_New_Testament>.

Cranfield, C.E.B. 1975. *A Critical and Exegetical Commentary on the Epistle to the Romans.* 2 vols. 6th ed. ICC. Edinburgh: T & T Clark.

Currie, Gregory. 2006. 'Why Irony Is Pretence.' Pages 111–33 in *The Architecture of the Imagination.* Edited by Shaun Nichols. Oxford: Oxford University Press.

Dahl, Nils. 2002. 'Paul's Letter to the Galatians: Epistolary Genre, Content, and Structure.' Pages 117–42 in *The Galatians Debate: Contemporary Issues in Rhetorical and Historical Interpretation.* Edited by Mark Nanos. Peabody: Hendrickson.

Denniston, Dover. 1954. *The Greek Particles.* 2nd ed. Oxford: Clarendon.

deSilva, David. 2018. *The Letter to the Galatians.* New International Commentary on the New Testament. Grand Rapids: Eerdmans.

DeVries, Simon. 1985. *1 Kings.* World Biblical Commentary 12. Waco: Word Books.

Dews, Shelly, Ellen Winner, Joan Kaplan, Elizabeth Rosenblatt, Malia Hunt, Karen Lim, Angela McGovern, Alison Qualter, and Bonnie Smarsh. 1996. 'Children's Understanding of the Meaning and Functions of Verbal Irony.' *Child Development* 67.6:3071–85.

Dhont, Marieke. 2018. *Style and Context of Old Greek Job.* Supplements to the *Journal for the Study of Judaism* 183. Leiden: Brill.

Dhorme, Paul. 1926. *Le livre de Job.* ÉB. Paris: Gabalda.

Dickey, Eleanor. 1996. *Greek Forms of Address.* Oxford Classical Monographs. Oxford: Clarendon.

Dines, Jennifer. 2015. 'The Minor Prophets.' Pages 438–55 in *T&T Clark Companion to the Septuagint.* Edited by James K. Aitken. London: Bloomsbury.

Dodd, Brian. 1999. *Paul's Paradigmatic "I": Personal Example as Literary Strategy.* Journal for the Study of The New Testament Supplement Series 213 177. Sheffield: Sheffield Academic Press.

Driver, Samuel R., and George Buchanan Gray. 1958. *A Critical and Exegetical Commentary on the Book of Job.* Repr. International Critical Commentary. Edinburgh: T&T Clark.

Duling, D. 2008. '2 Corinthians 11:22: Historical Context, Rhetoric, and Ethnicity.' *HTS* 64.2:819–43.

Dunn, James. 1988. *Romans 1–8; Romans 9–16.* 2 vols. World Biblical Commentary 38a, 38b. Dallas: Word Books.

1993. *A Commentary on the Epistle to the Galatians.* Black's New Testament Commentaries. London: A & C Black.

1996. *The Epistles to the Colossians and to Philemon: A Commentary on the Greek Text.* New International Greek Testament Commentary. Grand Rapids: Eerdmans/Carlisle: Paternoster Press.

Elliott, Neil. 2004. 'Strategies of Resistance and Hidden Transcripts in the Pauline Communities.' Pages 97–122 in *Hidden Transcripts and the Arts of Resistance: Applying the Work of James C. Scott to Jesus and Paul.* Edited by Richard A. Horsley. Semeia 48. Atlanta: SBL.

Escandell-Vidal, Victoria, and Manuel Leonetti. 2014. 'Fronting and Irony in Spanish.' Pages 309–42 in *Left Sentence Peripheries in Spanish: Diachronic, Variationist and Comparative Perspectives*. Edited by Andreas Dufter and Álvaro S. Octavio de Toledo. Amsterdam: John Benjamins Publishing Company.

Fee, Gordon. 1987. *The First Epistle to the Corinthians*. New International Commentary on the New Testament. Grand Rapids: Eerdmans.

  2014. *The First Epistle to the Corinthians*. Rev. ed. New International Commentary on the New Testament. Grand Rapids: Eerdmans.

Fein, Ofer, Menahem Yeari, and Rachel Giora. 2015. 'On the Priority of Salience-Based Interpretations: The Case of Sarcastic Irony.' *Intercultural Pragmatics* 12.1:1–32.

Fitzgerald, John T. 1988. *Cracks in an Earthen Vessel: An Examination of the Catalogues of Hardships in the Corinthian Correspondence*. Society of Biblical Literature Dissertation Series 99. Atlanta: Scholars Press.

Fitzmyer, Joseph. 1993. *Romans: A New Translation with Introduction and Commentary*. Anchor Bible 33. London: Doubleday.

  2008. *First Corinthians: A New Translation with Introduction and Commentary*. Anchor Bible 32. New Haven: Yale University Press.

Forbes, Christopher. 1986. 'Comparison, Self-Praise and Irony: Paul's Boasting and the Conventions of Hellenistic Rhetoric.' *New Testament Studies* 32.1:1–30.

Fredriksen, Paula. 2017. *Paul: The Pagans' Apostle*. New Haven: Yale University Press.

Furnish, Victor. 1984. *II Corinthians: A New Translation with Introduction and Commentary*. Anchor Bible. Garden City: Doubleday.

Garland, David. 2003. *1 Corinthians. BECNT*. Grand Rapids: Baker Academic.

Geeraerts, Dirk. 2003. 'Caught in a Web of Irony: Job and His Embarrassed God.' Pages 37–55 in *Job 28: Cognition in Context*. Edited by Ellen Van Wolde.

Geiger, Michaela. 2018. 'Ambiguität und Ironie in Hi 40,6–32(MT).' Pages 30–49 in *Die Septuaginta – Geschichte, Wirkung, Relevanz: 6. internationale Fachtagung veranstaltet von Septuaginta Deutsch (LXX.D), Wuppertal 21.–24. Juli 2016*. Edited by Martin Meiser, Michaela Geiger, Siegfried Kreuzer, and Marcus Sigismund. Wissenschaftliche Untersuchungen zum neuen Testament 405. Tübingen: Mohr Siebeck.

Georgi, Dieter. 1986. *The Opponents of Paul in Second Corinthians*. Translated by Harold Attridge. Philadelphia: Fortress.

Gibbs, Raymond. 1986. 'On the Psycholinguistics of Sarcasm.' *Journal of Experimental Psychology: General* 115.1:3–15.

  2000. 'Irony in Talk Among Friends.' *Metaphor and Symbol* 15.1–2:5–27.

  2012. 'Are Ironic Acts Deliberate?' *Journal of Pragmatics* 44.1:104–15.

Gifford, E.H. 1886. *The Epistle of St. Paul to the Romans*. London: John Murray.

Giora, Rachel. 1997. 'Understanding Figurative and Literal Language: The Graded Salience Hypothesis.' *Cognitive Linguistics* 8.3:183–206.

2007. '"And Olmert Is a Responsible Man": On the Priority of Salience-Based yet Incompatible Interpretations in Nonliteral Language.' *Cognitive Studies* 14.3:269–81.

Giora, Rachel, and Ofer Fein. 1999. 'Irony Comprehension: The Graded Salience Hypothesis*.' *HUMOR: International Journal of Humor Research* 12.4:425–36.

Godet, Frédéric Louis. 1883. *Commentary on St. Paul's Epistle to the Romans.* Edited by Talbot W. Chambers. Translated by A. Cusin. New York: Funk & Wagnalls.

Good, Edwin. 1973. 'Job and the Literary Task: A Response.' *Soundings* 56.4:470–84.

——— 1981. *Irony in the Old Testament.* 2nd ed. Bible & Literature Series 3. Sheffield: Almond.

Gräßer, Erich. 1969. 'Das eine Evangelium: Hermeneutische Erwagungen zu Gal 1:6-10.' *Zeitschrift für Theologie und Kirche* 66.3:306–44.

——— 2005. *Der Zweite Brief an die Korinther.* Vol. 2. 2 vols. Ökumenischer Taschenbuchkommentar zum neuen Testament. Gütersloh: Gütersloher Verlagshaus.

Grice, H.P. 1989. *Studies in the Way of Words.* Cambridge: Harvard University Press.

Gruen, Erich S. 2009. *Diaspora: Jews Amidst Greeks and Romans.* Cambridge: Harvard University Press.

Haiman, John. 1990. 'Sarcasm as Theatre.' *Cognitive Linguistics* 1.2:181–205.

——— 1998. *Talk Is Cheap: Sarcasm, Alienation, and the Evolution of Language.* New York: Oxford University Press.

Hall, J. 1981. *Lucian's Satire. MCS.* New York: Arno.

Halliwell, S. 2008. *Greek Laughter: A Study of Cultural Psychology from Homer to Early Christianity.* Cambridge: Cambridge University Press.

Hammerstaedt-Löhr, A., M. Konkel, H. Löhr, and K. Usener. 2011. 'Jezekiel / Ezechiel / Hesekiel.' Pages 2849–992 in *Septuaginta Deutsch: Erläuterungen und Kommentare zum griechischen Alten Testament.* Edited by Martin Karrer and Wolfgang Kraus. Vol. 2. 2 vols. Stuttgart: Deutsche Bibelgesellschaft.

Hancock, Jeffrey. 2004. 'Verbal Irony Use in Face-to-Face and Computer-Mediated Conversations.' *Journal of Language and Social Psychology* 23.4:447–63.

Häner, T. 2019. 'The Exegetical Function of the Additions to Old Greek Job (42,17a-e).' *Biblica* 100.1:34–49.

Hansen, G. Walter. 1989. *Abraham in Galatians: Epistolary and Rhetorical Contexts.* Journal for the Study of The New Testament Supplement Series 213 29. Sheffield: Sheffield Academic Press.

Harris, Murray. 2005. *The Second Epistle to the Corinthians: A Commentary on the Greek Text.* New International Greek Testament Commentary. Grand Rapids: Eerdmans.

Hartley, John E. 1991. *The Book of Job.* Repr. New International Commentary on the Old Testament. Grand Rapids: Eerdmans.

Hays, Richard B. 1985. '"Have We Found Abraham to Be Our Forefather According to the Flesh?" A Reconsideration of Rom 4:1.' *Novum Testamentum* 27.1:76–98.

Heckel, Ulrich. 1993. *Kraft in Schwachheit: Untersuchungen zu 2. Kor 10-13*. Wissenschaftliche Untersuchungen zum neuen Testament 2.56. Tübingen: Mohr Siebeck.

Héring, Jean. 1967. *The Second Epistle of Saint Paul to the Corinthians*. Translated by P.J. Allcock and A.W. Heathcote. Eugene: Wipf & Stock.

Herzog II, William. 1994. 'Dissembling, a Weapon of the Weak: The Case of Christ and Caesar in Mark 12:13–17 and Romans 13:1–7.' *Perspectives in Religious Studies* 21.4:339–60.

Hoffman, Yair. 1996. *A Blemished Perfection: The Book of Job in Context*. *Journal for the Study of The New Testament* Supplement Series 213. Sheffield: Sheffield Academic Press.

Holland, Glenn. 1993. 'Speaking like a Fool: Irony in 2 Corinthians 10–13.' Pages 250–64 in *Rhetoric and the New Testament: Essays from the 1992 Heidelberg Conference*. Edited by Thomas Olbricht and Stanley Porter. *Journal for the Study of The New Testament* Supplement Series 213 90. Sheffield: Sheffield Academic Press.

1997. 'Paul's Use of Irony as a Rhetorical Technique.' Pages 234–48 in *The Rhetorical Analysis of Scripture: Essays from the 1995 London Conference*. Edited by Stanley Porter and Thomas Olbricht. Journal for the Study of The New Testament Supplement Series 213 146. Sheffield: Sheffield Academic Press.

2000. *Divine Irony*. Selinsgrove: Susquehanna.

Hopkinson, Neil. 2008. *Lucian: A Selection*. Cambridge Greek and Latin Classics. Cambridge: Cambridge University Press.

Horsley, Richard. 1998. *1 Corinthians*. Abingdon New Testament Commentaries. Nashville: Abingdon.

Hughes, Philip. 1962. *Paul's Second Epistle to the Corinthians*. London: Marshall, Morgan & Scott.

Hurd, John Coolidge. 1965. *The Origin of 1 Corinthians*. London: S.P.C.K.

Hurley, Robert. 2006. 'Ironie dramatique dans la mise en intrigue de l'empire en Romains 13, 1–7'. *Studies in Religion/Sciences Religieuses* 35.1:39–63.

Ingram, Virginia. 2017. 'The Book of Job as a Satire with Mention of Verbal Irony.' *St Mark's Review* 239:51–62.

Jackson, David R. 2010. '"Who Is This Who Darkens Counsel?": The Use of Rhetorical Irony in God's Charges against Job.' *The Westminster Theological Journal* 72.1:153–67.

Janzen, J. Gerald. 1985. *Job. Interpretation*. Atlanta: Knox.

Jewett, Robert. 2007. *Romans: A Commentary. Hermeneia*. Minneapolis: Fortress.

Johnson, Lee A. 2017. 'Paul's Letters Reheard: A Performance-Critical Examination of the Preparation, Transportation, and Delivery of Paul's Correspondence.' *Catholic Biblical Quarterly* 79.1:60.

Jónsson, Jakob. 1965. *Humour and Irony in the New Testament: Illuminated by Parallels in the Talmud and Midrash*. Reykjavík: Bókaútgáfa Menningarsjóds.

Käsemann, Ernst. 1942. 'Die Legitimität des Apostels: Eine Untersuchung zu II Korinther 10–13.' *Zeitschrift für die neutestamentliche Wissenschaft und die Kunde der älteren Kirche* 41:33–71.

——. 1963. 'Introduction to Ferdinand Christian Baur: Ausgewählte Werke in Einzelausgaben.' Edited by Klaus Scholder. 4 vols. *Historisch-kritisch Untersuchungen zum neuen Testament mit einer Einführung von Ernst Käsemann*. Stuttgart: Friedrich Fromman.

——. 1980. *Commentary on Romans*. Edited by Geoffrey Bromiley. Translated by Geoffrey Bromiley. 4th ed. Grand Rapids: Eerdmans.

Katz, Albert. 2009. 'On the Science and Art of Sarcasm.' Pages 81–96 in *Disguise, Deception, Trompe-l'oeil: Interdisciplinary Perspectives*. Edited by Leslie Boldt-Irons, Corrado Federici, and Ernesto Virgulti. Studies on Themes and Motifs in Literature 99. New York: Peter Lang.

Katz, Albert N., and Penny M. Pexman. 1997. 'Interpreting Figurative Statements: Speaker Occupation Can Change Metaphor to Irony.' *Metaphor and Symbol* 12.1:19–41.

Keaney, J.J., and Robert Lamberton. 1996. *[Plutarch] Essay on the Life and Poetry of Homer*. American Philological Association 40. Atlanta: Scholars Press.

Kee, Doyle. 1980. 'Who Were the "Super-Apostles" of 2 Corinthians 10–13.' *Restoration Quarterly* 23.2:65–76.

Kepper, M., and M. Witte. 2011. 'Job / Das Buch Ijob / Hiob.' Pages 2041–126 in *Septuaginta Deutsch: Erläuterungen und Kommentare zum griechischen Alten Testament*. Edited by Martin Karrer and Wolfgang Kraus. Vol. 2. 2 vols. Stuttgart: Deutsche Bibelgesellschaft.

Kierkegaard, Søren. 1966. *The Concept of Irony: With Constant Reference to Socrates*. Translated by Lee Capel. London: Collins.

King, Justin. 2018. *Speech-in-Character, Diatribe, and Romans 3:1-9: Who's Speaking When and Why It Matters*. Biblical Interpretation Series 163. Leiden: Brill.

Klauck, Hans-Josef. 1986. *2. Korintherbrief*. Kommentar zum neuen Testament. Würtzberg: Echter.

Knox, Wilfred. 1939. *St Paul and the Church of the Gentiles*. Cambridge: Cambridge University Press.

Kooij, A. van der 2016. 'Esaias / Isaias / Jesaja.' Pages 559–73 in *Einleitung in die Septuaginta*. Edited by Siegfried Kreuzer. Handbuch zur Septuaginta 1. Gütersloh: Gütersloher Verlagshaus.

Kooij, A., van der and F. Wilk. 2011. 'Esaias / Das Buch Jesaja. Einleitung.' Pages 2484–504 in *Septuaginta Deutsch: Erläuterungen und Kommentare zum griechischen Alten Testament*. Edited by Martin Karrer and Wolfgang Kraus. Vol. 2. 2 vols. Stuttgart: Deutsche Bibelgesellschaft.

Koole, Jan Leunis. 1997. *Isaiah III: Isaiah 40–48*. Vol. 1. 3 vols. Historical Commentary on the Old Testament. Kampen: Kok.

Kovaz, David, Roger Kreuz, and Monica Riordan. 2013. 'Distinguishing Sarcasm from Literal Language: Evidence from Books and Blogging.' *Discourse Processes: A Multidisciplinary Journal* 50.8:598–615.

Kowatch, Kristy, Juanita M. Whalen, and Penny M. Pexman. 2013. 'Irony Comprehension in Action: A New Test of Processing for Verbal Irony.' *Discourse Processes* 50.5:301–15.

Kraft, Robert, ed. 1974. *The Testament of Job. Texts and Translations 5; PS 4.* Missoula: Society of Biblical Literature & Scholars' Press.

Kremendahl, Dieter. 2000. *Die Botschaft der Form: Zum Verhältnis von Antiker Epistolographie und Rhetorik im Galaterbrief.* Novum Testamentum et orbis antiquus 46. Freiburg: Vandenhoeck & Ruprecht.

Kreuz, Roger, and Sam Glucksberg. 1989. 'How to Be Sarcastic: The Echoic Reminder Theory of Verbal Irony.' *Journal of Experimental Psychology: General* 118.4:374–86.

Kreuz, Roger, and Richard Roberts. 1995. 'Two Cues for Verbal Irony: Hyperbole and the Ironic Tone of Voice. *Metaphor & Symbolic Activity* 10.1:21–31.

Kumon-Nakamura, Sachi, Sam Glucksberg, and Mary Brown. 1995. 'How about Another Piece of Pie: The Allusional Pretense Theory of Discourse Irony.' *Journal of Experimental Psychology: General* 124.1:3–21.

Kynes, Will. 2012. *My Psalm Has Turned into Weeping, Job's Dialogue with the Psalms.* Berlin, Boston: De Gruyter.

Lagrange, M. 1931. *Saint Paul, épître aux Romains.* Études bibliques. Paris: J. Gabalda et Fils.

Lampe, G.W.H. 1968. *A Patristic Greek Lexicon.* Oxford: Clarendon (accessed via Thesaurus Linguae Graecae).

Lane, Melissa. 2006. 'The Evolution of Eirōneia in Classical Greek Texts: Why Socratic Eirōneia Is Not Socratic Irony.' Pages 49–83 in *Oxford Studies in Ancient Philosophy XXXI: Winter 2006.* Edited by David Sedley. Vol. 31. Oxford: Oxford University Press.

2010. 'Reconsidering Socratic Irony.' Pages 237–59 in *The Cambridge Companion to Socrates.* Edited by Donald Morrison. Cambridge: Cambridge University Press.

Lateiner, Donald. 1995. *Sardonic Smile: Nonverbal Behavior in Homeric Epic.* Ann Arbor: University of Michigan.

Lauber, Stephan. 2017. 'Ironie im Ijob-Buch.' Pages 156–73 in *«Darum, Ihr Hirten, Hört das Wort des Herrn» (Ez 34,7.9): Studien zu Prophetischen und weisheitlichen Texten.* Edited by Christoph Gregor Müller and Matthias Helmer. Fuldaer Studien 21. Freiburg: Herder.

Levy, Harry. 1976. *Lucian: Seventy Dialogues. The American Philological Association Series of Classical Texts.* Norman: University of Oklahoma.

Lichtenberger, Hermann. 2017. 'Da lachen ja die Engel! Humor im neuen Testament.' Pages 95–112 in *Religion und Humor.* Edited by Hans Martin Dober. Göttingen: Vandenhoeck & Ruprecht.

Lietzmann, Hans. 1923. *An die Galater: Erklärt von Hans Lietzmann.* Tübingen: Mohr Siebeck.

1931. *An die Korinther I & II.* 3rd ed. Handbuch zum neuen Testament 9. Tübingen: Mohr Siebeck.

1949. *An die Korinther I-II. HNT 9.* Tübingen: Mohr Siebeck.

Lightfoot, J. B. 1876. *St. Paul's Epistle to the Galatians: A Revised Text with Introduction, Notes and Dissertations by J.B. Lightfoot.* 2nd ed. London: Macmillan.

Lim, Sung. 2015. 'A Double-Voiced Reading of Romans 13:1–7 in Light of the Imperial Cult.' *HTS Theological Studies* 71.1:1–10.

Lim, Timothy H. 1987. '"Not in Persuasive Words of Wisdom, but in the Demonstration of the Spirit and Power".' *Novum Testamentum* 29.2:137–49.

Linss, Wilhelm C. 1998. 'The Hidden Humor of St Paul.' *Currents in Theology and Mission:* 25: 195–99.

Longenecker, Richard. 1990. *Galatians. WBC 41.* Grand Rapids: Zondervan.

2016. *The Epistle to the Romans: A Commentary on the Greek Text.* New International Greek Testament Commentary. Grand Rapids: Eerdmans.

Loubser, J.A. 1992. "A New Look at Paradox and Irony in 2 Corinthians 10-13." *Neotestamentica* 26.2:507–21.

Lucariello, Joan. 1994. 'Situational Irony: A Concept of Events Gone Awry.' *Journal of Experimental Psychology: General* 123.2:129–45.

Luciani, Didier. 2009. 'L'ironie vétéro-testamentaire: de Good à Sharp.' *Ephemerides theologicae Lovanienses* 85.4:385–410.

Lust, Johan. 2016. 'Jezekiel / Ezechiel / Hesekiel.' Pages 613–32 in *Einleitung in die Septuaginta.* Edited by Siegfried Kreuzer. Handbuch zur Septuaginta 1. Gütersloh: Gütersloher Verlagshaus.

MacKenzie, R.A.F. 1959. 'Purpose of the Yahweh Speeches in the Book of Job.' *Biblica* 40.2:435–45.

Mackie, E.C. 1892. *Luciani: Menippus et Timon.* Cambridge: Cambridge University Press.

MacLeod, M.D. 1991. *Lucian: A Selection. Classical Texts.* Warminster: Aris & Phillips.

Malherbe, Abraham J. 1980. 'Mē Genoito in the Diatribe and Paul.' *Harvard Theological Review* 73.1–2:231–40.

Manson, T.W. 1962. 'Romans.' Pages 940–54 in *Peake's Commentary on the Bible. Edited by Matthew Black.* London: Thomas Nelson and Sons.

Marshall, John W. 2008. 'Hybridity and Reading Romans 13.' *Journal for the Study of the New Testament* 31.2:157–78.

Martin, Ralph. 2014. *2 Corinthians.* 2nd ed. World Biblical Commentary 40. Grand Rapids: Zondervan.

Martyn, J. Louis. 1997. *Galatians: A New Translation with Introduction and Commentary.* Anchor Bible 33A. New York: Doubleday.

Matera, Frank. 2003. *II Corinthians: A Commentary. The New Testament Library.* London: Westminster John Knox.

McClelland, S.E. 1982. '"Super-Apostles, Servants of Christ, Servants of Satan': A Response." *Journal for the Study of the New Testament* 14:82–87.

McLay, Tim. 2003. *The Use of the Septuagint in New Testament Research.* Grand Rapids: Eerdmans.

Meier, Mischa (Bielefeld). 2006. 'Kalokagathia.' Edited by Hubert Cancik, Helmuth Schneider, Manfred Landfester, Christine Salazar, and Francis Gentry. *Brill's New Pauly.* Available from <https:// referenceworks.brillonline.com/entries/brill-s-new-pauly/kalokagathia-e607270?s.num=0&s.f.s2_parent=s.f.book.brill-s-new-pauly&s.q= Kalokagathia>.

Michel, Otto. 1978. *Der Brief an die Römer. 5. bearb.* Kritisch-exegetischer Kommentar über das neue Testament 4. Göttingen: Vandenhoeck & Ruprecht.

Minchin, Elizabeth. 2010a. "From Gentle Teasing to Heavy Sarcasm: Instances of Rhetorical Irony in Homer's *Iliad.*" *Hermes: Zeitschrift für klassische Philologie* 138.4:387–402.

——— 2010b. 'The Expression of Sarcasm in the Odyssey.' *Mnemosyne: Bibliotheca Classica Batava* 4.63:533–56.

Mitchell, Margaret. 1991. *Paul and the Rhetoric of Reconciliation: An Exegetical Investigation of the Language and Composition of 1 Corinthians.* Vol. 28. Hermeneutische Untersuchungen zu Theologie. Tübingen: J.C.B. Mohr Siebeck.

Montgomery, James. 1951. *The Books of Kings.* Edited by Henry Snyder Gehman. International Critical Commentary. Edinburgh: T & T Clark.

Moo, Douglas. 1996. *The Epistle to the Romans.* New International Commentary on the New Testament. Grand Rapids: Eerdmans.

——— 2013. *Galatians.* 3 vols. Baker Exegetical Commentary on the New Testament. Grand Rapids: Baker Academic.

Morris, Leon. 1988. *The Epistle to the Romans.* Leicester: Eerdmans.

Moule, C.F.D. 1953. *An Idiom Book of New Testament Greek.* Cambridge: Cambridge University Press.

Muecke, D.C. 1969. *The Compass of Irony.* London: Methuen & Co.

——— 1982. *Irony and the Ironic.* 2nd ed. New York: Methuen & Co.

Mullins, Terence. 1972. 'Formulas in New Testament Epistles.' *Journal of Biblical Literature* 91.3:380–90.

Murphy-O'Connor, Jerome. 1996. *Paul: A Critical Life.* Oxford: Clarendon.

——— 2009. *Keys to First Corinthians: Revisiting the Major Issues.* Oxford: Oxford University Press.

——— 2010. *Keys to Second Corinthians: Revisiting the Major Issues.* Oxford: Oxford University Press.

Murray, John. 1967. *The Epistle to the Romans: The English Text with Introduction, Exposition and Notes.* Lenski's Commentary on the New Testament. London: Marshall, Morgan & Scott.

Mußner, Franz. 1974. *Der Galaterbrief.* HKT 9. Freiburg: Herder.

Nanos, Mark. 2002. *The Irony of Galatians: Paul's Letter in First-Century Context.* Minneapolis: Fortress.

Naselli, Andrew David. 2017. 'Is Every Sin Outside the Body except Immoral Sex? Weighing Whether 1 Corinthians 6:18b Is Paul's Statement or a Corinthian Slogan.' *Journal of Biblical Literature* 136.4:969–87.

Newell, Lynne. 1992. 'Job: Repentant or Rebellious.' Pages 441–56 in *Sitting with Job: Selected Studies on the Book of Job*. Edited by Roy B. Zuck. Eugene: Wipf and Stock.

Ngunga, Abi, and Joachim Schaper. 2015. 'Isaiah.' Pages 456–68 in *T&T Clark Companion to the Septuagint*. Edited by James K. Aitken. London: Bloomsbury.

Nikolakopoulos, Konstantin. 2001. 'Aspekte der ‚paulinischen Ironie' am Beispiel des Galaterbriefes.' *Biblische Zeitschrift* 45.2. Ferdinand Schöningh:193–208.

Nordgren, Lars. 2015. *Greek Interjections: Syntax, Semantics and Pragmatics. TL 273*. Berlin: Walter de Gruyter.

Novenson, Matthew. 2016. 'The Self-Styled Jew of Romans 2 and the Actual Jews of Romans 9–11.' Pages 133–62 in *The So-Called Jew in Paul's Letter to the Romans*. Edited by Rafael Rodríguez and Matthew Thiessen. Minneapolis: Fortress.

Nygren, Anders. 1952. *Commentary on Romans*. Translated by Carl Rasmussen. London: SCM.

Oestreich, Bernhard. 2012. *Performanzkritik der Paulusbriefe*. Wissenschaftliche Untersuchungen zum neuen Testament 296. Tübingen: Mohr Siebeck.

Okamoto, Shinichiro. 2002. 'Politeness and the Perception of Irony: Honorifics in Japanese.' *Metaphor and Symbol* 17.2:119–39.

Olley, John W. 2009. *Ezekiel: A Commentary Based on Iezekiēl in Codex Vaticanus*. Septuagint Commentary Series. Leiden: Brill.

Omanson, Roger L. 1992. 'Acknowledging Paul's Quotations.' *The Bible Translator* 43.2:201–13.

Oswalt, John. 1998. *The Book of Isaiah: Chapters 40–66*. New International Commentary on the Old Testament. Grand Rapids: Eerdmans.

Parsons, Gregory W. 1992. 'Literary Features of the Book of Job.' Pages 35–50 in *Sitting with Job: Selected Studies on the Book of Job*. Edited by Roy B. Zuck. Eugene: Wipf and Stock.

Pawlak, Matthew C. 2018. 'Consistency Isn't Everything: Self-Commendation in 2 Corinthians.' *Journal for the Study of the New Testament:* 360–82.

——— 2019. 'How to Be Sarcastic in Greek: Typical Means of Signaling Sarcasm in the New Testament and Lucian.' *HUMOR: International Journal of Humor Research* 32.4:545–64.

——— 2021. 'Is Galatians an Ironic Letter?: Θαυμάζω, Ancient Letter Writing Handbooks, and Galatians 1:6'. *Novum Testamentum* 63.2:249–70.

Pelham, Abigail. 2010. '*Job* as Comedy, Revisited.' *Journal for the Study of the Old Testament* 35.1:89–112.

Pexman, Penny M. 2008. 'It's Fascinating Research: The Cognition of Verbal Irony.'' *Current Directions in Psychological Science* 17.4:286–90.

Pexman, Penny M., Todd R. Ferretti, and Albert N. Katz. 2000. 'Discourse Factors That Influence Online Reading of Metaphor and Irony.' *Discourse Processes* 29.3:201–22.

Pfeiffer, Robert Henry. 1953. *Introduction to the Old Testament*. Repr.; Rev. ed. London: Black.

Pinheiro, Marília Pulquério Futre. 2012. 'Irony, Satire and Parody in Lucian's 'The Dead Come to Life, or The Fisherman.' *Trends in Classics* 4.2:296–315.

Piskorska, Agnieszka. 2016. 'Echo and Inadequacy in Ironic Utterances.' *Journal of Pragmatics* 101:54–65.

Plank, Karl. 1987. *Paul and the Irony of Affliction. Semeia.* Atlanta: Scholars Press.

Plummer, A. 1915. *A Critical and Exegetical Commentary on the Second Epistle of St. Paul to the Corinthians.* International Critical Commentary. Edinburgh: T & T Clark.

Pogoloff, Stephen. 1992. *Logos and Sophia: The Rhetorical Situation of 1 Corinthians.* Society of Biblical Literature Dissertation Series 134. Atlanta: Scholars Press.

Popa-Wyatt, Mihaela. 2014. 'Pretence and Echo: Towards an Integrated Account of Verbal Irony.' *International Review of Pragmatics* 6.1:127–68.

Porter, Stanley. 1991. 'The Argument of Romans 5: Can a Rhetorical Question Make a Difference?' *Journal of Biblical Literature* 110.4:655–77.

——— 1992. *Idioms of the Greek New Testament.* 2nd ed. Biblical Languages: Greek 2. Sheffield: Sheffield Academic Press.

Reumann, John. 1955. 'St Paul's Use of Irony.' *Lutheran Quarterly* 7.2:140–45.

Ritter-Müller, Petra. 2000. *Kennst du die Welt? – Gottes Antwort an Ijob: Eine sprachwissenschaftliche und exegetische Studie zur ersten Gottesrede Ijob 38 und 39.* Altes Testament und Moderne 5. Münster: Lit.

Roberts, J. H. 1991. 'ΘΑΥΜΑΖΩ: An Expression of Perplexity in Some Examples from Papyri Letters.' *Neotestamentica* 25.1:109–22.

——— 1992. 'Paul's Expression of Perplexity in Galatians 1:6: The Force of Emotive Argumentation.' *Neotestamentica* 26.2:329–38.

Robertson, David A. 1973. 'Book of Job: A Literary Study.' *Soundings* 56.4:446–69.

Rockwell, Patricia. 2001. 'Facial Expression and Sarcasm.' *Perceptual and Motor Skills* 93.1:47–50.

——— 2007. 'Vocal Features of Conversational Sarcasm: A Comparison of Methods.' *Journal of Psycholinguistic Research* 36.5:361–69.

Rodríguez, Rafael. 2016. 'Romans 5–8 in Light of Paul's Dialogue with a Gentile Who "Calls Himself a Jew".' Pages 101–32 in *The So-Called Jew in Paul's Letter to the Romans.* Edited by Rafael Rodríguez and Matthew Thiessen. Minneapolis: Fortress.

Rusten, Jeffery, and I.C. Cunningham, eds. 1993. *Theophrastus: Characters.* Loeb Classical Library. Cambridge: Harvard University Press.

Schellenberg, Ryan. 2013. *Rethinking Paul's Rhetorical Education: Comparative Rhetoric and 2 Corinthians 10–13.* 10. Atlanta: Society of Biblical Literature.

——— 2016. 'Paul, Samson Occom, and the Constraints of Boasting: A Comparative Rereading of 2 Corinthians 10–13*.' *Harvard Theological Review* 109.4:512–35.

——— 2018. 'Did Paul Refuse an Offer of Support from the Corinthians?' *Journal for the Study of the New Testament* 40.3:312–36.

Schlatter, A. 1928. 'Der frühere Brief an die Korinther.' *Erläuterungen zum neuen Testament.* Vol. 2. 3 vols. Stuttgart: Calwer.

Schmeller, Thomas. 1987. *Paulus und die „Diatribe": Eine vergleichende Stilinterpretation.* Neutestamentliche Abhandlungen 19. Münster: Aschendorffsche Verlagsbuchhandung GmbH & Co.

Schmidt, Hans. 1963. *Der Brief des Paulus an die Römer.* THNT 6. Berlin: Evangelische Verlaganstalt.

Schmithals, Walter. 1971. *Gnosticism in Corinth: An Investigation of the Letters to the Corinthians.* Translated by John Steely. Nashville: Abingdon.

Schmitz, Leonhard. 1873. 'Alexander Numenius.' Page 123 in *Dictionary of Greek and Roman Biography and Mythology.* Edited by W. Smith. Vol. 1. 3 vols. London: John Murray.

Schrage, Wolfgang. 1991. *Der erste Brief an die Korinther.* 4 vols. Evangelisch-katholischer Kommentar zum neuen Testament 7. Braunschweig: Benziger.

Schreiner, Thomas. 1998. *Romans.* Grand Rapids: Baker Academic.

Schröter, Jens. 2013. *From Jesus to the New Testament: Early Christian Theology and the Origin of the New Testament Canon.* Translated by Wayne Coppins. Waco: Baylor.

Schütz, Roland. 1958. *Humor und Ironie bei Jesus und Paulus.* Freies Christentum 29. Frankfurt: Deutscher Bund für Freies Christentum.

Seto, Ken-Ichi. 1998. 'On Non-Echoic Irony.' Pages 239–56 in *Relevance Theory: Applications and Implications.* Edited by Robyn Carston and Seiji Uchida. Pragmatics and Beyond 37. Amsterdam: John Benjamins.

Shead, Andrew. 2015. 'Jeremiah.' Pages 469–86 in *T&T Clark Companion to the Septuagint.* Edited by James Aitken. London: Bloomsbury T&T Clark.

Shelley, Cameron. 2001. 'The Bicoherence Theory of Situational Irony.' *Cognitive Science* 25.5:775–818.

Siebenmann, Paul Charles. 1997. 'The Question of Slogans in 1 Corinthians.' Ph.D. diss. Texas: Baylor University.

Siegert, Folker. 1985. *Argumentation bei Paulus: Gezeigt an Röm 9–11.* Wissenschaftliche Untersuchungen zum neuen Testament 34. Tübingen: Mohr Siebeck.

Sim, Margaret. 2016. *A Relevant Way to Read: A New Approach to Exegesis and Communication.* Cambridge: James Clarke & Co.

Simpson, Paul. 2003. *On the Discourse of Satire: Towards a Stylistic Model of Satirical Humour.* Amsterdam: John Benjamins.

Smith, Jay E. 2010. 'Slogans in 1 Corinthians.' *Bibliotheca Sacra* 167.665:68–88.

Smyth, Herbert. 1959. *Greek Grammar.* Cambridge: Harvard University Press.

Spencer, Aída Besançon. 1981. 'The Wise Fool (and the Foolish Wise): A Study of Irony in Paul.' *Novum Testamentum* 23.4:349–60.

Sperber, Dan. 1984. 'Verbal Irony: Pretense or Echoic Mention.' *Journal of Experimental Psychology: General* 113.1:130–36.

Sperber, Dan, and Deirdre Wilson. 1978. 'Les ironies comme mentions.' *Poétique* 36:399–412.

1981. 'Irony and the Use–Mention Distinction.' Pages 295–318 in *Radical Pragmatics*. Edited by Peter Cole. New York: Academic Press.

1995. *Relevance: Communication and Cognition*. 2nd ed. Oxford: Blackwell.

1998. "Irony and Relevance: A Reply to Seto, Hamamoto and Yamanashi." *Relevance Theory: Applications and Implications*. Edited by Robyn Carston and Seiji Uchida. Pragmatics and Beyond 37. Amsterdam: John Benjamins.

Spotorno, Nicola, Anne Cheylus, Jean-Baptiste Van Der Henst, and Ira A. Noveck. 2013. 'What's Behind a P600? Integration Operations during Irony Processing.' *PLOS ONE* 8.6:1–10.

Stowers, Stanley. 1981. *The Diatribe and Paul's Letter to the Romans*. Society of Biblical Literature Dissertation Series 57. Chico: Scholars Press.

1984. 'Paul's Dialogue with a Fellow Jew in Romans 3:1-9.' *The Catholic Biblical Quarterly* 46.4:707–22.

1994. *A Rereading of Romans: Justice, Jews, and Gentiles*. New Haven: Yale University Press.

Sumney, Jerry. 1990. *Identifying Paul's Opponents: The Question of Method in 2 Corinthians*. Journal for the Study of the New Testament Supplement Series 40. Sheffield: Sheffield Academic Press.

Sundermann, Hans-Georg. 1996. *Der schwache Apostel und die Kraft der Rede. 575*. Frankfurt am Main: Peter Lang.

Thiessen, Matthew. 2016. *Paul and the Gentile Problem*. New York: Oxford.

Thiselton, Anthony. 1973. 'Meaning of Sarx in 1 Corinthians 5:5: A Fresh Approach in the Light of Logical and Semantic Factors.' *Scottish Journal of Theology* 26.2:204–28.

2000. *The First Epistle to the Corinthians: A Commentary on the Greek Text*. New International Greek Testament Commentary. Grand Rapids: Eerdmans.

Thorsteinsson, Runar M. 2003. *Paul's Interlocutor in Romans 2: Function and Identity in the Context of Ancient Epistolography*. Stockholm, Sweden: Almqvist & Wiksell International.

Thrall, Margaret. 1994. *The Second Epistle to the Corinthians: A Critical and Exegetical Commentary*. 2 vols. International Critical Commentary 32B. Edinburgh: T&T Clark.

Utsumi, Akira. 2000. 'Verbal Irony as Implicit Display of Ironic Environment: Distinguishing Ironic Utterances from Nonirony.' *Journal of Pragmatics* 32.12:1777–806.

Van Voorst, Robert. 2010. 'Why Is There No Thanksgiving Period in Galatians? An Assessment of an Exegetical Commonplace.' *Journal of Biblical Literature* 129.1:153–72.

Vlastos, Gregory. 1987. 'Socratic Irony.' *The Classical Quarterly* 37.1:79–96.

Vonach, A. 2011. 'Jeremias / Das Buch Jeremia.' Pages 2696–814 in *Septuaginta Deutsch: Erläuterungen und Kommentare zum griechischen Alten Testament*. Edited by Wolfgang Kraus and Martin Karrer. Vol. 2. 2 vols. Stuttgart: Deutsche Bibelgesellschaft.

Waite, Maurice, ed. 2013. 'Irony.' *Pocket Oxford English Dictionary*. Oxford: Oxford University Press.

Wallace, D.B. 1996. *Greek Grammar Beyond the Basics: An Exegetical Syntax of the New Testament*. Grand Rapids: Zondervan.

Wan, Sze-kar. 2008. 'Coded Resistance: A Proposed Rereading of Romans 13:1–7.' Pages 173–84 in *The Bible in the Public Square: Reading the Signs of the Times*. Edited by Cynthia Briggs Kittredge, Ellen Bradshaw Aitken, and Jonathan Draper. Minneapolis: Fortress.

Warning, Rainer. 1985. 'Reading Irony in Flaubert.' *Style* 19.3:304–16.

Warren, L. 2013. 'Towards Redefining Socratic Irony.' *Akroterion* 58:1–17.

Watts, John. 1987. *Isaiah 34-66*. World Biblical Commentary 25. Waco: Word Books.

Weiss, Johannes. 1910. *Der erste Korintherbrief*. 9th ed. Kritisch-exegetischer Kommentar über das neue Testament 5. Göttingen: Vandenhoeck & Ruprecht.

West, M.L. 1965. 'Tryphon De Tropis.' *The Classical Quarterly* 15.2:230–48.

Whedbee, William. 1977. 'Comedy of Job.' *Semeia* 7:1–39.

White, John. 1971. 'Introductory Formulae in the Body of the Pauline Letter.' *Journal of Biblical Literature* 90.1:91–97.

Wilckens, Ulrich. 1978. *Der Brief an die Römer*. 3 vols. Evangelisch-katholischer Kommentar zum neuen Testament 6. Zürich: Benziger.

Williams, James G. 1971. 'You Have Not Spoken Truth of Me: Mystery and Irony in Job.' *Zeitschrift für die alttestamentliche Wissenschaft* 83.2:231–55.

Willis, Wendell Lee. 1985. *Idol Meat in Corinth: The Pauline Argument in 1 Corinthians 8 and 10*. Eugene: Wipf & Stock.

Wilson, Deirdre. 2006. 'The Pragmatics of Verbal Irony: Echo or Pretence?' *Lingua* 116.10:1722–43.

——— 2013. 'Irony Comprehension: A Developmental Perspective.' *Journal of Pragmatics* 59A:40–56.

——— 2017. 'Irony, Hyperbole, Jokes and Banter.' Pages 201–20 in *Formal Models in the Study of Language: Applications in Interdisciplinary Contexts*. Edited by Joanna Blochowiak, Cristina Grisot, Stephanie Durrleman, and Christopher Laenzlinger. Springer.

Wilson, Deirdre, and Dan Sperber. 1992. 'On Verbal Irony.' *Lingua* 87.1:53–76.

——— 2012. *Meaning and Relevance*. Cambridge: Cambridge University Press.

Witherington III, Ben. 1995. *Conflict and Community in Corinth: A Socio-Rhetorical Commentary on 1 and 2 Corinthians*. Grand Rapids: Eerdmans.

Woodland, Jennifer, and Daniel Voyer. 2011. 'Context and Intonation in the Perception of Sarcasm.' *Metaphor and Symbol* 26.3:227–39.

Wooten, Cecil (trans.). 1987. *Hermogenes' On Types of Style*. Chapel Hill: University of North Carolina.

Yao, Jun, Jie Song, and Michael Singh. 2013. 'The Ironical Chinese Bei-Construction and Its Accessibility to English Speakers.' *Journal of Pragmatics* 55:195–209.

Zahn, T. 1910. *Der Brief des Paulus an die Römer.* 2. Aufl. Kommentar zum
  neuen Testament 6. Leipzig: A. Deichert.
Zmijewski, Josef. 1978. *Der Stil der paulinischen "Narrenrede": Analyse der
  Sprachgestaltung in 2 Kor 11,1–12,10 als Beitrag zur Methodik von
  Stiluntersuchungen neutestamentlicher Texte. Bonner Biblische Beiträge
  52.* Köln–Bonn: Peter Hanstein.

INDEX OF ANCIENT SOURCES

1. Septuagint / Hebrew Bible

2. New Testament

3. Ancient Sources

INDEX OF MODERN AUTHORS

SUBJECT INDEX

For EU product safety concerns, contact us at Calle de José Abascal, 56–1°,
28003 Madrid, Spain or eugpsr@cambridge.org.

www.ingramcontent.com/pod-product-compliance
Ingram Content Group UK Ltd.
Pitfield, Milton Keynes, MK11 3LW, UK
UKHW010248140625
459647UK00013BA/1720